MASS ATROCITY, COLLECTIVE MEMORY, AND THE LAW

MASS ATROCITY, COLLECTIVE MEMORY, AND THE LAW

Mark Osiel

TRANSACTION PUBLISHERS
New Brunswick (U.S.A.) and London (U.K.)

First paperback printing 2000

Copyright © 1997 by Transaction Publishers, New Brunswick, New Jersey 08903. Revised edition of *University of Pennsylvania Law Review,* Vol. 144, No. 2

This book is printed on acid-free paper that meets the American National Standard for Permanence of Paper for Printed Library Materials.

Library of Congress Catalog Number: 96-50097
ISBN 1-56000-322-7 (cloth) • 0-7658-0663-0 (paper)
Printed in the United States of America

Library of Congress Cataloging-in-Publication Data

Osiel, Mark.
  Mass atrocity, collective memory, and the law / Mark Osiel.
    p. cm.
  Includes bibliographical references and index.
    ISBN: 1-56000-322-7 (cloth) • 0-7658-0663-0 (paper)
    1. War crime trials—Moral and ethical aspects. 2. War crime trials—Social aspects. 3. Memory—Social aspects. I. Title.
JX5433.083 1997
341.6'9'01—dc21   96-50097
                                                                        CIP

To the Memory of Carlos Nino

CONTENTS

Preface and Acknowledgments

Serious attempts at dialogue between lawyers and sociologists rarely get very far. To oversimplify a bit, this is because lawyers begin by asking what choices we should make as a society in designing our institutions, while sociologists tell us (or, at least, their explanations imply) that we really don't have any choices to make, after all. Contemporary legal scholars thus strike sociologists as naive day-dreamers. Sociologists, in turn, strike academic lawyers as sullen and lacking imagination. As someone who wears both professional hats, I have often had both reactions to each sort of colleague—and sometimes to myself.

I have not transcended this perennial difficulty. Whether I have briefly side-stepped it is for the reader to judge. My relatively optimistic conclusions will reveal that I have preferred to risk erring on the side of the lawyers. After all, social science utterly failed to predict virtually all of the most momentous developments of our century, from the rise of fascism and the gulag to the extermination of European Jewry and the demise of communism. It is scarcely surprising, then, that social science as we know it also proves of little use in helping us grapple with the legal ramifications of such events, in their aftermath.

Even so, I owe my greatest debt to the spirited fraternity of fellow teachers at Harvard's Committee on Social Studies, from whom I was able to gather intimations of what American sociology, with better fortune, might have become. Such an imaginary discipline would abandon its pretension to scientific prediction. It would concern itself instead with identifying practical possibilities for a better world. To that end, it would ravage through modern history at large to uncover the reasons for prior successes and failures at social improvement. It would stay close to the ground of historical experience, while exploring how a particular social practice or institution might be reimagined and reconstructed. This book was written in the spirit of such a mode of social inquiry.

* * *

For information about the Buenos Aires trials of military officers, I am grateful to the several Argentine judges, prosecutors, military officers, defense counsel, journalists, and social scientists who shared their observations of these proceedings. Although I sought to maintain neutrality during all interviews, several of my informants, particularly within the Alfonsín administration, became personal friends, and ultimately wished to learn my legal opinion on several questions, some discussed herein, since their resolution was being debated within government circles at the time. I thus found myself being drawn into the controversy willy-nilly as something of a participant, albeit an extremely minor one. I mention this as a matter of scholarly ethics, since one such official claims to have been influenced by the views I expressed.

The rolling hills and green pastures of the Iowa countryside provided a comfortable vantage point (albeit an incongruous one) from which to contemplate such horrible events with a measure of scholarly perspective. I wish to thank the citizens and taxpayers of that state for making this possible.

Generous support for the present research was provided by The Iowa Law Foundation, Harvard's Program in Ethics and the Professions, and Columbia Law School's Human Rights Program.

For their helpful comments, I thank Virginia Dominguez, Kenneth Cmiel, Tulio Halperin, Jeffrey Herf, Linda Kerber, Kenneth Kress, Peter Novick, Robert C. Post, Michael Schudson, the Iowa Legal History Workshop, and especially Eliza Willis. Charles Maier, Michael Marrus, Jaime Malamud, and Lawrence Douglas generously shared with me their own unpublished works on related matters.

A considerably shorter version of this study first appeared as an article in the *University of Pennsylvania Law Review*. I am grateful to Irving Louis Horowitz for proposing that it might be of interest to a wider readership, and to the *Law Review* editors for authorizing republication.

Mark J. Osiel
Iowa City, Iowa

I have spent many nights sleeping in the plazas of Buenos Aires with a bottle of wine, trying to forget.... I am afraid to be alone with my thoughts.

> Argentine Captain Adolfo Scilingo, confessing to having thrown thirty people from a navy helicopter during the "dirty war."[1]

Publicly coming forward to give such testimony is a way of returning to a horrible past that we are trying to forget.

> Argentine President Carlos Saúl Menem, responding to Scilingo's public confession.[2]

The struggle of man against power is the struggle of memory against forgetting.

> Milan Kundera[3]

Introduction

This study concerns the role of criminal trials in democratic transitions. Such trials and transitions are judged in various ways by lawyers, activists, and scholars. We ought to evaluate transitions to democracy with greater attention to the kind of public discussion they foster concerning the human rights abuse perpetrated by authoritarian rulers, recently deposed. We should evaluate the prosecution of these perpetrators in light of how it influences such public deliberation.

To that end, the law's conventional concerns with deterrence and retribution will receive less emphasis. The rules designed to keep these concerns at center stage will sometimes need to be compromised. Such compromises are necessary and appropriate, I suggest, in the aftermath

---

1 Quoted in Calvin Sims, "Argentine Tells of Dumping 'Dirty War' Captives into Sea," *N.Y. TIMES,* Mar. 13, 1995, at A1, A8. Sergeant Víctor Armando Ibáñez made similar confessions. "Confessions of a Dirty Warrior," *Harper's Mag.*, July 1995, at 15 (translating and reprinting an interview published in the April 24, 1995 issue of *La Prensa*). A leading Argentine journalist has written a book on such death flights, based on lengthy interviews with Scilingo. Horacio Verbitsky, *El Vuelo* (1995).

2 Quoted in Calvin Sims, "National Nightmare Returns to Argentine Consciousness," *N.Y. Times,* Apr. 5, 1995, at A1, A6; see also "Argentina: The Unspoken Past," *N.Y. Times,* Mar. 21, 1995, at A20 (noting that "authorities have actively discouraged public discussion of what went on").

3 Milan Kundera, *The Book of Laughter and Forgetting* 3 (Michael H. Heim trans., 1980).

of large-scale brutality sponsored by an authoritarian state. At such times, the need for public reckoning with the question of how such horrific events could have happened is more important to democratization than the criminal law's more traditional objectives. This is because such trials, when effective as public spectacle, stimulate public discussion in ways that foster the liberal virtues of toleration, moderation, and civil respect. Criminal trials must be conducted with this pedagogical purpose in mind. I seek to show how that can be done.

Trials of those responsible for large-scale state brutality have captured the public imagination in several societies. Insofar as they succeed in concentrating public attention and stimulating reflection, such proceedings indelibly influence collective memory of the events they judge. More subtly, they influence even our underlying notions of what memory is about, what it is for. It is only a small exaggeration to say, as two political theorists recently have, that the cumulative effect of such trials, from Nuremberg and Buenos Aires to the current proceedings in the Hague, is that "the process of how people are made to vanish has become a distinctive feature of postwar conceptions of what memory is."[4]

By highlighting official brutality and public complicity, these trials often make people willing to reassess their foundational beliefs and constitutive commitments, as few events in political life can do. In the lives of individuals, these trials thus often become, at very least, an occasion for personal stock-taking. They are "moments of truth," in several senses. Specifically, they present moments of transformative opportunity in the lives of individuals and societies, a potential not lost upon the litigants themselves. Prosecutors and judges in these cases thus rightly aim to shape collective memory of horrible events in ways that can be both successful as public spectacle and consistent with liberal legality. In defending this view, I examine aspects of the Nuremberg and Tokyo trials, as well as the Eichmann prosecution and more recent trials in Argentina and France.

Such trials cannot summon up a "collective conscience" of moral principles shared by all. At such moments, no such consensus on fundamentals is likely to exist. Neither can it be easily created. But

---

4 Avishai Margalit and Gabriel Motzkin, "The Uniqueness of the Holocaust," 25 *Philosophy and Public Affairs* 64, 83 (1996) (emphasis added).

criminal trials may nevertheless contribute significantly to a certain, underappreciated kind of social solidarity, arising from reliance on procedures for ensuring that moral disagreement among antagonists remains mutually respectful, within the courtroom and beyond.

To this end, judges and prosecutors can profit from closer attention to the "poetics" of legal storytelling, i.e., to the way in which an experience of administrative massacre can be framed within the conventions of competing theatrical genres. The task of comparative historical sociology is therefore to understand why certain narrative tropes were employed by prosecution and defense in particular trials, and to assess the varying degree to which these were successful in influencing collective memory—both national and international—of the disputed events, often many years thereafter. The answers to these empirical questions will prove helpful in designing future prosecutions of administrative massacre, I contend.

In a nutshell, the record of these trials suggests that defense counsel will tell the story as a tragedy, while prosecutors will present it as a morality play. The judicial task at such moments, however, is to employ the law of evidence, procedure, and professional responsibility to recast the courtroom drama in terms of the "theater of ideas," where large questions of collective memory and even national identity are engaged. By helping to put these questions in issue, courts contribute to social solidarity of the sort just described.

Principles of liberal morality can be most effectively inculcated in a society traumatized by recent fratricide if the proceedings are conducted in this fashion. To maximize their pedagogic impact, such trials should be unabashedly designed as monumental spectacles. Though rarely acknowledged, considerations of dramaturgy have proven quite valuable to this end. This is because these are "liberal show trials," conducted by what have been called "moral entrepreneurs"[5] and "activists of memory."[6]

The approach advocated here necessarily involves courts in questions of historical interpretation and moral pedagogy generally

---

5   On the concept of moral entrepreneurship, as applied to efforts at shaping social memory, see Nachman Ben-Yehuda, *The Masada Myth: Collective Memory and Mythmaking in Israel* 287-92 (1995).

6   Tzvetan Todorov, "The Abuses of Memory," 1 *Common Knowledge* 6, 22 (1996).

regarded as beyond their professional competence. It also assumes their capacity to influence political culture and social norms in powerful ways. For both reasons, it will be controversial. This study therefore concentrates on responding to the ethical objections and practical obstacles to orchestrating prosecutions of administrative massacre with a view to realizing so ambitious an agenda.

All societies have founding myths, explaining where we come from, defining what we stand for.[7] These are often commemorated in the form of "monumental didactics," public recountings of the founders' heroic deeds as a national epic. Some societies also have myths of *re*founding, marking a period of decisive break from their own pasts, celebrating the courage and imagination of those who effected this rupture.

Myths of founding and refounding often center on legal proceedings or the drafting of legal documents: the Magna Carta (for Britain),[8] the trial and execution of King Louis XVI (for France),[9] and the Declaration of Independence[10] and the Constitutional Convention (for the United States).[11] "Our country's birthday," reminds Mary Ann Glendon, "commemorates the formal signing of a legal document—a bill of grievances in which rebellious but fussily legalistic colonists recited their complaints, [and] claimed that they had been denied 'the rights of Englishmen.'"[12]

---

7 Mircea Eliade, *Myth and Reality* 4-5, 30-38 (Ruth N. Anshen ed., Willard R. Trask trans., 1963) (examining the purpose of "foundation myths" in society).

8 On the many and conflicting invocations of the Magna Carta in subsequent English political history, by both the left and the right, see Anne Pallister, *Magna Carta: The Heritage of Liberty* 32-38, 51-62, 73, 89 (1971).

9 Susan Dunn, *The Deaths of Louis XVI: Regicide and the French Political Imagination* (1994) (examining the shifting place of this event in French memory).

10 On how American memory of the Declaration of Independence has changed several times, in light of shifting political contexts, see Michael Kammen, *A Season of Youth: The American Revolution and the Historical Imagination* 55-65 (1978).

11 On the place of the U.S. Constitution in the collective memory and popular culture of Americans, see Michael Kammen, *A Machine That Would Go of Itself: The Constitution in American Culture* (1986).

12 Mary Ann Glendon, *A Nation Under Lawyers: How the Crisis in the Legal Profession Is Transforming American Society* 259 (1994). The act of founding often becomes the focal point for later disputes about its meaning and bearing, if any, on contemporary disputes that find their way into courtrooms. As Milner Ball observes, "[t]he courts are the paradigmatic spaces where the dramatic narrative of our beginning

To considerable extent, such formations and transformations of collective identity are legally induced. They are not confined to the distant past, moreover. Two recent examples: In Australia, the white population has recently come to refocus its national identity around a "discovery" or rehabilitation of the country's aboriginal population.[13] At the same time, aborigines themselves have increasingly come to refocus their relations with the white majority population around several highly successful legal interactions with it: a well-publicized lawsuit vindicating indigenous claims to traditional lands and a law consolidating these claims.[14] These legal events have, in turn, come to be celebrated both in indigenous ceremony and in best-selling musical recordings.[15]

A second, recent example: In August 1996, former South Korean dictators Chun Doo Hwan and Roh Tae Woo were convicted of mutiny and treason, arising from their military coup and the later massacre of some 200 student protesters. Their prosecution was widely seen as part of an effort to refound the nation on new principles by retelling the story of those years. "We want to cut ourselves off from a history that legitimized coups and military dictatorships," said one Korean legislator. To this end, he argued, "We need a new history. This means not only redefining the [student protesters] as a democratic movement, but also punishing those who suppressed it."[16] An Asian journalist adds,

---

is recurred to and augmented." Milner S. Ball, *The Promise of American Law* 62 (1981).

13   Paula Hamilton, "The Knife Edge: Debates About Memory and History," *in Memory and History in Twentieth-Century Australia* 9, 13-14 (Kate Darian-Smith & Paula Hamilton eds., 1994).

14   *Mabo v. Queensland,* 175 C.L.R. 1, 2 (Austl. 1992) (holding that "the Meriam people are entitled as against the whole world to possession, occupation, use and enjoyment of the lands of the Murray Islands"); Native Title Act, No. 110 (1993) (Austl.) (setting forth Parliament's objectives of providing for the recognition and protection of native title).

15   Two such songs, composed and performed by an interracial rock group, have become hits on the Australian pop music charts. The group's name is Yothu Yindi. The songs are entitled *Mabu* and *Treaty.* The first of these appears on the album *Freedom* (Hollywood Records 1993), the second on *Tribal Voice* (Hollywood Records 1992).

16   Andrew Higgins, "When the Buck Stops at the Very Top," *The Guardian* (London) Jan 20 1996 (quoting Sohn Hak Kyu, parliamentary spokesperson for the New Korea Party); reprinted in *World Press Review* June 1996, at 12.

the spectacle of the two former rulers, dressed in prison uniforms like common criminals and standing powerless before the three judges, riveted the nation. South Koreans gathered around television sets in homes, stores, and offices to watch the unfolding of a drama that has become a symbol of the political transformation that South Korea has undergone in the past three years. The trial has been viewed by many South Koreans less as a hearing on the specific crimes committed more than a decade ago by aging military leaders than as a pivotal step toward the establishment of the rule of law by a country trying to cleanse itself of its brutal and corrupt past.[17]

All these examples, past and present, suggest that acts asserting legal rights or officially stigmatizing their violation have often become a focal point for the collective memory of whole nations. These acts often become secular rituals of commemoration. As such, they consolidate shared memories with increasing deliberateness and sophistication.[18] These events are both "real" and "staged." In this regard, they seem to problematize the very distinction between true and false representations of reality.[19]

Law-related activities of this sort contribute to the kind of social solidarity that is enhanced by shared historical memory. In the last half century, criminal law has increasingly been used in several societies with a view to teaching a particular interpretation of the country's history, one expected to have a salubrious impact on its solidarity. Many have thought, in particular, that the best way to prevent recurrence of genocide, and other forms of state-sponsored mass brutality, is to cultivate a shared and enduring memory of its horrors—and to employ the law self-consciously toward this end.

---

17   Sandra Suguwara, "South Korean Court Sentences Ex-Rulers To Prison, Death," *Washington Post,* Aug. 26, 1996, at A01.

18   Daniel Dayan & Elihu Katz, *Media Events: The Live Broadcasting of History* 211-13 (1992) (examining official efforts to influence collective memory through television broadcasts of major public events); see also Ana Maria Alonso, "The Effects of Truth: Re-Presentations of the Past and the Imagining of Community," 1 *J. Hist. Sociology* 33, 40 (1988) ("Social groups form images of themselves in relation to a set of founding events and re-enact this shared link to a collective past in public ceremony .... [Hence,] social memory is integral to the creation of social meaning.").

19   Jean Baudrillard, *Simulations* 5-6 (Paul Foss et al. trans., 1983).

To do this effectively has increasingly been recognized to require some measure of *son et lumière*, smoke and mirrors, that is, some self-conscious dramaturgy by prosecutors and judges, I contend. For instance, western Allies in postwar war crimes trials deliberately strove "to *dramatize* the implacable contradiction between the methods of totalitarianism and the ways of civilized humanity through a worldwide *demonstration* of fair judicial procedure."[20]

This book examines six recurring problems that have arisen from efforts to employ criminal prosecution to influence a nation's collective memory of state-sponsored mass murder.[21] Some of these suggest the task's impossibility; others, its undesirability. First, such efforts can easily sacrifice the rights of defendants on the altar of social solidarity. Second, they can unwittingly distort historical understanding of the nation's recent past. Third, they may foster delusions of purity and grandeur by encouraging faulty analogies between past and future controversies, readings of the precedent that are often too broad, sometimes too narrow.

Fourth, they may fail by requiring more extensive admissions of guilt, and more repentance, than most nations are prepared to undertake. This is because efforts at employing law to instill shared memories sometimes require substantial segments of a society to accept responsibility for colossal wrongs and to break completely with cherished aspects of its past. Fifth, legal efforts to influence collective memory may fail because such memory—almost by nature—arises only incidentally; it cannot be constructed intentionally. Sixth, even if collective memory can be created deliberately, perhaps it can be done

---

20   Peter J. Fliess, 78 *Am. J. Int'l L.* 256, 256 (1984) (reviewing Richard L. Lael, *The Yamashita Precedent: War Crimes and Command Responsibility* (1982)) (emphasis added).

21   I focus primarily on the legal response to the Argentine dirty war, in which between 10,000 and 30,000 citizens were murdered by the country's officer corps. Over 500 officers were indicted, and some two dozen convicted (including six junta members and individual torturers), before military uprisings forced an end to further trials. On this history, see Martin E. Andersen, *Dossier Secreto: Argentina's Desaparecidos and the Myth of the "Dirty War"* (1993); Alison Brysk, *The Politics of Human Rights in Argentina* (1994); Ronald Dworkin, "Introduction" to *Comisión Nacional Sobre la Desaparición de Personas, Nunca Más: The Report of the Argentine National Commission on the Disappeared* at xi (1986) [hereinafter *Nunca Más*].

only dishonestly, that is, by concealing this very deliberateness from the
intended audience.

These obstacles establish the moral and empirical limits within
which any liberal account of law's contribution to collective memory
must maneuver.[22] I discuss each obstacle in turn, drawing on the now
considerable experiences of Germany, Japan, France, Israel, and
Argentina.[23] My primary aim is to clarify the nature of these six

---

22 Several of these obstacles would also present problems for *any* effort to influence
collective memory, by whatever means (that is, other than by legal proceedings). The
relative efficacy of the law in this regard, compared with alternative methods of shaping
memory (such as the news media, educational institutions, cinema, and so forth) will not
be examined here. But see Heide Fehrenbach, *Cinema in Democratizing Germany:
Reconstructing National Identity After Hitler* 148-68 (1995). I here examine only the
law's potential contribution, largely in isolation from the rest.

By "the law," I shall primarily refer to criminal prosecution, including strategic
decisions by counsel on both sides and by the court. I will also allude occasionally to
legislation and executive orders, although these will be of decidedly secondary concern.
Still another crucial use of law to influence collective memory has involved litigation
aimed at creating or increasing access (by historians and journalists) to government
records documenting administrative massacres in the past. Such litigation has recently
become particularly important in societies undergoing transition from nondemocratic
to democratic rule, including the former Eastern Bloc states.

Important as well has been the statutory provision in many criminal codes making
"disparagement of the memory of the dead" an offense. Eric Stein, "History Against
Free Speech: The New German Law Against the "Auschwitz"—and Other—"Lies","
85 *Mich. L. Rev.* 277, 294 (1986). In West Germany, such a provision was employed,
for instance, to prosecute individuals and publications that had denied the occurrence
of the Holocaust. *Strafgesetzbuch* [STGB] §189 (F.R.G.) (prohibiting the disparagement
of the memory of the deceased); Stein, *Id.* at 294-95 (relating the prosecution of a
teacher who had denied the existence of concentration camps and that Jews had been
killed in the Third Reich). More recently, several western societies, including Germany,
Belgium, France, Austria, Sweden, and the Netherlands, have enacted criminal
provisions specifically prohibiting "Holocaust denial." Deborah E. Lipstadt, *Denying
the Holocaust: The Growing Assault on Truth and Memory* 219-22 (1993). These
statutes are often justified expressly in terms of a societal interest in preserving
collective memory of that event. Stein, *Id.* at 316-18.

23 For Germany, I discuss the Nuremberg prosecution of German leaders before the
International Military Tribunal; for Japan, the Tokyo War Crimes trial; for France, the
prosecutions of Klaus Barbie and Paul Touvier; for Israel, the trial of Adolph Eichmann;
for Argentina, the trial of the military juntas convicted of ordering the deaths of many
citizens during the dirty war of the mid- to late-1970s. In each case the conduct judged
by the courts involved large-scale official brutality against large numbers of victims,
perpetrated by thousands of military and police officers, occupying several bureaucratic
levels, over a long period of time, enjoying considerable collaboration by civilians.
Notwithstanding the considerable differences between these several historical
experiences, I shall treat them for present conceptual purposes as examples of what
Hannah Arendt described as "administrative massacres." Hannah Arendt, *Eichmann in*

problems and to illustrate the ways in which they arise. In hopes of fostering their wider recognition and consideration, I offer only the most confessedly provisional suggestions for their resolution.

Administrative massacre, as I shall use the term, entails large-scale violation of basic human rights to life and liberty by the central state in a systematic and organized fashion, often against its own citizens, generally in a climate of war—civil or international, real or imagined. Mass murder is the most extreme of a broader class of harms inflicted during such episodes; these episodes routinely involve massive numbers of other war crimes and crimes against humanity, such as enslavement of labor (for example, of Korean "comfort women" by the Japanese army and of Jews by the Nazis). My premise is that state criminality of this nature, on this scale, poses special problems—in its immediate aftermath—for new democratic rulers seeking to reconstruct some measure of trust, social solidarity, and collective memory of the recent past. I assess the extent to which criminal law may effectively address these problems.

These problems take various shape in differing circumstances. For this reason, occasional forays are necessary into a wide range of historical experience and efforts by social theorists, of competing persuasions, to make sense of it. The strengths and weaknesses of liberal philosophy, in guiding the law's response to administrative massacre and in influencing memory of it, are a central concern in this regard. The criminal law is widely and correctly thought to embody assumptions about human nature and society that are primarily liberal.[24]

It follows that a sophisticated critique of criminal law, of its response to a given problem, issues very quickly into an indictment of liberalism itself. For this reason, the most influential recent criticisms

---

Jerusalem: A Report on the Banality of Evil 288-91 (Penguin Books, rev. & enlarged ed. 1977) (1963).

24 By "liberal" I mean a theory based on the moral autonomy and rational capacity of individual persons and their corresponding rights to equal concern and respect by fellow citizens and the state. Both critics and defenders of criminal law, as a response to social deviance, routinely characterize it as based on such liberal premises. George Fletcher, *Rethinking Criminal Law* at xix (1978); H.L.A. Hart, *Punishment and Responsibility* at preface (1968); Alan W. Norrie, *Law, Ideology, and Punishment: Retrieval and Critique of the Liberal Ideal of Criminal Justice* at xiii (1991); Michael S. Moore, "The Moral and Metaphysical Sources of the Criminal Law," in *Criminal Justice: NOMOS XXVII*, at 11, 14 (J. Roland Pennock & John W. Chapman eds., 1985).

of liberalism, by communitarians and postmodernists, will recurrently arise. My aim will be to see how much light such critics can shed on the law's limits and possibilities in this area.

The qualified defense of liberal law that ultimately emerges, of its conceptual resources for coping with these six problems, operates by way of a comparative history, not a conceptual analysis or metatheoretical speculation. I examine the historical experience of administrative massacre in light of what alternative theories have to say about the law's capacity to grapple with it. Conversely, I assess the theories themselves in terms of the practical successes and failures revealed by the comparative history of efforts to bring the perpetrators of administrative massacre to justice.[25]

But first it is necessary to ask: What is at stake here? How would the obstacles just mentioned, if insurmountable, limit the capacity of liberal law to respond adequately to state-sponsored mass brutality? What would be lost if these obstacles prevented the law from effectively fostering a shared memory of such events? How might the criminal law, by cultivating shared memory of administrative massacre through prosecution of its perpetrators, contribute significantly to social solidarity? For that matter, what is the proper place of such solidarity—law-induced or otherwise—within a liberal society?

---

25 In adopting this approach, I have relied upon Neil J. Smelser, *Comparative Methods in the Social Sciences* 72-150 (1976). For an application, see Mark J. Osiel, "Lawyers As Monopolists, Aristocrats, and Entrepreneurs," 103 *Harv. L. Rev.* 2009, 2065 (1990).

Part I.

**HOW PROSECUTION ASSISTS COLLECTIVE MEMORY
AND HOW MEMORY FURTHERS SOCIAL SOLIDARITY**

connect to movie

"social dramas": cultural performances involving the who disruption, self-examination, and reconciliation of a society by of legal or other ritual procedures. These are designed to enhance the group's ability

> to scrutinize, portray, understand, and then act on itself.... As heroes in our own dramas, we are made self aware, conscious of our consciousness. Since social dramas suspend normal everyday role playing, they interrupt the flow of social life and force a group to take cognizance of its own behavior in relation to its ... own values, even to question ... the value of those values. In other words, [such] dramas induce and contain reflexive processes and generate cultural frames in which reflexivity can find a legitimate place.[22]

Alongside such Promethean aspirations, the traditional purposes of criminal law—deterrence and retribution of culpable wrongdoing—are likely to seem quite pedestrian. Moreover, those committed to keeping such concerns at the center of judicial attention—that is, professionally scrupulous lawyers—are likely to come off as plodding dullards, distracted by doctrinal trivia from the issues of truly "historic" importance before them. This was, in fact, precisely the verdict reached on Hausner by Hannah Arendt.[23] Hausner himself had aimed to become "the impresario of a national-historic production."[24] But for Arendt,

---

22 Victor Turner, *From Ritual to Theatre* 75, 92 (1982). Although Turner lists the Dreyfus trial among the episodes exemplified by his concept of social drama, see *id.* at 70, his theory confessedly stresses how legal procedures at such times "maintain the *status quo*," *id.* at 10, and "reassert and reanimate the overarching values shared by all." *Id.* at 75. But while this is sometimes the case, more common in the episodes examined in this study (as in the Dreyfus trial itself) has been the intention, often partly successful, of permanently altering the institutional status quo and transforming existing values.
   Turner's account of trials as social dramas is heavily Durkheimian in theoretical inspiration. Hence the present account will seek to show the limits of Durkheim's sociology in grappling with the impact of the criminal proceedings examined here. Turner views the agonistic strife aroused by such trials as leading necessarily either to reconciliation among warring parties or to secession by one of them. As we shall see, however, there is a third possibility: the reconstruction of social solidarity through public deliberation over continuing *dis*agreement, a process by which rules constrain conflict within nonlethal bounds, inspiring increasing mutual respect among adversaries.
23 Hannah Arendt, *Eichmann in Jerusalem: A Report on the Banality of Evil* 5, 8, 124-25, 276-79 (1962).
24 Segev, *supra* note 14, at 338.

Eichmann's trial failed as drama, due to the studied mediocrity of its principal protagonist.[25]

The real question, however, is not whether the prosecutor made a compelling hero, or the defendant a compelling villain. The question is whether it is right to seek such operatic virtuosity from proceedings of this sort in the first place, as Arendt apparently did.[26]

As an aim for criminal law, the cultivation of collective memory resembles deterrence in that it is directed toward the future, where enhanced solidarity is sought. But like retribution, it looks to the past, to provide the narrative content of what is to be shared in memory. Stated most modestly, its purpose is, as Thomas Scanlon puts it, "to achieve a general state of mind in the country in which the unacceptability of these acts is generally recognized, so that the perpetrators become pariahs, ... having done something that cannot be sustained and accepted."[27]

Collective memory, as I shall use the term,[28] consists of the stories

---

25   Arendt, *supra* note 23, at 9, 287.

26   On Arendt's aestheticized conception of politics as performance, long noted by scholars, see Lisa J. Disch, *Hannah Arendt and the Limits of Philosophy* 21, 83-84, 161 (1994).

27   Tape of Human Rights and Deliberative Democracy: A Conference in Honor of Carlos Santiago Nino, Presented at Yale Law School (Sept. 23-24, 1994).

28   Collective memory consists of past reminiscences that link given groups of people for whom the remembered events are important, that is, the events remain significant to them later on. The memory is later invoked to help define what such people have in common and to guide their collective action. As the events in question recede further into the past and those who experienced them directly no longer remain alive, the "memory" becomes, more precisely, a memory of memory, that is, a memory of what others have told future generations about their pasts. On this temporal distinction, see Amos Funkenstein, "Collective Memory and Historical Consciousness," 1 *Hist. & Memory* 5, 9 (1989).

Once survivors are no longer available to offer individualized accounts of their personal and sometimes idiosyncratic experiences, the "mass production of memory" by the state and its legal institutions increasingly becomes a realistic possibility and, for some, a terrible danger. Michael Geyer & Miriam Hansen, "German-Jewish Memory and National Consciousness," in *Holocaust Remembrance, supra* note 18, at 175, 178 (noting that younger Germans remember the Nazi years only by way of their subsequent representations in cinema and official ceremonies and concluding that "what we have witnessed over the past two decades is the creation of a public *through* these collective rituals and representations of remembering").

Collective memory is a woolly concept, often used casually as a metaphor, albeit an evocative one, for other things. An analytical philosopher would have no difficulty distinguishing at least ten different usages of the term in current social thought. Ian

a society tells about momentous events in its history, the events that most profoundly affect the lives of its members and most arouse their passions for long periods. This category of events prominently includes wars, revolutions, economic depressions, large-scale strikes and riots, and genocides—as well as the legal proceedings often arising from such upheavals.[29] These events are also distinguished by the tendency for recollection of them to "hover over" subsequent events, providing compelling analogies with later controversies of the most diverse variety. When a society's members interpret such an event in common fashion, they derive common lessons from it for the future.[30]

When the event has been deeply divisive for a society, however, its memory will later evoke the same disagreements and consolidate the

---

Hacking, *Rewriting the Soul: Multiple Personality and the Sciences of Memory* 3 (1995) (noting the recent profusion of uses of collective memory and that this abundance reflects, in itself, a phenomenon of considerable interest). Discussion could profit from conceptual clarification of the term collective memory. But that is not the aim of this study. My concerns are primarily pragmatic. I shall here employ the concept as an ideal type, for its heuristic value alone, in hopes of assessing just what this value might be.

29   This list is decidedly focused on the "great events" of modern societies. The collective memory of peasant societies, by contrast, has often remained centered on seasonal events and hence dependent on a cyclical conception of time. Françoise Zonabend, *The Enduring Memory: Time and History in a French Village* 139 (Anthony Forster trans., 1984) ("The present ... is reconstituted by reference to the past—a stable, lasting and well-ordered period, a time outside the reach of Time."). In such traditional societies, the content of shared memory—as recounted in social gatherings and interviews with anthropologists—remains remarkably uninfluenced by even the largest catastrophes suffered by the nation-state in which peasants reside. James Fentress & Chris Wickham, *Social Memory* 96 (1992) (noting that peasants "tend to stress their social identity through images of resistance to the state, which are peculiarly unlikely to get into Great Events history").

30   The idea of collective memory need not imply that the collectivity—the nation, the class, or the ethnic group—possess memories independent of those held by its members, although the concept has sometimes been interpreted in this way. F.C. Bartlett, *Remembering* 296-98 (1932) ("It is not theoretically impossible that the organization of individuals into a group should literally produce a new mental unit which perhaps feels, knows and remembers in its own right."). There is both an individual and a social component to many memories. Large-scale sociopolitical events like an administrative massacre, for instance, are experienced and hence remembered differently, in certain respects, by each of the surviving individuals affected. But many other aspects of their experiences, and the sentiments evoked, will have been shared by fellow citizens and will be recognized as such. This is the sense in which I shall speak here of collective memory. For a useful discussion of these issues, see Elizabeth Tonkin, *supra* note 4, at 104-06.

same social divisions that it involved. The Dreyfus trial in France is the clearest case. In more recent French memory the Algerian war occupies a similar place, much like the Vietnam War in American memory.[31] In both societies, memory of the war arouses strong emotions.

But these emotions differ radically between various social groups. Hence no common commemoration of such events is possible. It appears that to commemorate events has required an attempt to "sacralize them and [thereby] remove them from the category of debatable," as Sally Falk Moore observes.[32] Only commemoration can, to some degree, "resist the passage of time and transmit the sense of the event to generations who did not live it."[33] In this respect, these military conflicts are remembered very differently from the First or Second World War, in either country. Divisive memory surely threatens the "pacific" virtues of cohesion and solidarity. But it may also undermine the martial virtues, those required for unity and courage against external threats. "The final lesson of Vietnam," George Bush thus observed in his inaugural address, "is that no great nation can long afford to be sundered by [such] a memory."[34]

There is yet a third scenario. Sometimes the memory of a major legal event will initially unify the nation that experienced it, but later be interpreted so differently by contending factions that its memory becomes divisive. American memory of the Declaration of Independence suffered this fate, for instance, in the last decades of the eighteenth century. "By the end of John Adams's administration," writes an historian,

> partisan politics had grown so nasty that ideological opponents could not
> disentangle their sense of the present from their remembrance of the past.

---

31   The memory of these wars is compared by David L. Schalk, *War and the Ivory Tower* (1991). The highly divisive impact of the O.J. Simpson verdict on American race relations has been persuasively analysed similar terms. See Paul Gewirtz, "Victims and Voyeurs: Two Narrative Problems at the Criminal Trial," in *Law's Stories: Narrative and Rhetoric in the Law* 135, 156 (Peter Brooks and Paul Gewirtz eds., 1996).

32   Sally Falk Moore, "Introduction," in *Moralizing States and the Ethnography of the Present* 1 (Sally Falk Moore, ed., 1993).

33   Robert Frank, "Troubles de la mémoire française," in *La Guerre d'Algérie et les Français* 606 (Jean-Pierre Riouz, ed., 1990).

34   President George Bush, Inaugural Address, Jan. 1988, reprinted in Gerald Pomper et. al., eds., *The Election of 1988* 210 (1989).

Unable to celebrate the Fourth of July together, they held separate processions, separate dinners, and heard separate orations—a situation that continued until the Federalist party died out ....[35]

More recently, the same deterioration of shared memory has occurred regarding the "Battle of the Alamo," the 1836 siege of the compound by Santa Ana's forces. For well over a century that event was publicly remembered as "a moment of glory during which freedom-loving Anglos, outnumbered but undaunted, spontaneously chose to fight until death rather than surrender to a corrupt Mexican dictator."[36] Increasingly, however, many Latino residents of nearby San Antonio, who now compose well over half the City's population, have come to see the event as "a brutal example of U.S. expansionism, the story of a few white predators taking over what was sacred territory and half-willingly providing, with their death, the alibi for a well-planned annexation."[37] As is now customary, each side invokes the law in support of its favored reading of history. "Demonstrations, parades, editorials, and demands for various municipal and court orders—including one blocking the streets now leading to the Alamo—punctuate the debate between increasingly angry parties."[38]

Collective memory—both the divisive and solidifying sorts—plays a much greater role in the political discourse of some societies than others. It plays considerably more of a role in Europe, it is often observed, than in our own society.[39] Anthropologists have long noted

---

35 Michael Kammen, *A Season of Youth: The American Revolution and the Historical Imagination* 40 (1978).

36 Michel Rolph-Trouillot, *Silencing the Past: Power and the Production of History* 9 (1995).

37 *Id.*

38 *Id.*

39 In this regard, the United States resembles other frontier and immigrant societies, whose members often retain stronger memories of their disparate lands of origin than of their common, new-found home. The shallowness of historical memory in the United States is a central theme of Michael Kammen's recent work. Michael Kammen, *Mystic Chords of Memory* 9-10 (1991); Michael Kammen, *A Machine That Would Go of Itself: The Constitution in American Culture* 13 (1986).

In the 19th century, many European political theorists, novelists, and psychologists viewed social and political disorder as reflecting a loss of shared memory. Richard Terdiman, *Present Past: Modernity and the Memory Crisis* (1993); Walter Benjamin, *Illuminations*, trans. Harry Zohn, 83 (1969); M. Christine Boyer, *The City of Collective*

that in premodern societies authoritative stories about the past often serve as "the legal charter of the community," functioning to "integrate and weld together the historical tradition, the legal principles, and the various customs," thereby providing "for cohesion, for local patriotism, for a feeling of union."[40]

But this insight into the role of the past in non-Western societies was derived from the early legal history of the West itself.[41] This suggests that the way our law uses memory of the past—whether burying or unearthing it—may not be altogether unique or culturally idiosyncratic. In turn, the anthropological study of collective memory in far-off lands may now shed some important light on law in Western society itself.

There are two very different ways in which the law in general, and criminal prosecution of administrative massacre in particular, might contribute to social solidarity. The first views legal proceedings as drawing upon an already-existing consensus within a country regarding its first principles and as employing that consensus to infuse a single, shared interpretation of its recent past. Solidarity results from the awareness of a common history judged by common standards, a history from which unequivocal lessons for future conduct will be learned by all.

The second view does not expect legal proceedings to draw upon, nor even necessarily to produce any society-wide consensus on such matters. Legal proceedings produce a different kind of solidarity, founded on a different basis. The proceedings are founded on civil dissensus. They produce the kind of solidarity embodied in the

---

Memory 23-29 (1994).

But it is a misconception, partially perpetuated by recent communitarianism, that people in preliterate societies have better developed memories and more detailed recall—presumably because they cannot turn to documents as a mnemonic crutch—than those in modern, literate societies. Ulric Neisser, "Literacy and Memory," in *Memory Observed: Remembering in Natural Contexts* 241, 241-42 (1982) (rejecting the notion that "illiterate people have particularly good memories to compensate for being unable to write things down").

40 Bronislaw Malinowski, *Magic, Science, and Religion* 116-17 (1954).

41 Peter Burke, "History as Social Memory," in *Memory: History, Culture and the Mind* 97, 109 (Thomas Butler ed., 1989); see also M.T. Clanchy, *From Memory to Written Record: England 1066-1307*, at 146-48, 297 (Blackwell Publishers, 2d ed. 1993) (1979) (discussing the place of such charters in early British society); P.H. Sawyer, *Anglo-Saxon Charters: An Annotated List and Bibliography* (1968).

increasingly respectful way that citizens can come to acknowledge the differing views of their fellows.

I will sketch each of these two accounts of law's service to solidarity before examining how the six problems mentioned above may undercut each of them.   I conclude that criminal prosecution of administrative massacre can only contribute significantly to social solidarity of the second sort and that this is precisely the kind of solidarity to which a liberal society should aspire.

Chapter 1.

Crime, Consensus, and Solidarity

Upon recounting, the stories that constitute collective memory can contribute to social solidarity by evoking in citizens the common values that Durkheim called the collective conscience.[1] "For Durkheim," writes Garland,

> the rituals of criminal justice—the court-room trial, the passing of sentence, the execution of punishment—are, in effect, the formalized embodiment of the *conscience collective.* In doing justice, and in prosecuting criminals, these procedures are also giving formal expression to the feelings of the community—and by being expressed in this way those feelings are both strengthened and gratified.[2]

Punishment, Garland continues, "is a social occasion which simultaneously structures individual sentiment and gives it cathartic release."[3] Criminal prosecutions play a special role in this process.

> The *conscience collective* is protected by a strict code of penal law, which—unlike most law in modern society—*does* evoke deep-seated emotions and a sense of the sacred. Thus in a world of secular diversity, punishment continues to protect a residual sphere of sacred values, and draws its force and significance from this fact.[4]

---

1 Emile Durkheim, *The Division of Labor in Society* 79 (George Simpson trans., 1964) (defining the collective conscience as "the totality of beliefs and sentiments common to average citizens of the same society"). The normative implications of Durkheim's criminology have been partially developed by Jean Hampton, who argues "that the moral education which punishment effects is at least part of punishment's justification." Jean Hampton, "The Moral Education Theory of Punishment," 13 *Phil. & Pub. Aff.* 208, 208 (1984); see also Joel Feinberg, "The Expressive Function of Punishment," in *Doing and Deserving: Essays in the Theory of Responsibility* 95, 98 (1970).

2 David Garland, *Punishment and Modern Society* 67 (1990).

3 *Id.* at 68.

4 *Id.* at 57.

Indeed,

> handed down by our leading institutions with an aura of *gravitas* and
> moral seriousness, these decisions set the tone for the public's response
> at the very moment that they claim to express it.... [Such judicial
> decisions] prefigure popular sentiment and give it a degree of definition
> which it would otherwise lack. As James Fitzjames Stephen once put
> the point: "... the sentence of law is to the moral sentiment of the public
> in relation to any offense what a seal is to hot wax."[5]

Modern societies are held together not only by common values, of
course.   More important is the functional interdependence and
convergent interests created by a division of labor between members of
various occupational groups.[6]   Law's purpose is now primarily
"restitutive," as reflected in the growth of private litigation in contract
and tort.[7] An astringent version of liberalism is therefore prepared to
reject as romantic sentimentality the notion that modern social order
rests, in any significant measure, on shared values, that is, on what
Durkheim labels mechanical solidarity.[8]   In this view, social
solidarity—as mutual recognition of our interdependence—is better
served not by attempting to reaffirm shared principles but by
suppressing our principled disagreements and "forgetting" the political
conflagrations to which they may historically have given rise.[9]

---

5   *Id.* at 58.

6   Durkheim, *supra* note 1, at 147 (contending that "the ties which bind us to society
and which come from the community of beliefs and sentiments are much less numerous
than those which result from the division of labor" and that "co-operative law
express[es] ... the links which the division of labor brings about").

7   *Id.* at 112, 133-43, 147.

8   The leading exponent of this view is Niklas Luhmann.   Luhmann, *The
Differentiation of Society* (Stephen Holmes & Charles Larmore trans., 1982) (arguing
that modern industrial society consists of separate institutional spheres, each governed
by different principles, lacking any single normative order encompassing them all and
that the purpose of law is to regulate the interaction between these spheres, not to
subject them and their differing logics to any single coherent moral vision); see also
Ernest Gellner, *Conditions of Liberty* 96 (1994) ("Social co-operation, loyalty, and
solidarity do not now presuppose a shared faith. They may, in fact, presuppose the
absence of a wholly shared and seriously, unambiguously upheld conviction. They may
require a shared doubt.").

9   Stephen Holmes is the most vigorous contemporary exponent of this reading of
liberalism.   Stephen Holmes, "Gag Rules or the Politics of Omission," in

This view spurns Durkheim's confidence in law's capacity to evoke a collective conscience. But it resembles Durkheim's position, paradoxically, in assuming that dissensus on central normative questions is necessarily at odds with social solidarity. It assumes that if agreement cannot be reached here, solidarity must be found elsewhere: in the division of labor, i.e., in the cooperative mechanisms which a differentiated economy imposes and on which its continued operation relies).

The range of policy choice, in the aftermath of administrative massacre, is thus reduced to one between different forms of consensus: to remember (in the same way) or to forget. "Forgetting" becomes a metaphor for a political truce, a *modus vivendi.* "The French never *really* forgot," as historian Robert Paxton notes of Vichy collaboration; rather, "there was a tacit agreement not to tear one another apart."[10] Once the issue is framed this narrowly, the question becomes simply whether solidarity is better served by consensus in memory or consensus in oblivion.

To be sure, there remains the metaquestion of how much mechanical solidarity—how much common commitment to substantive moral principles—is necessary in a modern, pluralistic, industrial society. But virtually all versions of liberalism acknowledge that general commitment to a core of shared principles is necessary if modern society is "not to disintegrate," as one theorist summarizes, "into a heap of mutually antagonistic and self-seeking individuals."[11] These moral principles may derive historically from religion, but are now most strongly embodied in criminal law, according to Durkheim.[12] Once principles and stories are widely shared, they become what

---

Constitutionalism and Democracy 1 (Jon Elster & Rune Slagstad eds., 1988) (arguing that liberal society must sometimes suppress controversial topics to avoid conflict). He applies this approach to recent Eastern European developments in "The End of Decommunization," *E. Eur. Const. Rev.*, Summer-Fall 1994, at 33 (praising the decision of most new Eastern European democracies to dispense with criminal trials or massive purges of former communist elites). See also Bruce Ackerman, *The Future of Liberal Revolution* 84 (1992) (arguing that Eastern European states should burn their files on domestic informers and members of the secret police).

10   Judith Miller, *One, By One, By One: Facing the Holocaust* 141 (1990) (emphasis added).

11   Lewis A. Coser, *Masters of Sociological Thought* 132 (2d ed. 1977).

12   Durkheim, *supra* note 1, at 80-82, 109.

Durkheim called "social facts," which can be as genuine in their consequences as material facts.[13]

We know very little, however, about how moral ideas sometimes come to be widely adopted as societal ideals. Though they are sometimes helpful, clearer concepts and better normative theories are neither necessary nor sufficient for progress of this sort. Durkheim's followers have hinted at one promising approach: the ritual elevation of attempted "turning points" in a nation's history. At such times, "morality is formed in emotionalized collective states in which actors are attracted by ideals and lifted beyond themselves.... [Such] moments of collective effervescence transform or create social structures and interpersonal bonds."[14]

But if social rituals generally evoke shared values that endure, how could "turning points" in a society's history—when existing values are reconsidered and revised—ever serve as the focal point of ritual commemoration? The short answer (argued at greater length herein) is: When the need for a new beginning is widely felt, the very process of critical reassessment—to which the dramatic power of liberal show trials can contribute—may itself be symbolically treated (and later commemorated) as a decisive moment of collective refounding. As one scholar notes of this process:

> The choice of a single event clearly provides a better opportunity for ritualized remembrance than a gradual process of transition does. The master commemorative narrative thus presents these events as turning points that changed the course of the group's historical development .... In turn, selection of certain events as turning points highlights the ideological principles underlying the master commemorative narrative by dramatizing the transitions between periods. [Such events] not only reflect the social and political needs of the group ... but also become active agents in molding the group's needs.[15]

---

13 Emile Durkheim, *The Rules of Sociological Method* 1-13 (George E.G. Catlin ed., Sarah A. Solovay & John H. Mueller trans., 8th ed. 1966). For a recent discussion, see Margaret Gilbert, *On Social Facts* 237-54 (1989).

14 Stephen P. Turner, "Introduction: Reconnecting the Sociologist to the Moralist," in *Emile Durkheim: Sociologist and Moralist* 1, 19 (Stephen P. Turner ed., 1993) (parsing Durkheim's sociological theory of religious ritual).

15 Yael Zerubavel, *Recovered Roots: Collective Memory and the Making of Israeli National Tradition* 9 (1995) (emphasis omitted).

Some disagreement always exists over what the shared principles are and how far they reach. Do they extend, for instance, only to mutual recognition of one another's basic moral rights, or also into conceptions of the good life and attendant ideals of virtuous character? In any event, it is clear (indeed, almost tautological) that in a liberal society these common principles must be primarily liberal ones. Foremost among them is respect for fundamental liberties of the individual against encroachment by others, whether public or private.[16] Individualism, in this sense, provides modern society with "the basis of our moral catechism."[17]

The individualism of those within modern Western society is not presocial in origin, derived from a state of nature (any more than it is antisocial or antiegalitarian in normative thrust). Rather, the modern individualism that Durkheim revered is itself the product of societal differentiation and complexity. It results from the social process by which persons come to differ from one another through membership in multiple groups and organizations, voluntary and involuntary. The overlapping and cross-cutting nature of such allegiances generates conflicting demands on the person, conflicts that each must manage and resolve to her own satisfaction, in pursuit of psychological stability and personal integrity.[18]

Violence against individuals violates their moral rights to life and to physical integrity. Administrative massacre involves violent acts on a massive scale. Acts of violence evoke in citizens strong feelings of resentment and indignation toward the wrongdoer. Prosecuting

---

16   Steven Lukes, "Durkheim's 'Individualism and the Intellectuals'," 17 *Pol. Stud.* 14, 14 (1969). Contemporary "Durkheimians" often reject his conclusion here, contending that collective conscience and social solidarity rest entirely on the residue of *non*-liberal values and practices. Robert N. Bellah, "The Idea of Practices in *Habits*: A Response," in *Community in America* 269, 271 (Charles H. Reynolds & Ralph V. Norman eds., 1988). Much closer to Durkheim's spirit in this regard, however, is the interpretation offered by Mark S. Cladis, *A Communitarian Defense of Liberalism: Emile Durkheim and Contemporary Social Theory* 9 (1992).

17   Lukes, *supra* note 16, at 21; see also Durkheim, *supra* note 16, at 172 ("As all the other beliefs and ... practices [in modern society become] less and less religious, the individual becomes the object of a sort of religion. We erect a cult in behalf of personal dignity....").

18   This conception of individualism was developed by George H. Mead. George H. Mead, *Mind, Self & Society* 149-292 (Charles W. Morris ed., 1934).

wrongdoers also evokes—more important to Durkheimians—an awareness of *sharing* these sentiments with others, that is, of belonging to a community whose members are united by this very convergence and periodic reinvigoration of moral sentiment.[19] In criminal trials, prosecutors—as spokesmen for "the people"—tell the stories through which such sentiments are elicited and such membership consolidated. In affirming criminal convictions, appellate courts draw upon "the ritual attitude of sacred respect" for themselves and for the moral traditions they invoke.[20]

In the Argentine military trials President Raul Alfonsín's legal advisors, highly literate in social theory, hoped to put Durkheim's undoubted insights to work. They even invoked his theoretical terminology. Carlos Nino wrote,[21] for instance, that prosecution of the juntas "is required in order to inculcate in the collective conscience and in the consciences of the groups concerned that no sector of the population stands above the law."[22] Prosecution, in other words, was not necessary primarily for retribution (in which Nino did not believe)[23] nor for deterrence (which lies beyond the reach of the law when the criminals control the state). Prosecution was also at odds with "rehabilitation" of the officers corps as an institution. Reform of military education, for instance, would require active cooperation from the very officers most vulnerable to the criminal sanction.

The trial of the military juntas would tell a liberal story, hoped prosecutors and presidential aids, one that would strengthen public commitment to principles of liberal morality, embodied in criminal law

---

19   Durkheim, *supra* note 1, at 102 (arguing that "crime brings together upright consciences and concentrates them"). In other words, "each time the community moves to censure some act of deviation, then, and convenes a formal ceremony to deal with the responsible offender, it sharpens the authority of the violated norm and restates where the boundaries of the group are located." Kai T. Erikson, *Wayward Puritans* 13 (1966).

20   Dominick LaCapra, *Emile Durkheim: Sociologist and Philosopher* 289 (1972). LaCapra observes of Durkheim in this regard that "[t]he vision of a society based upon truth and justice and able to reconcile reason and the ritual attitude of sacred respect was vital to Durkheim's idea of structural reform in modern society." *Id.*

21   Nino was also a professor of legal philosophy and criminal law.

22   Carlos S. Nino, "Transition to Democracy, Corporatism and Constitutional Reform in Latin America," 44 *U. Miami L. Rev.* 129, 136 (1989).

23   Carlos S. Nino, "A Consensual Theory of Punishment," 12 *Phil. & Pub. Aff.* 289, 300 (1983).

and egregiously violated in the dirty war. The trial, in other words, was in substantial part a self-conscious attempt to "apply" Durkheimian social theory. Argentine liberals understood the application of Durkheim's ideas not so much to entail strapping the patient down for emergency transfusions of liberal fluids, as laying the groundwork for concurrent reforms in political institutions.[24] As Alfonsín would announce (in a speech drafted by Nino), "the full and free exercise of democratic citizenship, individual liberties and social solidarity, must now provide the foundation for constructing a modern society."[25]

Editorial sympathizers with the Alfonsín government adopted a similar idiom in defending the proceedings. One wrote of the televised proceedings, for instance, that

> the victims, as witnesses, appeal not only to the judges but implicitly to the community at large. Each victim, finally rescued from oblivion, seeks recognition of the essential humanity that was denied him. For this reason, the trial, as an event in the life of the entire community, not only furthers legal justice but also, at the same time, helps to reconstruct the nation's ethical foundations.[26]

Nino, would later strike a similarly Durkheimian chord in reflecting on what the junta trial had accomplished. "The moral consciousness of society seems to have been deeply affected by these trials.... The months of testimony regarding the atrocities made a perceptible impact in the minds of the people."[27] "In its sober and thorough decisions, [the court] set forth principles conducive to the reestablishment of the rule of law ...."[28] The trial had served to "awaken the dormant legal consciousness."[29]

---

24 On several of these proposed reforms, see Carlos S. Nino, "The Debate over Constitutional Reform in Latin America," 16 *Fordham Int'l L.J.* 635, 636-37, 646-49 (Michael E. Roll trans., 1993).

25 Raul Alfonsín, "Speech Before Delegates of the National Committee of the *Unión Cívica Radical* "(Jan. 12, 1985), in *Alfonsín: Discursos Sobre el Discurso* 11, 14 (Luis Aznar et al. eds., 1986) (translation by author).

26 Hugo Vezzetti, *"El Juicio: Un Ritual de la Memoria Colectiva,"* 7 *Punto de Vista* 3, 5 (1985) (translation by author).

27 Carlos Nino, *Radical Evil on Trial* 90 (1996).

28 *Id.*

29 *Id.* Nino here refers favorably to, and extrapolates from, Shklar's defense of the

might become decisive for creating and consolidating the very specific sort of collective conscience required by a modern liberal society. During that episode, "many who thought they had little in common joined in intellectual and moral communion as they felt the 'horror' of the trespass against Dreyfus's rights."[42] Simply put, mechanical solidarity was achieved—and remains possible—through the felt sharing of liberal principle.

It is ironic, however, that the Dreyfus trial would lead Durkheim to realize how liberalism could supplant religion as the collective conscience of a modern society, fostering the sort of mechanical solidarity it required. For although that famous trial fostered considerable solidarity among Dreyfus's supporters (the liberals) and among his opponents (the antiliberals), it engendered only the deepest divisions between supporters and opponents, divisions that were to endure and infect French politics for decades.[43]

For these three reasons, as well as others examined herein, Durkheim offers only the most uncertain help in understanding criminal law's potential contribution to social solidarity in times of deep political division and societal trauma. But the solidarity that can result from a shared code of substantive morality, periodically reinvigorated by punishing those agreed to have violated its first principles, is not the only sort. Solidarity is a concept that admits of several conceptions.[44]

---

42   Cladis, *supra* note 16, at 22 (interpreting Durkheim's reflections on the period).

43   On the divisions introduced or exacerbated by the Dreyfus trial, see H.R. Kedward, *The Dreyfus Affair: Catalyst for Tensions in French Society* 2, 9, 13 (1965). On the trial's enduring legacy for French politics, see François Furet, *In the Workshop of History* 220 (Jonathan Mandelbaum trans., 1984) (arguing that the French right saw in the country's 1940 defeat "an opportunity for taking long-awaited revenge on the Republic" and "availed itself of the national debacle to take its revenge for ... the Dreyfus affair").

44   On the distinction between concepts and conceptions, central to the jurisprudence of Ronald Dworkin, see Dworkin, *Law's Empire* 71-72 (1986); Ronald Dworkin, *Taking Rights Seriously* 134-36 (1977).

Chapter 2.

Solidarity Through Civil Dissensus

Durkheim's conception of mechanical solidarity pertains only when virtually all members of society share a particular view of justice: their fundamental ideas about how other members should be treated, ideas quintessentially embodied in their criminal law.

This condition is conspicuously absent in many societies, particularly in societies just emerging from experiences of large-scale administrative massacre. Thus, prosecution of its perpetrators cannot hope to establish collective memory upon shared moral intuitions already deeply felt and culturally encoded, requiring only an occasion for their easy evocation.[1] As ritual expressions of collective conscience, trials for administrative massacre have decidedly *not* been, as we shall see, simple and unmediated reflections of moral sentiments universally felt within society toward the accused—the frequent assumption of foreign observers to this effect notwithstanding.

Episodes of large-scale administrative massacre, like the Holocaust and the Argentine dirty war, do disrupt social solidarity in decisive ways. This is amply recognized by many citizens—surviving victims, passive bystanders, and (at least low-level) collaborators alike—who find themselves asking one another in the wake of such traumatizing events: What sort of place *is* this that such things could happen? What trust can we ever again place in fellow citizens and political leaders who allowed such horrors to occur? Given the pervasiveness with which our society's official norms were betrayed by so many, why should we ever put confidence in anyone but our most intimate kith and kin? Julian Barnes's fictional prosecutor reflects, for instance, that "one part of his job, every day now, on television, was to help expunge that fear [of repression], to reassure people that they would never have to give in to

---

1   This may be, in fact, more generally true of other trials. Sally F. Moore, "Explaining the Present: Theoretical Dilemmas in Processual Ethnography," 14 *Am. Ethnologist* 727, 729 (1987) ("[A legal] event is not necessarily best understood as the exemplification of an extant symbolic or social order.... Events may show a multiplicity of social contestations and the voicing of competing cultural claims.").

it again."[2] The Argentine lawyers who prosecuted the military juntas described their professional tasks and self-understanding in similar terms.[3]

Citizens of former Soviet Bloc societies, for instance, now concern themselves with such questions as: "How is basic trust to be established when memories persist of neighbors informing on neighbors, friends on friends and husbands on wives?"[4] When such questions become both inescapable and unanswerable, social solidarity of any but the most crudely economistic sort threatens to collapse entirely. That threat of collapse is no mere sociological abstraction; it begins to haunt the most minor, daily interactions in profound and perplexing ways, as memoirs of these periods reflect.[5] People watch one another, in even the most private settings, with hair-trigger sensitivity to the possibility of betrayal. The fragile tissue of social life wears precariously thin.

Deliberation requires a measure of trust in one's interlocutors. In the aftermath of administrative massacre, this is at low ebb. Because social antagonists do not trust one another, they are strongly tempted to prefer alternatives to deliberation. At such times, the formalized rules

---

2   Julian Barnes, *The Porcupine* 74 (1992).

3   Interview with Luis Moreno Ocampo, Assistant Prosecutor, in Buenos Aires, Argentina (Aug. 1987).

4   Michael T. Kaufman, "Lurching Toward Democracy," *N.Y. Times,* May 14, 1995, §7 (Book Reviews), at 8. Even when the good faith of family members could be assumed, the danger of inadvertent slips posed further problems for intra-familial trust. "Nobody confided their doubts to their children," writes Nadezhda Mandelstam of the Stalinist era, for "suppose the child talked in school and brought disaster to the entire family?" Quoted in Adam Hochschild, *The Unquiet Ghost: Russians Remember Stalin* 16 (1994).

5   Carlos Nino, *Un País al Margen de la Ley* 54-55, 131-34, 270-71 (1990); Juan Corradi, "The Culture of Fear in Civil Society," in *From Military Rule to Liberal Democracy in Argentina* 113, 119-28 (Monica Peralta-Ramos & Carlos Waisman eds., 1987); Ernest Gellner, "Trust, Cohesion, and the Social Order," in *Trust: Making and Breaking Cooperative Relations* 142, 142 (Diego Gambetta ed., 1988); see also Jaime Malamud-Goti, *Game Without End: Terror, Justice and the Democratic Transition in Argentina* (forthcoming 1996) (manuscript at 142-62, 175- 85) (describing how a pervasive distrust and fear of betrayal by government informers infected all but Malamud-Goti's most intimate familial relations during the military dictatorship and following years); Carina Perelli, "*Memoria de Sangre:* Fear, Hope, and Disenchantment in Argentina," in *Remapping Memory* 39, 45 (Jonathan Boyarin ed., 1994) (observing how the climate of fear tended "to curb the impulse to provide assistance and comfort to one's neighbors, coworkers, or fellow students; to forego caring or sharing for the sake of staying alive.").

riminal trial permit a kind of deliberation between otherwise
it participants. The resulting deliberation itself can begin to
generate a measure of trust. When "institutions are designed to
facilitate deliberative approaches to political conflict," writes a political
theorist, "they can help to generate ... desirable forms of trust. Trust, in
other words, is one of the important transformative effects that
democratic institutions can have upon the interests and identities of
participants."[6]

A central aim of "the rule of law" itself, after all, has always been
to lessen the risk of conferring trust, by lending assurances to
expectations about how others will behave.[7] Creating trust is thus a
longstanding purpose of legal rules and institutions. They can restore
trust both between individual disputants and throughout society at large.
It should not seem so strange, then, to examine the trials of Eichmann
and Videla in light of their potential contribution to restoring social trust
and solidarity.

One strand of neo-Durkheimian criminology recognizes the limits
of legal rituals for restoring fractured solidarity in societies torn by
internal conflict. At such times legal rituals cannot merely "express"
emotions inertly, as Garland observes. Rather,

> they arouse them and organize their content; they provide a kind of
> didactic theatre through which the onlooker is *taught* what to feel, how
> to react, which sentiments are called for .... Rituals—including the
> rituals of criminal justice—are ceremonies which, through the
> manipulation of emotion, prompt particular value commitments on the
> part of the participants and the audience and thus act as a kind of
> sentimental education ....[8]

He concludes, "like all rituals of power, punishments must be carefully
staged and publicized if they are to have their intended results."[9] Like
other rituals, they can "*modify* social reality by modifying the agents'

---

6 Mark E. Warren, "Democracy and Trust," 1-2 (paper presented at the American
Political Science Association Conference, San Francisco, Aug. 30, 1996).

7 Niklas Luhmann, "Trust," In *Trust and Power: Two Works by Niklas Luhmann* 34
(1979).

8 David Garland, *Punishment and Modern Society 67* (1990) (emphasis added).

9 *Id.* at 80.

representation of it."[10]

A traumatized society that is deeply divided about its recent past can greatly benefit from collective representations of that past, created and cultivated by a process of prosecution and judgment, accompanied by public discussion about the trial and its result. Thus, the internal dynamics of this process, especially the implications of the choices it entails for all parties, are very significant.

Durkheim grasped none of this. Yet it is this constructive process rather than any finished judicial product or authoritative pronouncement that is the most important contribution of criminal prosecution to social solidarity at such times.[11] Hence, Tullia Zevi, president of Italy's Jewish communities, remarks concerning the war crimes trial of Erich Priebke: "'The verdict is in some ways irrelevant .... What is important is the trial.'"[12] This importance consists in the way it forces those telling competing stories to join issue with each other.

As Gewirtz observes, "Thinking about the trial as narrative or storytelling can bring fresh attention to the communicative exchanges central to [it], directing us to the fact that the trial is centrally an arena of speakers and listeners, that the trial's search for truth always proceeds by way of competing attempts to shape and present narratives for particular audiences, that the form of telling and the setting of listening affect everything, that telling and listening are complex transactions that jointly create meaning and significance."[13]

In trials involving administrative massacre, at least, we should start by conceding that the criminal courtroom will inevitably be viewed as

---

10   Pierre Bourdieu, *Language and Symbolic Power* 128 (1991) (emphasis added).

11   Laura Nader & Harry F. Todd, Jr., "Introduction" to *The Disputing Process: Law in Ten Societies* 1, 22 (Laura Nader & Harry F. Todd, Jr. eds., 1978) ("People who write about the judicial process and the judicial decision as if the outcome were solely the product of a third party, a judge, miss the sociological relevance of the courtroom as an interactive arena.").

12   Celestine Bohlen, "Italy Opens Trial in Wartime Massacre in Rome," *N.Y. Times,* Dec. 8, 1995, at A4. Priebke is a former SS captain accused of the 1944 killing of 335 people outside Rome. The event is considered the worst atrocity that occurred in Italy during World War II. Zevi adds, "'What do I care if Priebke ends up under house arrest, or in prison for life?'" *Id.* Priebke was later acquitted on grounds of having obeyed superiors' orders.

13   Paul Gewirtz, "Victims and Voyeurs: Two Narrative Problems at the Criminal Trial," in *Law's Stories: Narrative and Rhetoric in the Law* 136-37 (Peter Brooks and Paul Gewirtz eds., 1996).

providing a forum in which competing historical accounts of recent catastrophes will be promoted. These accounts search for authoritative recognition, and judgments likely will be viewed as endorsing one or another version of collective memory. To ignore this fact is to become entranced and deceived by our own (otherwise defensible) abstractions: professional, doctrinal, and jurisprudential. Better to face facts, to learn to live with the reality that such trials will necessarily be read for their "larger lessons," as monumental didactics. Let us turn this admittedly unsettling circumstance into an opportunity for liberal legality, for fostering solidarity of a liberal sort.[14]

Simmel offered the first hints of how certain kinds of disputes might foster solidarity. He observed that sometimes, as one commentator notes:

> The very act of entering into conflict with an antagonist establishes relations where none may have existed before.... Once relations have been established through conflict, other types of relations are likely to follow.... Conflict, for Simmel, just as crime for Durkheim, brings out the need for application of rules that, had no conflict occurred, might remain dormant and forgotten .... Those who engage in antagonistic behavior bring into consciousness basic norms governing rights and duties of citizens. Conflict thus intensifies participation in social life. This very consciousness of the need for rules governing their behavior makes the contenders aware that they belong to the same moral universe.[15]

---

14   Robert Hariman, "Introduction" to *Popular Trials: Rhetoric, Mass Media, and the Law* 1, 8 (Robert Hariman ed., 1990) ("Rather than seeing popular trials as odd or embarrassing moments in legal practice, we should recognize how they provide opportunities to articulate ideas important to our larger understandings of legal interpretation and the role of law in society.").

15   Lewis A. Coser, *The Functions of Social Conflict* 121, 123-24, 127 (1956) (parsing Georg Simmel, *Conflict and the Web of Group Affiliations* 26 (Kurt H. Wolff trans., 1955) and then offering examples from legal disputes over property and contract, as well as the law of war). Albert Hirschman recently argued, to similar effect, that "the community spirit that is normally needed in a democratic market society tends to be spontaneously generated through the experience of tending the conflicts that are typical of that society." Albert O. Hirschman, "Social Conflicts As Pillars of Democratic Market Society," 22 *Pol. Theory* 203, 216 (1994).

Not *all* such conflicts are functional, of course. Neither Simmel nor Coser, however, offer much guidance in distinguishing functional from dysfunctional conflict, *ex ante* or even *ex post*. Their simple point, moreover, should not be subsumed under some grand Hegelian process whereby devastating conflict becomes indispensable to social progress, through the cunning dialectic of history. It is nevertheless true, as

This argument about the unifying effects of conflict applies even in Durkheim's citadel of consensus: the criminal courtroom. The court becomes a privileged site for conflicting accounts of recent history and the memories of it that citizens should preserve. At such times, the "circumstances of politics" are the following: people differ radically on their judgments of recent history (that is, on what went wrong and who is responsible), and yet share the view that some resolution of this disagreement must be reached among themselves for the country to set itself back on track.[16] At the end of World War II, for instance, both conservative and liberal political leaders in Japan—despite their many differences over the nature of needed change—agreed that there existed a crucial 'connection between clarification of "the causes of defeat" and building a new "moral Japan."'[17]

At such times, if opposing factions do not reach some resolution, the social solidarity that they all seek cannot be restored. Each is thus obliged—by circumstance, not shared morality—to engage the other in hopes of persuading a more general public, and perhaps even an immediate opponent, of the superiority of a favored historical account. To be persuasive to anyone, one must display a measure of civility, even toward those one would prefer, in ideal circumstances, simply to kill or suppress.[18]

Deliberative Democratization

Rules of criminal procedure and professional responsibility seek to ensure, among other things, a measure of civility in the courtroom, a civility achieved even in the midst of heated conflict. Such civility is not primarily a matter of decorum or politeness, but of compliance with

---

Lawrence Whitehead famously observed, that sometimes "the major advances in civilization are processes which all but wreck the societies in which they occur." *Id.* at 210.

16 Jeremy Waldron, "The Circumstances of Politics," (paper presented at the American Political Science Association Conference, New York, N.Y., Sept. 2, 1994).

17 Herbert P. Bix, 'The Shōwa Emperor's "Monologue" and the Problem of War Responsibility,' 18 *Journal of Japanese Studies* 295, 311 (1996).

18 On the role of civility in liberal discourse, see Mark Kingwell, *A Civil Tongue: Justice, Dialogue, and the Politics of Pluralism* (1995).

rules requiring parties to treat one another with respect, as equal participants in a common task of truth-seeking. Through such "rules of engagement,"[19] each party comes to learn, at the very least, what its opponent actually thinks and most deeply cares about. Through this process, dangerous misconceptions about "the other" are overcome.

The adversary system, although roundly condemned by many today for stirring needless bitterness and antagonism, is nevertheless highly functional where conflict between parties has already reached a point of deep mutual incomprehension. At such times, the adversary system is indispensable, in Lon Fuller's words, as "a means by which the capacities of the individual may be lifted to the point where he gains the power to view reality through eyes other than his own."[20] Fuller further notes that

> an effective consensus cannot be reached unless each party understands fully the position of the others.... At the same time, since an effective consensus requires an understanding and willing cooperation of all concerned, no party should so abandon himself in advocacy that he loses the power to comprehend sympathetically the views of those with different interests.... This implies not only tolerance for opposing viewpoints, but tolerance for a partisan presentation of those viewpoints, since without that presentation they may easily be lost from sight.[21]

At the very least, through adversarial exchanges, when constrained by civility rules, we achieve a sense of lived experience that is mutual. With better luck, we gain some appreciation of how someone could, sincerely and in good faith, come to think so differently from us about something so fundamental to us both.[22]

---

19   On how other legal rules, such as the law of defamation, similarly aim to foster civility as a norm of public discourse and seek to make such civility a feature of national identity, see Robert Post, "Managing Deliberation: The Quandary of Democratic Dialogue," 103 *Ethics* 654 (1993).

20   Lon L. Fuller, "The Adversary System," in *Talks on American Law* 34, 47 (Harold J. Berman ed., Vintage Books 2d ed. 1971) (1961).

21   *Id.* at 46.

22   This appreciation can, in turn, produce agreement on questions of constitutional structure among those retaining radically different comprehensive doctrines of the good. On how this happens, see John Rawls, "The Domain of the Political and Overlapping Consensus," in *The Idea of Democracy* 245, 255 (David Copp et al. eds., 1993).

On how procedural protections of dignified exchange foster a significant measure

The experience of disagreement itself, although often unpleasant and divisive in many ways, nonetheless creates a kind of joint understanding: that we have both faced the issues dividing us, that we are united in caring deeply about them and about what the other thinks of them. The phenomenology of this interpersonal experience nowhere has adequately been captured in social or political theory. But who among us can deny having had it, and having found it not altogether unpleasant?

So long as we follow the rules of civility that govern the discursive enterprise, we are (in an underappreciated sense) united by it, drawn willy-nilly into a form of solidarity—albeit not the mushier sort favored by Durkheim and current communitarians.[23] A measure of social unity is achieved, neither "on the mystical model of fusion," with its risky political romanticism, nor "on the legal model of the contract,"[24] the classic solution of liberal theory.

We form attachments to our adversaries not only through procedures establishing agreement on how to disagree, but through the actual human experience of the resulting exchanges, provided they conform to these civility rules. Through such exchanges, we need not transcend our differences on matters of ultimate concern. We need not come to love our adversaries in Aristotelian friendship. We may continue to view them much as we view our appendix: an object without which we could very easily go on living and that only imperils us with the prospect of its eruption, an object whose condition cannot be entirely ignored as long as it remains part of us.

In this spirit, opposing parties greet each other not with a fraternal

---

of satisfaction among civil litigants, even when they do not prevail, see E. Allan Lind et al., "In the Eye of the Beholder: Tort Litigants' Evaluation of Their Experiences in the Civil Justice System," 24 *Law & Soc'y Rev.* 953, 971-73, 981 (1990). See also W. Lance Bennett & Martha S. Feldman, *Reconstructing Reality in the Courtroom* 171 (1981) ("When people say that trials are objective and impartial means of producing legal judgments, what they really mean is that trials rely on a standardized means of packaging and analyzing information: the story.... [In the litigants' view,] protection of the justice process only holds if all parties in an adjudication have the same capacity to present and judge stories.").

23   On the many affinities (and some important disaffinities) between Durkheim and contemporary communitarians, see Mark S. Cladis, *A Communitarian Defense of Liberalism: Emile Durkheim and Contemporary Social Theory* 170-75, 276-79 (1992).

24   Alain Finkielkraut, *The Defeat of the Mind* 72 (1995).

embrace, nor even a businesslike handshake, but rather with a nod of mutual acknowledgment, initially grudging, that they will occupy the same society— reluctantly but inescapably—for the foreseeable future. It has become fashionable to disparage so limited a view of what the members of a society can hope to share with one another as reflective of a merely "procedural republic." But such a republic would better be viewed as a noble aspiration and hard-won achievement for societies whose histories have been as recurrently fratricidal as Argentina's.

Solidarity of this sort, then, does not claim to provide any recipe for societal happiness. Through the debate on which it is predicated, however, we may reluctantly come to acknowledge that there is a legitimate place in ongoing public discussion for the views, and hence their spokesmen, that we initially regarded as odious and contemptible.

Just such a change has been observed in a study of the "Waldheim affair" in Austria, concerning the former President's participation in wartime atrocities. At first, "the confrontational nature of this vehicle of memory made people shun the past, rather than explore it."[25] As the affair developed, however, "'what began as a vitriolic confrontation had evolved into a positive debate.'"[26] In such debates, we often expect to remain profoundly at odds over our attributions of blame for recent national horrors and about what should be done to prevent their recurrence. But we are united in the hope of ultimately achieving a measure of agreement on certain issues—if not now, then at some future point. As seasoned participants report, this process of solidarity through dissensus happens routinely in democratic politics.[27]

Such solidarity can happen, as well, in the courtroom, or through a process of discussion initiated there but continued elsewhere. It can occur even if the discussion begins only under duress: because one party to the debate, the defendants, are forced to justify themselves, in

---

25 Judith Miller, *One, By One, By One: Facing the Holocaust* 286 (1990).

26 *Id.* at 86 (quoting Leon Zelman, a Polish Jew who survived three and a half years at Mauthausen, Auschwitz, and other camps).

27 Consider, for instance, the considerable mutual respect and appreciation—indeed friendship—that developed between Senators Edward Kennedy and Orrin Hatch through their many years of work on the Senate Judiciary Committee. Neil A. Lewis, "Orrin Hatch's Journey: Strict Conservative to Compromise Seeker," *N.Y. Times,* Mar. 2, 1990, at A12.

response to prosecutorial accusation.[28] "Democracy begins in conversation," John Dewey said.[29] The act of conversation presupposes a measure of respect for the rational and deliberative capacities of one's interlocutor, as Jürgen Habermas contends.[30]

Respect need not always be a precondition for dialogue, however; it can also be its result. This must be our response to those who assume that a criminal trial can only reinforce existing attitudes of respect for human rights, attitudes that must already be effectively in place for the punishment to have this confirmatory effect.[31]

Unlike an "ideal speech situation,"[32] in which debate must be entirely unconstrained, a real discussion between non-hypothetical antagonists requires the restraint of civility rules.[33] These rules (of

---

28 Whether this process of social learning is successfully set in motion depends on many factors unrelated to law itself, such as how the mass media report the trial, the degree of forbearance opposing counsel show toward each other's adversarial excesses, the structure of the political system, and many other contingent circumstances. Much depends, as well, on the degree of "obligation one feels to the contested memory." Iwona Irwin-Zarecka, *Frames of Remembrance: The Dynamics of Collective Memory* 81 (1994).

29 *Dialogue on John Dewey* 58 (Corliss Lamont ed., 1959) (quoting James T. Farrell's recollections of Dewey's remarks).

30 2 *Jürgen Habermas, The Theory of Communicative Action* 46, 86, 187, 262-66 (Thomas McCarthy trans., 1981).

31 This view has been proposed by Thomas Scanlon. Tape of Human Rights and Deliberative Democracy: A Conference in Honor of Carlos Santiago Nino, Presented at Yale Law School (Sept. 23-24, 1994) (currently available on videotape from the Schell Center for Human Rights).

32 Jürgen Habermas, *Justification and Application: Remarks on Discourse Ethics* 56-59 (1993).

33 On such rules, see Robert C. Post, "Between Democracy and Community: The Legal Constitution of Social Form," in *Democratic Community: NOMOS XXXV*, at 163, 168-69 (John W. Chapman & Ian Shapiro eds., 1993). Several readers of this manuscript have observed a resemblance here between the civility rules explicitly governing legal process and those tacitly governing faculty meetings at many American law schools. In the latter settings, even those who radically disagree on substantive questions nevertheless implicitly agree, when debating our differences, to eschew *ad hominems*, to appeal to normative standards that we profess to share, to refrain from escalating the terms of a localized dispute into a decisive battle in "the culture wars," and to engage respectfully the arguments of those whose views, in more intimate settings, we would confess to finding loathsome. But for these unstated discursive conventions, many of which we import from our experience in legal practice, faculty meetings at many American law schools would quickly degenerate into fratricidal conflagrations, as they routinely do in the humanities and social sciences.

evidence, procedure, and professional ethics) serve as "enabling constraints."[34] By permitting an orderly sequence of exchanges, they enable a discussion to occur that would otherwise never take place. Without such rules, the parties would refuse to sit down together, or when they did, would quickly descend to vitriolic name-calling, theological incantation, or outright violence. Seen in this light, "the entire law of evidence, and much of the law of procedure," as Gewirtz observes, "is really a law of narrative—a law of narrative transactions."[35]

A criminal trial is one useful way to begin a discussion with an initially unwilling interlocutor. It also formulates the discussion in the favored terms of liberal morality, as this is the moral theory underpinning most of our criminal law.[36] At very least, this is a hypothesis worth considering.[37] Let us call this the "discursive" conception of how criminal prosecution might strengthen social solidarity.[38] It is more consistent with what we currently know about

---

34   This definition is employed by Bernard Yack, to describe a distinctive feature of liberal theory developed by Benjamin Constant and Niklas Luhmann. Bernard Yack, "Toward a Free Marketplace of Social Institutions: Roberto Unger's "Super-Liberal" Theory of Emancipation," 101 *Harv. L. Rev.* 1961, 1967 & n.12 (1988).

35   Gewirtz, *supra* note 13, at 136.

36   On the liberal foundations of criminal law, according to both liberalism's defenders and critics, see George Fletcher, *Rethinking Criminal Law* at xix (1978); H.L.A. Hart, *Punishment and Responsibility* at preface (1968); Alan W. Norrie, *Law, Ideology, and Punishment: Retrieval and Critique of the Liberal Ideal of Criminal Justice* at xiii (1991); Michael S. Moore, "The Moral and Metaphysical Sources of the Criminal Law," in *Criminal Justice: NOMOS* XXVII, at 11, 14 (J. Roland Pennock & John W. Chapman eds., 1985).

37   It is somewhat unclear what would count as convincing evidence that this type of solidarity had become established in a given society, beyond the fact that its members were no longer slaughtering one another. But this methodological problem is shared with the Durkheimian-communitarian conception of solidarity. The present study therefore limits itself to examining the extent to which each of these types of solidarity would be impaired by the six obstacles discussed.

38   Several influential theorists currently stress the importance of public discourse and the legal rules protecting it, as the basis for any legitimate authority in a modern democracy. Cass Sunstein, *Democracy and the Problem of Free Speech* (1993); Seyla Benhabib, "Deliberative Rationality and Models of Democratic Legitimacy," 1 *Constellations* 26, 26 (1994) (arguing that "legitimacy in complex modern democratic societies must be thought to result from the free and unconstrained public deliberation of all about matters of common concern"). On how legal rules settling procedures for public discourse also tacitly shape national identity, see Bruce Ackerman, "Constitutional Politics/Constitutional Law," 99 *Yale L.J.* 453, 477 (1989); Post, *supra*

the formation of collective memory, I shall contend, for that process proves to be "more like an endless conversation than a simple vote on a proposition," as one historian puts it.[39]

Writing just before his early death, Nino would describe the aims and achievements of the Argentine military trials in similar terms:

> The trials promote *public deliberation* in a unique manner. Public deliberation counteracts the authoritarian tendencies which had led, and continue to lead, to a weakening of the democratic system and massive human rights violations. All public deliberation has this effect, but even more so when the subject of the public discussion is those very authoritarian tendencies. The disclosure of the truth through the trials feeds public discussion and generates a collective consciousness and process of self-examination. Questions like, "Where were you, Dad, when these things were going on?" become part of daily discourse. The contrast between the legality of the trials and the way the defendants acted is prominently noticed in public discussion and further contributes to the collective appreciation of the rule of law. Public discussion also serves as an escape valve for the victims' emotions and promotes public solidarity which, in turn, contributes to the victims recovering their self-respect ....[40]

Nino continues that

> this type of value-searching deliberation was evident in the debates surrounding the trials in Argentina. The accusations, the defenses, judicial decisions, and arguments taking place among society were precisely about the role of the military and other groups in a democratic society, the moral limits for the achievement of certain goals (quite often society cited the legal manner in which terrorism was fought in European countries as a counterexample), the rule of law (the most common conciliatory argument was that the military could have achieved the same

---

note 33, at 678. On the contribution of open public debate to social solidarity, see Jürgen Habermas, "Justice and Solidarity," in *The Moral Domain* 224, 244-45 (Thomas Wren ed., 1990).

39   John Thelen, "Memory and American History," 75 *J. Am. Hist.* 1117, 1127 (1992); see also *id.* at 1119 (observing that collective memory "is not made in isolation but in conversations with others that occur in the contexts of community, broader politics, and social dynamics.").

40   Carlos Nino, *Radical Evil on Trial* 147 (1996).

ds through summary trials and open death sentences under appropriate laws which sanctioned such actions), and the advantages of a division of power to protect human rights (it was often said that, even in the degraded democracy of Isabel Peron, there were fewer violations of human rights than under the military).[41]

Nino here displays an unsullied optimism about the role of universal reason in politics. This optimism is equally conspicuous in his more philosophical writing and draws vigorous criticism from leading theorists on that account.[42] The "solidarity" of which Nino speaks in this passage expressly rests upon the achievement of agreement throughout Argentine society about how to judge the military's conduct in the dirty war. Nino assumes that unconstrained discussion and public deliberation could lead to no other result. He may well be correct that "reason prevailed" in most of the discussions, public and private, to which he alludes. But it did not prevail in all of them, by any means, nor in all of the most important ones, that is, among citizens with power to influence future events.[43]

The solidarity that I anticipate (and observed) in contrast, presumes no such agreement, but merely civil engagement in disagreements by way of procedures entailing display of respect for one's adversary, respect that may be entirely procedural (and a matter of rule-following) at the outset but that often tends to grow into something more substantive—if not between the most unreconstructed of antagonists, then among the larger numbers of their more moderate sympathizers. There is a kind of solidarity, in other words, in continuing exchanges that result in the mutual recognition that agreement on a question of common concern is strongly desirable and ultimately possible, even if only at some uncertain point in the future.

Social scientists are quick to tell us these days that invocations of shared values, in social theory no less than in national politics, are often merely "pious allusions,"[44] which "greatly overstate the degree of

---

41   *Id.* at 133.

42   Nino Conference, *supra* note 31 (particularly the remarks of Bernard Williams).

43   On hostile reaction to the trials among military and conservative circles, including (initially) many elite newspapers, see Horacio Verbitsky, *Civiles y Militares: Memoria Secreta de la Transición* 95-108, 171-94, 371-82 (2d ed. 1987).

44   Sally Falk Moore, "Introduction," In *Moralizing States and the Ethnography of the*

shared value commitments."[45] Such commonalities are partly fictional, to be sure. But the fiction they offer to the disputing process is surely a salubrious one. It enables opposing parties to argue with one another as if they actually did share fundamental principles, as if they differed only about how these should be interpreted and applied to a particular context. By appealing to norms that all claim to share, norms embodied in a legal system for which all profess respect, the fiction of common values serves to limit the scope and intensity of controversy within mutually tolerable bounds.

It may be true, as the social scientists insist, that "even people who talk as though they fully endorsed and agreed upon the ideals of national unity do not necessarily mean the same thing by it."[46] Yet surely the central truth here is that even the deepest disagreements are channeled into a single conceptual framework, providing common terms. This common framework offers the basis for discursive engagements that would be impossible if participants did not share its repertory. Through such discussions, in turn, the fiction of shared values can often be slowly pushed in the direction of "social fact." The civility rules of legal fora, combined with the substantive rules of criminal law, provide one such framework.

Every form of social solidarity has its privileged institutional locus, Durkheim implied. Mechanical solidarity finds its favored locale in the church, especially a legally "established" one, where core values can be evoked and authoritatively interpreted with a maximum of symbolic resonance throughout the furthest reaches of a society.[47] The economy offers the institutional center for organic solidarity.[48] The division of labor involved in a modern economy makes far-flung sectors of the

---

Present 1 (Sally Falk Moore, ed., 1993).

45 Steven Lukes, "Political Ritual and Social Integration," 9 *Sociology* 289, 298 (1975).

46 Michael Herzfeld, *Anthropology Through the Looking Glass* 152 (1989).

47 Emile Durkheim, *The Division of Labor in Society* 75-76, 159-173 (George Simpson trans., 1964). Mechanical solidarity "comes from a certain number of states of conscience which are common to all the members of the same society." *Id.* at 109. "It is a product of the most essential social likenesses ...." *Id.* at 106. Such solidarity "can be strong only if the ideas and tendencies common to all the members of the society are greater in number and intensity than those which pertain personally to each member." *Id.* at 129.

48 *Id.* at 131.

population and their diverse productive activities increasingly dependent upon one another—and increasingly *aware* of such interdependence, partly due to periodic disruption in the ever-lengthening chain of commercial exchange.

The result is an awareness of attachment to, and a fate shared with others who are and will remain anonymous, but whose differing activities are meaningfully related to one's own, Durkheim inferred.[49] The law remains essential to such attachments, not by codifying a consensus on fundamental morality, but simply by providing a key symbolic code through which complexity is reduced, agreements reached, and attachments formed.[50]

But it is the polity, especially the freedoms of press and speech integral to democratic politics, that constitute the institutional foundation of discursive solidarity. Such solidarity arises from, and consists of, the attachments formed (often unwittingly) through the vigorous exercise of these rights that a liberal society will most prominently display—and to which its adherents should aspire.[51] It is the memory of our discursive engagements themselves, no less than our memory of the events we discuss, that establishes such solidarity between us. Engagements of this sort can occur as much around a dinner table, and on neighborhood street corners, as on the stage of "high" politics.

Discursive solidarity is not the third act in some social-evolutionary drama. Like the other two varieties, it is best viewed as an ideal type, a conceptual construct not expected to provide the sufficient conditions of solidarity in any actual society.[52] We may expect all three varieties to be instantiated within a given country, in

---

49   *Id.* at 55-56, 61-62.

50   Niklas Luhmann, *The Differentiation of Society* 122-137 (Stephen Holmes & Charles Larmore trans., 1982); Talcott Parsons, "Law As an Intellectual Stepchild," in *Social System and Legal Process* 11, 12 (Harry M. Johnson ed., 1978).

51   Bernard Crick, *In Defense of Politics* 24 (1962):
  Diverse groups hold together ... because they practise politics—not because they agree about 'fundamentals', or some such concept too vague, too personal, or too divine ever to do the job of politics for it. The moral consensus of a free state is not something mysteriously prior to or above politics: it is the activity (the civilizing activity) of politics itself. *Id.*

52   For a discussion of this method, see Max Weber, *The Methodology of the Social Sciences* 90 (Edward A. Shils & Henry A. Finch eds., trans., 1949).

different degree, at a particular point in time. All three, moreover, may be necessary and desirable in the modern world, in relations within and between national societies. Contemporary societies "require solidarity between their members on more than one level."[53]

The three types of solidarity vary as well in the significance they ascribe to the differences between individuals, and between various groups, within a society. Mechanical solidarity requires a denial, even an active suppression, of differences between individuals and subgroups in order to preserve the sharing of a single normative order among them.[54] Organic solidarity requires a preservation and cultivation of differences between individuals and subgroups in order to enhance efficiency and productivity.[55] Discursive solidarity, by contrast to both, requires neither the permanent denial nor affirmation of difference. It involves simply a recognition that a society's members often disagree radically regarding their conceptions of justice and the good and that they nevertheless recognize a need to settle upon a common scheme of association and cooperation. Rules requiring civility in the management of disagreements provide a useful device for reaching this end.

Narrative Conflict in a Liberal Voice

Postmodernist accounts of narrative typically view the cacophony of alternative tales about the same large-scale event, and the resulting conflict between them, as valuable in themselves. The proliferation of "little narratives," each by performative utterance, ensures that no single "grand meta-narrative" will ever consolidate itself as *the* collective memory of an event.[56] Such a consolidation would entail, on this view, an effective "end to narration, by revealing the meaning of narratives."[57] The *force* of narratives, however, is not "synonymous with the meaning

---

53 Maeve Cooke, "Selfhood and Solidarity," 1 *Constellations* 337, 350 (1995).

54 Durkheim, *supra* note 47, at 129-31.

55 *Id.* at 131-32.

56 Jean-François Lyotard, *The Postmodern Condition: A Report on Knowledge* at xi, 27-33, 60 (Geoff Bennington & Brian Massumi trans., 1984); Jochen Mecke, "Dialogue in Narration (the Narrative Principle)," in *The Interpretation of Dialogue* 195, 213 (T. Maranhão ed., 1990).

57 Bill Readings, *Introducing Lyotard: Art and Politics* 63 (1991).

that may be found in them."[58] Narratives are valuable regardless of their persuasiveness, because they involve "argumentation whose purpose is to bring to light and provoke contestation over implicit rules that constrain the production of new ideas and determine the boundaries of political communities."[59]

In brief, leading postmodernists seek to sever the link that liberalism seeks between moral argument and conflict reduction, between political deliberation and agreement production.[60] On this view, the law should not seek to banish all ambiguity, even regarding the wrongfulness of genocidal conduct or the culpability of its perpetrators. The inescapability of cognitive and moral ambiguity is the very essence of the postmodern condition—hence the doubts and disagreement to which law perpetually gives rise. It is therefore wrong to endow anyone's story about a collective event with authoritative status, for the same reason that it is wrong to endow political power with moral legitimacy: the worst abuses of power are always committed by those most convinced of the moral superiority of their cause, their civilization, or their theory of history.[61]

Jacques Vergès, defense counsel for Klaus Barbie, subtly appealed to this pervasive preoccupation, fostered by leading postmodernists, turning it to his client's advantage. Vergès's public rhetoric about the prosecution sought to equate the serene confidence of the criminal law,

---

58   *Id.*

59   Lisa J. Disch, *Hannah Arendt and the Limits of Philosophy* 9 (1994) (parsing Lyotard, *The Postmodern Condition*, at xxiv). Several commentators have noted the anarchistic sensibility that such a normative ideal entails. Todd May, *The Political Philosophy of Poststructuralist Anarchism* 3 (1994); Michael Walzer, "The Politics of Michel Foucault," in *Foucault: A Critical Reader* 51, 61 (David Hoy ed., 1986). For a leading defense of postmodernist politics, so conceived, see Bonnie Honig, *Political Theory and the Displacement of Politics* 2 (1992) (decrying the preoccupation of political theory with "the juridical, administrative, [and] regulative tasks of stabilizing moral and political subjects, building consensus, maintaining agreements, or consolidating communities and identities"). Roberto Unger's views on such issues are similar. Roberto Unger, *Social Theory* 22 (1987).

60   Honig, *supra* note 59, at 2-5, 14-15; Deena Weinstein & Michael A. Weinstein, *Postmodern(ized) Simmel* 115- 29 (1993); William E. Connolly, *Identity\Difference* x (1991) (Democracy, properly understood, should not "equate concern for human dignity with a quest for rational consensus. It opens political spaces for agonistic relations of adversarial respect.").

61   The strains of anarchism are again strong here. May and Walzer, *supra* note 59.

in its judgment against his client, with that of French colonialism, now recognized to have perpetrated grave injustices in the name of lofty principles, those of Western civilization.[62]

The same principles of French culture invoked against his client, Vergès suggested, had been invoked against the Algerians and other victims of French power.[63] As this incident amply reveals, the logic of the postmodernist celebration of contested memory applies no less to the "disruptive" narratives of Nazi war criminals than to those of ethnic minorities or battered wives. After all, the only "counter-hegemonic narrative" publicly offered in Argentina, in opposition to that of Alfonsín and his liberal courts, was that of the officer corps, a story about military victory in a just war against foreign-inspired subversion.[64]

In contrast, the liberal view defended here values civil dissension as a means for developing some solidarity in a deeply divided society. It occupies a midpoint on the continuum between the postmodernist celebration of permanent disruption, as an end in itself,[65] and the Durkheimian veneration of settled consensus over moral fundamentals, with its denial of continuing disagreement among reasonable people at the end of the day. On the present account, the contested character of collective memory is cause neither for celebration nor despair, but a challenge to liberal solidarity and an opportunity for its conscious cultivation by dramaturgical design.

Official correction of collective memory by criminal law remains subject to an intensely practical constraint: those with an interest in

---

62   Alain Finkielkraut, *Remembering in Vain: The Klaus Barbie Trial and Crimes Against Humanity* 32-36 (Roxanne Lapidus & Sima Godfrey trans., 1992).

63   *Id.*

64   Ejército Argentino, *El Derecho a la Libertad* (1980); Ramon J.A. Camps, *El Poder en la Sombra: El Affaire Gravier* (1983); Interviews with Argentine Military Officers, in Buenos Aires, Argentina (June-Aug. 1985).

65   Postmodernists generally think that political institutions should help bring to the surface conflicts that presently lie dormant, conflicts that are merely "suppressed," in their view. Honig, *supra* note 59, at 2-17. The liberal perspective adopted here, by contrast, assumes that existing Western democracies already succeed in raising social conflicts to the surface of political life in ample abundance, without the need to incite such conflicts any further; political institutions, in this view, need only provide a receptive forum for deliberative discussion and resolution of these conflicts.

collective forgetting must not get their way.[66] In analyzing these trials, there is a danger of over-subtlety (to which we intellectuals incline), that must be resisted. The point of such proceedings is not so much to make people remember what they have repressed and would prefer to forget—the psychoanalytical angle[67]—but rather to confront those with something to hide with evidence they have tried to keep from coming to light.[68] In postwar Germany, for instance, "the extinction of memory," as Adorno wrote, "is far more the accomplishment of an all too wide awake consciousness than of its weakness in the face of ... unconscious processes."[69]

Still, one should not infer that the simple task of locking up enough of the people with blood on their hands is the exclusive concern of criminal trials. No less important to the political efficacy of these proceedings is the way in which they are orchestrated and symbolized, I suggest. As Clifford Geertz observes, "the real is as imagined as the imaginary."[70] "This prejudice ... that the dramaturgy of power is external to its workings, must be put aside."[71]

During periods of democratization, political conflict often extends to the question of how the prior regime and those who served it should be remembered, and how the law should be employed to that end. Sometimes, as in the recent murder prosecution of East German border guards, this conflict finds its way into the criminal courts.[72] It has been

---

66 This point is made with particular cogency by one Argentine who lost several family members during the dirty war. Noga Tarnopolsky, "Murdering Memory in Argentina," *N.Y. Times,* Dec. 12, 1994, at A19.

67 Several have examined West Germany's postwar self-scrutiny—particularly the limits on that process—in psychoanalytic terms. Dominick LaCapra, *Representing the Holocaust* (1994); Eric L. Santner, *Stranded Objects: Mourning, Memory, and Film in Postwar Germany* (1990).

68 I am grateful to Jeffrey Herf for this observation. For much the same point, see Saul Friedlander, "Some German Struggles with Memory," in *Bitburg in Moral and Political Perspective* 27, 29 (Geoffrey H. Hartman ed., 1986).

69 Theodor Adorno, "Was bedeuter Aufarbeitung der Vergangenheit," in *Theodor Adorno: Gesammelte Schriften* 10:2 (1977).

70 Clifford Geertz, *Negara: The Theatre State in Nineteenth-Century Bali* 136 (1980).

71 *Id.*; see also Umberto Eco, "Semiotics of Theatrical Performance," *Drama Rev.,* Mar. 1977, at 107, 113 ("It is not theatre that is able to imitate life; it is social life that is designed as a continuous performance and, because of this, there is a link between theatre and life.").

72 Tina Rosenberg, *The Haunted Land: Facing Europe's Ghosts After Communism*

especially apparent in the former Soviet Bloc in recent years.[73]

The recovery of a more accurate past, the correction of collective memory, is an integral aspect of democratization. "Indeed, there is a striking correlation," observes Timothy Garton Ash, comparing the recent history of Central European states, "between the degree of facing up to the past, however clumsily, and the state of progress from dictatorship to democracy. Which is cause and which effect is a moot point; they go together."[74] Describing this process in the former Soviet Union, David Remnick notes, with only slight exaggeration, that "the return of history to the intellectual and political life of the people of the Soviet Union was the foundation of the great changes ahead."[75]

Thus, changes in collective memory, through official efforts to revise historical understanding (by executive order, legislation, or litigation), can have monumental consequences for social and political structure. What, then, are the foreseeable obstacles to efforts at employing the law toward this end?

261-305 (1995); Kif A. Adams, "What Is Just?: The Rule of Law and Natural Law in the Trials of Former East German Border Guards," 29 *Stan. J. Int'l L.* 271, 295-300 (1993).

73   The Hungarian novelist and sociologist György Konrad observes, for instance: "'Today only the dissenters [that is, those who opposed Communist oppression] conserve the sentiment of continuity. The others must eliminate remembrances; they cannot permit themselves to keep the memory.... Most people have an interest in losing memory.'" Cécile Wajsbrot & Sébastien Reichmann, *Europe Centrale* 84 (1991).

74   Timothy G. Ash, "Central Europe: The Present Past," *N.Y. Rev. Books,* July 13, 1995, at 21, 22.

75   David Remnick, *Lenin's Tomb: The Last Days of the Soviet Empire* 41 (1993); see also Misha Glenny, *The Rebirth of History* (1990).

Part II.

**LEGAL SHAPING OF COLLECTIVE MEMORY:
SIX OBSTACLES**

Chapter 3.

Defendants' Rights, National Narrative, and Liberal Memory

Is liberal jurisprudence inherently at odds with any effort to orchestrate prosecution as public spectacle, for social didactics? What is the proper place within an avowedly liberal legal theory for dramaturgical concerns about reaching a desired audience?

None, many liberals would say. They would agree, of course, that a gripping story is to be preferred to a wearisome one, *ceteris paribus*. But unfortunately—many liberals hasten to add—other things rarely turn out, on careful inspection, to be truly equal after all. What makes for a good "morality play" tends not to make for a fair trial.[1] And if it is the simplifications of melodrama that are needed to influence collective memory, then the production had best be staged somewhere other than in a court of law.[2] A call for monumental didactics is all too likely to be mistaken as an invitation for histrionic bellicosity and sanctimonious grandstanding—vices to which certain members of our profession are not altogether immune.[3]

Even so, there is nothing especially pernicious, in principle, about efforts to shape the dynamics of criminal proceedings for maximal dramaturgical effect. Theatrics of this sort are, after all, part of the

---

1 The Nuremberg proceedings were condemned in precisely these terms by contemporary commentators. Their views are summarized in William J. Bosch, *Judgment on Nuremberg: American Attitudes Toward the Major German War-Crimes Trials* 36-39, 51, 110-11, 153, 236 (1970).

2 Buruma offers a typical statement of this view:
Just as belief belongs in church, surely history education belongs in school. When the court of law is used for history lessons, then the risk of show trials cannot be far off. It may be that show trials can be good politics ... but good politics don't necessarily serve the truth.
Ian Buruma, *The Wages of Guilt: Memories of War in Germany and Japan* 142 (1994). Furthermore, "political trials produce politicized histories." *Id.* at 166.

3 Julian Barnes warns of this danger. The prosecutor, returning home from a day of particularly dramatic but underhanded point-scoring against the deposed dictator in the dock, is greeted by his wife, who pronounces his performance "worthy of American television." She adds: "It was vulgar and dishonest, contemptuous of the law, and you behaved like a pimp." Julian Barnes, *The Porcupine* 111-12 (1992).

standard repertoire of any effective courtroom lawyer.[4] Theatrics are not, however, thought to be a legitimate part of the judicial repertoire, even when rendering judgment against violations of basic human rights.

There is reason to wonder whether justice to the defendant, however heinous his wrongs, has been compromised when it can be said, as does one Israeli historian, that "the trial was only a medium, and Eichmann's role was simply to be there, in the glass booth; the real purpose of the trial was to give voice to the Jewish people, for whom Israel claimed to speak."[5] Another Israeli scholar adds that "Eichmann rather swiftly became peripheral to his own trial, which was deliberately designed to focus more comprehensively on the Nazi crimes against the Jews."[6] Those initially willing to testify in his defense were deterred from so doing by threat of prosecution for their own wartime activities.[7] Surely, they would have sought to tell a different tale.

In the trial of Klaus Barbie, "pent-up feelings were vented as those who had suffered took revenge on history."[8] Although the prosecutor and court relied almost entirely on documentary evidence in developing their legal arguments, the trial was orchestrated to highlight very different evidence for the mass audience: "The witnesses ... were the

---

4   Moreover, some historians contend that the professional pleader of the 13th century was in origin a "remembrancer [who used] the poetic technique of the singer of tales to recall the forms of his 'tales' or pleadings." M.T. Clanchy, "Remembering the Past and the Good Old Law," 55 *History* 165, 175 (1970). Other historians have traced the origins of such "memory officials," and the courts' reliance on them, to ancient Greece. Jacques Le Goff, *History and Memory* 63 (Steven Rendall & Elizabeth Claman trans., 1992).

5   Tom Segev, *The Seventh Million: The Israelis and the Holocaust* 358 (1993). Segev writes that Israeli Prime Minister "David Ben-Gurion often emphasized that the man Adolf Eichmann was of no interest to him; he was concerned only with the historic importance of the trial itself." *Id.* at 327. One of Ben-Gurion's principal goals in holding the trial "was to remind the countries of the world that the Holocaust obligated them to support the only Jewish state on earth." *Id.*; see also Hannah Arendt, *Eichmann in Jerusalem* 4-5 (Penguin Books, rev. & enlarged ed. 1977) (1963) (describing the courtroom architecture as "not a bad place for the show trial David Ben-Gurion ... had in mind" and Ben-Gurion as "the invisible stage manager of the proceedings").

6   Moshe Halbertal, "The Seventh Million: The Israelis and the Holocaust," *New Republic*, Oct. 18, 1993, at 40, 43 (book review).

7   Robert K. Woetzel, *The Nuremberg Trials in International Law with a Postlude on the Eichmann Case* 249 (2d impression rev. 1962).

8   Henry Rousso, *The Vichy Syndrome: History and Memory in France Since 1944* 214 (Arthur Goldhammer trans., 1991).

heroes of the trial because they gave, symbolically, faces to the dead, who were on everyone's mind."[9]

Such observations suggest the first of six reasons for skepticism—namely, the risk of sacrificing the defendants' rights on the altar of social solidarity—about what law might do for collective memory of administrative massacre.

The primary limit that liberalism imposes on storytelling in criminal trials is the principle of personal culpability: the requirement that no defendant be held responsible for the wrongs of others beyond his contemplation or control.[10] This entails a judicial duty to focus on a very small piece of what most observers will inevitably view as a much larger puzzle, to delimit judicial attention to that restricted place and period within which the defendant willfully acted.

Episodes of administrative massacre, however, generally involve many people acting in coordinated ways over considerable space and time, impeding adherence to this stricture. Moreover, to tell a compelling story, one that will persuade its intended audience that it is not unfairly singling out a serviceable scapegoat, the state (in the person of the prosecutor) must be able to paint the larger tableaux. Hence the recurrent tension, of which trial participants have often been well aware, between the needs of persuasive storytelling and the normative requirements of liberal judgment.[11]

This tension has manifested itself in diverse ways during various prosecutions for administrative massacre. In prosecuting Eichmann, Ben-Gurion wanted, above all else, to retell the story told at Nuremberg in an entirely different way.[12] This retelling would conceive the offense as a "crime against the Jewish people," rather than against "humanity"—the latter concept an invention of the secular Enlightenment. Ben-Gurion's retelling was "ideologically rooted in the Zionist disappointment with liberalism," as an Israeli legal scholar

---

9 *Id.*

10 George Fletcher, *Rethinking Criminal Law* 459-63, 492-95, 509-11 (1978).

11 The Israeli trial court, for instance, repeatedly reproached the prosecutor for seeking to expand the narrative frame with evidence of Nazi wrongs that could not be traced to Eichmann's acts. *Attorney-Gen. of Israel v. Eichmann,* 36 I.L.R. 5, 18-19 (Isr. Dist. Ct. 1961).

12 Pnina Lahav, "The Eichmann Trial, the Jewish Question, and the American-Jewish Intelligentsia," 72 *B.U. L. Rev.* 559-61 (1992).

observes.[13] It was designed to reflect the Zionist view that liberalism, with its aim of moral universalism, had misled the Jews into seeking assimilation within gentile societies, rather than reestablishing their own.[14]

What better way to dramatize the link that Zionism asserted between assimilation's failure and the occurrence of the Holocaust than by a story about how Eichmann's actions assaulted the flesh of the Jewish people, not merely the liberal morality of the assimilated? For Israelis, this made for a powerful and persuasive story. Yet the narrative was willfully and unabashedly antiliberal, not merely in violating *nulla poena sine lege*, but in its very definition of the offense as one committed against a particular ethnoreligious community. In myriad ways, Ben-Gurion sought to frame the courtroom narrative in expressly communitarian terms, as a tale about the Jewish community's collective victimization, suffering, resistance, resurrection (from the ashes of failed assimilation), and, finally, redemption as a powerful nation-state.

Eichmann's seeming "banality" admittedly became the absorbing focus for Hannah Arendt and later generations of non-Israeli intellectuals.[15] But for Israelis themselves (and many other observers) his pedestrian, non-demoniac character simply made him boring.[16] It became that much easier to concentrate their attention upon the very different and more compelling drama told by his victims—the survivor-witnesses (whose narratives Arendt found entirely beside the point, leaving her largely unmoved).[17] That the Nuremberg judgment appears in virtually every casebook and treatise on international law,

---

13   *Id.* at 560.

14   *Id.* at 559-68. Ben-Gurion probably had other intentions of a more partisan nature as well. But I am here concerned only with his success in using the trial to reshape the memory and meaning of the Holocaust for Israelis.

15   See, e.g., David Luban et al., "Moral Responsibility in the Age of Bureaucracy," 90 *Mich. L. Rev.* 2348, 2359-60 (1992).

16   Alex Ross, "Watching for a Judgment of Real Evil," *N.Y. Times,* Nov. 12, 1995, §2, at 37, 40 (noting that Eichmann's courtroom persona was "lackluster," due to his "evasive pedantry").

17   Virtually all Israeli studies of the Eichmann trial, and of its legacy for that nation, focus upon this. Segev, *supra* note 5, at 345-66; Haim Gouri, "Facing the Glass Booth," in *Holocaust Remembrance: The Shapes of Memory* 155 (Geoffrey H. Hartman ed., 1994).

while the Eichmann judgment appears in virtually none, would not have troubled Ben-Gurion in the least, one suspects. He was playing to a different audience, and he chose his theatrical techniques accordingly.[18]

In the Nuremberg and Tokyo trials, illiberalism took another form. Defendants complained that the narrative of the courtroom was being framed too broadly. The Charter for the Tokyo trial, for instance, provided that "the tribunal shall not be bound by technical rules of evidence ... and shall admit any evidence that it deems to have probative value."[19] Apart from the unchecked discretion this approach granted the courts, its effect may have been, as Justice Pal argued in dissent, to "operate practically against the defense only."[20]

The breadth of relevant evidence followed from the breadth of the conspiracy charge, covering over a decade. As a legal historian recently observed:

> The court's discussion of the case is largely a historical narrative of the unfolding of this conspiracy rather than an examination of each defendant's conduct. The problem ... is that a narrative structure built around a conspiracy theory inevitably emphasizes the actions of the "conspirators" as an abstract collectivity, and operates to obscure the precise connection of specific individuals to particular events.[21]

He continues, "the basic strategy, then, ... was not to delineate clearly the culpable conduct of each defendant, considered as an individual, but rather to establish participatory linkage between each defendant and a

---

18   In this regard, Arendt was right to note "the almost universal hostility in Israel to the mere mention of an international court which would have indicted Eichmann, not for crimes 'against the Jewish people,' but for crimes against mankind committed on the body of the Jewish people." Arendt, *supra* note 5, at 7.

19   *Tokyo Charter*, art. 13, cited in Richard H. Minear, *Victors' Justice: The Tokyo War Crimes Trial* 118 (1971). A similar provision appeared in the London Charter for the International Military Tribunal at Nuremberg. *Id.* at 118.

20   *U.S. Dep't of State, Pub. No. 2613, Trial of Japanese War Criminals* 12, 39, 42 (1946) (Pal, J., dissenting). American tribunals employed similarly relaxed evidentiary rules, allowing hearsay, unsworn statements, and "facts of common knowledge" in all postwar proceedings against Japanese defendants. Philip R. Piccigallo, *The Japanese on Trial: Allied War Crimes Operations in the East, 1945-1951* 38 (1979).

21   David Cohen, "Beyond Nuremberg: Individual Responsibility for War Crimes," in *Human Rights in Transitions* (Robert Post & Carla Hesse eds., forthcoming 1997). In my view, Cohen's charge in this regard is entirely accurate, and devastating.

historical flow of collective activity.... This was done without specifying the criteria which would render such participation culpable."[22] In short, the court's narrative successfully simplified some highly complicated events into an intelligible, coherent, and evocative story. But in so doing, it failed to adhere to liberalism's requirement that criminal liability be conditioned on a showing of individual culpability.

By contrast, in the Buenos Aires trials, military defendants complained that the law's framing of their conduct was far too narrow to judge it fairly. Defense counsel sought to situate the military's conduct in a wider context of the collapse of public order during the last years of Peronist rule. On this account, the military's victims were actually perpetrators and aggressors in the larger conflict, which entailed a virtual state of war by leftist guerrillas, supported in key ways by a web of sympathizers.[23] On this framing of the tale, the military's conduct represented only the self-defense of Argentine society, a response proportionate to the serious threat that this society had faced. The court employed traditional rules of evidence, however, to prevent this contextualizing effort, to the considerable detriment of the defendants' case, many believed.[24]

A key question, then, is whether compelling collective memory may be purchased only at the exorbitant price of fairness to individual defendants. An affirmative answer is suggested by the fact that those most enamored of harnessing the law to the construction of collective memory are generally those most hostile to liberal morality.[25]

Any talk of monumental didactics evokes the fear of Stalinist "show trials," those degradation rituals[26] in which every invocation by

---

22   *Id.*

23   Lieutenant Colonel Carlos Horacio Dominguez offers an elaborate legal argument to this effect in *La Nueva Guerra y el Nuevo Derecho: Ensayo para una Estrategia Jurídica Contrasubversiva* (1980).

24   On how criminal law permits alternative temporal framings of a defendant's act, allowing admission or exclusion of exculpatory evidence, see Mark Kelman, "Interpretive Construction in the Substantive Criminal Law," 33 *Stan. L. Rev.* 591, 616-20 (1981). For a sociological perspective on this problem, see Erving Goffman, *Frame Analysis* (1974).

25   I refer to cultural anthropologists and Durkheimian sociologists, who are decidedly communitarian in their ethical theory.

26   Harold Garfinkel, "Conditions of Successful Degradation Ceremonies," 61 *Am. J.*

defendants of procedural protections is recharacterized by the court as further evidence of their seditious character as "enemies of the people." Milner Ball states the conventional wisdom: "Insofar as it is made a platform for moralizing or a forum for educating, a trial is not a trial. Trials may indeed have an educative effect, but they have this effect when, instead of deliberately undertaking to teach, they treat the parties as individuals."[27]

In Defense of Liberal Show Trials

Liberal legal theorists will thus be tempted quickly to reject the cultivation of collective memory as a defensible objective when prosecuting those responsible for administrative massacre. But that conclusion would be premature and unfounded. The orchestration of criminal trials for pedagogic purposes—such as the transformation of a society's collective memory—is not inherently misguided or morally indefensible. The defensibility of the practice depends on the defensibility of the lessons being taught—that is, on the liberal nature of the stories being told. Whether show trials are defensible depends on what the state intends to show and how it will show it. Liberal show trials are ones self-consciously designed to show the merits of liberal morality and to do so in ways consistent with its very requirements.

Those requirements do not include a purely proceduralist version of the rule of law, as Shklar rightly argued in defending the Nuremberg

---

Soc. 420, 420 (1956). On Stalin's purge trials, especially on prosecutorial vituperation of defendants and their legal "'evaluation from the point of view of class expediency,'" see Aleksandr I. Solzhenitsyn, *The Gulag Archipelago* 1918-1956, at 308 (Thomas P. Whitney trans., 1973) (quoting N.V. Krylenko, Stalin's Prosecutor General). See also Lon L. Fuller, "Pashukanis and Vyshinsky: A Study in the Development of Marxian Legal Theory," 47 *Mich. L. Rev.* 1157, 1161-62 (1949) (defining show trials as "sham legal proceedings, repeatedly used in the USSR and other communist countries ... designed to dramatize specific political campaigns and/or eliminate prominent individuals"). For the standard, entirely pejorative connotation of the term "show trial," based on the Soviet experience, see *A Dictionary of Politics* 454-55 (Walter Laqueur ed., 1971).

27   Milner S. Ball, *The Promise of American Law* 56 (1981); see also Robert Hariman, "Introduction" to *Popular Trials: Rhetoric, Mass Media, and the Law* 3 (Hariman ed., 1990) (arguing that "the more a trial appears to be a scene or product of public controversy and rhetorical artistry, the less legitimate it appears").

trial. The rule of law, so understood, could be satisfied even in highly authoritarian regimes.[28]   To strengthen substantive norms of liberal conduct (against gross cruelty, for instance), courts might have to revise procedural rules during a democratic transition, partly compromising the protections they afford. Moreover, other cases of administrative massacre examined here suggest that the procedural revisions necessary to enhance a trial's impact on collective memory—such as admitting evidence bearing on wider, historical interpretations—often prejudice the prosecution far more than the defense. What justifies such revisions does not turn on which side's interests are prejudiced by them.

Their justification rests simply on their capacity to make for telling a better story about where the country should be heading.   The Nuremberg trial was therefore justified, she argued, as a "great legalistic drama"[29] that would help postwar Germany refound itself and base its new Constitution on principles of justice. The trial was justified, in purely consequentialist terms, to the extent that it "reinforced dormant legal consciousness" among the German people.[30] Nuremberg should therefore be defended *as* a political trial, unabashedly so. What mattered most, at such times and places at least, was not to insulate legal institutions from politics, but rather to ensure that they were placed in service of the *right kind* of politics. The present study is little more than an elaboration and defense of Shklar's argument in this regard. But I am more concerned than she with the practical question of 'how to do it.' After all, any good lawyer would surely react to a such a proposal with our proverbial refrain: the devil is in the details.

"What is the cost for the individual and for society," asks one anthropologist, "when there is no meaningful framework for publicly exploring traumatic memories of political violence?"[31] That question

---

28   Judith Shklar, *Legalism: Law, Morals, and Political Trials* 150 (1986). For further analysis of this problem in historical context, see Mark J. Osiel, "Dialogue with Dictators: Judicial Resistance in Argentina and Brazil," 20 *Law & Social Inquiry* 481 (1995).

29   Shklar, *Id.* at 169. My interpretation of Shklar's critique of "legalism" has profited from a recent paper by Lisa J. Disch, "Exploring the 'Territory Between History and Ethics': Judith Shklar on Narrative and Political Theory," (paper presented at the American Political Science Association Conference, San Francisco, Aug. 30, 1996).

30   Shklar, *supra* note 28, at 156.

31   Rubie S. Watson, "Memory, History, and Opposition Under State Socialism: An Introduction," in *Memory, History, and Opposition Under State Socialism* 1,

sounds no less powerfully in a liberal society than in any other.

A liberal society, to be sure, cannot officially endorse any full-bodied conception of the good.[32] Hence its law, as an expression of state power, cannot aspire to provide its members a fully coherent way of life. In other words, individual rights establish side-constraints that the state must respect. Liberalism is a theory neither about "the meaning of life,"[33] nor about the ends in service of which these rights must be exercised. The legal storytelling in which courts necessarily engage, reproaching some and commending others, cannot seek to teach citizens how to exercise their moral autonomy, other than to respect the like autonomy of others. In this sense, the lessons taught by a liberal society and its law are necessarily and deliberately incomplete. The common culture of a liberal society can be only "loosely coherent."[34]

Even so, a liberal state may employ a "show trial" for administrative massacre to display the horrific consequences of the illiberal vices and so to foster among its citizens the liberal virtues (including respect for basic individual rights, deliberative capacity, and toleration). "There is no reason to think that liberal citizens come about naturally ...."[35] As Macedo contends, "We need to avoid making the mistake of assuming that liberal citizens—self-restrained, moderate, and reasonable—spring full-blown from the soil of private freedom."[36]

A criminal trial is a congenial public opportunity for collective mourning of the victims of administrative massacre. It provides a ritual that is helpful for family members and a sympathetic public in coming to terms with melancholia in even the most traumatic cases.[37] Just

---

13 (Rubie S. Watson ed., 1994).

32   John Rawls, *A Theory of Justice* 395-411, 446-49 (1971).

33   Charles E. Larmore, *Patterns of Moral Complexity* 69-90 (1987).

34   Stuart Hampshire, *Morality and Conflict* 149 (1983). I later develop this point regarding the relationship between official narratives, sanctioned by criminal law, and "private" memories of personal experiences, which are often the basis for civil damage suits.

35   Stephen Macedo, "Transformative Constitutionalism and the Case of Religion: Defending the Moderate Hegemony of Liberal Constitutional Values," in *Constitutional Politics and Constitutional Studies* (Sotirios Barber & Robert George eds., forthcoming 1996).

36   *Id.* Joseph Raz adopts a similar view in *The Morality of Freedom* 196-97 (1986).

37   Peter Homans, *The Ability to Mourn* 261-348 (1989). As a ritual, mourning involves a condition of grief that is repeated and expressed in a "reduced, normatively

because a liberal state cannot dictate the terms on which the victims' lives could be lived does not preclude the state from providing an occasion that serves for mourning their wrongful taking.

The liberal state can thus provide an institutional mechanism for mourning not only the deprivation of a victim's abstract moral rights, but the fully-developed life she might have lived in exercising those rights. In so doing, criminal law contributes significantly to the social solidarity that is based on shared commitment to liberal principles of mutual respect and concern among individuals. This communal mourning is one important role that collective memory may legitimately play in a liberal society, or within a society aspiring to liberalize itself.

With this provisional answer in mind, we can begin to assess how the law might properly contribute to the formation of such memory, particularly of national catastrophes like the Argentine dirty war. I shall speak of law's legitimate tasks in this regard as those of liberal memory. Is it possible, when prosecuting perpetrators of administrative massacre, to craft evidence and legal argument in a way that stimulates public discussion of the underlying issues, influencing the ensuing debate so as to foster liberal morality and solidarity? That is our central question.

Liberal stories are ones that, in treatment of their characters, reward the liberal virtues and condemn illiberal vices. Cruelty is a cardinal vice in this regard;[38] respect for individual life and liberty, the cardinal virtue.[39] All else is commentary.[40] Liberal virtues are those dispositions of character that a liberal society must cultivate in its members in order to function effectively and to keep social conflict within tolerable bounds.

First and foremost, a liberal society must inculcate the disposition to respect the moral rights of others, that is, the rights that liberal morality accords to all persons. The stories that criminal courts tell

---

controlled, and socially supported form." Dominick LaCapra, *Representing the Holocaust* 199 (1994).

38   Judith N. Shklar, *Ordinary Vices* 44 (1984).

39   Recent efforts to find a place for virtue within liberalism include Stephen Macedo, *Liberal Virtues* 131-62 (1990) and William A. Galston, *Liberal Purposes* 237 (1991).

40   There is more to most contemporary versions of liberal theory than individual rights against others or to civic and political participation, of course. But whether a liberal society also requires social provision of "primary goods" or essential social "capabilities" is tangential to present purposes.

must celebrate this virtue and chastise the correlative vice. The law accomplishes this only when courts and juries themselves respect the law, that is, when they adhere to legal rules reflecting liberal principles of procedural fairness and personal culpability as conditions of criminal liability. The most gripping of legal yarns must hence be classified as a failure if its capacity for public enthrallment is purchased at the price of violating such strictures.

But within these principled constraints, liberals have plenty of good stories to tell. As Yack observes:

> If man is, as MacIntyre insists, "... a story-telling being," ... then we should expect men and women to turn theories, even liberal theories which insist on impersonal and antitraditional criteria, into the basis for new stories.... The French turned liberty from tradition into a female figure, symbolic of the Republic's virtues and energy. American colonists turned Lockean liberal principles into didactic stories with which to educate their children.... Similarly, the Kantian categorical imperative has generated stories that celebrate moral courage, while social contract theories have encouraged stories that celebrate the virtues associated with self-reliance.[41]

But notice that a liberal story, on Yack's representative account, does no more than illustrate principles, the validity of which do not derive from the story itself or from the character-virtues of those enacting it. Stories allow the listener to intuit directly the moral lessons embedded in them. Rather than being required to "act on principle," that is, in conscious awareness of moral duties discerned from the story's proper interpretation, stories allow us to apprehend these lessons in an unmediated way: from the very vivacity of their immediate impact on the listeners' sentiments.[42] "Ideally, a story should be

---

41 Bernard Yack, "Liberalism and Its Communitarian Critics: Does Liberal Practice "Live Down" to Liberal Theory?," in *Community in America* 147, 151-52 (Charles H. Reynolds & Ralph V. Norman eds., 1988). Yack's reference to liberty as a female figure alludes to an early effort of liberal iconography to translate republican ideas into pictorial imagery with which citizens could readily identify. On this effort, see Maurice Agulhon, *Marianne into Battle: Republican Imagery and Symbolism in France, 1789-1880* (Janet Lloyd trans., 1981).

42 Adam Z. Newton, *Narrative Ethics* 13 (1995) ("[By eliminating] the mediatory role of reason, narrative situations create an immediacy and force, framing relations ... that bind narrator and listener .... These relations will often precede ... understanding, with

self-explanatory," Gallie notes.[43]

Thus, stories appear primarily a crutch, on Yack's account, for those who cannot yet reason abstractly, who must emulate the concrete lives of "role models" because they have not yet learned to formulate their aspirations at any level of generality, their moral ideals in more universalistic terms. Just as we rely increasingly on pictures for assisting memories as we age,[44] so we initially learn (in childhood) our society's moral principles by way of stories, not moral argument.[45] It is thus scarcely surprising that, in seeking direction or instructing our children, most of us turn more readily to biblical parables than to Kant's *Prolegomena*.

From this perspective, liberalism uses stories primarily "to evoke the psychological reality behind political thought, and to jar recognition."[46] They do so by appealing to the emotions and, in this way, help "provide the force to do as reason commands."[47] Stories can, as well, provide empirical data illustrating what justice or some other virtue requires in a given situation. But stories and abstract theory, on this view, remain different entities, distinct ways of knowing, each in its conceptually watertight cubbyhole.

There is a second and more sophisticated view of the relation between storytelling and legal theory, compatible with liberalism but not monopolizable by it. This approach does not see the two activities as logically separate, essentially different in nature. Rather, it stresses the element of theorizing already inherent in storytelling and,

---

consciousness arriving late, after the assumption or imposition of intersubjective ties.").

43   W.B. Gallie, *Philosophy and the Historical Understanding* 23 (1964).   Gallie further states that: "It is only when things become complicated and difficult—when in fact it is no longer possible to *follow* them—that we require an explicit explanation of what the characters are doing and why. But the more skillful the story-teller, the rarer will be the intrusion of such explicit explanations." *Id.* at 22-23.

44   Mihaly Csikszentmihalyi & Eugene Rochberg-Halton, *The Meaning of Things: Domestic Symbols and the Self* 63-69, 112 (1981).

45   On the salience of storytelling in the moral education of young children, see Gallie, *supra* note 43, at 24-25; Paul Harris, "Developmental Aspects of Children's Memory," in *Aspects of Memory* 132, 143-50 (Michael M. Gruneberg & Peter Morris eds., 1978).

46   Nancy Rosenblum, "The Democracy of Everyday Life," In *Liberalism Without Illusions: Essays on the Liberal Theory and Political Vision of Judith N. Shklar* 27 (Bernard Yack ed., 1996).

47   Anthony Kronman, "Leontius' Tale," in *Law's Stories: Narrative and Rhetoric in the Law* 54, 56 (Peter Brooks and Paul Gewirtz eds., 1996).

conversely, the element of narrativity inherent in good theorizing. Let us examine each in turn.

First, in deciding how one will recount a set of brute facts, one must at least tacitly select some genre according to which they will be organized. Otherwise, one will be left with merely a chronology that begins and ends at points in time and space which are entirely arbitrary. Without recourse to the conventions of some genre, one will not have a genuine story. A story must have a plot, providing an intelligible beginning, middle, and end, located within a meaningfully delimited spatial context, a given community.

The formal elements of a criminal offense provide the minimally necessary elements for telling a legal story of administrative massacre. The offense itself will often also be situated within a larger narrative of national crisis and rejuvenation. When prosecutors select one among several available offenses with which to indict a defendant, they are necessarily relying on a theoretical construct which will greatly determine how the story of his actions will be told in court.

Conversely, narrative contributes to theory beyond merely illustrating how to act on a given principle. The complexities of character and context involved in any densely described story serve to bring to light dilemmatic features that moral and legal theory will inevitably have missed. "The great intellectual challenge of telling stories," Shklar observed, is that in contrast to more abstract forms of theory unchastened by it, storytelling "does not rationalize the irrationality of actual experience and of history. Indecision, incoherence, and inconsistency are not ironed out or put in brackets."[48]

In the face of inescapable uncertainties, practical judgment—for which theoretical acumen provides little guidance—is required to discern the relevant particulars and accurately to weigh their moral valences, before deciding how to act. The "situation sensitivity" of the common law has made Anglo-American courts, when operating in good form, relatively adept at storytelling of this kind. This sensitivity has allowed the law's theoretical elements, its analytical concepts, to enlarge and contract in light of the moral valences of the particular story that "had to be told" in the case at hand. Conceived in this way, then, liberal storytelling is something that judges do routinely.

---

48 Shklar, *supra* note 38, at 230.

If nothing else, liberalism is very much engaged in telling the story of liberalism, the "origin" stories of Locke, Jefferson, and Madison, as well as the "horror" stories about communal intolerance—large (Stalin and Hitler) or small (tribes and towns).[49] The latter stories offer particularly resonant support for "the liberalism of fear,"[50] which is more centrally concerned with preventing the *summum malum* of oppressive cruelty than with articulating and aiming for any *summum bonum*.

In a liberal society, prosecutors (especially in their closing arguments) and courts (in their opinions) tell stories about individual rights: the myriad forms of the human flourishing that the exercise of such rights permits and that their violation wrongly forecloses. Liberal courts thus tell a story in which men are portrayed as autonomous subjects, choosing to conduct themselves in this way or that.

The Value of Liberal Fictions

There is an irreducibly "fictive" element here: the legal fiction that men, in obeying or breaking the law, are exercising an inalienable capacity for autonomous choice. By representing men as autonomous choosers, liberal law seeks to *make* them so—recognizing all the while that this entails forcing freedom upon some who would prefer to surrender it (to priests, parents, marital partners, or military superiors). Liberal stories in criminal cases thus always involve "side-shadowing";[51] that is, they allude to unrealized possibilities more appealing and more defensible than what transpired. The story always

---

49   I owe this observation to Michael Schudson.

50   Judith Shklar, "The Liberalism of Fear," In *Liberalism and the Moral Life* 21, 38 (Nancy Rosenblum ed., 1989).

51   Michael A. Bernstein, *Foregone Conclusions: Against Apocalyptic History* 7-8 (1994). As Bernstein notes:

> To concentrate on the sideshadowed ideas and events, on what did not happen, does not cast doubt on the historicity of what occurred but views it as one among a range of possibilities, a number of which might, with equal plausibility, have taken place instead.... To keep the claims of both the event and its unrealized alternatives in mind may be more perplexing as a theoretical formulation than as an ongoing act ....

Id.

runs: the defendant was not fated to perform his dastardly deeds; he was free to do otherwise, and should have.

But liberal courts do not merely apply first principles set in stone. While they seek to preserve the normative "integrity" of their community over time, judicial stories also involve a continual effort to rework legal rules and principles "in their best light"—to clarify and refine extant norms in the course of applying them to disputes regarding their scope and meaning.[52]   The story of the litigants and their immediate dispute is thereby woven into a larger story about the community, its history, and its evolving normative commitments. The story of what the parties did to one another is subsumed within a broader tale about what communal norms required of them and how these norms got to be the way they are. In recounting the tale of the crimes the juntas had ordered, the obedience of their underlings, and the suffering of their victims, the military trials in Argentina told such liberal stories.

Compelling stories about the country's past—legal and otherwise—aid our remembrance not only of the events themselves, but also of the moral judgments we ultimately reached about them, often through discussions of these events with friends and fellow citizens. The principles on which we based these judgments are thus kept firmly in mind. In this way, memory of the events themselves also comes to be influenced by memory of subsequent debate about how to judge their perpetrators and accomplices.

Both views of liberal storytelling, as mnemonic device or as prompting deeper development of existing concepts, enable us—the listeners—to maintain the proper measure of critical distance from the teller. These approaches help us to ask such questions as: Was that really his motive? Did he accurately understand the motives of other characters? Did he correctly grasp the situation he faced and what it required of him?

The best of modern drama does not encourage complete identification with its characters. Far from it. Bertolt Brecht's

---

52   This formulation follows Dworkin's account of how judges resemble the authors of a "chain novel." Dworkin, *Law's Empire* 228-38 (1986). It is modeled on Rawls' account of the "constructive" process of "reflective equilibrium" by which we bring our principles into harmony with our settled moral judgments, and vice versa. Rawls, *A Theory of Justice* 46-53 (1973).

influential idea of the "alienation effect" involves precisely such a self-conscious effort by the dramatist to encourage a measure of impartial detachment by the audience from even the most appealing characters.[53] It is a theatrical device for inducing the audience to confront the dramatic character and his social world—and that of the audience itself—in a critical and self-critical fashion. The objective is a form of "acting where the transformation of consciousness"—of the viewer into the mind and situation of the character—"is not only intentionally incomplete but also revealed as such to the spectators, who delight in the unresolved dialectic."[54]

By contrast, when a legal author today tells us that her narrative can communicate "the inexpressible, the inexplicable"[55] (that is, inexplicable in strictly normative or analytical terms), we often find her smuggling in "the indefensible" as well. As we are called upon to enter empathetically into her imaginative universe, we are tacitly asked to leave our critical faculties at the door. Such authors resemble the Zambian tribe whose members insist, even when testifying in court, on relating events uninterrupted, for fear that the spell cast by the storyteller will be broken. "Beware the judge who asks a witness to clarify a point!" reports one leading Africanist. "The witness will go back to the beginning of the tale and start over."[56]

Liberalism rightly rejects the uncritical celebration of storytelling, so fashionable in current legal scholarship,[57] as no substitute for rational assessment of evidence and argument—and as often no more than self-display.[58] The resulting "meditations" less often resemble the

---

53   Bertolt Brecht, "Alienation Effects in Chinese Acting," in *The Modern Theatre: Readings and Documents* 276, 277-78 (Daniel Seltzer ed., 1967).

54   Richard Schechner, *Between Theater and Anthropology* 9 (1985).

55   James B. White, *The Legal Imagination* 863 (1973).

56   Jennifer A. Widner, *Building the Rule of Law: What Commonwealth Africa Tells Us About Constructing Judicial Independence* 67 (July 1995) (unpublished manuscript).

57   The literature here is enormous. See, e.g., Kathryn Abrams, "Hearing the Call of Stories," 79 *Cal. L. Rev.* 971 (1991); Symposium, "Legal Storytelling," 87 *Mich. L. Rev.* 2073 (1989).

58   See, e.g., Larry Alexander, "What We Do, and Why We Do It," 45 *Stan. L. Rev.* 1885, 1895 (1993) (noting that "critical race theory typically consists of narratives purporting to reveal how it feels to be the oppressed[,] ...coupled with ... an implicit claim that these experiences are self-certifying"). For further critique, see Daniel A. Farber & Suzanna Sherry, "Telling Stories out of School: An Essay on Legal

soliloquies of Hamlet than the solipsism of Narcissus. The very people who uphold anecdotes about their personal experience as significant to legal and policy debates are often the first to decry the use of complacent anecdotes aimed at countering statistical arguments about deteriorating socioeconomic conditions. "'For example,' is no proof," goes a Yiddish proverb.[59] This is not to reinstate the old opposition between reason and rhetoric, with the latter understood as merely a matter of style and persuasive skill. As a form of rhetoric, storytelling has a legitimate, if delimited place in public deliberation.

In contrast to liberal memory, communitarian and conservative accounts of didactic storytelling view narratives as *constituting* the teaching, not merely illustrating it or helping to develop it. "Through its recitation," argues Paul Ricoeur, "a story is incorporated into a community which it gathers together."[60] The factual details are seen as valuable in themselves, apart from the more general principles that they may reflect. It is in the emotional savoring and shared experiencing of these resonant details that the historical continuity of a genuine community is thought to consist.[61] Shared stories themselves define the nature and boundaries of the group to whom the stories belong.

In liberal stories, by contrast, the characters generally are not large groups, let alone entire societies. As Halbwachs observes: "Ordinarily,... the nation is too remote from the individual for him to consider the history of his country as anything else but a very large framework with which his own history makes contact at only a few

---

Narratives," 45 *Stan. L. Rev.* 807, 854 (1993) (concluding that while legal storytelling "can play a useful role in legal scholarship," it is a method weak in truthfulness and typicality, as well as reason and analysis).

59   *Yiddish Proverbs* 21 (Hanan J. Ayalti ed., 1949).

60   Paul Ricoeur, 3 *Time and Narrative* 347 (Kathleen Blamey & David Pellauer trans., 1988).

61   This conception of communal narrative defines the "premodern" condition, according to Lyotard: "[A] collectivity that takes narrative as its key form of competence," he contends, "finds the raw material for its social bond not only in the meaning of the narratives it recounts, but also in the act of reciting them." Jean-François Lyotard, *The Postmodern Condition: A Report on Knowledge* at 22 (Geoff Bennington & Brian Massumi trans., 1984). For a defense of the continuing relevance of this conception of communal narrative, see Robert N. Bellah et al., *Habits of the Heart: Individualism and Commitment in American Life* 153 (1985) (arguing that "[i]n order not to forget [its] past, a community is involved in retelling its story, its constitutive narrative").

points."[62] But there are certain events, he acknowledged, that "alter group life."[63] These are of such moral magnitude that they become "imbued with the concerns, interests, and passions of a nation."[64] Such transformative events may involve triumphs or catastrophes. Administrative massacre decidedly exemplifies the latter. In our century it has become the quintessential catastrophe for the collective memory of many societies. "An experience like that undergone by Argentina in the last decade," writes historian Halperin,

> turns terror into one of the basic dimensions of collective life. This necessarily redefines the horizon on which the experience of every Argentine is played out. His relation to his country, to his city, to his street cannot remain untouched after having come to see them as places where death always lurks.[65]

When a society suffers trauma on this scale, its members will often seek to reconstruct its institutions on the basis of a shared understanding of what went wrong. To that end, they conduct surveys, write monographs, compose memoirs, and draft legislation.

But mostly, they tell stories. The "telling and retelling" of a people's central stories constitute its collective identity, Gottsegen writes.[66] "The story's heroes, and the principles for which they stand, will become exemplary, and in every age youths will be exhorted to be

---

62   Maurice Halbwachs, *The Collective Memory* 77 (Francis J. Ditter, Jr. & Vida Y. Ditter trans., 1992). Collective memory of such events "differs from history in ... [that] it retains from the past only what still lives or is capable of living in the consciousness of the groups keeping the memory alive." *Id.* at 80. Halbwachs was greatly influenced by Durkheim. Mary Douglas, *Introduction* to *id.* at 1, 6-9.

63   Halbwachs, *supra* note 62, at 58.

64   *Id.*

65   Tulio Halperin Donghi, "El Presente Transforma el Pasado: El Impacto del Reciente Terror en la Imagen de la Historia Argentina," in *Ficción y Política: La Narrativa Argentina Durante el Proceso Militar* 71, 72 (René Jara & Hernán Vidal eds., 1987) (translation by author). After stating this view, which he describes as widely held in Argentina, Halperin argues that it can easily distort the historiography of earlier periods. *Id.*

66   Michael G. Gottsegen, *The Political Thought of Hannah Arendt* 100-01 (1994). Gottsegen is parsing Hannah Arendt in this passage, describing part of her argument in Hannah Arendt, *On Revolution* 200-14 (1963). The indispensability of shared stories and storytelling for a society's self-preservation is a common theme in literary forays into social analysis. Mario Vargas Llosa, *The Storyteller* (Helen Lane trans., 1989).

like them."[67] It was a dramaturgical decision on Alfonsín's part to conduct the trial of the military juntas, for instance, in a single oral proceeding, susceptible to television coverage.[68] (In Argentina, legal proceedings are normally conducted largely on paper, and witnesses are examined at various times, rather than sequentially, as the investigating magistrate must pursue several proceedings simultaneously.)[69]

This aspect of Alfonsín's approach to the junta trial, for instance, greatly enhanced its persuasive power, as its intellectual architects intended. It is almost impossible to imagine any way in which this procedural reorganization could have compromised the legal protections of the accused. Adoption of an uninterrupted oral procedure made for a more compelling public spectacle, in short, without making for any less justice. This sensitivity on the part of its legal planners to dramatic didactics in no way reduced the junta prosecution to a Stalinist "show trial."[70]

The liberal requirement of procedural fairness to the perpetrators of administrative massacre is a greater problem for the Durkheimian account of law's contribution to solidarity than for the discursive. The discursive conception, after all, finds nothing threatening to social solidarity in zealous advocacy by defense counsel, that is, in its attempt to offer an alternative narrative. That counternarrative is directed not at eliciting retributive moral sentiments (universally shared by the community), but at questioning whether the defendants can be punished in a manner consistent with the community's law.

More dramatically, the counternarrative will often suggest that the defendants' cause was just, however much at odds with positive law, or that their acts should be viewed in a "larger historical context" which is extenuating. Such a counternarrative would not seek merely to introduce reasonable doubt concerning the elements of the prosecution's

---

67 Gottsegen, *supra* note 66, at 100-01.

68 Interview with Presidential Legal Advisors, in Buenos Aires, Argentina (July 20, 1985).

69 Historically, this was standard practice throughout the civil law world. John H. Langbein, *Comparative Criminal Procedure: Germany* 67 (1977).

70 On "show trials," see *The Great Purge Trial* (Robert C. Tucker & Stephen F. Cohen eds., 1965) (discussing the series of show trials during Stalin's Great Purge of the Communist Party during 1936-1938); Arkady Vaksberg, *Stalin's Prosecutor: The Life of Andrei Vyshinsky* (Jan Butler trans., 1991).

story, but rather to tell a different one altogether, one that is more compelling in moral and historical terms. That brings us to the second problem.

Chapter 4.

Losing Perspective, Distorting History

What I want, so far as it is possible, is an objective political debate over the history of both German states. Penal laws, any penal laws, are fundamentally unsuited to resolving historical problems.

> Egon Krenz, Politburo member and former Gen. Sec. of the Communist Party of the German Democratic Republic, at his 1996 trial for manslaughter of border escapees.[1]

There can be no one historical narrative that ... renders perfect justice (just as perhaps there is no judicial outcome that can capture the complexity of history)... On the other hand ... The historian would like to do justice; the judge must establish some version of history... If good judges and historians shun these tasks, they will be taken on by prejudiced or triumphalist ones.

> Charles Maier, historian[2]

The relation between criminal judgment and historical interpretation is problematic in myriad ways. Krenz says, in short, that the two tasks are radically different and should not be addressed in the same forum. Maier 'responds' that these tasks are indeed distinct, but ultimately inextricable. So we must get on with reconciling the two as best we can. The tension between what I take to be the truth in both statements is the subject of the present chapter.

---

1 Quoted in Stephen Kinzer, "We Weren't Following Orders, But the Currents of the Cold War," *N.Y. Times*, March 24, 1996, at 16. Similar views are commonly expressed even by those with no interest in apologetics or self-exculpation. Tzvetan Todorov, for instance, has complained, with respect to the French court's opinion concerning Klaus Barbie, that "what is especially worth criticizing is not that they wrote bad history, it's that they wrote history at all, instead of being content to apply the law equitably and universally." In *Memory, the Holocaust, and French Justice* 114, 120 (Richard J. Golsan ed., 1996).

2 Charles Maier, "Doing Justice, Doing History: Political Purges and National Narratives after 1945 and 1989," 14-15 (paper presented at "In Memory: Revisiting Nazi Atrocities in Post-Cold War Europe. International Conference to Commemorate the Fiftieth Anniversary of the 1944 Massacres around Arezzo").

Maier ultimately gets the better of the argument. But he concedes that the majority view has been otherwise. For instance, after 1989, he notes, "the societies of Eastern Europe have chosen to separate the tasks of political justice and historical representation. Only the Germans have persisted in trying to attempt both tasks, and the results so far are also problematic."[3] The prevailing opinion is now that the attempt to combine the two endeavors is very likely to produce poor justice or poor history, probably both.

If the law is to influence collective memory, it must tell stories that are engaging and compelling, stories that linger in the mind because they are responsive to the public's central concerns.

This proves difficult. The central concerns of criminal courts, when trying cases of administrative massacre, are often decidedly at odds with the public's interest in a thorough, wide-ranging exploration of what caused such events and whose misconduct contributed to them. Courts can easily distort such public understanding either by excessive narrowness ("legalistic" blinders) or by excessive breadth (straying beyond their professional competence). A frequent form of distortion combines the worst of both: It presents a professionally correct conclusion, perfectly suitable for traditional legal purposes, as something much more, that is, as an "official history" of the entire conflagration.

The trial court in the *Eichmann* case was well aware of these dangers. It expressly disavowed such historiographic or didactic aims as beyond its ken. The first paragraph of its opinion thus struck a tone of professional modesty, observing that:

> The desire was felt—readily understandable in itself—to give, within the limits of this trial, a comprehensive and exhaustive historical account of the events of the catastrophe, and, in so doing, to emphasize also the signal feats of heroism of the Ghetto-fighters .... Others again sought to regard this trial as a forum to clarify questions of great import ....
>
> ... [But] the Court ... must not allow itself to be enticed to stray into provinces which are outside its sphere. The judicial process has ways of its own ... whatever the subject-matter of the trial. Were it not so, ... the trial would otherwise resemble a rudderless ship tossed about on the

---

3   *Id.* at 14.

waves.

... The Court does not possess the facilities required for investigating general questions of the kind referred to above. For example, to describe the historical background of the catastrophe, a great mass of documents and evidence has been submitted to us, collected most painstakingly and certainly out of a genuine desire to delineate as complete a picture as possible. Even so, all this material is but a tiny fraction of the extant sources on the subject.... As for questions of principle which are outside the realm of law, no one has made us judges of them and therefore our opinion on them carries no greater weight than that of any person who has devoted study and thought to these questions.[4]

The court here admirably identifies a genuine problem: that many citizens look to the court, and to the evidence it will gather and assess, to help answer large questions that have recently become the center of public concern (and private anguish), questions over which it can claim no monopoly of expertise. Yet even as the court seeks to delimit its professional tasks, to reject any role as history teacher or scholar, it cannot quite contain itself from proclaiming the trial's "educational significance" and "educational value."[5] The court remains Delphically silent about what this educational significance consists of and about how to resolve possible tensions between the trial's positive educational

---

4 *Attorney Gen. of Israel v. Eichmann,* 36 I.L.R. 5, 18-19 (Isr. Dist. Ct. 1961). The court had offered these questions:

How could this happen in the full light of day, and why was it just the German people from whom this great evil sprang? Could the Nazis have carried out their evil designs without the help given them by other peoples in whose midst the Jews dwelt? Would it have been possible to avert the catastrophe, at least in part, if the Allies had displayed a greater will to assist the persecuted Jews? ... What is the lesson which the Jews and other nations, as well as every man in his relationship to others, must learn from all this?

Id. at 18.

Similarly, the London Charter for the International Military Tribunal at Nuremberg avowed the desire of its drafters to influence historical memory, in seeking to "make available for all mankind to study in future years an authentic record of Nazi crimes and criminality." *U.S. Dep't of State, Pub. No. 3080, Report of Robert H. Jackson, United States Representative to the International Conference on Military Trials* 6 (1945).

5 Both statements appear in *Eichmann,* 36 I.L.R., *supra* note 4, at 19. Recognizing the apparent tension between its claims, the court then seeks to clarify how it views its educational function, asserting that although the record "will certainly provide valuable material for the research worker and the historian, ... as far as this Court is concerned all these things are merely a by-product of the trial." *Id.*

effect and the other, more conventional aims of a criminal proceeding.

At the very least, the judges are acutely aware that their judgment will inevitably be viewed as *making* history and that their judgment will itself be subject to historiographical scrutiny. Justice Jackson's opening statement at Nuremberg acknowledged this explicitly: "The record on which we judge these defendants today is the record on which history will judge us tomorrow."[6] Even after Julius and Ethel Rosenberg had been executed, Felix Frankfurter penned a dissent to the Supreme Court's denial of a stay. He acknowledged that to dissent "after the curtain has been rung down upon them has the appearance of pathetic futility."[7] Even so, he added, "history also has its claims."[8] It is those claims to which judges feel obliged to respond in the cases discussed here. The only problem—characteristic of these cases—is that Frankfurter almost certainly got those claims largely wrong, as recent historiography on the *Rosenberg* case suggests.[9]

The *Eichmann* court's vague claim about the trial's educational value is very modest compared to the more extravagant proclamations of national "catharsis" and "collective psychoanalysis" by the intellectuals mentioned above.[10] Even so, many historians have concluded that at such times the law unwittingly provides more *mis*education than accurate historical instruction.[11]

---

6   2 *Trial of the Major War Criminals Before the International Military Tribunal* 101 (1947).

7   *Rosenberg v. United States*, 346 U.S. 273, 310 (1953) (Frankfurter, J., dissenting).

8   *Id.* Frankfurter's dissent inevitably focused almost entirely on procedural defects in the trial, but he concluded that such defects undermined confidence in the result.

9   Ronald Radosh, "The Venona Files," *New Republic,* Aug. 7, 1995, at 25, 25-27 (summarizing the famous Venona intercepts between Soviet and American Communist Party officials, decoded by the Army Signal Intelligence Service and recently declassified, clearly establishing that Julius Rosenberg, although not his wife, spied for the Soviets). In this study the term "historiography" refers broadly to all scholarship by professional historians rather than (as in some current discussion) more narrowly to historians' writings about the nature of historical writing.

10   See, respectively, Paula K. Speck, "The Trial of the Argentine Juntas," 18 *U. Miami Inter-Am. L. Rev.* 491, 533 (1987) and Henry Rousso, *The Vichy Syndrome* 210 (Arthur Goldhammer trans., 1991).

11   See, e.g., Christopher R. Browning, "German Memory, Judicial Interrogation, and Historical Reconstruction: Writing Perpetrator History from Postwar Testimony," in *Probing the Limits of Representation: Nazism and the "Final Solution"* 22, 26 (Saul Friedlander ed., 1992); Letter from Professor Herbert A. Strauss to Professor Eric Stein, in "Correspondence on the "Auschwitz Lie"," 87 *Mich. L. Rev.* 1026, 1029 (1989).

The concept of historical distortion is itself somewhat problematic, to be sure, and must be scrutinized before employable in assessing judicial forays into telling a national story. As Schudson warns:

> The notion that memory can be "distorted" assumes that there is a standard by which we can judge or measure what a veridical memory must be. If this is difficult with individual memory, it is even more complex with collective memory where the past event or experience remembered was truly a different event or experience for its different participants. Moreover, where we can accept with little question that biography or the lifetime is the appropriate or "natural" frame for individual memory, there is no such evident frame for cultural memories. Neither national boundaries nor linguistic ones are as self-evidently the right containers for collective memory as the person is for individual memory....[12]

Hence the contours of the story itself will determine the precise nature and identity of the collective subject that is presumably to do the remembering. The collectivity cannot tell the historian when or how "its" story begins or ends, for it is the historian whose conclusions about the origins and nature of that collectivity determine, in considerable measure, how it itself is configured and defined. Hence, Schudson concludes, "Memory *is* distortion since memory is invariably and inevitably selective. A way of seeing is a way of not seeing, a way of remembering is a way of forgetting, too."[13]

Still, we should not abandon the concept of distortion altogether.[14] Rather, we should apply it reflexively, in both directions. What will be

---

12 Michael Schudson, "Dynamics of Distortion in Collective Memory," in *Memory Distortion: How Minds, Brains, and Societies Reconstruct the Past* 347 (Daniel L. Schacter ed., 1995) (emphasis added). Examining postwar memory of WWII in Japan, one scholar of Japanese history makes a similar point: "No single ... chronology can be produced by a summary of the infinite series of differently remembered personal pasts. There are too many variants of the way the 'little history' of individuals connects with the 'big history' of the nation-state." Carol Gluck, "The Past in the Present," in *Postwar Japan As History* 64, 78 (Andrew Gordon ed., 1993). On the reciprocal influence of individual experience on collective memory, and vice versa, over time, see Nathan Wachtel, "Remember and Never Forget," in *Between Memory and History* 307, 334 (Marie-Noëlle Bourguet et al. eds., 1986).

13 Schudson, *Id.* at 348.

14 Schudson agrees. Michael Schudson, *Watergate in American Memory* 206 (1992).

viewed as a distortion from the perspective of either profession may be entirely legitimate in light of the distinct purposes of the other. Inevitably, the law will often treat past events in ways that will constitute distortion from the standpoint of historiography. But if courts distort history, so too historians can distort the law—often in ways that make lawyers howl or cringe. The most notorious example among historical treatments of administrative massacre is surely the conclusion, reached by Ernst Nolte, that Hitler was entitled to treat the Jews as his enemy since leading Zionist Chaim Weitzmann—in a late 1939 speech after the outbreak of war—had expressly "declared war" on the Third Reich by announcing that Jews would support Britain in the imminent conflict.[15]

The second source of skepticism about law's potential contribution to collective memory is the converse of the first. Just as we properly wonder whether liberal morality will be sacrificed in the interests of historical storytelling, we may also suspect that judges—when faithful to liberal law and professional ethics—may make poor historians and lousy storytellers. To be sure, Western legal scholarship and historiography initially set out, in the Middle Ages, on surprisingly parallel tracks, employing similar methods, seeking similar objectives.[16] But their professional paths have long since diverged in many ways.

Even so, one still encounters refreshing reminders of these common concerns. Good judges and historians continue to display similar virtues, argues Maier. "Moderation, trustworthiness, common sense, sensitivity to context and the limits of human action, life experience, the capacity to address what is particular as well as what is general ... these comprise the catalogue of historiographical and jurisprudential virtues alike."[17] The appeal of these virtues lingers on among both young and old, within both disciplines, despite all the disdain heaped upon them in recent decades by adherents of radical history, critical legal studies, and the economic analysis of law.

---

15   Ernst Nolte, "Between Historical Legend and Revisionism? The Third Reich in the Perspective of 1980," in *Forever in the Shadow of Hitler?* 1, 8 (James Knowlton & Truett Cates trans., 1993).

16   Donald R. Kelley, "Clio and the Lawyers: Forms of Historical Consciousness in Medieval Jurisprudence," 5 *Medievalia et Humanistica* 25, 26-28 (1974).

17   Maier, *supra* note 2, at 4. For a similarly Aristotelian defense of judicial virtue, see Anthony Kronman, *The Lost Lawyer* 53-108 (1993).

Both courts and (traditional) historians try to establish a measure of "integrity" in the history of a community by linking events in its past with its present situation. This presents acute problems when judging administrative massacre. Can a single, coherent narrative be written of a nation's experience with large-scale massacre (by either judges or historians), when its members must be divided into perpetrators, victims, and bystanders, each with its own perspective on what happened? Yes, answers Maier, despite the problems he acknowledges this entails. "Historians and judges presuppose an underlying community, even one at war with itself. Therein, too, lies their shared challenge."[18]   The question, however, is whether their common presupposition is defensible, and if so, on what basis.

To influence collective memory through legal proceedings, it is helpful for prosecutors to be familiar with accepted genres of storytelling. In other words, prosecutors must discover how to couch the trial's doctrinal narrative within "genre conventions" already in place within the particular society.[19]   These conventions are by no means universal and will often require some rather fine-grained "local knowledge" of "the plot structures of the various story types cultivated in a given culture."[20]

For instance, a prosecution of Emperor Hirohito could easily have been staged—without distortion of brute facts[21]—to draw upon the dramatic conventions of Kabuki, within which the "death of kings" is a recurrent and evocative theme.[22]   Attentiveness to cultural particularities of this sort, however, is a virtue for which liberal legal

---

18   Maier, *Id.* at 5.

19   Bernard S. Jackson, "Narrative Theories and Legal Discourse," in *Narrative in Culture* 23, 30 (Christopher Nash ed., 1990) ("Every society ... has its own stock of substantive narratives, which represent typical human behavior patterns known and understood .... This is the form in which social knowledge is acquired and stored, and which provides the framework for understanding particular stories presented to us in discourse.").

20   Hayden White, *The Content of the Form: Narrative Discourse and Historical Representation* 43 (1987).

21   Searle coined the term "brute facts." Such facts exist independently of human observation. John R. Searle, *The Construction of Social Reality* 2-3 (1995).

22   Masao Yamaguchi, "Kingship, Theatricality, and Marginal Reality in Japan," in *Text and Context: The Social Anthropology of Tradition* 151, 169-75 (Ravindra K. Jain ed., 1977).

and political theory—with its longings for Enlightenment universalism—have not always evinced sufficient respect. In addition, "lawyers have masked the real importance of generic considerations," notes Robert Ferguson, "through their appeals to the common sense of a situation. But common sense, as anthropologists have begun to show, is basically a culturally constructed use of experience to claim self-evidence."[23]   In fact, by ignoring the lawyers on their team, Occupation authorities in Japan proved quite savvy in formulating several key policies, even the most transformative, in terms of existing indigenous concepts and categories.[24]

The promise of liberal storytelling will quickly founder if it turns out that the very things that make the story *liberal*—its moral universalism or impartial detachment, for instance—deprive its characters of the concreteness and particularity that make a good *story*, a vivid yarn. It is the vivid particularity of characters and events in good literature that makes it singularly apt as a setting for Aristotelian ethics, that is, for its teaching and analytical development.[25]   In contrast, *liberal* theory has rarely placed comparable emphasis on the particularities of historical context or individual character. Kant, for instance, viewed "examples" and the stories in which they were formulated as devices useful only for instructing us in how to apply moral principles and motivating such compliance.[26]

The common law method of Anglo-American courts, of course, has

---

23   Robert Ferguson, "Untold Stories in the Law," in *Law's Stories: Narrative and Rhetoric in the Law* 84, 87 (Peter Brooks and Paul Gewirtz eds., 1996) (citation to Clifford Geertz omitted).

24   Japanese historian Ienaga Saburō reports, for instance, that for scholars like himself "'cooperation with the Occupation's policy for reforming the teaching of history was an unexpected opportunity to put previously held beliefs into practice.'" Arthur E. Tiedemann, "Japan Sheds Dictatorship," in *From Dictatorship to Democracy: Coping with the Legacies of Authoritarianism and Totalitarianism* 179, 194 (John H. Herz ed., 1982). Conversely, Tiedemann adds: "For almost every proposed reform there was found a Japanese who long before the occupation had developed a commitment to the concept involved." *Id.*

25   Martha C. Nussbaum, *Love's Knowledge: Essays on Philosophy and Literature* 148-67 (1990).

26   Kant's view differed, between his *Groundwork of the Metaphysics of Morals* and his *Critique of Pure Reason*, over whether examples could accomplish merely the second or also the first of these two tasks. Charles E. Larmore, *Patterns of Moral Complexity* 2-3 (1987).

always prized judicial "situation sensitivity" to the infinite factual variation in the configurations presented by particular disputes.[27] But the sensitivity of liberal jurisprudence to particularity is driven by concerns with being fair and just, not with being spellbinding. The two aims may well be at odds, as many have long supposed. Justice requires predictability, as through like treatment of like cases; a compelling story, by contrast, requires an ever-present element of surprise, to keep the listener on edge. As Gallie observes:

> The conclusion of a good story—a conclusion which we wait for eagerly—is not something that could have been or should have been foreseen.
>
> ... We can imagine almost any good story being presented, and probably ruined, as either a cautionary tale or as the illustration of a moral homily.... In the homily the persons and early incidents of the story will be introduced somewhat in the manner of instantial or factual premises from which, in conjunction with appropriate wise saws and moral principles, the conclusion of the story—the exemplification of the appropriate moral lesson—can be deduced. But in this process the conclusion will, of course, have lost all its virtue *as the conclusion of a story*. Inevitably it will have become a foregone conclusion, possibly to be assimilated with moral profit, but certainly not to be awaited with eagerness and excitement.[28]

The solution to this problem would be simple if we could accept Durkheim's account of how criminal trials contribute to social solidarity. What sustains public attentiveness to such trials, on his account, is not any uncertainty about their likely result (or even morbid curiosity about their grisly details). In fact, any great uncertainty of this kind could easily vitiate the retributive sentiments of resentment and indignation against the accused that such proceedings are to evoke among the public. In support of Durkheim's view, there is little evidence the general public much cares for unpredictability in its favored narratives or for psychological complexity in the characters who people them. After all, it is generally not terribly difficult to

---

27   On the judicial virtue of "situation sense," see Karl N. Llewellyn, *The Common Law Tradition: Deciding Appeals* 60-61 (1960).

28   W.B. Gallie, *Philosophy and the Historical Understanding* 24 (1964).

anticipate the conclusion of most popular novels or television dramas. Nor is complex "character development" exactly the strength of, say, John Grisham's novels.[29]

Although eminently predictable and populated by stick-figure characters, such narratives maintain the attention of millions of readers and viewers every day.   This simply could not occur if much particularity of character or uncertainty of result were necessary to make a story compelling for most audiences, as Gallie and Nussbaum imply. If stories must capture the popular imagination before they can foster social solidarity, the most simplistic of narratives have little trouble in doing so. The problem, for present purposes, is precisely that trials for administrative massacre typically *lack* the simplicity of plot, character, and *dénouement* that most popular narratives involve—and seem to require for their very popularity.

Eichmann's character traits *alone* have evoked thousands of pages of scholarly commentary, much of it confessedly perplexed, beginning with Arendt's observations of his trial. Moreover, the panoramic sweep of the events at issue precludes the defendant from continuously occupying center stage. Arendt stated the problem succinctly:

> A show trial needs even more urgently than an ordinary trial a limited and well-defined outline of what was done and how it was done. In the center of the trial can only be the one who did—in this respect, he is like the hero in the play ....[30]

The discursive account of how criminal trials contribute to social solidarity can more easily accommodate the complexity of character and uncertainty of result that make for great literature, according to Gallie and Nussbaum.[31] These very complexities and uncertainties

---

29   Michiko Kakutani, "Chasing Ambulances Before Dreams," *N.Y. Times*, Apr. 28, 1995, at C33 (reviewing John Grisham, *The Rainmaker* (1995), and commenting on "the leadenness of Mr. Grisham's prose, the banality of his characters and the shocking predictability of his story").

30   Hannah Arendt, *Eichmann in Jerusalem: A Report on the Banality of Evil* 9 (Penguin Books, rev. & enlarged ed. 1977) (1963); see also Jackson, *supra* note 19, at 29 (describing an empirical study of juror receptivity to competing accounts which found that "as structural ambiguities in stories increased, credibility decreased, and vice versa").

31   I here reject any conventional, pejorative distinction between high art and low. As

become the object of day-to-day curiosity and concern, the subject of private discussion and public debate, consistent with the ideal of discursive democracy. The question, however, is whether such lengthy and complex tales can sustain the public's interest at all, or for very long, that is, whether Durkheimian desires for moral certainty and narrative closure will assert themselves prematurely. The record here is quite mixed, allowing little empirical basis for generalization.[32]

Are Liberal Stories Boring?

By nature, many nonliberals suspect, liberal stories (and, by implication, liberal lives) must be boring. This is due to the procedural scrupulousness with which liberal law protects the rights of the villain, against whom the audience's collective conscience could otherwise be unrestrainedly loosed.[33] If liberal stories carry any dramatic power, it may be precisely because of their understatement, because of judicial aversion to self-conscious dramaturgy. To some extent, at least, it is the very absence of declamatory histrionics that makes such stories compelling, when recounted in their quiet, impersonal way by judicial opinions.[34] But, compelling to whom, one must ask? To liberal jurisprudents alone?

The criminal law may present a dramatic persona of either majesty or sobriety. Uncertainty between the two, over how justice should project its public image, has long informed our assumptions about the proper rhetorical style of legal argument and opinion-writing. It has

Young observes, monuments of commemoration, which are often "unabashedly figurative, heroic, and referential" to some historical reality, must necessarily flout contemporary standards of aesthetic sophistication. James E. Young, *The Texture of Memory* 11-12 (1993).

32 See Chapter 5, "Legal Judgment as Precedent and Analogy," *infra* at text accompanying notes 54-69.

33 A recent argument to this effect is offered by Francis Fukuyama, *The End of History and the Last Man* 288- 89, 312 (1992). But see Richard E. Flathman, *Willful Liberalism* (1992) (arguing for a more spirited, creative ideal of liberal personhood); Nancy L. Rosenblum, *Another Liberalism* (1987) (same).

34 On the impersonal character of legal authority in modern western society, see *Max Weber on Law in Economy and Society* 301-21 (Max Rheinstein ed., Edward Shils & Max Rheinstein trans., 1967).

even informed debates about the law's proper architectural style. Hence the recurrent vacillation, in the design of courthouses, over "whether authority should be displayed with splendor"—to inspire awe and obedience, at risk of seeming insensitivity to the misery of the accused—"or dissimulated with a self-disciplined and severe austerity."[35]

On one hand, a cold, nondescript courtroom may not maximally summon up the law's potential majesty. So too, a highly self-restrained style of legal storytelling may make poor theatre.[36] It may thus fail to evoke the retributive sentiments that Durkheim considered central to the solidarity-enhancing function of criminal law.

On the other hand, an austere courthouse deprives the state of its theatrical advantage, its ritual power to define symbolically the proceedings within. Such a courtroom therefore more easily facilitates an equal exchange of views between the public's prosecutor and the accused. This is more compatible with the discursive ideal. The businesslike atmosphere of the modern courthouse is also more consistent with the unpretentious spirit of a commercial republic, whose members are held together largely in Durkheimian recognition of their economic interdependence and by a Rawlsian "overlapping consensus" concerning basic constitutional structure.[37]

Lacking the majesty of traditional rituals of state power, however, liberal-legal stories may become dull.[38] Experience of prosecutions for

---

35   Katherine F. Taylor, *In the Theater of Criminal Justice: The Palais de Justice in Second Empire Paris* 94 (1993). Taylor observes how, according to the "splendor" school of 19th-century French architects, "the rich ambiance of the courtroom inspires the desire to fuse with the society that the courtroom represents, and so unites the diverse constituencies in the courtroom in social solidarity." *Id.* at 102. Taylor rightly notes the Durkheimian premises of this architectural strategy. *Id.* On representations of justice in sculpture and portraiture, see Dennis E. Curtis & Judith Resnik, "Images of Justice," 96 *Yale L.J.* 1727, 1729-31 (1987) and M. Christine Boyer, *The City of Collective Memory: Its Historical Imagery and Architectural Entertainments* 7 (1994).

36   Herbert A. Eastman, "Speaking Truth to Power: The Language of Civil Rights Litigators," 104 *Yale L.J.* 763, 766 (1995) (observing the rhetorically pallid character of plaintiffs' pleadings even in civil rights suits alleging the most egregious—and potentially dramatic acts—of misconduct).

37   John Rawls, "The Domain of the Political and Overlapping Consensus," in *The Idea of Democracy* 245, 255 (David Copp et al. eds., 1993).

38   A distinguished novelist highlights this possibility in his fictional account of the prosecution of a deposed communist dictator in an unidentified Balkan country. Three

administrative massacre suggests, in particular, that liberal-legal stories are likely to dwell on what many listeners regard as meaningless minutiae.[39] Novelist Rebecca West, covering the first "historic" Nuremberg trial for *The New Yorker*, found it insufferably tedious.[40] Her reaction was not uncommon. As one reporter notes,

> It was the largest crime in history, and it promised the greatest courtroom spectacle. [But] with their cheap suits and hungry faces, these indistinguished men did not look like the archcriminals of the age.
> What ensued was an excruciatingly long and complex trial that failed to mesmerize a distracted world. Its mass of evidence created boredom, mixed occasionally with an abject horror before which ordinary justice seemed helpless .... Its finale, 10 messy hangings and a surreptitious suicide, was less than majestic. Its one legacy seemed to be the celebrity of Albert Speer ... who escaped death with gestures of ambiguous atonement.[41]

In orchestrating such a trial there may be some trade-off between the goals of didactic spectacle and adherence to liberal principle. Yet one should not exclude the possibility that the trial may fail in both respects. Nuremberg (and, even more, the Tokyo trial) appear to have been both boring and illiberal at once, on many accounts.

---

young adults are watching the televised trial. One wishes to leave. The following exchange ensues:
"No, I want to watch. We've got to."
"We've got to. It's our history."
"But it's BORING."
"History often is when it happens. Then it becomes interesting later."
"You're such a philosopher, Vera. And a tyrant."
Julian Barnes, *The Porcupine* 100 (1992).

39   Even prosecutor Taylor conceded, regarding the first Nuremberg trial: "As month after month passed ... [the] press and public lost interest in the case as a 'spectacle.'" He immediately adds, significantly, that "the judicial foundations of the trial were strengthened by this very fact." Telford Taylor, "The Nuremberg War Crimes Trials," *Int'l Conciliation Papers,* Apr. 1949, at 243, 262.

40   Rebecca West, "Extraordinary Exile," *New Yorker*, Sept. 7, 1946, at 34, 34; see also Joseph E. Persico, *Nuremberg: Infamy on Trial* 203 (1994) ("The papers back home were no longer giving heavy daily play to a trial that, no matter how sensational the evidence, had already gone on for six weeks. Reporters had begun scrambling for fresh angles.").

41   Alex Ross, "Watching for a Judgment of Real Evil," *N.Y. Times,* Nov. 12, 1995, §2, at 37.

One is thus led to question whether it was really the principled commitment of such proceedings to liberalism that made them fail as social drama, any more than a principled commitment to dullness could have made them liberal. The dramaturgical decisions that made them dull do not seem to be ones that made the proceedings any more consistent with liberal legality. At the very least, no one has even begun to demonstrate such a connection. There is nothing necessarily illiberal in the efforts of courts and prosecutors to give a little thought to props and décor, mise-en-scène and pacing of action, character development and narrative framing, stage and audience.[42]

Hannah Arendt's dismay at Eichmann's "banality" betrayed a disappointment that the defendant, in refusing "to play the villain," failed to provide the dramatic tension for which she had hoped. The prosecutor, in his preoccupation with painting a larger tableau, failed to keep his *dramatis persona* at center stage.

Also, when a politically resonant ritual is called for, it seems that lawyers often make poor performers. One historian even argues that medieval Italy's reliance on lawyers for its historical records and "myths of origin," rather than on the superior narrative skills of clerics and chroniclers (common elsewhere in medieval Europe) seriously undermined the public legitimacy of its kings.[43] Social theorists from Weber to Foucault, moreover, contend that as Western law became ever more rational, formalized, and demystified, public trials and punishments increasingly lost their capacity to serve as spectacles, to "enchant" and captivate the public imagination by evoking deeply shared moods and sensibilities.[44]

---

42 John R. Brown, *Effective Theatre* (1969); George McCalmon & Christian Moe, *Creating Historical Drama* (1965).

43 Chris Wickham, "Lawyers' Time: History and Memory in Tenth- and Eleventh-Century Italy," in *Studies in Medieval History* 53, 70 (Henry Mayr-Harting & R.I. Moore eds., 1985).

44 *From Max Weber: Essays in Sociology* 352-57 (H.H. Gerth & C. Wright Mills eds., trans., 1948) (observing the historical trend toward "disenchantment" of political authority and legal ritual); Michel Foucault, *Discipline and Punish* 32-72 (Alan Sheridan trans., Vintage Books 1979) (1975) (describing how "the spectacle of the scaffold" was gradually displaced by a more diffuse system of "carceral" surveillance, whose rituals of social control were less dramatic). But see Michael Lynch & David Bogen, *The Spectacle of History: Speech, Text, and Memory in the Iran-contra Hearings* 17 (1996).

Worse yet, prosecutors may labor under a particularly onerous burden, relative to defense counsel, in dramatizing their favored narrative, allowing their adversary more easily to capture the public eye and imagination. In the Barbie trial, for instance, prosecutors rightly believed that "an unpaid debt to the dead bound them to the truth."[45] Barbie's defense counsel, "on the other hand was free. No debt tied him to the past; he was in a position to plant suspense in the very heart of the ceremony of remembering and to substitute the delicious thrill of the event"—especially the threat to reveal the pro-German complicity of currently prominent figures in French public life—"for the meticulous reassessment of the facts."[46]

The upshot was that the press and public, like Finkielkraut himself, quickly tired of the prosecution and plaintiffs, (the intervenors, Barbie's surviving victims), due to "the thirty-nine lawyers whose thirty-nine closing speeches talked the audience into a stupor" over a nine-day period.[47] "Instead of making an impression, they made people yawn. Rather than satisfying the appetite for the new, they rehashed, *ad nauseam*, the same tired formulas."[48]

Accounts of the Barbie trial by even the most scrupulously liberal commentators and scholars have been more deeply drawn into the mental universe of defense counsel, Jacques Vergès, with "his promise of scandal, his steamy reputation, and his consummate art of mystery," the qualities for which he came to be "adulated in the media."[49] Even

---

45   Alain Finkielkraut, *Remembering in Vain: The Klaus Barbie Trial and Crimes Against Humanity* 65 (Roxanne Lapidus & Sima Godfrey trans., 1992).

46   *Id.* Legal rules contributed directly to the problem in at least one small way. French law, like English common law until about 150 years ago, exempts the criminal defendant from any duty to swear an oath. The result, as presiding Judge Boulard at Touvier's trial put it, is that "only the accused has the right to lie." Quoted in Henry Rousso, "What Historians Will Retain From the Last Trial of the Purge," in Golsan, *supra* note 1, at 163, 165.

47   *Id.* at 63.

48   *Id.* at 65.

49   *Id.* at 66. Despite his best efforts to elude ensnarement by Vergès's rhetorical stratagems, Finkielkraut—a philosophical journalist of liberal inspiration—clearly is no less entranced by Barbie's lawyer, on whom his book largely centers, than he is repulsed by him. *Cf.* Guyora Binder, "Representing Nazism: Advocacy and Identity at the Trial of Klaus Barbie," 98 *Yale L.J.* 1321, 1355-72 (1989) (lavishing enormous attention on Vergès's defense strategy and its postmodernist implications, and noting, at 1356, that "Vergès is known for his effective use of the media as a forum for his controversial

so discerning an observer as Todorov was clearly persuaded by much of Vergès argument against the trial's rendition of French history. He observes, for instance, "it's a fact that Barbie tortured Resistance fighters, but they did the same when they got their hands on a Gestapo officer. The French army, moreover, systematically resorted to torture after 1944, in Algeria for example; no one has ever been condemned for crimes against humanity as a result."[50] Selective enforcement of this sort violates the principle of equal protection, Todorov contends. Thus he is not saying that the "bad guys" have good arguments only when the public spotlight is shifted from strictly legal questions to ones of historical interpretation. He also suggests that when courts seek to write national history, the law's own purposes easily come to be mocked.

Boredom as such is, then, by no means the most serious problem here. The problem is that boredom tends to settle selectively upon the shoulders of those whose story is most truthful, most faithful to the past, and most vital to a legal cultivation of liberal memory. In Barnes's fictional (but entirely plausible, even compelling) treatment of such a trial,[51] the former dictator gets all the best lines, successfully upstaging and embarrassing the public prosecutor at key points. In fact, the facility with which this diversion, this "hijacking," of narrative direction can be decisively accomplished—once traditional procedural and evidentiary rules are relaxed (to enable judicial rewriting of the period's official story)—is the organizing premise of his entire book.

What, then, is the response to the suspicion that liberal stories must fail as public pedagogy because, insofar as they focus on a simple "moral," they are sure to drive people from the courtroom, or from "court TV"?

First, many stories—from nursery tales to "Star Wars" movies—adopt a simple view of morality, yet succeed in winning the hearts of large publics, of all ages. Second, liberal stories do not have to be conceived as straightforward homilies. Their morality need not be stark and simplistic. The best stories, liberal and otherwise, almost always involve dilemmatic situations, where the central character is

---

clients' views").

50   Tzvetan Todorov, "The Touvier Trial," in Golsan, *supra* note 1, at 169, 176. See also Todorov, "The Abuses of Memory," 1 *Common Knowledge* 6, 23-25 (1996).

51   Barnes, *supra* note 38.

constrained by circumstance to "do wrong," to some degree, any way she turns.[52] Her moral problem then becomes how to minimize such wrongdoing.

Resolving that problem turns out to require "situational judgment" regarding the weight of competing principles at stake. Exercising such judgment is, of course, difficult and complex. This very complexity is often what engages us as listeners, drawing us into the character's world by way of "rational empathy"[53] with her and the difficulty of the choice she must make. When courts tell the first, simpler kind of tale with success, they foster Durkheim's mechanical solidarity. Whey they tell the second, more complex sort of story, they can further discursive solidarity. Which type of story they should try to tell in a given case depends on the circumstances at hand, examined later.

Misfocusing on Minutiae

Judicial assessment of men like Eichmann and Argentine General Videla often seems to place questions at the center of legal analysis that, from any other standpoint, would surely be of marginal concern. Distortions in collective memory of administrative massacre would thus follow if courts were to train public attention upon such purely professional concerns.[54] For instance, the Argentine prosecutors and judges felt professionally obligated to occupy themselves for a considerable time with establishing the juntas' liability for such offenses as forgery and property theft.[55] This was surely a curious and digressive inclusion in a proceeding whose drama was presumably to center upon a condemnation of the unrepentant slaughter of thousands.

---

52 For an example, see Shklar's analysis of "Rosa," the central character in Nadine Gordimer's *Burger's Daughter* (1979). Judith N. Shklar, *Ordinary Vices* 21-22 (1984)

53 Judith Shklar, "Injustice, Injury, and Inequality: An Introduction," In *Liberalism and the Moral Life* 13, 26 (Nancy Rosenblum ed., 1989).

54 Henry Rousso, "Ce que les historiens retiendront des vingt-trois journées du procès," *Libération,* Apr. 20, 1994, at 4-5 (observing that "the Touvier trial was meant to be an important lesson in history, yet it sometimes got stuck in the quagmire of infinite details relative to the facts or to judicial definitions, making one lose sight of the general picture").

55 Interview with Judge Andrés D'Alessio, in Buenos Aires, Argentina (Aug. 1987).

In the Nuremberg trial, such misfocus arose because the London Charter had given jurisdiction to the International Military Tribunal not for all Nazi crimes against humanity, but only for those undertaken in preparation for, and in service of aggressive war.[56] This jurisdictional peculiarity required prosecutors to weave the Holocaust into a larger story that was primarily about perverted militarism. Justice Robert H. Jackson (United States Chief Prosecution Counsel) thus argued that "the crime against the Jews, insofar as it is a crime against humanity and not a war crime as well, is one which we indict *because of* its close association with the crime against peace."[57]

This way of framing the story seemed to imply that the extermination of European Jewry had not been for the defendants a central end in itself, i.e., a central goal independent of its relation to aggressive war. In so arguing, Jackson unwittingly perpetrated what would be viewed only a few years later as a severe historical distortion. To maintain his indictment within the Tribunal's restricted jurisdiction, Jackson was led to argue that

> the Jews ... were used as exemplars of Nazi discipline; and their persecution eliminated an obstacle to aggressive war. His reasoning, of course, is question-begging—how can such annihilation be understood as a "measure in preparation for war"?—and historically suspect. Scholars of the Holocaust have amply demonstrated how ethnic genocide not only did not serve any military end, but effected the channeling away of critical resources from the war effort. Yet the very vulnerabilities of Jackson's argument highlights his attempts to translate Nazi crimes into an idiom familiar to the law, and to enlist the evidence of such atrocities into an argument about renegade militarism.[58]

It is true that prosecutors explicitly referred to other causes of the Holocaust. But given the Tribunal's delimited jurisdiction, such references were irrelevant, perhaps even exculpatory, in their legal import. That these other explanations nonetheless found their way into

---

56   William J. Bosch, *Judgment on Nuremberg: American Attitudes Toward the Major German War-Crimes Trials* 119 (1970).

57   XIX *International Military Tribunal* 470-71 (1946).

58   Lawrence Douglas, "Film As Witness: Screening 'Nazi Concentration Camps' Before the Nuremberg Tribunal," 105 *Yale L.J.* 449, 479 (1995).

the prosecution's narrative confirms a central point of this study: that if courts are to influence collective memory of such historical episodes in persuasive ways, they must admit a wider range of evidence and argument than are often cognizable within strictly legal terms. Otherwise, the reality they seek to construct is likely to serve very poorly as a plausible and compelling basis for rewriting the national story. In fact, it borders on the obscene to resolve so historiographically momentous and morally weighty a question as "the cause of the Holocaust"—for purposes of collective memory—on the basis of so narrow and peculiarly professional a preoccupation as the terms of a treaty's jurisdictional provision.

Moreover, by indicting the Nuremberg defendants for the offense of "conspiracy" (to wage aggressive war), Allied prosecutors appeared to adopt a particular historical interpretation—a "conspiratorial view of history"—one that (by its particular implausibility) threatened to discredit the trial's potential contribution to collective memory.[59] In their public statements, prosecutors labored to explain the meaning of conspiracy in legal doctrine and to distinguish it as a term of art from the more conventional understanding prevalent among historians and the wider public.

Judging from contemporaneous accounts, such efforts at public explanation, however conscientious, were largely unsuccessful.[60] These efforts also cast the profession in the unappealing position of appearing to lecture others about the "true" meaning of a concept that most listeners were quite convinced they already understood. This discrepancy between lay and legal understandings of conspiracy worked to discredit the conspiracy indictment and conviction of the Tokyo defendants even more than those at Nuremberg.[61] Much of the conduct

---

59   Judith N. Shklar, *Legalism* 172 (1964). Summarizing the receptive reaction of American public opinion, Bosch notes that "popular faith in Nuremberg, which at times espoused a 'devil theory' of history and which hoped that the Tribunal would be a 'once-and-for-all' antidote to the world's ills, revealed the American propensity for oversimplifying complex questions of foreign affairs." Bosch, *supra* note 56, at 233.

60   Bosch, *supra* note 56, at 113.

61   For one version of these definitional disparities, see Richard H. Minear, *Victors' Justice: The Tokyo War Crimes Trial* 128-33 (1971) (asserting that the Tokyo defendants' activities amounted to a legal conspiracy but not a historical, common-sense conspiracy). On objections to the Tokyo conspiracy indictment by defense counsel and the dissenting Justices, see Philip R. Piccigallo, *The Japanese on Trial: Allied War*

of the Japanese simply could not be clearly characterized in laymen's terms as a "conspiracy to wage aggressive war," considering the complex regional rivalries and balance of power politics (involving several major powers) preceding the war in the Pacific.[62] For many laymen, the idea of conspiracy inevitably evoked the vision of a small cabal, scheming together in a single room, plotting out in meticulous detail everything that would later transpire.[63]

But of course, "history reveals on its every page the importance of contingencies—accidents, coincidences or other unforeseeable developments," as Gallie observes.[64] The legal concept of conspiracy, in its exceptional "looseness and pliability,"[65] fully acknowledges this fact, conceptually accommodating the need to disaggregate a lengthy period of activity by many contributors into a series of interlocking conspiracies, some of which may be characterized as a "chain," others as a "wheel." Far from a rare and improbable scenario in human affairs, the legal concept of conspiracy is frequently overinclusive, and consequently unfair to defendants, as judges and legal scholars have long acknowledged.[66] Even so, careful historians generally conclude,

---

Crimes Operations in the East, 1945-1951 22-23, 29-31(1979).

62 Conservative Japanese intellectuals have consistently argued, for instance, that Japan was forced to fight the United States and Britain after they imposed a blockade on oil imports. For recent arguments to this effect by Japanese legal scholars, see C. Hosoya et al., "Preface" to *The Tokyo War Crimes Trial: An International Symposium* 7, 8-9 (C. Hosoya et al. eds., 1986); Kojima Noburu, "Contributions to Peace," in *The Tokyo War Crimes Trial, supra,* at 69, 76-78. See also Paul W. Schroeder, *The Axis Alliance and Japanese-American Relations* 124, 221-28 (1958) (suggesting that Japan had several legitimate reasons for entering the Axis Alliance, including a need to end its diplomatic isolation and a desire to prevent the war in Europe from consuming the Pacific). Justice B.V.A. Röling, in dissent, even found such arguments *legally* compelling. B.V.A. Röling, *The Tokyo Trial and Beyond* 85-86 (Antonio Cassese ed., 1993).

63 On the receptivity of extremist political movements to conspiracy theories of this sort, see Richard Hofstadter, "The Paranoid Style in American Politics," in *The Paranoid Style in American Politics and Other Essays* 3, 4-6, 35-39 (1965).

64 Gallie, *supra* note 28, at 133.

65 George E. Dix & M. Michael Sharlot, *Criminal Law: Cases and Materials* 582 (1987).

66 See, e.g., *Krulewitch v. United States,* 336 U.S. 440, 445 (1949) (Jackson, J., concurring) (characterizing conspiracy as an "elastic, sprawling and pervasive offense" that is typically employed when there is insufficient evidence to prosecute for the substantive offense); Phillip E. Johnson, "The Unnecessary Crime of Conspiracy," 61 *Cal. L. Rev.* 1137, 1141-46 (1973) (arguing that criminal defendants may be unjustly

as does Maier regarding the conspiracy trials of Italian terrorists in the late 1970s, that "judicial proceedings tend to impose a coherence on fragmentary testimony, attributing a degree of intentionality and group organization in search for cohesive narrative and explanation."[67]

Trials of administrative massacre have introduced still other distortions into historical understanding and, thereby, into collective memory. Early historiography of the Holocaust was based largely on the record assembled by Allied prosecutors. The prosecutors did not conceal their aspiration to do just that. Executive trial counsel at Nuremberg, Robert G. Storey, spoke openly of this purpose: "the making of a record of the Hitler regime which would withstand the test of history."[68]

Wooed by the lawyers in this way, it is scarcely surprising that the first generation of postwar historians proved inattentive to the idiosyncratic nature of the law's concerns.[69] What came to be known among historians as "the Nuremberg view" or as "perpetrator history," for instance, focused almost exclusively on the intentions and ideologies of top leaders, an emphasis understandably reflected in the record of the legal proceedings against them.[70]

The prosecution's preoccupation with the intentional acts of top figures followed naturally from its desire to convict such figures of particular criminal offenses. But it was neither natural nor inevitable that historians of the period should have concentrated their attention to

---

punished when the conspiracy doctrine is used to expand the scope of the criminal law).

67   Maier, *supra* note 2, at 9, citing the work of the Italian historian of memory, Alessandro Portelli.

68   Hannah Arendt, *Eichmann in Jerusalem: A Report on the Banality of Evil* 253 (Penguin Books, rev. & enlarged ed. 1977) (1963).

69   Browning notes, for instance, that for early postwar historiography, "[t]he evidentiary base was above all the German documents captured at the end of the war, which served ... the prosecutors at postwar trials. The initial representation of the Holocaust perpetrators was that of criminal minds, infected with racism and antisemitism, carrying out criminal policies through criminal organizations." Christopher R. Browning, "German Memory, Judicial Interrogation, and Historical Reconstruction: Writing Perpetrator History from Postwar Testimony," in *Probing the Limits of Representation, supra* note 11, at 22, 26. Browning also observes how the enduring possibility of criminal indictment influenced the stories told by members of Police Battalion 101 concerning their participation in one large-scale slaughter of Jews. *Id.* at 29.

70   *Id.* at 26.

similar effect. Historians followed the lawyers' lead in this regard not only because the lawyers' documents were those most readily available, but at least partly because the then-prevalent conception of "the historian as neutral judge"[71] established a natural affinity between how courts and historians understood their respective callings.

Only years later did historians come to realize how the evidentiary focus of the criminal proceedings had unwittingly skewed their analysis in favor of what came to be known as the "intentionalist" interpretation of the period.[72] This focus subtly drew attention away from institutional dynamics and the "machinery of destruction," particularly the crucial role of minor bureaucrats and functionaries at all levels of German society.[73]

---

71   Peter Novick, *That Noble Dream: The "Objectivity Question" and the American Historical Profession* 596 (1988).   On this view, "the historian's conclusions are expected to display the standard judicial qualities of balance and evenhandedness. As with the judiciary, these qualities are guarded by the insulation of the historical profession from social pressure or political influence, and by the individual historian avoiding partisanship ...." *Id.* at 2.

72   Historical debates came to be "fought less by means of scholarly than legalistic arguments," one historian recently complained. "The highly emotionalized debate about ... whether a formal order by Hitler for the policy of genocide was necessary illuminates this tendency ...." Hans Mommsen, 'Search for the "Lost History"? Observations on the Historical Self-Evidence of the Federal Republic,' in *Forever in the Shadow of Hitler?*, *supra* note 15, at 101, 108.

This was not the first time that the history of large-scale administrative massacre had been written under the heavy influence of legal claims against its perpetrators. Roberto González-Echevarría, "The Law of the Letter: *Garcilaso's* Commentaries and the Origins of the Latin American Narrative," 1 *Yale J. Criticism* 107, 108-15 (1987) (observing that several early histories of the Spanish conquest of America were written in the form of legal arguments).

Uncritical reliance by historians on legal testimony is not confined to historiography concerning administrative massacre.   Robert F. Berkhofer, Jr., *Beyond the Great Story: History As Text and Discourse* 151 (1995) (criticizing two influential recent books for "purport[ing] to reproduce the popular culture of the common people" from the legal records of the Inquisition, ignoring the likely effect of "the Inquisitorial power structure that produced and preserved the words in the first place" and to whose interrogators the recovered testimony was calculated to appeal).

73   Browning, *supra* note 69, at 26-27; see also David Bankier, *The Germans and the Final Solution* 89-100 (1992); Christopher Browning, *Ordinary Men: Reserve Police Battalion 101 and the Final Solution in Poland* at xvii (1992) (describing the battalion as composed of grass-roots civilians who became "professional killers").   The Tokyo trial similarly skewed historical understanding in Japan of the country's wartime wrongdoing in the direction of "the individualist theory of history," according to scholars, leading to the neglect of institutional and structural sources requiring more fundamental reform.   Steven T. Benfell, "The Construction and Change of Japanese

The problem would have been aggravated if judges deliberately tried to make their stories compelling as monumental didactics, as national narrative. After all, "successful narratives often foreground individual protagonists and antagonists rather than structures, trends, or social forces," Schudson notes.[74] Yet since individual leaders come and go, it is precisely such structures and forces—their analysis and critique—that should occupy the center stage of public deliberation in the aftermath of large-scale administrative massacre.

As in Germany, the extent of public collaboration with Nazi policies has been discovered in France. These discoveries have compelled a similar reassessment of the initial focus of postwar French criminal courts on a few top elites. Despite early outbursts of mass vigilantism, criminal prosecutions in the years immediately following the War were limited to the most high-ranking Vichy officials and intellectual defenders of Nazi collaboration.[75] The decision to confine the scope of legal retribution in this way reflected the Gaullist story that the French nation had been substantially united in opposition to German suzerainty.[76]

A leading French historian proudly proclaims that sophisticated scholars in his country have, in this century, almost entirely abandoned the antiquated notion of writing history in the pedagogic or "epideictic" mode. History, he implies, should not concern itself with ascribing praise or blame to individuals, but rather with tracking long-term social and institutional change.[77] Perhaps it is no coincidence, then, that it took the work of non-French historians, published decades after the

---

National Identity," (paper presented at the American Political Science Association Conference in Chicago, Sept. 2, 1995).

74   Schudson, *supra* note 12, at 357.

75   Herbert R. Lottman, *The Purge* 132-68 (1986); see also Diane Rubenstein, *What's Left?: The Ecole Normale Supérieure and the Right* 137-63 (1990) (describing the trials of collaborationist journalists and intellectuals).

76   In his August 25, 1944 speech to liberated Paris, De Gaulle proclaimed that the city had been "'freed by itself, by its own people with the cooperation and support of the whole of France ... of the eternal France.'" R.J.B. Bosworth, *Explaining Auschwitz and Hiroshima: History Writing and the Second World War, 1945-1990*, at 112 (1993); see also *id.* at 112-13 (describing "the Gaullist line of the naturally united French, apart from a few criminals, resisting to a man and a woman").

77   Pierre Nora, "Between Memory and History: *Les Lieux de Mémoire*," 26 *Representations* 7, 11-12 (1989).

War, to disprove the Gaullist myth of a nation united in Resistance, to demonstrate the pervasiveness of collaboration at many levels of French society.[78] It required two decades of litigation to compel correction of French schoolbooks, so that they would describe the roundup of Jews for deportation as an entirely French, not German, operation.[79]

Master Narrative by Legal Decree?

The immediate upshot of such historiography, however, was to discredit the story that early postwar French courts had sought to tell at De Gaulle's urging: that a handful of collaborationists—Laval, Pétain, and a few intellectual journalists—had sold out the good and noble nation. The recently renewed efforts at prosecution of French war criminals, although still focused on a handful of high-ranking collaborationists, has been inspired, in part, by these historical revelations and the pall they cast on early efforts to protect such individuals from public scrutiny.[80] Such prosecutions have also relied increasingly on historical scholarship and the expert testimony of

---

78 Bertram M. Gordon, *Collaborationism in France During the Second World War* (1980); John F. Sweets, *Choices in Vichy France: The French Under Nazi Occupation* (1986). See generally Michael R. Marrus & Robert O. Paxton, *Vichy France and the Jews* (1981) (describing how the French Vichy government "energetically persecuted Jews" with policies that were "usually supported by French public opinion"); Zeev Sternhell, *Neither Right Nor Left: Fascist Ideology in France* (David Maisel trans., 1986) (describing the penetration of France by fascist ideas); Marcel Ophüls, *The Sorrow and the Pity* (Mireille Johnston trans., 1972) (discussing life in a French city under Nazi occupation). Such collaboration has only recently received official recognition. Marlise Simons, "Chirac Affirms France's Guilt in Fate of Jews," *N.Y. Times*, July 17, 1995, at A1 (quoting French President Jacques Chirac officially affirming, for the first time, that "the criminal folly of the occupiers was seconded by the French, by the French state"). Paxton and Gordon are American, Marrus is Canadian, Sternhell is Israeli, and Ophüls is a German Jew.

79 Judith Miller, *One, By One, By One: Facing the Holocaust* 145 (1990) ("'The textbooks are now impeccable,'" reports Serge Klarsfeld, who spearheaded the litigation, "'but it was one hell of a battle.'").

80 On the success of conservative French bishops at harboring Paul Touvier for over forty years in a series of monasteries while the French state publicly sought his apprehension and prosecution, see René Rémond et al., *Touvier et l'eglise* (1992); Ted Morgan, "The Hidden Henchman," *N.Y. Times*, May 22, 1994, §6 (Magazine), at 31. A fictionalized treatment is offered by Brian Moore in *The Statement: A Novel* (1996).

professional historians, reversing the earlier pattern of reliance.[81]   In short, the judicial preoccupation with identifying and punishing a small subset of culpable elites told a story that first led historians astray for many years and then enabled them, upon finding a more fitting focus, to discredit persuasively the courts' accounts as national narrative.

In focusing on the acts and intentions of these very top elites, the courts not only missed the macropicture: the story of mass collaboration and institutional support for administrative brutality. They also missed the micropicture: the story of the victims—the human experience of uncomprehending suffering that official brutality produced.   It is that experience which many historians now seek to recapture and to place at the center of any narrative about the period.[82] At Nuremberg there was little testimony by surviving victims of the concentration camps and entirely nothing about their felt experience of life there or its emotional aftermath.

It is this confessedly subjective experience—irrelevant to criminal law, though not to civil claims—that oral historians have only recently sought to explore.   In this respect, scholars have perceived a need to overcome what they perceive as a 'legal' concern with the factual accuracy of personal testimony in order to apprehend its historical significance.   That is, these scholars try to grasp the meaning of the period's most traumatic events through the continuing memory of those who lived through its trauma.   One such scholar writes:

> Testimonies are often labelled as 'subjective' or 'biased' in the legal proceedings concerning war crimes.   The lawyers of war criminals have asked the most impertinent questions of people trying to find words for a shattered memory that did not fit into any language ... to describe those days and months in which the only chance of survival was to forget that there had ever been a world of goodness, warmth, and beauty.... The fault is not theirs, but lies with a certain method of argument on the part of the lawyers ....   They demand precise statements of facts, and in this

---

81   Tony Judt, "The Past Is Another Country: Myth and Memory in Postwar Europe," *Daedalus,* Fall 1992, at 83, 98 (noting that early postwar myths of massive resistance to Nazism unraveled on account of "the work of professional scholars working in relative obscurity, their conclusions and evidence surfacing into the public realm only when a particularly egregious case ... caught the headlines").

82   Lawrence L. Langer, *Holocaust Testimonies: The Ruins of Memory* (1991).

way deny that in the concrete process of remembering, facts are enmeshed within the stories of a lifetime.... A lawyer's case is after all merely another kind of story ....

... It is not the task of oral historians to give the kind of evidence required in a court of law.... [Some historians attempt to uncover] the way in which suffering is remembered and influences all other memory.... One is dealing with an effort to create a new kind of history that cannot be used as legal evidence since it explicitly records subjective experience.[83]

Such historians adopt what can fairly be described as a reverential attitude toward the personal "testimony" of their informants, particularly when testifying about the extreme trauma that history has inflicted upon them. This attitude of sanctity is deeply at odds with the skeptical, scrutinizing posture of any competent cross-examiner, such as defense counsel at the trials we are considering.

Not surprisingly, at the Argentine junta trial, witness-survivors found themselves facing questions concerning, for instance, their membership in guerrilla groups, questions identical to those their abductors had asked them under torture. The witnesses, of course, found such questions deeply offensive; the experience of public testimony was thus personally degrading, rather than empowering.[84]

But their experiences here may simply reveal an inherent limitation of criminal proceedings (that is, those consistent with liberal ideals of due process) as a vehicle for fostering reverential public attitudes toward such victims and their stories and for endowing their narratives with authoritative meaning. A similar problem arose in the case against John Demjanjuk. As Novick observes:

Much of the outrage which greeted the Israeli Supreme Court's overturning the verdict ... was a result of the Court having based its decision on its plausible view that, while there was no question of subjective bad faith [by Demjanjuk's victim-accusers], fifty-year-old memories, however "sacred," were fallible. The decision was thus,

---

83   Selma Leydesdorff, "A Shattered Silence: The Life Stories of Survivors of the Jewish Proletariat of Amsterdam," in *Memory and Totalitarianism* 145, 147-48 (Luisa Passerini ed., 1992).

84   Interview with Renee Epelbaum, President of *Madres de la Plaza de Mayo, Linea Fundadora*, in Buenos Aires, Argentina (July 1987).

literally, "sacrilege."[85]

In sum, contemporary historians, whether focused on impersonal structures of complicity or intimate survivors' sensibilities, have found that the legal record of Nuremberg and other such trials, gathered with a view to criminal prosecution, is not particularly useful for current purposes of description or explanation.

Lawyers and even legal scholars, examining these proceedings many years later, have been largely deaf to such shifts in historical sensibilities, lamenting only that Nuremberg has not been taken more seriously as binding legal precedent.[86] As legal advocates we are intimately familiar with how to use the historical record to support a particular interpretation of the law. But we are almost entirely blind to how our legal interpretations, and the records they create in a given dispute, may favor—subtly but decisively—one of the competing historical interpretations of a period.

Lawyers are not the only professionals creating problems for historical interpretation and public understanding of such events. Just as the law, with its special preoccupations, can easily lead historians astray for long periods, so too can it derail journalists, who infuse misunderstandings directly into collective memory. When political leaders are acquitted in a criminal proceeding, they choose (unsurprisingly) to interpret this legal result as a complete vindication of their story. Their claims to this effect, in turn, are widely disseminated throughout society by the mass media.

But the failure of a jury to find guilt "beyond a reasonable doubt" is, in fact, well short of vindication of the defendant's story. Insofar as legal standards governing the burden of proof in criminal proceedings have uncritically infiltrated public deliberation about unrelated matters, the quality of such deliberation is degraded.[87] This posed a threat to any effort at reading historical lessons from the Touvier trial, for instance: "if France was 'in the dock' along with Touvier, France could also be

---

85   Peter Novick, "Pseudo-Memory and Dubious "Lessons": The Holocaust in American Culture" 2 (Apr. 1995) (paper presented at the Project for Rhetoric of Inquiry Symposium, University of Iowa).

86   Steven Fogelson, "Note, The Nuremberg Legacy: An Unfulfilled Promise," 63 *S. Cal. L. Rev.* 833 (1990).

87   Frederick Schauer, "Slightly Guilty," *U. Chi. Legal F.* 83, 83 (1993).

acquitted along with Touvier, a distinct if disquieting possibility given the fragile legal construct on which his prosecution rested."[88]

The collective memory of administrative massacres in several famous cases has been distorted because the frequent acquittal of some defendants is mistakenly read as an authoritative endorsement of the stories the defendants had offered to the court.[89] Tried for the murder of some 200 student protesters, South Korean dictator Chun Doo Hwan was acquitted for lack of substantial evidence that he gave the order to shoot. Though convicted on other charges (mutiny and treason) and sentenced to death, Chun's murder acquittal was "angrily denounced" by relatives of the massacre's victims.[90] "They are murderers," charged Kin Gyong Chon, one such relative. "How could murderers be pardoned in this way?" However much we might sympathize with the speaker, his statement makes several mistakes, to which the unnecessary infusion of legal language has contributed.

Even where the prosecution prevails entirely at final judgment, some contend that press reports may seem to favor the defense by inevitably focusing on its scoring of small points, however insignificant to central issues.[91]

---

88   Leila S. Wexler, "Reflections on the Trial of Vichy Collaborator Paul Touvier for Crimes Against Humanity in France," 20 *Law & Soc. Inquiry* 191, 217 (1995); see also Jennifer Merchant, "History, Memory, and Justice: The Touvier Trial in France," 23 *J. Crim. Just.* 425 (1995).

89   For a particularly egregious example of this mistake, see Kate Millett, *The Politics of Cruelty: An Essay on the Literature of Political Imprisonment* 230 (1994) (contending that since some of the junta defendants were acquitted of certain offenses, "the results of the Argentinean trial are deplorable, virtually an exoneration of the military and all its brutality, ... an outcome ... very reassuring not only for the Argentinean military but for all other military regimes in the region").

It would be difficult to write a sentence about the trial that is more mistaken in both its general point and all of its details. Still, a distinguished sociologist manages to do so, observing—in a chapter- length analysis of the dirty war and its aftermath—that "in Argentina, as elsewhere in Latin America, the military, when it gave up power, managed to protect itself from retribution." Daniel Chirot, *Modern Tyrants* 286 (1994). Chirot makes no mention of the trials of the junta members or other officers, the indictment of hundreds more, the successful civil suits, or the purging of many top generals and admirals.

90   Sandra Sugawara, "Seoul Court Convicts Top Industrialists," *Washington Post*, Tuesday, Aug. 27, 1996, at A01. At the time of this writing, Chun's sentence was pending on appeal.

91   Robert A. Kahn, "Holocaust Denial Litigation in Canada" 19-21 (July 3, 1995) (paper presented at the Law and Society Association Conference). Kahn studied the

Misreading acquittals as historical vindication is one of a larger set of obstacles to the law's effective influencing of collective memory: because few citizens can be expected to read the judicial opinion (or to follow closely the proceedings that produce it), much of any story that the courts recount about an episode of administrative massacre must be filtered through the mass media. The media, however, have a short list of narrative genres—each with conventions of its own—that simplify and stereotype the story of liberal legality in ways largely unconducive to public deliberation and discursive democracy.[92]

The trial of the Argentine juntas offers another telling example of how the law often focuses on issues ancillary to the larger claims of history and collective memory. In prosecuting the juntas, the courts lavished enormous time and attention on the question of which doctrine of "indirect authorship," among the several authorized by law, ought best be invoked to link the acts of the subordinates to the intentions of the superiors.[93] This question proves quite fascinating for legal theorists, and it consequently preoccupied Alfonsín's advisor-philosophers for a considerable time.[94]

The question was irrelevant, however, in the larger public debate, since no one seriously questioned that the subordinates' wrongful acts had been authorized by their superiors. Public advocates for the disappeared, as well as for military officers, may have agreed on very

---

Canadian trial of Ernst Zundel for "Holocaust Denial" and its treatment by the Canadian press. He concludes: "Even as the revisionists are proven wrong on point after point, an air of revisionism lingers in the courtroom and media." *Id.* at 29. The trial thus "reinforced the idea that a legitimate debate [is] under way" between Holocaust deniers and their accusers. *Id.* at 22.

92 For sociological study of this process, see Herbert J. Gans, *Deciding What's News: A Study of CBS Evening News, NBC Nightly News, Newsweek, and Time* (1979). On how the news media distort the representation of criminal trials, see Philip Schlesinger & Howard Tumber, *Reporting Crime: The Media Politics of Criminal Justice* 207-47 (1994); Barbie Zelizer, *"Covering the Body": The Kennedy Assassination, the Media, and the Shaping of Collective Memory* 49-98 (1992); David A. Harris, "The Appearance of Justice: Court TV, Conventional Television, and Public Understanding of the Criminal Justice System," 35 *Ariz. L. Rev.* 785, 785 (1993).

93 "Argentina: National Appeals Court (Criminal Division) Judgment on Human Rights Violations By Former Military Leaders (Excerpts)," 26 *Int'l Legal Materials* 317, 327 (1987).

94 Malamud-Goti has since conceded that this emphasis was misplaced. Interview with Jaime Malamud-Goti, in Buenos Aires, Argentina (Aug. 1987).

little. But they agreed that this central question, preoccupying the courts, was entirely superfluous to a historical assessment of the period, and hence to its place within national memory. Given such disparities between the claims of law and memory, it did not strike many Argentines as particularly strange that one of the junta defendants would even announce to the court that he was prepared to accept "the judgment of history" (that is, of disinterested historians, presumably), but not that of the tribunal.[95]

No less than the right, those on the left, including most of Argentina's historians and social scientists, found the legal narrative of the junta trial largely unpersuasive as the basis for memory of the period. They insisted that it was wrong for the President to condemn the political culture of the general population. That culture was the finest legacy of Peronism, from its days as a genuine mass movement. Specifically, there was no good reason why ordinary people should express even minimal respect for legal institutions that had historically been highly corrupt and almost entirely inaccessible to people of their socioeconomic status.[96] Confronted with this unpleasant, daily reality, such people might be forgiven for thinking "the rule of law" a cynical abstraction. Their lack of reverence for the judicial system should not, then, be bemoaned as an ethical failure on their part; the President's implication to that effect only added new insult to existing injury.

But particularly offensive to the left (including the Peronist left) was the insistence of the Alfonsín government and the prosecutors on

---

95 *"Galtieri Espera el Juicio de Dios y de la Historia,"* El Diario del Juicio (Buenos Aires), Sept. 30, 1985 (translation by author) (quoting Gen. Leopoldo Galtieri). General Roberto Viola similarly proclaimed during the trial that "the judgment of history will be highly unfavorable towards the prosecutor's conduct." *El Diario del Juicio* (Buenos Aires), Oct. 22, 1985 (translation by author). Admiral Emilio Massera also expressed a willingness to be judged only by history. Emilio Massera, Speech Delivered at the Chamber of Public Relations, Plaza Hotel, Buenos Aires, Argentina (Apr. 1978).

96 On the extreme inaccessibility of Argentine courts to most citizens of moderate means for ordinary dispute resolution, see "Argentina," in Mauro Cappelletti & Bryant Garth, 3 *Access to Justice,* 179 (1978). It should scarcely be surprising, then, that most Argentines hold a negative view of the courts, see Gallup Institute of Argentina, *Estudio de Opinión Acerca de la Justicia en Argentina,* (indicating that in 1990 49% of the population believed that the judicial system was either "bad" or "very bad."). Cited in Mark Unger, "Judicial Reform: Inequality, Democratization, and Latin America's Courts," 5 (paper presented at the American Political Science Association Conference, San Francisco, Sept. 1, 1996).

viewing the dirty war not in terms of social struggle and its suppression, but as the deprivation of individual rights, an insistence rightly seen as based upon the law's liberal premises. For Argentine leftists, who view liberal law as an illegitimate expression of class power, the problem with the government's approach to memory construction

> arises from the idea or the experience of political violence as the chaotic and intractable opposite of law.... [This] opposition of the order of law and the chaos of violence ... led to the omission of collective motivation not only of victimizers (national security doctrine as political program) but of victims as well, who were defended as individuals whose human rights had been violated rather than as political activists (a concept that even the prosecution refused to contemplate).[97]

The result of the government's approach was that "the collective nature of the experience, of agency, and of guilt together have remained obscured and forgotten, ... incomprehensible and inutterable."[98] In short, "because they saw the crimes ... as resulting from the suspension of [the] legal system, [they] were adamant that their investigations should be understood within a context of legal concepts and language."[99] The effect was harmful, even perverse: The legal language used to protest terror in these documents is itself exclusionary: it "colludes with the deeds they 'expose.'"[100] In fact, "the goals of the

---

97 Julie Taylor, "Body Memories: Aide-Memoires and Collective Amnesia in the Wake of the Argentine Terror," in *Body Politics: Disease, Desire, and the Family* 192, 198 (Michael Ryan & Avery Gordon eds., 1994). Taylor's remarks here mirror criticisms offered by the military defendants themselves and the defense counsel, who similarly accused the court of ignoring left-wing political activities and sympathies of many of the disappeared. For a critique (similar to Taylor's) of Italy's courts, in their treatment of prosecutions of the Red Brigades, see Alessandro Portelli, "Oral Testimony, the Law, and the Making of History: The 'April 7' Murder Trial," *Hist. Workshop J.* 5, 9-11, 15, 31 (1986) (criticizing judicial narratives, in applying legal concepts of conspiracy, for denigrating and denying mass support for the Red Brigades among students and workers as a genuine social movement).

98 Taylor, *supra* note 97, at 202. Taylor's argument here will be familiar to American readers. Stuart A. Scheingold, *The Politics of Rights* 203-19 (1974) (observing drawbacks of conceiving organized struggles for social change in terms of individuals' rights).

99 *Id.* at 193.

100 *Id.* at 196.

Repression ... found its echo in the law."[101]

For those who shared this view, including many leaders of human rights groups, the dirty war was defined by social forces of class oppression—international capitalism and its domestic, military representatives—battling forces of mass resistance, the guerrillas and their sympathizers.[102] Both the defendants and the victims were agents of objective historical forces, not mere bearers (or deniers) of individual civil rights. The national narrative had to be told in these larger terms.

One need not accept Taylor's leftist views here to accept her critique of lawyerly hubris. For many such leftists, the junta trial would have been more persuasive *as law* if the government had not also sought to portray it as the new "official story"—as collective memory by legal mandate.[103] By trying to use the trials to shape collective memory, rather than solely to find the legal truth and justice, their value—limited, but important—was undermined.

It was the aspiration to combine matters of legal and historical judgment—to settle them at once, and by the state-that weakened the trial's ultimate persuasiveness as either. Many Argentines of leftist sympathies, no less than Alfonsín, favored severe punishment of the military. For them, the junta trial would have been more compelling had it been staged and publicly defended in a way that kept its ambitions within more modest bounds. It would have been more compelling had liberal law not sought to do what, for the left, it necessarily could not do (that is, offer persuasive social analysis).

---

101   *Id.* at 197.

102   Alison Brysk, *The Politics of Human Rights in Argentina* 139 (1994) (observing that the Madres have "adopted an analysis of human rights that posits a direct relationship between capitalism, imperialism, and repression, and a stance of implacable opposition to the Radical government" of Alfonsín). Class analysis of the dirty war is equally common in the social science literature. Guillermo O'Donnell, *¿Y a Mi, Que Me Importa?: Notas Sobre Sociabilidad y Política en Argentina y Brasil* 20-24 (1984); David Pion-Berlin, *The Ideology of State Terror: Economic Doctrine and Political Repression in Argentina and Peru* 104 (1989); William C. Smith, *Authoritarianism and the Crisis of the Argentine Political Economy* 249 (1991).

103   The government itself, in an official report documenting the disappearances, found that the National Commission on the Disappeared's "first steps within the framework of the precise powers laid down for it by the Decree, stimulated immediate public response in an incredible process of reconstructing public memory." *Comisión Nacional Sobre la Desaparición de Personas, Nunca Más: The Report of the Argentine National Commission on the Disappeared* 429 (1986).

In Praise of Law's 'Superficiality'

The utility of legal rules, particularly in a society deeply divided over conceptions of justice, is precisely that they often allow agreement about how to handle a matter (such as punishing Argentine officers) without requiring agreement on the precise reasons for doing so.[104] The criminal law's very "superficiality" as social-historical analysis of administrative massacre is thus its cardinal virtue. To employ it primarily to shape collective historical memory, then, is to risk depriving ourselves of its more modest, traditional contribution by discrediting it altogether. Those for whom the liberal state, newly reestablished, inspired only the most precarious support—which in Argentina meant both the left and right—were willing to accord it qualified legitimacy for the essential tasks of ensuring social order and public provision, but not for the writing of a liberal "official story" that they could not endorse.

A similar concern with misfocusing of historical attention arose in the French prosecutions of Klaus Barbie and Paul Touvier, for different doctrinal reasons. Because the statute of limitations had expired for all their offenses except crimes against humanity, both trials focused almost exclusively on the defendants' conduct toward Jews.[105]

But scholars of the period concurred that this had not been Barbie's or Touvier's principal concern or responsibility. As Rousso notes, the court's exclusive attention to offenses that were still chargeable against Barbie and Touvier led to neglecting the fact that the primary role of the Milice was the battle against the Resistance:

> Memories, which now enjoyed the symbolic support of the law, began to crystallize .... Judges found themselves forced to write history and pronounce historical judgment in the historian's place. In this role they were profoundly uncomfortable, as a glance at the records of the Fauvisson, Touvier, and Barbie cases makes clear. The courts in many cases were forced to rely on shaky interpretations of events, and thus the

---

104   Cass R. Sunstein, "Incompletely Theorized Agreements," 108 *Harv. L. Rev.* 1733, 1735-36 (1995).

105   Leila S. Wexler, "The Interpretation of the Nuremberg Principles by the French Court of Cassation: From Touvier to Barbie and Back Again," 32 *Colum. J. Transnat'l L.* 289, 323-25, 331-33 (1994).

trials unintentionally exacerbated the existing tension between memory, history, and truth.[106]

Touvier's defense counsel, Jacques Trémolet de Villers, hoped that the tension between collective memory and the search for legal truth might work to his client's advantage. Indeed, it had the desired effect in public debate of pitting spokesmen for the Resistance, irritated by the trial's curious "misfocus," against members of the Jewish community.[107] Touvier's attorney then sought to discredit the legal proceedings in the public mind by highlighting this genuine discrepancy between the law's concerns and history's claims, claims for which most laymen had greater sympathy. That is, the discrepancy between the law's need for an offense with which the defendant could still be charged, on one hand, and history's concern with the relative importance or "centrality" of particular motives and events to the period in question, on the other, became a potent weapon of Touvier's attorney to discredit the trial.

Again, the issue of "centrality" would remain entirely irrelevant to the law were the law not universally seen in such cases as necessarily engaged in writing history. The recent French trials hence struck many Frenchmen as peculiar in their "overemphasis" upon the Jews, just as the Nuremberg trial has since struck many as equally peculiar in its tendency to minimize the predominantly Jewish origins of the Holocaust's victims.[108]

Collective memory in France had come, by this point in time, to center on Resistance heroism. A legal proceeding that seemed to minimize the importance of that movement, and its repression by pro-German collaborators, was highly unlikely to find a sympathetic

---

106   Rousso, *supra* note 10, at 160-61; see also John Dixon, "Manipulators of Vichy Propaganda: A Case Study in Personality," in *Vichy France and the Resistance* 41-61 (Roderick Kedward & Roger Austin eds., 1985); Wexler, *supra* note 105, at 349. On the role of the Milice, see John F. Sweets, *The Politics of Resistance in France, 1940-1944* 27 (1976).

107   Alain Finkielkraut characterizes the view of many Frenchmen during the Barbie trial in the following terms: "'Why do the Jews want to monopolize the status of victim? people say. This is their new greed, they say.'" Miller, *supra* note 79, at 117.

108   See, e.g., Michael R. Marrus, *The Holocaust in History* 4 (1987) (observing that, in contrast to the Eichmann trial, crimes against the Jews "never assumed a prominent place" at Nuremberg); Lawrence Douglas, "The Memory of Judgment" 7 *History and Memory* 100, 114 (1996) (noting "the failure of the Nuremberg trial [to] adequately ... address Nazi genocide" of the Jews).

national audience.   Here, the collective memory of national resistance—exaggerated by nationalist hubris to be sure—was shrewdly invoked and opportunistically deployed to weaken public receptivity to prosecution.   The public spotlight was thereby deflected from the inherent wrongfulness of Barbie's acts.[109] The French court was only able to stir up a hermeneutic hornet's nest, not to shape decisively a shared interpretation of these acts. The tribunal was then constrained to "adopt" the least persuasive reading of the acts' historical significance (that is, Barbie against the Jews), thus undermining its authority as national storyteller.

If there is a lesson here, it is surely that when collective memory has already become comfortably entrenched, the law's efforts to excavate and scrutinize it are only likely to discredit the law and its professional spokesmen.[110]   Just when we are tempted to say that memory is ephemeral, a feather in changing political winds, we find that sometimes it attaches itself to particular interpretations for long periods and with great tenacity. How does it do so, we then ask?

In the Barbie case, a direct and insurmountable conflict arose between the requirements of historical truth and those of social solidarity. The law was forced to choose between the two, just as in the Dreyfus trial a century before. Gaullists had deliberately constructed postwar solidarity in France on the basis of a self-flattering myth of united resistance.   The courts, informed by the best recent historiography, could not fail to attack and discredit this myth.

---

109 Barbie was convicted for his role in the deportation of French Jews. "Judgment of December 20, 1985," Cass. crim., 1986 J.C.P. II G, No. 20,655, 113 *J. du Droit Int'l* 127, 127 (1986). But Barbie was publicly known and reproached primarily for his role in the death of Resistance hero Jean Moulin. Alice Y. Kaplan, "Introduction" to Alain Finkielkraut, *Remembering in Vain: The Klaus Barbie Trial and Crimes Against Humanity* ix, xv-xvi (Roxanne Lapidus & Sima Godfrey trans., 1992).

110 Not only lawyers, but even professional historians—though not publicly perceived at most times as highly partisan—often fail to dislodge deeply entrenched collective memories. This is especially clear where historical reinterpretation entails displacing self-congratulatory recollections with self-critical ones. In the Enola Gay controversy at the Smithsonian, for instance, the professionals' "version of history contrasted ... sharply with the lived experience of American veterans, whose personal narratives ... constituted a collective memory of unimpeachable authority." Michael J. Hogan, "The Enola Gay Controversy: History, Memory, and the Politics of Presentation," in *Hiroshima in History and Memory* 200, 212 (Michael J. Hogan, ed., 1996). The professionals lost.

The defense could draw upon such historiography no less than the judges and prosecution.   Although Robert Paxton served as a prosecution witness in the Barbie trial, his scholarship, which revealed the pervasiveness of collaborationism,[111] offered at least equal support for the defense in its effort to portray the defendant's wrongs as enabled by the support of many other now-influential Frenchmen.

The law's difficulty in "getting its history right" is further complicated by the fact that historians themselves are certain to disagree about the relative centrality and significance of particular individuals and events in the larger tableau of administrative massacre. "Such irresolution, which no amount of factual information can resolve, allows for a proliferation of possible narrations of this past," as Friedlander notes regarding the Holocaust.[112]   Just as the law's requirements necessarily focused on certain aspects of German and French wartime history over others, so too the more recent demands within Germany for the restoration of national identity have tended to displace the acts of Eichmann and judgments against the Nuremberg defendants from historical centrality. In both cases, the perceived needs of the present came to dominate interpretation of the past.

Historians have their favored tropes: tragedy, triumph, subordination, resistance to subordination, irony, and so forth. Scholarly debate often consists of disagreements over which such master trope best "fits and justifies" the known facts of a given place and period.[113] Criminal law has its own favored trope: the vindication of society's basic norms protecting individuals' rights to life and liberty against whoever, by his conduct, denies them. Thus, when law and lawyers consciously aspire to influence collective memory, they enter into   competition   with   historiography   and   historians,   who understandably respond by criticizing the law and defending the centrality of their favored tropes. Postmodernist historians accept the

---

111   Michael R. Marrus & Robert O. Paxton, *Vichy France and the Jews* (1981).

112   Saul Friedlander, *Memory, History, and the Extermination of the Jews of Europe* at ix (1993).

113   The terminology of "fit and justify" is that of Ronald Dworkin. Dworkin, *Law's Empire* 239 (1986). The meaning of "justify" in the present context, however, does not imply any approval of the conduct so classified. In this normatively neutral sense, to justify is "to confirm or support by ... evidence," or "to adjust to exact shape, size, or position." 8 *Oxford English Dictionary* 329, 330 (2d ed. 1989).

resulting multiplicity of narratives as salubrious. They graciously concede that their profession should not adopt a proprietary attitude toward the past. But when challenged by non-scholars, most historians assert their special expertise in such matters, bristling at the suggestion that mere laymen should presume to meddle.

This attitude is abundantly revealed in the reaction of German historians to Habermas's writings in the "historians' debate." The same proprietary attitude is even more conspicuous in the official statements of the Organization of American Historians and the American Historical Association during the Enola Gay controversy at the Smithsonian.[114] Professional historians are now eager to show how the representation of reality is a social construction, that is, when they are challenging what they view as the "dominant" one (such as the U.S. veterans' view of Hiroshima), a representation often endorsed by the state and its law.

But historians suddenly draw back from social constructivism when challenged by laymen who do not share the debunking, delegitimizing agenda of the professionals and who wish to tell a story of their own. In the Smithsonian incident, leftist and liberal historians (favoring a more critical assessment of Truman's decision) found themselves asserting just the sort of claims to "power/knowledge" that they invariably denounce in their histories of other professions. In fact, one could almost say, more polemically, that through their considerable efforts at political influence, they sought to impose their own "regime of truth," in Foucault's terms. But this would be an exaggeration, since theirs was to be a "regime" of more open discussion. Even so, their considerable lobbying efforts in that controversy made clear that "critical" historians can prove quite willing to deploy the state's "hegemonic" political and legal institutions to their narrative ends.[115]

---

114 On these statements, see Hogan, *supra* note 110, at 217-220. Hogan, like most professional historians, is entirely sympathetic with these official positions.

115 *Id.* at 210-225 (describing the considerable lobbying efforts of both professional associations to counter the political influence of veterans organizations and the mass media in the Enola Gay controversy.)

Legal Precedent vs. Historical 'Uniqueness'

One aspect of historical interpretation has caused the criminal law considerable embarrassment: whether, and in what respects, the Holocaust is "unique." Certain scholars of Jewish history have cared a great deal about establishing the "unprecedented" and inherently "incomparable" character of the Holocaust, resisting its use as an analogy to lesser crimes.[116] In some such quarters, the very idea of comparing the Holocaust to earlier or subsequent episodes of administrative massacre (even for analytical and scholarly purposes) is regarded as obscene, "an affront to the memory" of the six million.

However, lawyers, including some who have devoted their professional lives to prosecuting Nazi war criminals, will find this notion puzzling to the point of incomprehensibility.[117] In fact, the concept of historical incommensurability is almost uncognizable in legal terms. As lawyers, if we were compelled to conclude from historical investigation and comparative analysis that the events judged at Nuremberg were utterly incommensurable, we would be driven to the corollary conclusion that the legal rules developed from that experience must be very strictly construed; this approach would make them inapplicable to virtually all subsequent experiences of administrative massacre, since such experiences are almost invariably "distinguishable" in significant ways. Those who decry the dangers of comparison presumably do not desire this result. (Lawyers have had no

---

116 Lucy S. Dawidowicz, *The Holocaust and the Historians* 11-21 (1981).

117 See, e.g., Telford Taylor, *Nuremberg and Vietnam: An American Tragedy* 122-53 (1970) (comparing war crimes in both World War II and the Vietnam War in light of international law as developed by the four Geneva Conventions of 1949). For a defense of such comparisons, for both conceptual and theoretical purposes, see Charles S. Maier, *The Unmasterable Past: History, Holocaust, and German National Identity* 69-71 (1988) ("Comparison is a dual process that scrutinizes two or more systems to learn what elements they have in common, and what elements distinguish them. It does not assert identity; it does not deny unique components."). On how the comparative analysis of genocide arguably illuminates the Holocaust's distinctiveness, see Edward T. Linenthal, *Preserving Memory: The Struggle to Create America's Holocaust Museum* 228 (1995) (describing the views of Michael Berenbaum, Director of the U.S. Holocaust Museum, and stating that the representation of various groups of victims of the Holocaust in the museum "serves as a way to portray Jewish uniqueness *through* comparison with various others").

special corner on this insight, moreover.[118])

Historians and political analysts became increasingly dismayed, however, that the Nuremberg court would subsume the most unparalleled features of the defendants' wrongs under longstanding doctrines in the law of war, reducing the Holocaust merely to one among several methods employed for the "waging of aggressive war." By training and temperament (that is, by *déformation professionel*), it seemed, prosecutors and judges were inclined to tell a tale of continuity, even when the facts before them struck most laymen as involving a violent rupture with all prior experience.[119]

After all, courts generally downplay the elements of uniqueness in the facts before them, subsuming these under more general, preexisting concepts and precedents. These are avowedly extended, if at all, only in the most modest and guarded ways.[120] The problem of "representing the Holocaust," an event unintelligible through prior understandings of human conduct, has become a central concern—seen almost as an insurmountable obstacle—for virtually all serious scholarly disciplines.[121] The law does not even recognize it as a problem.[122]

---

118   Todorov similarly observes, with reference to the Holocaust generally (not its specifically legal dimensions): "It is impossible to affirm that the past should serve as a lesson and at the same time affirm that it is absolutely incomparable with the present: what is singular teaches us nothing applicable for the future." Todorov, *supra* note 50, at 17.

119   This gap between lay and lawyerly perceptions of the Holocaust is an important but neglected theme in Arendt's classic work on the Eichmann trial. Arendt, *supra* note 30, at 253-54; see also Douglas, *supra* note 58, at 122 (arguing that "the extraordinary effort to accommodate the Holocaust to prior conceptions of justice resulted in a failure to *see* the Holocaust in its full malignity" and attributing this failure to the legal concept of precedent).

120   Richard Wasserstrom, "Postscript: Lawyers and Revolution," Address at the Annual Convention of the National Lawyers Guild (July 6, 1968), in 30 *U. Pitt. L. Rev.* 125, 129 (1968) ("Law seeks to assimilate everything that happens to that which has happened.... The lawyer's virtually instinctive intellectual response when he is confronted with a situation is to look for the respects in which that situation is like something that is familiar ....").

121   Anton Kaes, "Holocaust and the End of History: Postmodern Historiography in Cinema," in *Probing the Limits of Representation, supra* note 11, at 206, 207 (noting that "[t]he insistence on the impossibility of adequately comprehending and describing the final solution has by now become a *topos* of Holocaust research"). For a representative example, see the observation of Julia Kristeva, that "our symbolic means find themselves hollowed out, nearly wiped out, paralyzed...Never has a cataclysm been more apocalyptically outrageous; never has its representations been assumed by so few

"Concerned as it must be with precedent, the Court treats the Holocaust in precisely the fashion rejected by so many scholars—as just another historical event about which unpopular claims can be made."[123] Its uniqueness is thereby denied simply by the way the legal question is posed.

The problem has reappeared in recent prosecutions for "Holocaust denial." Since the early 1960s, the Nuremberg proceedings have been criticized for failing to respect the Holocaust's specificity as a crime against the Jews.[124] Partially in response to that concern, legislation has been adopted in several Western countries criminalizing "Holocaust denial."[125] Such statutes are defended on the ground that the Holocaust's uniqueness warrants greater encroachment upon freedoms of speech and press than would be constitutionally acceptable concerning other statements that are also factually false, but nondefamatory.

This approach seeks to establish the Holocaust's uniqueness by legal fiat, however. It has thus been criticized as yet another instance of lawyerly encroachment on historiographical questions beyond the

---

symbolic means." Quoted in Jay Winter, *Sites of Memory, Sites of Mourning* 229 (1996).

122   In this regard, despite her hyperbolic and overheated prose, Hannah Arendt remains the most incisive critic of the law's failure.

> The Nazi crimes, it seems to me, explode the limits of the law; and that is precisely what constitutes their monstrousness. For these crimes, no punishment is severe enough .... This guilt, in contrast to all criminal guilt, oversteps and shatters any and all legal systems. That is the reason why the Nazis in Nuremberg are so smug.

"Letter to Karl Jaspers," in *Hannah Arendt Karl Jaspers: Correspondence 1926-1969*, at 54 (Lotte Kohler & Hans Saner eds., Robert Kimber & Rita Kimber trans., 1992).

123   Douglas, *supra* note 108, at 114.

124   For evidence of this failure, see 5 *Trial of the Major War Criminals Before the International Military Tribunal* 368-426 (1947), wherein the French prosecutors, responsible for presenting evidence of war crimes and crimes against humanity, included no evidence of the annihilation of European Jewry as one of the Nazis' transgressions. On this omission, see Douglas, *supra* note 108, at 120 (observing that the Nuremberg Tribunal adopted an "approach that placed the Holocaust on the margins of the legally relevant").

125   Deborah E. Lipstadt, *Denying the Holocaust: The Growing Assault on Truth and Memory* 219-22 (1993) (discussing legislation criminalizing "incitement to hatred; discrimination; or violence on racial, ethnic, or religious grounds").

professional competence of courts.[126]   Judges show themselves understandably uncomfortable about assuming this new role.

But the response to such unwelcome intrusions has sometimes been merely to employ legal fiat in service of the opposing claim: in *denying* the Holocaust's uniqueness. The 1985 West German provision thus criminalizes denial not only of the Holocaust, but also of another massive wrong that the legislators regarded as "comparable," the Soviet expulsion of German peoples from parts of Eastern Europe.[127] The German statute reinstates the earlier problem: treating the Holocaust as "morally equivalent" to other, lesser wrongs, only now doing so more explicitly.[128] In sum, it has proven difficult to employ the law in condemning Holocaust denial without also lending judicial authority to one or the other side of a legitimate scholarly dispute concerning historical uniqueness.

The difficulty of drafting Holocaust denial statutes suggests that law is likely to discredit itself when it presumes to impose any answer to an interpretive question over which reasonable historians differ. After all, in recent decades many historians and social scientists—on both the right and the left—have come to question and *de*emphasize the Holocaust's unique features.[129] These scholars have sought to reassess

---

126 Letter from Professor Herbert A. Strauss to Professor Eric Stein, in "Correspondence on the "Auschwitz Lie"," 87 *Mich. L. Rev.* 1026, 1029 (1989) ("The 'majority opinion' among scientific scholars must be formed in a scientific way, and every intervention of the judiciary power has to be rejected"). See also Todorov, *supra* note 50, at 8. Opposing a recent French statute prohibiting Holocaust denial, Todorov argues that though "the law should strike at libel or the inciting of racial hatred," still, "it is not up to the law to say what history is."

127 Eric Stein, "History Against Free Speech: The New German Law Against the "Auschwitz"—and Other—"Lies"," 85 *Mich. L. Rev.* 277, 307-08 (1986).

128 *Id.* at 309-14 (discussing the final compromise in the law's wording).

129 Although the conservative variants are today better known, there has long been a leftist version of the thesis that the Holocaust was the outgrowth of trends and social forces by no means unique to Germany, but latent within all modern capitalist societies. This thesis was first proposed by the early Frankfurt school, was elaborated by Hannah Arendt, and now finds many sympathizers among scholars in several fields. Zygmunt Bauman, *Modernity and the Holocaust* 9 (1989); Andreas Huyssen, *Twilight Memories: Marking Time in a Culture of Amnesia* 252 (1995). The affinity between the views of the far right and far left go further. The early history of Holocaust denial in France, at least, has been persuasively traced by scholars to the far left of the late 1960s and early 1970s. Nadine Fresco, "Negating the Dead," in *Holocaust Remembrance: The Shapes of Memory* 190, 192-98 (Geoffrey H. Hartman ed., 1994) (discussing the early life and later influence of Paul Rassinier—French author and former concentration camp

the idiosyncrasies of that experience, in both its methods and scope. Their entirely legitimate aim is to situate it within a comprehensive understanding of the horrors of our century, in light of the several genocides and many mass atrocities that preceded and followed it.[130]

The legal definition of "crimes against humanity" proved to be yet another locus of controversy in this regard. Early legal analysts of the Holocaust defined such conduct as involving ordinary criminal acts and intentions, committed for particular motives.[131] Underlying this doctrinal move was a crucial normative concern: to depict defendants as "common criminals"—no different in nature from garden variety murderers, despite their statesmanlike air and plumage. This move well served the goal of stripping high-ranking officials of their asserted immunity under international law. But this way of cognizing their conduct eventually came to be seen as "banalizing" or trivializing the unprecedented features of their wrong, minimizing its unique heinousness.[132]

The opposing approach, however, proved even more problematic. A definition more attentive to historical particularity was necessarily a narrower definition. By packing the most distinctive features of the Nazi Holocaust into the legal definition of "crimes against humanity," that offense became much harder to apply to the conduct of those not at the epicenter of the German extermination program, such as French collaborators acting under their own, purely French brand of anti-Semitism. In this way, efforts to reconceptualize crimes against humanity—aimed at redressing the prior problem—began to impede effective prosecution of their perpetrators. Such conceptual narrowing introduced new doctrinal requirements that are exceedingly difficult to meet, as the prosecution of Paul Touvier abundantly revealed.[133]

The Holocaust, like any historical event, is clearly unique in certain

---

inmate).

130 Klaus Barbie's defense counsel, Jacques Vergès, was to give this argument for "balance" special salience at Barbie's trial. See Chapter 8, "Making Public Memory, Publicly," *infra* text accompanying notes 108-117.

131 Jacques-Bernard Herzog, "Contribution à l'étude de la définition du crime contre l'humanité," 18 *Revue Internationale du Droit Penal* 155, 168 (1947); Wexler, *supra* note 105, at 356-57.

132 Wexler, *supra* note 105, at 358.

133 *Id.* at 359-62.

respects and all too commonplace in others. Thus, if one is asked simply, "Is the Holocaust unique?" the right answer has to be the law professor's proverbial response: "Why do you ask?" How one resolves the issue of uniqueness depends, in short, entirely on who is asking the question, and why she is asking it.   Perhaps one's purpose in asking is to endow the event with a mystical and ineffable aura, so that it can become the centerpiece of a new secular theology or national identity.[134] If so (and if the respondent shares this purpose), one's answer to the question of uniqueness will be very different than to someone whose purpose in asking is to prosecute a post-Nuremberg perpetrator of administrative massacre.

In sum, many see the criminal law as having strayed beyond its proper realm, thus embarrassing itself. It did so first by denying the Holocaust's uniqueness, when such uniqueness seemed obvious, later by blindly asserting it, when this obviousness was no more. From such mistakes, it is easy to see why many would conclude that courts ought therefore to stay out of the history game altogether.

The problem with that entreaty, as we shall see, is that courts are increasingly drawn into deciding historical questions unwittingly in ways they cannot entirely escape.[135]

For Historical "Balance,"
Against "Moral Equivalence"

The interested public has often found historians' accounts more persuasive than those of the courts, particularly the Tokyo and Nuremberg courts. This is primarily because historians are seen to be more concerned with "balance" in proportioning blame among all parties, including the courtroom accusers. To be sure, many historians today reject "balance" as a professional ideal, finding it either impossible or undesirable.[136] Public perception of historiography's

---

134 On how this purpose informs many arguments for its uniqueness, see Avishai Margalit and Gabriel Motzkin, "The Uniqueness of the Holocaust," 25 *Philosophy and Public Affairs* 65, 66 (1996).

135 See Chapter 8, "Making Public Memory, Publicly," *infra* text accompanying notes 7-22.

136 Novick, *supra* note 71, at 264-91, 421-62, 603-05.

tasks, however, still largely cleaves to this traditional ideal, as reflected in the remarks of Galtieri and Massera.[137]

Even avowedly leftist historians sometimes embrace the traditional ideal, at least when asked to serve as judges. Staughton Lynd, for instance, declined Bertrand Russell's invitation to sit on an international tribunal judging alleged U.S. war crimes in Vietnam.

> What I ask is that it [the tribunal] inquire into the acts of both sides and use the same criteria in evaluating the acts of one side that it uses in evaluating the acts of the other ... I believe that [what Russell proposes] amounts to judging one side (the N.L.F.) by its ends, the other side (the United States) by its means. Precisely this double standard is what I had thought all of us, in this post-Stalin era, wished to avoid.[138]

Realizing that the tribunal will be trying to write history, a task to which his desired participation is designed to contribute, Lynd invokes the historian's traditional professional ideal of balance, contrasting it with the tribunal's more partisan agenda.

For the Nuremberg and Tokyo courts, it mattered little to the validity of criminal proceedings against Axis leadership that Allied victors had committed vast war crimes of their own.[139] Unlike the law

---

137 See *supra* note 95.

138 Staughton Lynd, "The War Crimes Tribunal: A Dissent," 12 *Liberation,* Dec. 1967-Jan. 1968, at 76, 76-77. A leader of anti-war protests, Lynd taught history at Yale and wrote such early works as *American Labor Radicalism* (1973) and *Class Conflict, Slavery, and the United States* (1968). He later became a labor lawyer and community activist.

139 Hans J. Morgenthau, *Politics Among Nations* 218-19 (1954). Allied war crimes prominently included the saturation and fire bombing of civilian population centers such as Dresden, Hamburg, Tokyo, Yokohama, Hiroshima, and Nagasaki without discriminating between military and non-combatant targets. As one noted historian summarizes the data, the death toll of Japanese civilians from bombings of 66 cities was approximately 400,000. American military deaths in all of WWII were about 300,000. John W. Dower, *War Without Mercy: Race and Power in the Pacific War* 295-300 (1986). On Soviet war crimes, see Allen Paul, *Katyń: The Untold Story of Stalin's Polish Massacre* 103-17 (1991). If the Nuremberg trials produced poor historiography, this was due only partly to liberal law's inherent limitations. Surely more important was the fact that "for fifty years, the largest single participant in [the] war imposed a policy of almost total historical selectivity, while the other victors basked in the illusion of their own impartiality." Norman Davies, "The Misunderstood Victory in Europe," *N.Y. Rev. Books,* May 25, 1995, at 7, 11. In a spirit of Allied comity, "few historians were willing to ask if the country which played the major role in winning the war against Hitler might

of tort, criminal law has virtually no place for "comparative fault,"[140] no doctrinal device for mitigating the wrongdoing or culpability of the accused in light of the accusers'. Proposals to move criminal law very far in this direction rightly strike virtually all sensible people as quixotic, if not perverse.[141]

For the public, however, particularly in postwar Japan and West Germany, and among conservative Argentines, it mattered *greatly* in gauging the legitimacy of the trials that they seemed tendentiously selective, aimed at focusing memory in partisan ways. It mattered for such listeners that the defendants in all these episodes of administrative massacre had constituted only a single side to a two- or multi-sided conflict, one in which other parties had similarly committed unlawful acts on a large scale. This unsavory feature of the Nuremberg judgment has undermined its authority in the minds of many, weakening its normative weight. When Nuremberg's relevance to the dirty war as legal precedent was pointed out to him, for instance, one Argentine general observed: "Yes, but if the Germans had won the war, the trials would have been held not at Nuremberg, but in Virginia."[142] He was surely right.

Tu quoque is the conceptual peg on which this moral intuition is usually hung, but as a legal argument its scope is exceedingly narrow.[143]

---

also have played a part in causing it." *Id.* at 10.

140   Wayne R. LaFave & Austin W. Scott, Jr., *Criminal Law* 14 (2d ed. 1986) (stating that in criminal law "the contributory negligence of the victim is no defense"); Alon Harel, "Efficiency and Fairness in Criminal Law: The Case for a Criminal Law Principle of Comparative Fault," 82 *Cal. L. Rev.* 1181, 1184 (1994) (advocating a limited role for comparative fault within the criminal law).

141   For such proposals, see, e.g., K.N. Hylton, "Optimal Law Enforcement and Victims' Precaution," 27 *Rand Journal of Economics* 97 (1996) (arguing that often people become victims of crime because they have foolishly underinvested in their own protection) and Gary Becker, "Crime and Punishment: an Economic Approach," 76 *Journal of Political Economy* 1690 (1968).

142   Quoted in the remarks of Judge Andrés D'Alessio. Tape of "Human Rights and Deliberative Democracy: A Conference in Honor of Carlos Santiago Nino," Presented at Yale Law School (Sept. 23-24, 1994).

143   For a sweeping rejection of the *tu quoque* defense at Nuremberg, see 13 *Trial of the Major War Criminals Before the International Military Tribunal* 521 (1948) ("We are not trying whether any other powers have committed breaches of international law ... we are trying whether these defendants have."). The court nevertheless accepted much of the defense *sub rosa* where Allied activities were virtually identical to Axis illegalities, as in the common use of 'unlimited' submarine warfare. Otto Kirchheimer,

Kirchheimer describes its logic:

> Against the inherent assertion of moral superiority, of the radical
> difference between the contemptible doings of those in the dock and the
> visions, intentions, and record of the new master, the defendants will
> resort to *tu quoque* tactics.... [This] implies more an argument addressed
> *to the public at large and the future historian* than a legal defense. In
> asserting that an accident of history rather than an inherent quality of
> those who govern determines who should sit in judgment and who
> should be the defendant, it tries from the outset to devalue the meaning
> and import of the judgment.[144]

In so doing, it tries for too much. As an affirmative defense, such
an argument aims to be fully exculpatory. But *tu quoque* evidence can
be deployed more convincingly in mitigating a sentence. It closely
resembles "character evidence" in this regard. *To the extent* that
Japanese aggression throughout Asia, for instance, could be
convincingly viewed as partially a defensive response to a
still-pervasive Western imperialism there[145]—to which the testimony of
historians would be indispensable—this would suggest the non-
malicious character of Japanese actions and of those who directed them.
The law does not directly address such questions—whether praised as
reflecting "historical balance" or condemned as permitting "moral
equivalence." Thus it cannot insist on any bright lines here, as it does
between guilt and innocence.

If historical balance has strongly positive associations, "moral
equivalence" has strongly negative ones. But the two, though often
invoked in debate, are nowhere carefully defined or distinguished as a
conceptual matter. To judge from its usage in context, moral

Political Justice: The Use of Legal Procedure for Political Ends 338 (1961). Judicial
deliberation about *tu quoque* issues was explicit, but only recently acknowledged
publicly. B.V.A. Röling, *The Tokyo Trial and Beyond* 60 (Antonio Cassese ed., 1993).
Although a plaintiff must have "clean hands" for a civil suit in equity, there has never
been any analogous requirement for the party alleging criminal harm. The prevalence
of comparable misconduct by non-defendants is legally relevant only to establishing
prevailing international custom and the consistency of the defendant's conduct with
such custom.

144 Kirchheimer, *supra* note 143, at 336-37 (emphasis added).

145 Justice Röling, in dissent, found this argument partially persuasive. Röling, *supra*
note 143, at 889.

equivalence asserts the equal moral stature of accuser and accused. It thereby seeks to deny the moral standing of the accusers to assume the prosecutorial role. This is not the place for thorough analysis of the logical and historical errors in such assertions. For present purposes, two brief points are essential, however.

First, accusations of moral equivalence imply that legal proceedings are indefensible unless the accusers have "clean hands." The accused may be guilty of war crimes. But so are the accusers, after all. Since both are guilty of the very same offenses, their respective wrongdoing to each other "cancels out." There is no need even to assess their respective degrees of wrongdoing or culpability, the argument goes. It is wrong to seriously entertain comparative questions of measurement, moreover, where such horrendous misconduct has been perpetrated by both sides. This argument, significantly, exploits the binary logic of criminal liability (i.e., one is either guilty or not), turning it to dubious ends.

But criminal law has nowhere required that prosecutors or those they represent display clean hands. The burden of argument, at least, would thus seem to rest with those who would insist upon such cleanliness in the kind of case at issue: large-scale state brutality. The best argument to that effect would be that in these cases (unlike any others) the prosecution claims—explicitly or implicitly—not merely to be applying the law, but also writing authoritative history. To attain even minimal competence, any such historiography must strive for historical balance, i.e., to incorporate within the narrative frame the respective wrongs of all pertinent parties. This is not at all a preposterous claim, as I argue here throughout.

Second, however, the accusation of moral equivalence implies that if the wrongs done by accusers against accused were somehow "weighed" against those of the accused against the accusers, neither side would have an edge. This is a very different and much weaker argument, as applied to the cases in question. But proving my conclusion in this regard would require a lengthy discussion of the various "metrics" by which such comparative judgments would be made, followed by a their application to the several administrative massacres I examine. I could not begin to assay such an analysis here.

There is a second form of balance displayed by historiography,

particularly good biography, that legal judgments generally lack. This
is a rounded assessment of the strengths and weaknesses of the leading
characters. In criminal law, to be sure, evidence of good character is
admissible by the defense in mitigation of sanction, and even to
establish reasonable doubt regarding liability.[146] It may not be used,
however, to argue that the defendant's character is so virtuous as to
warrant his complete exemption from liability on this ground alone, if
he has culpably committed the wrongful act of which he is accused.

But these legal rules prove particularly troubling for defendants
who, like Marshall Pétain, had been national heroes for many years[147]
before (very late in life) disgracing themselves by complicity in
administrative massacre. The delimited relevance the law accords to
character evidence also deprives legal judgments of historical balance
when the defendant can plausibly claim, in the court of public opinion,
to have done much good in the very course of perpetrating his offense.

Pétain again provides a telling example:

> Every time [prosecutor] Mornet cited a concession granted to the
> Germans, Pétain's lawyers could cite a concession wrung from them.
> For every pro-Axis public act the lawyers could show a pro-Allied
> private one. The testimony bogged down into a balancing of profit and
> loss—exactly the chosen terrain of the defense.[148]

The law can easily discredit its judgments, when proclaiming these as
monumental didactics, by relegating such defensive efforts at historical
balancing beyond its framing of the story. Surely, such evidence is

---

146 In American law, for instance, the defendant may introduce evidence of good
character to establish that his mental state was not what the prosecution alleges it to have
been, and even to establish a reasonable doubt as to whether the defendant is the type
of person capable of committing the wrongful act. *Fed. R. Evid.* 404.

147 Stephen Ryan, *Pétain the Soldier* (1969).

148 Peter Novick, *The Resistance Versus Vichy: The Purge of Collaborators in
Liberated France* 176 (1968). Since Pétain's offenses had resulted in death for many
victims, his counsel could not claim that Pétain's "pro-Allied" actions legally "justified"
his collaborationist actions as a "lesser evil." On the longstanding exception to the
lesser evil defense for actions causing death, see George Fletcher, *Rethinking Criminal
Law* 787-89 (1978). Both Pierre Laval and René Bousquet made similar arguments
concerning their alleged efforts to mitigate the severity of Nazi policy. Denis
Peschanski & Henry Rousso, "Did Bousquet Falsify History in His Defense Plea?" in
Golsan, *supra* note 1, at 74, 76.

relevant to any effort to portray Pétain, for example, as an unscrupulous villain, pure and simple.[149]

A third form of concern about historical balance, also unacknowledged by criminal law, arises from the fact that citizens of aggressor nations suffer in many ways from wartime losses and the deprivations of defeat. These are often exacerbated by victors' misconduct. Such people therefore have an affinity for portrayals of the preceding events as a "tragedy,"[150] as a story of good people suffering evil acts on both sides, rather than a simpler tale of noble victims (their enemies) and nefarious victimizers (themselves).[151] As applied, criminal law tends to dichotomize the participants in just this way. It thereby conceals many pertinent moral complexities, denying the genuinely tragic dimension of these events,[152] a dimension that lingers

---

149 On the transformation of Pétain from hero to traitor, see Herbert R. Lottman, *Pétain: Hero or Traitor* (1985).

150 Moral philosophers generally understand a tragic situation as one in which an individual, when contemplating action, faces conflicting claims of right that are binding upon him, that is, not based upon some misunderstanding of his situation or his moral duties. Bernard Williams, "Ethical Consistency," in *Problems of the Self* at 166, 166 (1973). Many wars arise from situations in which all or most parties have some legitimate claims of right. Wars and the administrative massacres to which they often give rise also routinely present soldiers with such moral dilemmas, as through superior orders requiring commission of unlawful acts. Mark J. Osiel, *Obeying Orders* (forthcoming 1997).

151 Minear, *supra* note 61, at x ("'We need to rethink the causes of the Pacific war from what can only be described as a tragic view, one which takes no comfort in scapegoats and offers no sanctuary for private or national claims of moral righteousness ....'" (alteration in original) (quoting historian John W. Hall on the Tokyo trial)).

152 Only the vanquished tend to recognize this moral complexity and the consequent need for historical balance. This is the element of truth in the condemnation of the Nuremberg and Tokyo trials as "victors' justice." Among the victors, the general public characteristically *resists* any effort to infuse such balance into collective memory. It is only professional historians who sometimes favor it.

An example of this phenomenon is the recently failed effort by American historians to redress the perceived imbalance in public memory of the Hiroshima and Nagasaki bombings. The historians' attempts to depict those events in a way suggesting some moral complexity in the Smithsonian exhibition commemorating the 50th anniversary of the Second World War's end was successfully opposed by organizations of war veterans. David E. Sanger, "Coloring History Our Way," *N.Y. Times*, July 2, 1995, §6 (Magazine), at 30, 31 ("'The veterans want the exhibit to stop when the doors to the bomb bay opened. And that's where the Japanese want it to begin.'" (quoting a Smithsonian official, concerning the Enola Gay controversy)); "The History That Tripped over Memory," *N.Y. Times*, Feb. 5, 1995, at E5 (noting that critics claimed that

prominently in the memory of many survivors.

A fourth source of concern about historical balance involves the psychodynamics of reconciliation between antagonists—whether individuals, partisan groups, or nation-states. When offering an apology, one generally seeks forgiveness from the party who has been harmed. The process is interactive.[153] For instance, when an aged Japanese veteran recently sought to atone for his role in an especially vicious torture of a British officer, the latter saw fit (in fact, felt morally obliged) to come forward to accept the apology.[154] Only when apology succeeds in eliciting forgiveness does reconciliation occur. Such reconciliation is often a precondition to restoring relations of trust and interdependence.[155] For instance, recently the United Methodist Church formally apologized for its role in the massacre of some 200 Native American women and children.[156] In so doing, it expressly sought forgiveness from surviving members of the tribes in question. One Native leader promptly responded, "I'm satisfied. The church has supported the action, and now it's time to start the healing process."[157]

Negotiating this reconciliation can prove highly complex, since often each party will have valid grievances against the other. In such circumstances, apology is easiest when it is reciprocated, that is, when

the exhibit was a revisionist insult to the American soldiers who fought in the Pacific); see also Nicholas D. Kristof, "Japan's Plans for a Museum on War Mired in Controversy," *N.Y. Times*, May 21, 1995, at A4 (describing the similar disputes in Japan itself over whether to include material on its soldiers' extensive atrocities).

153   The best analysis of the interactional dimension of apology and forgiveness is offered by Beverly Flanigan, *Forgiving the Unforgivable* 7 (1992).

154   The British officer, Eric Lomax, recounts the story in *The Railway Man: A POW's Searing Account of War, Brutality and Forgiveness* (1995).

155   Japan's failure to apologize for its enslavement of Asian comfort women is thus often seen as an obstacle to better relations with its Asian neighbors. See, e.g., 'Lawyers Urge Government to Compensate "Comfort Women", *'Japan Pol'y & Pol.,* Jan. 30, 1995, available in LEXIS, News Library, Curnws File ("'Japan cannot build an honorable position in the international community without resolving the issue ....'") (quoting Koken Tsuchiya, Chairman, Japanese Federation of Bar Associations)).

156   Gustav Niebuhr, "132 Years Later, Methodists Repent Forebear's Sin," *N.Y. Times,* April 27, 1996, at A7 (describing the role of Methodist minister John M. Chivington in leading the 1864 massacre.)

157   *Id.* On the moral difficulties with any such effort by an individual to accept an apology for harms done to an entire group, see Peter Digeser, "Vicarious Forgiveness and Collective Responsibility: Who Has the Authority to Forgive?" (paper presented at the American Political Science Association Conference, San Francisco, Aug. 30, 1996).

X can acknowledge its wrongs against Y as Y acknowledges its against X. Reciprocity is particularly fitting where the adversaries have become "mutually implicated in each other's ... vices."[158] This is often true of war, as each side escalates its wrongdoing in retaliation for the enemy's wrongs, real or imagined.[159]

It is not surprising, then, that even the *Montonero* leader, Mario Firmenich, was impelled to apologize for the crimes of his guerrillas (two decades after the fact), immediately following a comparable apology by Army Chief Martín Balza (for the military's crimes against guerrillas and others in the dirty war).[160] Among antagonists who must go on living together in the same society, a judicial narrative perceived as "balanced"—in recognizing valid claims and wrongdoing on both sides—is best suited to facilitate reconciliation and reconstruction of social solidarity. An Israeli political theorist thus writes of the Oslo Accord with the P.L.O., 'the basis for reconciliation is the recognition that "You, too, have truly suffered, and we, too, are not without blame."'[161]

There is nothing in either the substance or process of criminal law, however, to facilitate such narrative balance and to help set in motion a process of reciprocal conciliation. On the contrary, the criminal law sets up a bright line between the parties, labeling one as victim, the other as wrongdoer.[162] It encourages attitudes in the former of righteous indignation, attitudes that the latter inevitably view in turn as self-righteous selectivity.

---

158 Donald W. Shriver, Jr., *An Ethic for Enemies: Forgiveness in Politics* 74 (1995).

159 In authorizing "reprisal" for war crimes, the law of armed conflict may aggravate this problem, as commentators have long noted. See, e.g., Paul Christopher, *The Ethics of War and Peace* 189-99 (1994); Michael Walzer, *Just and Unjust Wars* 207-22 (1977).

160 "Autocrítica a medias de Firmenich," *Clarín* (Buenos Aires), A1, May 3, 1995.

161 Noam J. Zohar, "Reconciliation and Forgiveness: On Amnesty, Reconciliation, and Bloodguilt," 13 (paper presented at the American Political Science Association, San Francisco, Aug. 30, 1996).

162 Private law at least allows the possibility of a counterclaim by the defendant. But a compulsory counterclaim must arise out of the same transaction as that on which the plaintiff's claim is based. *Fed. R. Civ.* P. 13. This presents a major obstacle when the events to be linked in this way by a single legal story cover vast expanses of time and space. One would be hard-pressed to say, for instance, that Japanese aggression on the Asian continent during the early 1930s was part of the same "transaction" or event as the United States' bombing of Nagasaki in 1945.

Moral and legal theory do little better in this regard than legal doctrine. They are preoccupied with notions of excuse and justification. In the present cases, however, the wrongs done by X to Y neither excuse nor justify those done by Y to X.[163] The bombing of Nagasaki does not excuse or justify the Rape of Nanjing, as all sensible people readily acknowledge. But this fact does not, in the minds of many Americans and Japanese, exhaust the possible range of moral links between the two events or their perpetrators. If legal doctrine and theory dismiss such widespread moral intuitions as misguided, the result is merely to limit the law's potential contribution to international reconciliation.

Consider in this light, the reaction of many Japanese to the American reluctance, as in the recent Smithsonian controversy, to debate openly the legality and moral defensibility of our use of nuclear weapons at the end of World War II. This reluctance "has fueled the self-righteousness of Japanese apologists for the Pacific War," observes one Asia specialist. "If Americans refuse to question *their* war record, they ask, then why should Japanese risk the reputation of Japanese soldiers by questioning theirs?"[164] No U.S. President, one might add, has ever visited Hiroshima or Nagasaki, or even expressed regrets for the decision to destroy them with nuclear weapons. It could be said that the result of the Smithsonian dispute shows that the American public is unwilling to allow its collective memory (and, by implication, its national identity) to be professionally reconstructed in ways requiring serious reckoning with major wrongs we have done to others.

In the aftermath of large-scale violence, the essential task of statesmanship often consists precisely in putting forth a formulation of

---

163 Moral theory has had virtually nothing to say about the element of *mutual* wrongdoing in many situations fitting for apology, and (by implication) forgiveness. Leading studies of forgiveness have little to say about reciprocity, while studies of reciprocity lack any discussion of forgiveness. Lawrence C. Becker, *Reciprocity* (1986); Jeffrie G. Murphy & Jean Hampton, *Forgiveness and Mercy* (1990).

164 Ian Buruma, "The War Over the Bomb," *N.Y. Rev. Books,* Sept. 21, 1995, at 26, 29. For instance, the head of the Japanese Veterans Association, Masao Horie, observed: "'At the 50th anniversary of the Dresden firebombing, ... I didn't hear the Allies apologizing. And the U.S. dropped atomic bombs on Hiroshima and Nagasaki and killed huge numbers of innocent Japanese people, and never apologized for this.'" Nicholas D. Kristof, "Why Japan Hasn't Said That Word," *N.Y. Times,* May 7, 1995, at E3.

national identity (or international community, as in the Marshall Plan) that allows former enemies to live together under a common regime. This entails a compelling narrative that restrains the powerful temptations toward an interminable cycle of recrimination and reprisal over the past. That is certainly how Abraham Lincoln, at least, understood his responsibilities in the aftermath of the Civil War.[165]

Elaine Scarry observes:

> Once those final labels [winner and loser] are designated and the war is over, it will cease to matter how the casualties ... were distributed .... [For] these verbal constructions will tend to be replaced by one in which the casualties ... collectively substantiate, or are perceived as the cost of, a single outcome: ... "The young America was maimed by the slavery of which it was necessary to rid itself violently: 534,000 died in the Civil War." Thus a Southern boy who may have believed himself to be risking and inflicting wounds for a feudal system of agriculture, and until the end of the war will have suffered much hardship and finally death for those beliefs, will once the war is over have died in substantiation of the disappearance of that feudal system and the racial inequality on which it depended.[166]

This process of redescription does not happen automatically or effortlessly, however, as Scarry seems to imply. Lincoln's pardons and amnesties of confederate soldiers, and even leaders, offered a legal device that helped later generations to retell the story of the war to one another in a conciliatory fashion: a narrative in which even the losers die for a just cause, and thereby rejoin the society of the winners. To

---

165   John G. Randall, "Introduction" to Jonathan T. Dorris, *Pardon and Amnesty Under Lincoln and Johnson*   xiii, xiv-xxi (1953).   In the interests of national reconciliation, Presidents Lincoln and Johnson both favored leniency toward those guilty of treason and sedition.   In December 1863 Lincoln proclaimed an amnesty for most who had taken up arms against the Union, provided they take an oath of future allegiance to it.   In 1868, Andrew Johnson extended the terms of amnesty, making it unconditional and universal in scope. *Id.*

166   Elaine Scarry, *The Body in Pain* 116-17 (1985). Zerubavel observes a similar process of mythic redescription in contemporary Israel regarding heroes who died in unsuccessful military campaigns, such as the Masada defenders and Bar Kokhba. "The display of readiness to sacrifice one's life for the nation is thus glorified as a supreme patriotic value that diminishes the significance of the outcome." Yael Zerubavel, *Recovered Roots: Collective Memory and the Making of Israeli National Tradition* 221 (1995).

accomplish this, the story must, of course, be extended to a later point of conclusion, from which the war's strictly military outcome becomes almost irrelevant to collective memory. In short, rewriting the national story by such legal devices as pardons, amnesties, and acts of clemency can sometimes greatly further the restoration of solidarity at such times. Great leadership partly consists precisely in knowing how and when to do so.

President Reagan's 1985 visit to the Bitburg cemetery offers a shining example how not to do so. On the President's retelling, the story of World War II was one of moral equality in the suffering of foot soldiers on both sides. This narrative framing was designed to provide a basis for agreement among Germans and Americans that would permit their joint commemoration of the War's end. Instead, the urge to force consensus provoked a reassertion of dissensus—impassioned but entirely civil. That very process of open disagreement, as Geoffrey Hartman observes, "gave us a chance—however unfortunate the occasion—to think matters through more honestly. It produced, for example, a speech by Richard von Weizäcker (President of the Federal Republic) that is really a public confession never before uttered at that level."[167] A better foundation for solidarity between Americans and Germans was thereby laid, even if (in fact, precisely because) a single, shared story could not be told in the way Reagan had sought to do.

Where to Begin the Story? Where to End?

The primary way defendants have sought to introduce greater balance into proceedings for administrative massacre has been to enlarge the temporal "frame" relevant to legal judgment (beyond that proposed by the prosecution). In this way, the narrative is made to encompass events both earlier and later in time. Defense counsel have often stressed the arbitrariness and indefensibility of the spatiotemporal borders established by courts, at the prosecution's behest. In this critique, they could easily draw theoretical sustenance today from leading postmodernists, who rightly observe that always there is

---

167   Geoffrey Hartman, *The Longest Shadow: In the Aftermath of the Holocaust* 67 (1996).

"another story 'waiting to be told' just beyond the confines of 'the end.' ... [T]he sequence of real events goes on: that's what it is to be 'real.'"[168]

The choice of where to begin the story and where to end it often determines who will play the villain, who the victim. Yet there are no consensual criteria for locating a story's beginning and end. In fact, sophisticated historians now readily concede that these temporal resting points "do not flow from the events but are in fact strategic ruptures chosen for specific purposes."[169] And people differ in their purposes.

Defendants in the Tokyo trial, for instance, sought to tell a tale that began not with Pearl Harbor, but with America's Lend-Lease policy and the blockade on Japan's lifeline of oil imports.[170] The story would begin not with the Japanese invasion of China, but earlier, with the Western colonialism throughout Asia that Japanese forces sought to displace. From within that narrative frame, Japan's conduct could be described as a "war of aggression" only through the grossest of historical oversimplification.

Just as the story would have a different beginning, it would have a different ending. It would end somewhat later than the prosecution preferred, not with Allied victory at Okinawa, but with the nuclear destruction of Hiroshima and Nagasaki, at a time when all but the final details of Japanese surrender had been resolved.[171] "Hiroshima and

---

168   Louis O. Mink, "Everyman His or Her Own Annalist," in *On Narrative* 233, 238 (W.J.T. Mitchell ed., 1981) (emphasis omitted) (quoting Hayden White); see also Zerubavel, *supra* note 166, at 221 (noting how selecting the points at which a story will begin and end "reveals how simple construction of boundaries confers a minimal fictive structure and meaning on an otherwise meaningless time flow").

169   Kenneth Cmiel, "After Objectivity: What Comes Next in History?" 2 *American Literary History* 170, 172 (1990) (parsing Hans Kellner, *Language and Historical Representation*, 1989).

170   See *supra* note 143.

171   Akira Iriye, *Power and Culture: The Japanese-American War, 1941-1945*, at 263-65 (1981). A wider spatiotemporal framing would not entirely have worked to mitigative effect, however. Prosecutors could easily have employed it to tell the story of Japan's enslavement of many thousands of women throughout its Asian empire into compulsory prostitution, for the entertainment of Japanese soldiers. George Hicks, *The Comfort Women: Sex Slaves of the Japanese Imperial Forces* (1994). Writes one Japanese historian, "the perfect opportunity for such reflection came during the postwar Allied occupation, but it was lost. Regrettably, at the Tokyo War Crimes Tribunal the voice of the Asian peoples who had suffered was not heard sufficiently." Yoshiaki Yoshimi, "Japan Battles Its Memories," *N.Y. Times*, Mar. 11, 1992, at A23.

Nagasaki," writes John Dower, "became icons of Japanese suffering—perverse national treasures, of a sort, capable of fixating Japanese memory of the war on what had happened to Japan and simultaneously blotting out recollection of the Japanese victimization of others. Remembering Hiroshima and Nagasaki, that is, easily became a way of forgetting Nanjing, Bataan, the Burma-Siam railway, Manila, and the countless Japanese atrocities..."[172]

Similarly, German historians now seek to enlarge the narrative framing of combat on the Eastern front, depicting the brutal methods of German forces as the first phase of Western resistance to what would soon prove to be Soviet imperialism into Eastern and Central Europe. This resistance bought the West essential time for regrouping, they suggest.[173] Had the Nuremberg trial been held a few years later than it was, defense counsel would likely have sought to make just such an argument. Notice, moreover, that these proffered enlargements of the legal-historical frame would not require that the court undertake large leaps across time and space—to Algeria and Vietnam in the early 1960s—of the sort employed in the defense of Klaus Barbie.[174]

If criminal law is to get into the business of condemning people for starting wars, it must be able to offer relatively clear criteria for determining when wars begin. This is a question to which historians have, with considerable justification, claimed greater professional expertise. And historians today, fifty years after its conclusion, do not

---

172 John W. Dower, "The Bombed: Hiroshimas and Nagasakis in Japanese Memory," in Hogan, *supra* note 110, at 116, 123.

173 This historical argument was introduced by Ernst Nolte, "The Past That Will Not Pass: A Speech That Could Be Written but Not Delivered," in *Forever in the Shadow of Hitler?*, *supra* note 15, at 18 and Andreas Hillgruber, *Zweierlei Untergang: Die Zerschlagung des Deutschen Reiches und das Ende des europäischen Judentums* (1986). It is implicitly critical of the story told by the Nuremberg court, and has in turn been adopted by conservative German politicians. See, for example, the recent letter signed by over 300 leading German conservatives, arguing that what ought to be commemorated on May 8 is not the Allied victory, but rather the Soviet "'expulsion by terror, oppression in the East, and the partition of our country.'" Nader Mousavizadeh, "States of Denial," *New Republic*, June 19, 1995, at 40, 42 (book review) (quoting the letter titled *Against Forgetting* in the *Frankfurter Allgemeine Zeitung*). The authors add that "'a view of history that ignores or represses this reality, or that compares it to other realities, cannot be the basis for the self-understanding of a confident people.'" *Id.*

174 See Chapter 8, "Making Public Memory, Publicly," *infra* text accompanying notes 108-117.

at all agree about when or where the Second World War began or ended.[175]

The upshot, then, is that the defendants' right to a fair hearing in such trials has often been compromised not only by indulgent relaxation of evidentiary rules (including legal relevance and hearsay) in favor of the prosecution, but also by hyperstringent enforcement of such evidentiary rules against the defense.

In viewing the criminal trial as a simplistic "morality play," Durkheim did not perceive how certain forms of criminality, such as large-scale administrative massacre, often cannot fairly be characterized as pitting the forces of unequivocal good against those of unequivocal evil. If courts could find a way to tell the tale as a genuine tragedy, alternately eliciting a measure of sympathy and antipathy for each side, dramatic tension would be enhanced, evoking more attention from the public. Such sustained attention would help stimulate the public discussion and collective soul-searching that is the primary contribution of criminal prosecution to social solidarity at such times, according to the discursive theory offered here.[176]

In the Argentine junta trial, the defendants' accusation of historical imbalance entailed the insistence that their conduct be viewed as an intelligible response, however excessive with the benefit of hindsight, to the genuine threat to public order presented by the leftist guerrilla movements. The temporal frame adopted by the court discredited the entire proceeding, in the view of the officer corps and most civilian conservatives, by not extending sufficiently backward in time to before the 1976 coup d'état (or outward in space, to the near-revolutionary situations in neighboring states like Brazil and Chile).[177]

---

175 John Keegan, *The Battle for History: Re-Fighting World War II* 27-29 (1995) (observing that historians differ over whether the War began in Europe in 1939 or in Asia in 1931, and over whether it ended in 1945 or later, with the demise of Western colonies in the East.)

176 See Chapter 2, "Solidarity Through Civil Consensus," *supra* notes 1-31 and accompanying text.

177 Horacio Lynch & Enrique Del Carrill, *Definitivamente—Nunca Más: La Otra Cara del Informe CONADEP* (1985). By contrast, the United Nations "Truth Commission" on El Salvador was expressly chartered to examine illegal violence by both the military and the FMLN, a fact that contributed to wider public acceptance of its conclusions, according to Thomas Buergenthal, one of its members. Thomas Buergenthal, "The United Nations Truth Commission for El Salvador," 27 *Vand. J.*

The Alfonsín government and its prosecutors were well aware of this danger and consciously sought to guard against it. They periodically reminded—through their public statements, and even in closing arguments at trial—that leaders of the leftist guerrilla groups were being simultaneously prosecuted as well, for many of the same offenses.[178]

This narrative frame quickly acquired the label of "The Doctrine of the Two Demons": that the country had been destroyed by similar extremisms of left and right, both equally hostile to liberalism and the rule of law, the rhetorical banner of the new democratic government. As a matter of dramaturgical strategy, this narrative was calculated to avoid giving offense either to military officers, who had escaped substantial involvement in the dirty war, or to surviving supporters of the *guerrilla*, who had already endured considerable suffering by illegal detainment, torture, and loss of family members through disappearance.[179] Thus, the doctrine of the two demons and the legal strategy it entailed were selected "to provide an adequate frame to reprocess memory without increasing the chasms that separated Argentine society," as one social scientist observes.[180]

But although this framing of the story made for "good law," in that it was entirely consistent with existing doctrine, it made for "poor history" in the eyes of those many people, mostly on the left, who felt it necessary—as a matter of historical balance—to stress the much greater measure of harm inflicted by the officer corps on Argentine

---

Transnat'l L. 497, 528 (1994). The Chilean truth commission adopted a similar approach. Despite the current preference of many new democracies for such commissions over criminal trials, commissions do not escape the controversy created by the question of how widely to define the scope of their inquiries. Activists in the human rights community, for instance, often challenge the inclusion of material concerning criminal conduct by leftist guerrillas, whose cause they consider more just. See, e.g., Jorge Mera, "Chile: Truth and Justice Under the Democratic Government," in *Impunity and Human Rights in International Law and Practice* 171, 174-75 (Naomi Roht-Arriaza ed., 1995).

178   Executive Decree No. 157/83.

179   Horacio Verbitsky, *Civiles y Militares: Memoria Secreta de la Transición* 57-66 (2d ed. 1987).

180   Carina Perelli, "*Memoria de Sangre*: Fear, Hope, and Disenchantment in Argentina," in *Remapping Memory* 39, 48 (Jonathan Boyarin ed., 1994).

society, in service of aspirations less noble than those of the *guerrilla*.[181]

In Argentina, as earlier in Japan and West Germany, the battle of interpretations between prosecution lawyers and spokesmen for "historical balance" was fought out in the elite press. Its wider influence beyond the upper middle classes cannot be presumed.[182] Historiography has often had no more influence than judicial proceedings in influencing non-elite memory of many such events, as historians themselves readily admit.[183] "The Enola Gay is flying solo on the Mall in Washington," an American journalist wryly observes, "without any serious examination of whether the bomb was needed to force Japan to surrender, a question that is debated more seriously today [by scholars], and with more compelling evidence, than at any time in postwar history."[184]

Like lawyers, professional historians must take a skeptical attitude toward the veracity of all sources. But popular memory of a community's catastrophes is often demonstrably inaccurate, even concerning fundamental facts of record. It is precisely these persistent deviations between the memories of those who were directly affected by such events and the later conclusions of elite professionals—both lawyers and historians—that have become a central focus of much current field work and reflection among scholars of collective memory.[185]

---

181   Interviews with human rights leaders, in Buenos Aires, Argentina (Aug. 1987).

182   We should recall, in this regard, the finding of survey researchers that while over half of Americans knew who presided over "The People's Court," fewer than 10% knew that the Chief Justice of the Supreme Court was William Rehnquist. "Can TV Rescue Rehnquist from Obscurity?," *Newsday* (N.Y.), June 28, 1989, at 64.

183   Keith Thomas, *The Perception of the Past in Early Modern England* 24 (1983); Yosef H. Yerushalmi, *Zakhor: Jewish History and Jewish Memory* 14-15 (1982). The recurrent resistance of popular memory to elite efforts at shaping it is examined in Chapter 7, "Constructing Memory with Legal Blueprints?" *infra* text accompanying notes 31-36.

184   Sanger, *supra* note 152, at 30. Sanger alludes especially to the recent scholarship of Barton Bernstein, Gar Alperowitz, Rufus Miles, Jr., and John R. Skates. Moreover, the text initially proposed by the Smithsonian historians for the 50th anniversary of the bombing of Hiroshima exhibit was not at all unsympathetic to President Truman; after weighing the arguments for and against his decision, it concludes that "the bombing of Hiroshima and Nagasaki ... played a crucial role in ending the Pacific War quickly." *Judgment at the Smithsonian* 117 (Philip Nobile ed., 1995).

185   See, e.g., James Fentress & Chris Wickham, *Social Memory* 91 (1992) (contending that "inaccurate memories ... shed a more unmediated light on social

On occasion, prosecutors of administrative massacre have felt obliged to tailor their legal approaches in light of what they thought would make a more persuasive story, on account of popular understandings of the period. Most notably, the chief American prosecutor at Tokyo, Joseph Keenan, was ordered not to indict Emperor Hirohito.[186] Prosecutors also encouraged some witnesses to mention the Emperor's role and presence at key meetings as little as possible, if at all.[187] The Occupation authorities, and General MacArthur in particular,[188] were convinced that the Japanese public, although willing to blame the Emperor's underlings, would not tolerate the punishment and consequent dethronement of Hirohito himself.

Japanese politicians and print media were already suggesting, in September 1945, that an Allied policy of publicizing Japanese war atrocities would "confront a Japanese countercampaign that called attention to the Allies own atrocious policies," particularly "the nuclear destruction of two essentially civilian targets," according to a leading historian of the period.[189] Direct censorship by Occupation authorities was necessary to squelch this incipient countercampaign.[190] Japanese

---

memory than accurate ones do: they are not, so to speak, polluted by 'real' past events"); Alessandro Portelli, *The Death of Luigi Trastulli and Other Stories* 2 (1991) (noting that "'wrong' tales ... allow us to recognize the interests of the tellers"). For an Argentine study of this phenomenon, see Lindsay DuBois, "Contradictory Memories of Dictatorship in Argentina" 4-5 (Dec. 1, 1994) (paper presented at the American Anthropological Association Conference) (noting how electoral supporters of former military officer Aldo Rico sometimes misremember the human rights abuses of the dirty war, 1975-1980, as having occurred during the *prior* military regime, that is, 1966-1973).

186   Minear, *supra* note 61, at 111 n.74.

187   *Id.* at 113-14.

188   Douglas MacArthur, *Reminiscences* 287-88 (1964) (noting MacArthur's fear that guerrilla warfare would break out if the Emperor were indicted, and that many thousands of U.S. troops would be needed to enforce the Allied Occupation); see also Minear, *supra* note 61, at 110-17 (analyzing the decision not to prosecute the Emperor as political, rather than based on the legal merits).

189   Dower, *supra* note 172, at 116, 117 (noting that Mamoru Shigemitzu, once and future prime minister, "authored an early internal memorandum explicitly proposing that the Japanese use the atomic bombs as counterpropaganda to Allied accusations of Japanese war crimes.").

190   *Id.* (noting that the Domei news agency and leading newspapers, such as *Asahi*, "naively attempted to balance the record of war behavior in this manner," triggering in turn increased censorship by the Occupation.)

understandings of recent history thus set serious limits on the choice of legal strategy, compromising the moral and legal integrity of the proceedings in crucial ways.[191]

These compromises also ensured that the "Tokyo Trial version of history," as it came to be derisively known, would ultimately be rejected—not only in Japan, but in much of the West as well.[192] It would be rejected not merely as morally and legally suspect,[193] but as poor historiography, on account of its unpersuasive and obviously opportunistic exclusion of a central character.[194] It is one thing to acknowledge that prosecutors have a legitimate range of dramaturgical discretion; it is quite another for them to attempt a staging of Hamlet without the prince.

The very effort to trim the legal proceedings in line with popular prejudice thus proved counterproductive, ultimately undermining the precarious legitimacy that such compromise had aimed to secure for the trials. Thus, criminal trials can fail to influence collective memory both when they *adhere* to the internal requirements of legal doctrine, ignoring popular understandings at odds with these requirements (the Barbie example), and conversely, when such trials *depart* from the law's own logic, deferring to such prejudices (the Hirohito example).

In the final analysis, neither historians nor legal advocates

---

191   On the much-belated explosion of debate and conflict over Hirohito's wartime role, in the months preceding and immediately following his death, see generally Norma Field, *In the Realm of a Dying Emperor* (1991).

192   Kojima Noboru, "Contribution to Peace," in *The Tokyo War Crimes Trial: An International Symposium* 69, 78, 109 (C. Hosoya et al. eds., 1986). See generally Minear, *supra* note 61 (presenting a widely disseminated example of this rejection of the Toyko Trial's version of history).

193   Minear, *supra* note 61, at 117 (quoting the dissenting opinion of Justice Henri Bernard, who argued that the Emperor's absence "was certainly detrimental to the defense of the accused").

194   MacArthur was strongly inclined to excuse the Emperor of all war crimes charges without even examining available evidence concerning Hirohito's actual wartime role. Herbert P. Bix, 'The Shōwa Emperor's "Monologue" and the Problem of War Responsibility," 18 *Journal of Japanese Studies* 295, 329 (1992). Perhaps the trial's greatest distortion (by understatement) of Japan's war crimes involved not its refusal to examine Hirohito's share of responsibility, but its exclusion of all evidence concerning Japan's extensive use of prisoners of war for bacteriological weapons experimentation. The U.S. apparently sought to preserve the secrecy of these experiments to learn their results and to keep them from the Soviets, according to some accounts. B.V.A. Röling, "Introduction" to *The Tokyo War Crimes Trial, supra* note 192, at 15, 18.

approach the past disinterestedly. While both bring contemporary concerns to bear upon their investigations, neither considers it defensible to ignore evidence disconfirming the story one initially wished to tell. Thus, despite the differences highlighted here, there are important similarities in how law and historiography approach the past. Legal advocates have always known that their inquiries were not disinterested; most historians have recognized this only recently.[195]

The very idea that the past has an integrity of its own, that it can be studied "for its own sake" and on the terms of its long-deceased denizens, that its interpretation should not be harnessed exclusively to present concerns, is a peculiarly modern notion, dating only from the late eighteenth century.[196] As professional commitment to that preoccupation has waned in the last two decades, the overlapping "moralizing" concerns of law and historiography have become ever more apparent. These emergent similarities make it more difficult to denounce judicial forays into national historical narrative as either a betrayal of internal professional scruple or an external encroachment on alien terrain.

The Durkheimian account of law's service to social solidarity encounters greater difficulty than the discursive in coping with the recurrent tension between the favored stories of lawyers, on one side, and historians or other interested parties, on the other. This is because the Durkheimian view presumes that only one story—the evocation of shared indignation for unambiguous breach of moral principles universally agreed upon—is compatible with social solidarity.[197]

The discursive conception, by contrast, makes no such assumption. It acknowledges that a plurality of interpretations may coexist within a pluralistic society, one whose members do not agree about the nature of

---

195   The long history of rear-guard action in resistance to this recognition is well told by Novick, *supra* note 71, at 38-39, 260-74, 295-301, 513-21. For an early statement of this view, see Carl L. Becker, *Everyman His Own Historian* 253-54 (1935) (arguing that "neither the value nor the dignity of history need suffer by regarding it as ... an unstable pattern of remembered things redesigned and newly colored to suit the convenience of those who make use of it").

196   Janet Coleman, *Ancient and Medieval Memories: Studies in the Reconstruction of the Past* 276, 291, 324 (1992); Thomas, *supra* note 183, at 1. For a recent effort to rehabilitate the ancient view, see Michael Oakeshott, "Present, Future, and Past," in *On History and Other Essays* 1, 7-19 (1983).

197   See generally Chapter 1, "Crime, Consensus, and Solidarity."

justice, and that such disagreement will inevitably extend to the meaning of the country's recent horrors.

On this account, courts may legitimately tailor the stories they tell in order to persuade skeptical publics of the merits of liberal morality. But they may not exclude incompatible stories from public hearing. Prosecutors and judges can strive to make the liberal story about these events more persuasive than its alternatives, yet cannot suppress them. In fact, the discursive view *requires* effective public presentation of counter-narratives in order to have any chance of refuting them, where they are inconsistent with the liberal one.[198] Other stories, such as those advanced by historians of various persuasions, have an entirely legitimate place within the public discussion of a liberal society. Law's proper contribution to social solidarity must be conceived in a way consistent with this fact.

---

198   See generally Chapter 2, "Solidarity Through Civil Dissensus."

Chapter 5.

Legal Judgment As Precedent and Analogy

This danger is the corollary of the preceding. We have just seen why it is wrong to yoke a society's understanding of its history tightly to present needs (for legal judgment). So too, it is wrong to address a society's present problems by exclusive reference to the lessons of its history, that is, to a privileged reading of its past.

There are opposing perils here. At one extreme lies the view, defended in legal thought by Savigny, that the study of history provides not "'merely a collection of examples but rather the sole path to the true knowledge of our own condition.'"[1] Nothing ever changes so drastically as to prevent the past from "rendering perennial its store of experience."[2] At the other extreme lies the view of history, including legal history, "as a burden man has to shoulder and of whose dead weight the living can or even must get rid of in their march into the future."[3] Modern technology and society change too dramatically, in this view, for history (including the history of legal judgments upon it) to offer meaningful prescriptions for future predicaments.

Criminal trials for administrative massacre can contribute, paradoxically, to errors of both sorts, at both ends of the continuum governing the past's pertinence to the present. Among victims of such horrific experiences, memories have often provided resonant analogies for the analysis of more current controversies.[4] Sympathetic others

---

1 Reinhart Koselleck, *Futures Past: On the Semantics of Historical Time* 38 (Keith Tribe trans., 1985) (quoting Friedrich K. von Savigny, 1 *Zeitschrift für Geschichtliche Wissenschaft* 4 (1815)).

2 *Id.* at 23 (attributing this view to Cicero and most other Hellenistic thinkers).

3 Hannah Arendt, *Between Past and Future* 10 (1961). Arendt does not defend this view.

4 To be sure, it is only the most vocal minority of surviving victims who generally assert a broad reading of the public lessons to be learned from their experiences. Langer's study of memory among Holocaust survivors reports, for instance, that the vast majority conclude that their personal experience is almost entirely insusceptible to description, that it confirms no moral theories, and that it offers no models for heroic emulation or redemption. Langer thus argues that most intellectual reflections on the Holocaust, in searching for its lessons, provide only false solace. Lawrence L. Langer, *Holocaust Testimonies: The Ruins of Memory* 162-205 (1991).

often will be inclined to accord considerable authority to such victims as natural spokesmen for the lessons of this momentous experience. "The recall of past evil [is] a critical source of empowerment," Hacking observes.[5] Of course, "no one wants *to be* a victim," Todorov reminds, but at such times "everyone wants to *have been* one...to aspire to the *status* of victim."[6] This is because the past becomes so powerful a metaphor in present debate. For this very reason, however, the past can be abused in various ways. Its "proper" interpretation—to which legal judgments may contribute—tends to be invoked as an all-purpose touchstone, purporting to offer answers to all future questions, however far afield. In the moral economy of victimhood, this is hyperinflation.

It might be said that this is one form of historical distortion that criminal prosecution can introduce into collective memory, and that this point is thus a refinement of the preceding. But what was at issue before was only historical understanding as such, the societal interest in preserving the past's integrity within our representations of it. What is at stake here, by contrast, is how such historical representations influence present policy, for better or worse, that is, how a past experience of administrative massacre, and our legal judgments upon it, should guide future politics. Broadly speaking, the dispute is about "the different ways of integrating the experience of the past into the texture of contemporary life."[7]

The more narrowly the experience is read for its "precedential value," the stronger the authority we accord its immediate victims to speak to us in its name. But the power this accords them sometimes proves intoxicating. As they begin to read the precedent more broadly, their right to assume its mantle, to speak with the special authority it affords—rather than simply with their own voices, as coequal

5   Ian Hacking, *Rewriting the Soul: Multiple Personality and the Sciences of Memory* 213 (1995). One might add that to have no memory is to lack an essential feature of personhood, on many accounts. On neurological disorders resulting in extreme memory loss, see generally Philip J. Hilts, *Memory's Ghost: The Strange Tale of Mr. M. and the Nature of Memory* (1995) (describing a famous patient who, through a surgical mistake, lost all prior memory and all capacity for subsequent memory, but who now has recurrent dreams in which he is a surgeon).

6   Tzvetan Todorov, "The Abuses of Memory," 1 *Common Knowledge* 6, 24 (1996).

7   Stephen Bann, *The Inventions of History* 101 (1990). For a thoughtful meditation on aspects of this problem, see Charles Maier, "A Surfeit of Memory? Reflections on History, Melancholy and Denial," 5 *History and Memory* 136 (1993).

citizens—is rightly called into question.

This presents the mobilized victim-survivor with a dilemma. At one extreme, she can preserve her monopoly over the collective memory only by reading its relevance so narrowly as to make its lessons inapplicable to even the most similar events (for example, another nearby episode of administrative massacre). At the other extreme, the victim-turned-activist can extrapolate the lessons of the events that caused her suffering into such universal terms as to make them applicable to innumerable public controversies. This can be done, however, only at the cost of abandoning any plausible claim to monopoly over invocation of the event from which these lessons are allegedly derived.

Too often, a sense of déjà vu—and the hope of refighting old battles with more successful results than the first time around—unwittingly substitutes for critical analysis of current predicaments. In several societies, this has proven a recurrent pathology in the aftermath of administrative massacre. To label it a pathology, of course, is not to deny the need for sympathetic understanding toward those permanently haunted by such events, those suffering its symptoms.

They resemble the central character in Jorge Luis Borges' well-known story, *Funes, the Memorious*, who can remember everything he has perceived.[8] Like Funes, we may become incapacitated for rational deliberation and principled action by a surfeit of memory. "What Funes has gained in memory," writes one Borges scholar, "he loses in the realm of general concepts ...."[9] Consumed by the wealth and resonance of narrative details, he lacks any "capacity to organize these into categories" or relate them to principles.[10] "And because his mind is always vividly recollecting to the level of pathology

---

8   Jorge L. Borges, "Funes, the Memorious," in *Ficciones* 107 (Anthony Kerrigan ed., 1962).

9   Gene H. Bell-Villada, *Borges and His Fiction* 97 (1981). This author diagnoses Funes's ailment as "a deep- seated incapacity for thinking in terms of general ideas." *Id.* at 101. Montaigne similarly remarked that "excellent memories are prone to be joined to feeble judgments." Michel de Montaigne, *The Complete Works of Montaigne* 22 (Donald M. Frame trans., Stanford Univ. Press 1958) (1580).

10   Bell-Villada, *supra* note 9, at 97.

... Funes can barely sleep."[11]   In short, lurid details of lived experience—no matter how moving and memorable the resulting stories—offer no guidance unless one can extract general principles facilitating conceptualization and comparison between past and present events.[12]

Extrapolated to the level of nation-states, the lesson is clear: overburdened by the weight of a catastrophic recent history, we are sometimes better off to forget. Nietzsche was surely right that "life in any true sense is impossible without forgetfulness .... We must know the right time to forget as well as the right time to remember, and instinctively see when it is necessary to feel historically and when unhistorically."[13]

This problem—the inability to forget, when forgetting is entirely appropriate—is, in a sense, the obverse of that dwelled upon by the psychohistorians: the repression or denial of memory, so that what is repressed, if not "worked through," later "returns" in the form of "acting-out."[14]   Obsession with memory can be as perilous as its repression, anamnesia as problematic as amnesia. "Hysterics," Breuer and Freud noted, "suffer mainly from reminiscences."[15]   One recent

---

11   *Id.* at 97-98; see also Naomi Lindstrom, *Jorge Luis Borges* 41 (1990) (observing that "the main issue examined in []Funes ... is ... the need to organize knowledge in the mind by means of judicious omission and the selective concentration of attention").

12   The best known versions of this process within current liberal theory are Dworkin on "law as integrity" and Rawls on "reflective equilibrium." Ronald Dworkin, *Law's Empire* 225-75 (1986); John Rawls, *A Theory of Justice* 48-51 (1973).

13   Friedrich Nietzsche, *On the Use and Abuse of History* 7-8 (Adrian Collins trans., Bobbs-Merrill Co. 1957) (1874).

14   The major works in this tradition, as applied to repressed memory of state-sponsored brutality, are those of Dominick LaCapra, *Representing the Holocaust* (1994); Alexander Mitscherlich & Margarete Mitscherlich, *The Inability to Mourn* (Beverley R. Placzek trans., 1975); Eric L. Santner, *Stranded Objects: Mourning, Memory, and Film in Postwar Germany* (1990). See also Eric L. Santner, "History Beyond the Pleasure Principle: Some Thoughts on the Representation of Trauma," in *Probing the Limits of Representation: Nazism and the "Final Solution"* 143, 150 (Saul Friedlander ed., 1992) (noting that "one can acknowledge the *fact* of an event, that is, that it happened, and yet continue to disavow the traumatizing impact of the same event").

15   Josef Breuer & Sigmund Freud, *Studies on Hysteria* 7 (James Strachey et al. trans., 1955). Primo Levi, who made a successful international literary career out of his inability to forget his time in Auschwitz, nevertheless experienced this mnemonic hypertrophy as a form of illness, one which may have proven fatal (he committed suicide in 1988). Levi notes:

author states the dilemma with particular poignancy:

> Pain can sear the human memory in two crippling ways: with
> forgetfulness of the past or imprisonment in it. The mind that insulates
> the traumatic past from conscious memory plants a live bomb in the
> depths of the psyche—it takes no great grasp of psychiatry to know that.
> But the mind that fixes on pain risks getting trapped in it. Too horrible
> to remember, too horrible to forget: down either path lies little health for
> the human sufferers of great evil.[16]

Criminal law can contribute to either mistake: as much through the
premature closure of a universal amnesty, as through interminable
proceedings aimed at rooting out every whiff of collaborative
impropriety. With so much talk in Argentina about the twin dangers of
"wallowing in the past" and "forgetting," it is scarcely surprising that
Funes himself now makes periodic appearance in Argentine discussions
of the dirty war and its memory.[17] As one Argentine historian rightly

---

> It has been observed by psychologists that the survivors of traumatic events are
> divided into two well-defined groups: those who repress their past *en bloc*, and
> those whose memory of the offense persists, as though carved in stone,
> prevailing over all previous or subsequent experiences. Now, not by choice but
> by nature, I belong to the second group. Of my two years of life outside the law
> I have not forgotten a single thing.

Primo Levi, *Moments of Reprieve* 10-11 (Ruth Feldman trans., 1986).

16   Donald W. Shriver, Jr., *An Ethic for Enemies: Forgiveness in Politics* 119 (1995).
Eric Stein formulates the dilemma in the terms of recent conservative German historians
concerning the need for national self-confidence:

> To allow the sense of responsibility to vanish from the collective memory would
> distort history and would harbor the danger of new excesses. [But] [t]o make
> people wallow in nightmares of guilt so as to impair the self-confidence of the
> young and their positive view of the future might bring about a destructive
> backlash against democratic institutions. The problem is one of a delicate
> balance; there is perhaps a modest role for law and the courts in helping to
> maintain it.

Eric Stein, "History Against Free Speech: The New German Law Against the
"Auschwitz"—and Other—"Lies"," 85 *Mich. L. Rev.* 321-22 (1986).

17   Eduardo Rabossi, *"Algunas Reflexiónes, a Modo de Prólogo,"* in *Usos del Olvido:
Comunicaciones al Coloquio de Royaumont* 7, 10 (Yosef H. Yerushalmi et al. eds.,
1989); Noga Tarnopolsky, "Murdering Memory in Argentina," *N.Y. Times,* Dec. 12,
1994, at A19 (noting the coincidence that the judge who recently awarded a $3 million
judgment to the one surviving family member of one of the disappeared shares the name
of Borges's fictional character, Funes, for whom, she writes "the burden of memory
becomes his torment and undoing, as it has been Argentina's").

cautions:

> The notion that terrible and extraordinary events are particularly fecund in historical lessons derives from a conception of history that expects to find it charged with meaning, like a good melodrama ..
>
> .. [But history] has little to teach us about the meaning of terror, apart from the obvious fact that it has been used many times before in the nation's crusades, and [our recent experience of] terror has little to teach us about our older history, except to record yet again that we generally prefer to forget all about it ....[18]

Like the Bourbons, we are unlikely to learn anything from such a past, on this account, even if we forget nothing of it. Like U.S. foreign policymakers in the mid-1960s, we may find that the seemingly straightforward lessons of World War II leave us conceptually ill-equipped for coping with the ensuing age—one of colonial insurrection, in which virtually all the rules of the geopolitical game were changed.[19] Those who remember the past receive no guarantee that it shall not be repeated, to them or by them, Santayana's famous platitude notwithstanding.[20] "If anything ... too sharp a sense of one's own victimization can easily lead to a compensatory urge to tyrannize over others, and those convinced of their unique victimhood are quite likely to prove tyrants both to themselves and to others if given a chance," one author has recently observed.[21]

---

18 Tulio Halperin Donghi, "El Presente Transforma el Pasado: El Impacto del Reciente Terror en la Imagen de la Historia Argentina," in *Ficción y Política: La Narrativa Argentina Durante el Proceso Militar* 71, 94 (René Jara & Hernán Vidal eds., 1987) (translation by author).

19 Yuen Foong Khong, *Analogies at War: Korea, Munich, Dien Bien Phu, and the Vietnam Decisions of 1965* 209-50 (1992).

20 Santayana observed: "Those who cannot remember the past are condemned to repeat it." 1 George Santayana, *The Life of Reason* 12 (1905).

21 Michael A. Bernstein, *Foregone Conclusions: Against Apocalyptic History* 88 (1994). Bernstein is specifically referring to particular demands by minority groups for changes in university curricula and to the statements offered by black U.C. Berkeley students who bragged of participating in the Los Angeles riots following the state-court acquittal of Rodney King's assailants.

Law Against Apocalyptic History

The notion of *in extremis veritas*, that the most essential truths—of broadest import and relevance—are discovered only through the most extreme tests at the darkest times, is surely "an unexamined and deeply false commonplace."[22] As Novick suggests of the Holocaust:

> Lessons for dealing with the sort of issues that confront us in ordinary life, public or private, are not likely to be found, I would think, in this most extraordinary of events. But ... Holocaust education, "confrontation" with the Holocaust, most recently, via viewing *Schindler's List*, is presented as a promising way of addressing a staggering array of social ills.[23]

This is an inherent danger of excessive reliance on storytelling, on the moral intuitions a poignant well-told story will arouse, at the expense of more careful, precise analysis.

If criminal prosecutions inevitably become the focus and forum for such lesson-mongering, they may simply be a mistake, a misguided expenditure of great effort, energy, and emotion. Judicial judgments possess a feature that makes them particularly vulnerable to abuse in this fashion: they do not merely pass judgment upon the past, but articulate social norms in ways designed to be binding upon the future. They authoritatively establish and reformulate the norms by which present activity is to proceed. For that reason, judicial judgments lend force to anyone who can persuasively invoke them—albeit by broad analogy—within the larger forum of political debate, interpreting them in support of a particular position on current controversies.

On the other hand, the law's preoccupation with precedent forces even the most extreme injustices, the most radical evil, to be apprehended in terms of something that has gone before, and hence to

---

22 *Id.* at 94. For instance, novelist Ernesto Sábato, in the prologue to the official report of the Argentine "truth commission," proclaims that "great catastrophes are always instructive." *Comisión Nacional Sobre la Desaparición de Personas, Nunca Más: The Report of the Argentine National Commission on the Disappeared* 6 (1986).

23 Peter Novick, "Pseudo-Memory and Dubious "Lessons": The Holocaust in American Culture" 13 (paper presented at the Project for Rhetoric of Inquiry Symposium, University of Iowa, April 1995).

be approached in a willfully "prosaic" way. This is normally seen as a vice by critics of liberal law, who view lawyers as plodding dullards, insistent on forcing every historical novelty into the Procrustean bed of professional tradition.[24]

But this lawyerly disposition can also be a virtue,[25] discouraging unduly apocalyptic interpretations of the past and extravagant readings of its relevance to quotidian questions. Criminal proceedings might actually serve as a useful counterweight to the pervasive tendency of political actors, especially partisan intellectuals, to exaggerate the scope of the "lessons" to be gleaned from such an "historic" experience, and to read the precedential value of those lessons far too capaciously.

When partisans invoke a legal precedent—"the lessons of Nuremberg," for instance—in political debate, they rarely confine their exhortations to an explication of the judicial record itself. But judges *invite* such expansive readings of their opinions when, in the interests of collective memory and monumental didactics, they admit evidence, or engage in fact-finding, beyond the scope of what is strictly necessary to apply the law. In short, judicial efforts at writing administrative massacre into the national narrative necessarily lend themselves to the most wide-ranging of later utilizations. The terrible episode and the courts' judgments upon it begin to "hover over" the most diverse of subsequent events and controversies, in ways that threaten to escalate the most routine disputes among reasonable people into apocalyptic conflagrations and holy wars.

The scope of history's teachings from such an episode, like those of a leading case and its judicial opinion,[26] must be treated as subject to

---

24   Hannah Arendt, *Eichmann in Jerusalem: A Report on the Banality of Evil* 276-79, 287-96 (Penguin Books, rev. & enlarged ed. 1977) (1963).

25   An eloquent, even poetic, defense of such prosaics is offered by Bernstein, *supra* note 21, at 120-22. See generally David G. Roskies, *Against the Apocalypse: Responses to Catastrophe in Modern Jewish Culture* (1984) (showing how Jewish writers and artists have reworked traditional genres and materials—prophetic, gnostic, cultic, and mystical—to represent historical catastrophe since the destruction of the Second Temple). The same is true regarding the capacity of traditional Christian and romantic traditions of bereavement to mediate the novel horrors of World War I. Jay Winter, *Sites of Memory, Sites of Mourning* 4 (1996). Despite its unprecedented elements of "multi-faceted dislocation, paradox, and the ironic," that war—like most before it—raised "timeless questions about the truncation of...lives, about promise unfulfilled, about the evanescence of hope." *Id.* at 224.

26   A classic statement of the omnipresent availability of both broad and narrow

a range of legitimate disagreement.[27] Discursive democracy requires that people be able to engage in a civil exchange of competing views about just what should be learned by whom from such a national experience. This fails to occur when the victims claim a monopoly over the meaning of the event, brooking no disagreement over its interpretation and the reach of its relevance. It also fails to occur when partially complicit parties treat the legal condemnation of others as irrelevant to a moral assessment of their own conduct during the period.

For an example of the first of these problems, consider the following pronouncement. Israeli President Menachem Begin told his Cabinet, on the eve of war in Lebanon: "'You know what I have done and what we have all done to prevent war and loss of life. But such is our fate in Israel. There is no way other than to fight selflessly. Believe me, the alternative is Treblinka.'"[28] To this use of collective memory, an Israeli philosopher responds:

> Such a commemoration enforces the hawkish psychology of paranoia corrected by aggression.... It is also handy for relaxing the moral demands made on [ourselves] .... this is a politically suicidal use of memory, that forgetfulness would better serve the national interest than [such] fatalism.... The memory of the Holocaust should be banished from political discourse. For the memory of such a nightmare is deranging. A political system cannot sanely function with Auschwitz as one of its central terms. If there are political lessons to be learned from the Holocaust, let the criminals ponder them, not the victims.[29]

---

readings of a legal precedent is presented by Karl N. Llewellyn, *The Bramble Bush: On Our Law and Its Study* 66-69 (1951).

27 Whatever their weaknesses in other respects, poststructuralist histories (beginning with Foucault's) at least never risk exaggerating the legitimate claims of the past upon the present. But they skirt this danger only by succumbing to a version of its opposite. All prior claims to truth are viewed, instead, as mere expressions of indefensible power; all alleged discoveries and resulting knowledge about the nature of "man" are dismissed as reflecting only the particular configuration of professional and disciplinary interests prevalent during specific historical periods, viewed as entirely discontinuous with our own.

28 Moshe Halbertal, "The Seventh Million: The Israelis and the Holocaust," *New Republic*, Oct. 18, 1993, at 40, 46 (book review).

29 *Id.*; see also LaCapra, *supra* note 14, at 63 (observing that "the Holocaust may serve as 'symbolic capital' or as a pretext for self-serving monumentalization"). Novick elaborates:

    Where once it was said that the *life* of Jews would be a "light unto the

In short, if collective memory of national tragedy will be invoked only for divisive, aggressive, or fatalistic purposes, it is better to forget, to institute an informal "gag rule" making such invocations taboo in debate of current policy.[30]

Begin's words, as Halbertal interprets them, reflect a disposition toward partisan use of the past that has had a partial analogue in postwar France, where this disposition has come to be called *résistantialisme*.[31] This is the belief that wartime resistance to the Nazis displayed the superior moral insight and courage of its participants in a way that authorizes them thereafter to speak for the nation with special moral authority on virtually any national controversy. In more sympathetic terms, it is the disposition to trust, and sometimes defer to, the conscience of those who displayed this virtue when it was most needed by the nation and most lacking in its officials.[32]

nations"—the bearer of universal lessons—now it is said to be the "darkness unto the nations" of the *death* of Jews that carries universal lessons. There is a good deal of confusion, and sometimes acrimonious dispute, over what these lessons *are*, but that has in no way diminished confidence that the lessons are urgent. Novick, *supra* note 23, at 9.

30 Begin's statement is also objectionable, from a religious perspective, in that it places the dead in the service of the living, viewing their memory not as intrinsically worthy of reverence, but worthy primarily in terms of its current utility. Alain Finkielkraut, *The Imaginary Jew* 54 (1994). But in a modern, secular society, especially one whose constitution rejects religious "establishment," the law cannot make such religious purposes the purpose of public commemoration. Moreover, secularists like myself would contend that the memory of the dead is often best honored by its invocation on behalf of principles they shared, fought for, or can be seen to have represented.

31 Henry Rousso, *The Vichy Syndrome: History and Memory in France Since 1944* 28-30, 59 (Arthur Goldhammer trans., 1991). A similar phenomenon has recently emerged in Eastern Europe. One journalist observes:

The struggle to define the past is one of the most important ways eastern Europeans compete for control of the present. These [competing] myths about the past are being constantly rewritten to fit the current political debate. Indeed, many political parties define themselves entirely in terms of the past: "We were the dissidents!" or "Trust us to be toughest on the Communists!" At times these claims are true. Often they merely reflect a very human forgetfulness of one's own complicity.

Tina Rosenberg, *The Haunted Land: Facing Europe's Ghosts After Communism* xiv-xv (1995).

32 Consider, for instance, the following 1943 editorial from *Combat*: "'On the morrow of the Liberation, France will pose this question to each of her sons: what did *you* do during the years of shame and misery? And it is on the basis of their answer ... that she will choose those who will have the honor of representing her.'" Peter Novick,

But in claiming to have spoken for the nation in its time of trial, such people could not very well acknowledge that most of the nation did not actually stand behind them in support. The French and Italian Communist Parties hence "had no objection to exaggerating the resistance record of the mass of the French or Italians, so long as they could themselves inherit the benefits of this illusion at the voting booth and in the national memory."[33]

The implication of *résistantialisme* is that active resistance to the unequivocal evil of state-sponsored mass murder provides the touchstone by which many later controversies may be understood and judged. This assumption, as Rousso observes, encouraged the making of many strained and faulty analogies between present and prior problems throughout postwar French history.[34] It also fostered simplistic "interventions" by the most prominent French intellectuals, invoking their *résistantialiste* credentials, in genuinely complicated matters of public policy on which they had little knowledge or, for that matter, moral sense.[35]

Like Begin's invocation of Treblinka to explain and justify the invasion of Lebanon (which might well have been defensible in other terms), this too was an abuse of collective memory. Public prosecutions of French collaborators were not employed to such didactic ends. But this was only because elite complicity had been so extensive as largely to foreclose their political possibility, until all but a handful of potential defendants had expired.[36] The French courts thus deserve no credit for not allowing the law's abuse by *résistantialisme*.

The Resistance Versus Vichy: The Purge of Collaborators in Liberated France 36 (1968).

33   Tony Judt, "The Past Is Another Country: Myth and Memory in Postwar Europe," *Daedalus,* 83, 91 (Fall 1992).

34   Rousso, *supra* note 31, at 28-30.

35   On the history of such intellectual interventions, see generally Tony Judt, *Past Imperfect: French Intellectuals, 1944-1956* (1992). For German analogues, see David C. Large, "Uses of the Past: The Anti-Nazi Resistance Legacy in the Federal Republic of Germany," in *Contending with Hitler: Varieties of German Resistance in the Third Reich* (David C. Large ed., 1991).

36   Robert O. Paxton, *Vichy France* 332-46, 381-83 (1972).

Debts to the Dead: A Dangerous Metaphor

In Argentina, there has been a similar and equally powerful tendency to view the dirty war, that is, its "proper understanding," as a moral guidepost to present and future controversies of the most disparate kind. This is especially true of Ms. Hebe de Bonafini, president of *Las Madres de Plaza de Mayo*. In her public pronouncements, she does not hesitate to invoke memory of the disappeared in service of controversies as far-afield as wage disputes between labor and management, and questions of foreign economic policy.[37]

Memory of the dirty war became, for such family members of the disappeared, a bloody shirt to be waved at every possible opportunity, to gain the moral high ground in political arguments of all sorts. Their profound suffering was taken (by themselves, if not generally by their opponents) to reflect the greater profundity of their moral and political insight, to confer not only spiritual strength, but also an ethical advantage in debate—an asserted superiority that, of course, did not at all follow from the fact of their greater suffering.

Family members of the disappeared were widely recognized as national spokesmen for human rights concerns, to be sure. For this reason, their leaders were understandably tempted to enhance their influence by turning virtually every political controversy into one "about human rights." The broader the reading given the dirty war as precedent, binding on the present, the greater the political power of those who could plausibly claim to invoke its memory. It is scarcely surprising, then, that other political contenders would seek to ally themselves with such groups, in hopes of benefiting from the considerable resonance the Madres and other human rights organizations enjoyed within Argentine politics in the mid-1980s. In this way, the Madres became closely allied with leftist political parties,

---

37 Alejandro Diago, *Hebe: Memoria y Esperanza* (1988). For a balanced assessment of Ms. Bonafini's leadership, superior to the already vast hagiographic literature, see Marifran Carlson, *Evil in the Southern Cone: Interviews with the Survivors and Witnesses of the Argentine Dirty War* (forthcoming 1997). See also Alison Brysk, *The Politics of Human Rights in Argentina* 73 (1994) (quoting Hebe de Bonafini in her objection to forensic exhumation techniques: "'We reject exhumations, because we want to know who the murderers are—we already know who the murdered are'").

who sought to use them for their own ends.[38]

These are highly sensitive matters, so it is important to be precise about what is objectionable here. There would have been nothing untoward had the Madres merely chosen to take up the particular political causes for which their loved ones had fought on the grounds that those causes were justified.[39] What is objectionable about invocations of the disappeared in contemporary Argentine debate is the implication that the country owes a moral debt to the victims and their families that can be repaid not by mourning, nor even by prosecution of the perpetrators, but only in deference to the beliefs of those who were murdered in the country's name. It was problematic enough to demand that the law punish all culpable parties. As Bernstein notes, "because it is so dismissive of temporal development and historical context, any ideology that endows victimhood with a singular authority to make claims upon others who were not themselves the agents of the injury strikes [us] as morally incoherent."[40]

Promiscuous use of collective memory in contemporary Argentina is not confined to the left, however. Sympathizers of the officer corps, for instance, soon founded an organization, Relatives and Friends of the Victims of Subversion, to commemorate soldiers killed by leftist guerrillas in the 1970s.[41] It holds religious masses in the soldiers' honor

---

38 Brysk, *supra* note 37, at 123-27, 129; Emilio F. Mignone, *Derechos Humanos y Sociedad: El Caso Argentino* 97-124 (1991). Such affiliations provoked a split within the Madres, and the formation of a subgroup (the *Fundadores*) which opposes what it regards as overbroad invocations of the dirty war's lessons. Each group marches separately, every Thursday, in the *Plaza de Mayo*. The chief organization of human rights lawyers, *Centro de Estudios Legales y Sociales*, was even infiltrated by active guerrilla groups. Brysk, *supra* note 37, at 118-21. One prominent lawyer-activist, for instance, was among the participants in a 1989 attack on the *La Tablada* garrison, during which over 40 people, including several draftees, were killed. *Id.*

39 Publications by the Madres and related groups often adopt this line. Deborah Norden provides several examples. Deborah L. Norden, Between Coups and Consolidation: Military Rebellion in Post-Authoritarian Argentina (1992) (unpublished Ph.D. dissertation, University of California, Berkeley). As Norden notes, "the radical factions of the Madres and Familiares injured their own credibility, by simultaneously portraying the disappeared as innocent victims of a cruel and unwarranted repression, and as heroes fighting for a just cause," a cause they often describe as "'the defeat of imperialism.'" *Id.* at 182.

40 Bernstein, *supra* note 21, at 93.

41 Familiares y Amigos de los Muertos por la Subversión, *Operación Independencia* (1988).

every month, officiated by sympathetic clergy. Speeches follow. In the mid-1980s, these speeches invariably denounced Alfonsín, the "liberals," "social democrats," "the Jews" behind him, and the "pornographic democracy" established by the new civilian administration.[42] The organization, its creators explained, was

> founded because of the increasing loss of memory by Argentine society concerning those who died in its defense. We have been moved by fear that the sacrifice of our loved ones' lives will be forgotten. We found this organization with the aim of permanently commemorating those who valiantly confronted subversive terrorism .... We also dedicate ourselves to the indefatigable defense of the moral, spiritual, and political values for which they gave their lives.[43]

Its goal, in short, is collective memory. Specifically, the goal is to restore a form of social solidarity in which shared remembrance and celebration of the victorious war against leftist terrorism would provide the common core of value-consensus. Until Menem's pardons, the ritual life of the organization focused on its denunciations of Alfonsín's military prosecutions.[44] The liberalism of the law thus became the symbolic centerpiece of its demonology. The continuing influence of "subversion" within the country's educational and cultural elite was also frequently decried at such gatherings.[45]

The enduring presence of subversion in these quarters was thought responsible for historical distortions of the dirty war disseminated by the courts, public schools, and mass media, who defamed those killed in the war against it. The military's defenders claimed that war must continue unabated in order to honor and preserve its good name, and to foster national memory of the cause its fallen members had served.

In short, the memory of their murdered loved ones made it impossible for either the Madres or the military's supporters to argue questions of current policy or national purpose apart from their perceived duties to the dead. All this inevitably suggests the "blood

---

42   Amos Elon, "Letter from Argentina," *New Yorker*, July 21, 1986, at 74, 82-83.

43   FAMUS, *supra* note 41, at acknowledgment page (translation by author).

44   Elon, *supra* note 42, at 82.

45   *Id.*

feud," an institution based on the all-consuming memory of a grievance originating in the distant past, that is, based on an inability to put aside what any reasonable person in a modern liberal society would prefer to forget.[46] Criminal trials originated largely to put an end to such processes, not to escalate them.

It is difficult to offer any rigorous criteria for classifying a particular invocation of memory as abusive or legitimate. In this chapter I could fairly be accused of having merely relabelled the problem, translating it from historical terms into jurisprudential ones (i.e., overbroad reading of precedent). But I have also offered examples that seem clearly to illustrate abuse, examples from which others may do better than I in extracting the implicit criteria by which we all (or almost all) reach this conclusion. And I have suggested some of the reasons why such overbroad readings arise and some of the political dynamics by which they work.

Within the law, readings of precedent that are grossly overbroad are quickly identified as such by all competent practitioners, on the basis of conventions we share regarding the nature of legal argument.[47] Such is not the case, however, beyond the courtroom, where shared conventions about what makes for an acceptable argument are often conspicuously lacking. This is particularly true in societies, such as Argentina, where the scope of political conflict has often extended to the most fundamental questions, such as the distribution of property, the allocation of capital, and the control of production—in short, the very structure of society itself.

While some succumb to overbroad readings of precedent, others

---

46   On blood feuds as quasilegal institutions, see William I. Miller, *Bloodtaking and Peacemaking: Feud, Law, and Society in Saga Iceland* 179-257 (1990). On the link between revenge and anamnesia (the inability to forget), see generally Rebecca N. Comay, "Redeeming Revenge: Nietzsche, Benjamin, Heidegger and the Politics of Memory," in *Nietzsche As Postmodernist* 21 (Clayton Koelb ed., 1990). Argentine sociologist Juan Carlos Torre recently predicted "that Argentine society would probably never come to terms with the dirty war but would 'continue with this open wound and carry it around with us for centuries.'" Calvin Sims, "Argentina to Issue New List of Missing in 'Dirty War'," *N.Y. Times,* Mar. 25, 1995, at A4. On some of the extremities to which this process now extends, including the adoption of Jewish names by German gentiles, see Jane Kramer, "Letter from Germany: The Politics of Memory," *New Yorker,* Aug. 14, 1995, at 48, 49-50.

47   Stanley Fish has emphasized this point in many of his writings. See, e.g., *Doing What Comes Naturally* (1989).

often fall victim to the opposite peril: too narrow a reading. This takes the form of a pervasive tendency toward self-flattering denial of one's own measure of complicity.[48] Since only a few will ever be prosecuted, the many who collaborated in myriad ways are discouraged from any serious self-examination. In fact, they often prominently join the ranks of the accusers, hurling invective at the former rulers whose policies they implemented and whose lies they feigned to believe.[49]

Those thus deluded view the trials of political and military chieftains merely as applying legal rules of properly delimited scope to those who have violated them. Such people should rather have understood the trials as embodying larger principles of liberal morality pertinent to assessing their own conduct. In short, these people underestimate the scope of the lessons properly to be learned from such legal proceedings. The danger here is not that the audience will prove unreceptive to the courtroom drama, but on the contrary, that it will prove all too responsive to the unduly circumscribed character of the narrative frame.

Thus, even when legal proceedings succeed in summoning up the collective conscience, as Durkheim hypothesized, they may do so only in a way that unduly narrows public understanding of the principles thereby reinvigorated. This peril was especially apparent in the French public's receptivity to the conviction of Klaus Barbie. As a German, putting Barbie in the dock enabled Frenchmen to point the accusatory finger at others, to evade any confrontation with the historical reality of French collaboration, and to reinvigorate the Gaullist myth of national purity.

Even when the defendant was unavoidably French, as in the trial of Paul Touvier, the French courts eagerly contributed to national efforts at moral evasion. They did so by interpreting the Nuremberg Charter to require the defendant to have acted in compliance with the orders of an Axis power.[50] Acts motivated by anti-Semitism of purely French inspiration were thereby excluded from the definition of "crimes

---

48 For an example, see Emilio F. Mignone, *Iglesia y Dictadura* (2d ed. 1986) (detailing the extensive complicity of the Catholic Church in the dirty war).

49 See *infra* text accompanying note 60.

50 Leila S. Wexler, "The Interpretation of the Nuremberg Principles by the French Court of Cassation: From Touvier to Barbie and Back Again," 32 *Colum. J. Transnat'l L.* 289, 323-25, 361-63 (1994).

against humanity."[51] Touvier was therefore criminally liable, as a matter of law, only to the extent that he was shown to have acted under German hegemony. Again, the story was told in such a way that the Germans became the real culprits, the French merely their long-suffering agents and grudging instruments.

Reading Precedent Restrictively

Criminal prosecution itself can facilitate self-deception through active misreading and misremembering. In eliciting and focusing the punitive sentiments of the many upon the very few, criminal trials tend not only to distort historical recollection by the general population, but also to discourage the discursive deliberation essential to liberal memory and solidarity. This is particularly apparent in how judicial condemnation of Germany's leaders at Nuremberg assisted many Central and Eastern Europeans—even those who had collaborated most extensively with Jewish deportations—to view themselves as victims of Nazism.[52]

A Japanese historian similarly observes that, "by thrusting the full responsibility onto the few who were executed, the Japanese effectively absolved themselves of any blame."[53] The past can have little relevance to the present when it is understood as a story about how the evil few led the innocent many astray. By declining to discuss official policies of the 1930s and 1940s, Japan has rendered many of its citizens virtually incapable of debating the question of when military power may defensibly be employed. Today, few students will engage in the discussion, on account of the pacifist reading of the War predominant among young Japanese.[54]

This is the wrong variety of societal self-reckoning. The nature and extent of collaboration under long- lasting despotic regimes ensures

---

51   Wexler offers an able doctrinal analysis and critique of how this legal conclusion was reached. *Id.* at 353-62.

52   Judt, *supra* note 33, at 87.

53   Yoshiaki Yoshimi, "Japan Battles Its Memories," *N.Y. Times*, Mar. 11, 1992, at A23.

54   On such attitudes, see Ian Buruma, *The Wages of Guilt: Memories of War in Germany and Japan* 92-111 (1994).

that "the line usually did not run clearly between Us and Them, but rather through the heart of each man and woman."[55] Alfonsín's top legal advisor, Malamud-Goti, now concludes that the danger of scapegoating a handful of aging elites is almost intrinsic to the bipolar logic of criminal law, with its insistence on dividing the world into mutually exclusive categories of people: legally, into guilty and innocent; sociologically, into blamers and blamed.[56]

These binary oppositions were deployed with brilliant casuistry by political elites in postwar France to minimize the moral questions raised by pervasive Nazi collaboration. Both De Gaulle and the metropolitan Resistance demanded prosecution of high-ranking Vichy officials.[57] To justify such prosecution as consistent with the law (of treason and sedition) required a finding that Pétain's Third Republic had been established by unconstitutional means.[58] But that conclusion entailed a corollary very convenient for collaborators not in the dock. Because the Vichy regime was illegal *ab initio*, none of its villainous acts—even those receiving *de facto* endorsement by a majority of Frenchmen—could be ascribed to France itself. Since it had come to power through defects of constitutional procedure, it could not be said to represent the true will of the French people.

Even if this France of innocent purity was a pure abstraction, it was *the law's* abstraction, hence highly authoritative when later invoked in

---

55 Timothy G. Ash, "Central Europe: The Present Past," *N.Y. Rev. Books,* July 13, 1995, at 21, 22 (paraphrasing Václav Havel).

56 But in seeing the problem as inherent in law, he explicitly assumes that legal discourse must retain its formalist contours. In other words, he assumes that even when courts judge administrative massacre, their deliberation and reasoning may entertain only such considerations recognized as relevant by positive law, not the wider range of factors admittedly indispensable to moral and political judgment of such events. Jaime Malamud-Goti, *Game Without End: Terror, Justice and the Democratic Transition in Argentina* 269-70 (manuscript, forthcoming 1996).

In this regard, he displays the jurisprudential commitment to positivist formalism. This commitment has long been characteristic of Latin American liberals. It is due to their considerable experience with the "naturalist" jurisprudence of courts during periods of authoritarian rule. Mark J. Osiel, "Dialogue with Dictators: Judicial Resistance in Argentina and Brazil," 20 *Law & Soc. Inquiry* 481, 495 (1995).

57 Herbert R. Lottman, *The Purge* 32-43 (1986).

58 On the arguments employed by French legal scholars to reach this conclusion, see Novick, *supra* note 32, at 21-24 (noting the "peculiar constitutional theory, which was to be the juridical foundation of the future Provisional Government, and, *pari passu,* of the purge").

political debate. It was the corollary of legal fictions thought necessary to convict the Nazis' most obvious henchmen. The very doctrines employed to ascribe legal responsibility to a few Frenchmen were thus increasingly employed in moral and political argument to absolve the rest. For instance, President François Mitterand's self-serving contention: "The Republic had nothing to do with this [Jewish deportation]. I do not believe France is responsible."[59] In this way, the trials themselves played into the propensity for self- deception, so powerful in the aftermath of collective catastrophe, by inviting an unduly narrow reading of their lessons.

The Argentine experience in this connection is similarly disconcerting. The trial of the Argentine juntas did not, by any means, put an end to manifestations of willful blindness about the pervasiveness of public sympathy for despotic rule. The very effectiveness of the junta trial in influencing present and future memory of the dirty war induced many Argentines to revise their *prior* memory of the period in more flattering terms. In the mid-1980s (shortly after public revelation of massive disappearances), Argentine sociologist Guillermo O'Donnell observed, when revisiting respondents he had interviewed years before during military rule, that:

> all of them "remembered" what they had told us before in a way that sharply contrasted with what they had actually told us. They were wrong, but evidently sincere, as they had been sincere before, in telling us, in the reinterviews, that they had always strongly opposed the regime and had never accepted its injunctions. In the first interviews those respondents had given distressing responses to our probings concerning the abductions, tortures and murders that were going on: these were only "rumors" or "exaggerations" and, at any event, "there must be some reason" why some persons were so victimized....
>
> ... They had rewritten their memories to fit [the] discovery [of what they felt they should have believed during the years of harsh repression]. The sense of continuity of their personal identity was preserved and, thus, they could look at the past without conscious guilt or shame. They ... had known little or nothing of those atrocities....
>
> ... This, at least, preserved them ... for the moment when it eventually

59   Marlise Simons, "Chirac Affirms France's Guilt in Fate of Jews," *N.Y. Times*, July 17, 1995, at A1, A3.

would become not too dangerous to "know" and, thus, to become indignant about what had happened.... [Through selective memory they imagined] that they had "always" been opposed to the regime ....[60]

It is scarcely surprising, then, that the military juntas felt they had been betrayed by a convenient failure in collective memory concerning the public connivance they had once enjoyed. In his closing statement to the court, Admiral Massera thus bitterly denounced the "fickleness" of Argentina's memory, a charge that O'Donnell's research painfully substantiates.[61] When a mass circulation newspaper in Buenos Aires first printed notice of numerous disappearances (tentatively testing the waters, in 1978), thousands of readers canceled their subscriptions.[62]

Discursive deliberation cannot get off the ground if people simply "tune out" messages they don't wish to hear. O'Donnell provides a reminder that "identification with the aggressor and blaming the victim," and their origins in rationalization and cognitive dissonance, were identified long ago in studies of Nazi Germany.[63] He might have added that the self-congratulatory revisionism which often follows, displayed by his interviewees, bespeaks a recurrent feature of transitions from authoritarianism to democracy. The French case is notorious in this regard: a substantial portion of the adult wartime survivors "remember" having assisted the Resistance in significant ways.[64]

---

60   Guillermo O'Donnell, "On the Fruitful Convergences of Hirschman's *Exit, Voice, and Loyalty* and *Shifting Involvements*: Reflections from the Recent Argentine Experience," in *Development, Democracy, and the Art of Trespassing* 249, 264-65 (Alejandro Foxley et al. eds., 1986). Malamud-Goti makes a similar observation regarding public enthusiasm for the junta trial: "Only in the sense of stifling a widely shared guilt, shame and anguish in the common knowledge that it was the same disappeared who we sought to censure did blame contribute to ... social solidarity." Malamud-Goti, *supra* note 56, at 259-60.

61   O'Donnell, *supra* note 60, at 264.

62   Hugo Vezzetti, *"El Juicio: Un Ritual de la Memoria Colectiva,"* 7 *Punto de Vista* 3, 5 (1985) (translation by author). The news article appeared in mid-1978.

63   O'Donnell, *supra* note 60, at 264. He is presumably alluding to the influential study by Mitscherlich & Mitscherlich, *supra* note 14, at 1-67, which sought to show that many Germans had managed to block out any memory of having glorified Hitler.

64   Stanley Hoffman, "Foreword" to Rousso, *supra* note 31, at vii, vii-viii.

Overcoming Willful Blindness

The only way in which trials for administrative massacre have been able to overcome such thick layers of willful blindness, as manifested by O'Donnell's interviewees, is by self-conscious use of powerful dramatical devices, particularly film. The quintessential case of its use was at Nuremberg, where Allied prosecutors showed "German Concentration Camps" to the Tribunal.[65] The film ends with footage of a bulldozer pushing enormous mounds of human bodies into a mass grave at Bergen-Belsen. When the court adjourned for the day at the completion of the showing, several of the defendants were seen stifling tears.[66] One scholar observes,

> whatever evasions and duplicities permitted a person to sweep the camps from his or her frame of vision cannot survive contact with the world captured on [this] film.... [It] does not simply instruct or produce visual knowledge of atrocity; rather, it overwhelms one's senses, creating an irrefutable imprint upon the mind, a trauma of sight.... The corpses force their memory upon the coward's mind.[67]

Where the perpetrators still hold considerable power, however, as did the Argentine military during the junta trial, prosecutorial stagecraft is more likely to work by understatement. It employs subtle appeals to conscience, rather than efforts to overpower the senses and defense mechanisms. Many mass graves had been uncovered in Argentina by the time of the junta trial. Yet no such cinematic images were employed to elicit support for the junta trial. Imagery of this sort had earlier been selectively broadcast as part of the "Truth Commission" report. However, it was preceded by remarks from Alfonsín's conservative Interior Minister, who "situated" the military's crimes in the context of the guerrilla violence.[68] Although Alfonsín allowed state television to

---

65   2 *Trial of the Major War Criminals Before the International Military Tribunal,* 104, 121, 431-33, 536 (1947) (originally shown at Nuremberg, 1945-1946).

66   Ann Tusa & John Tusa, *The Nuremberg Trial* 160 (1984).

67   Lawrence Douglas, "Film As Witness: Screening 'Nazi Concentration Camps' Before the Nuremberg Tribunal," 105 *Yale L.J.* 449 (1995). The same film was also shown at the Eichmann trial.

68   Brysk, *supra* note 37, at 71.

broadcast the junta trial, he insisted that coverage be confined to photographic images and exclude the harrowing oral testimony.[69] Nino confides that this was for fear of aggravating military tempers.[70]

Propensities for faulty analogy and self-deception, for overbroad and overly narrow readings of the precedent, pose problems for liberal law that are intertwined. On one hand, if the law contents itself with a narrow notion of responsibility, punishing only a small portion of culpable parties, it reinforces the powerful inclination of many others toward self-deception, that is, against any enduring recognition of their own, genuine moral failures and what might be learned from them.

On the other hand, if the law endorses a very broad reading of these moral failures and of their attendant lessons, it will necessarily be asked to accomplish things far beyond its power. It will then be condemned for failing to achieve them. Legal proceedings cannot, for instance, convict an entire society, unmask the international economic system allegedly responsible for the dirty war, or bring back the dead—all longstanding and continuing demands of *Las Madres de Plaza de Mayo* and their political sympathizers.[71]

Criminal law cannot further social solidarity if the story it tells exculpates most of the morally culpable parties—either through political prudence or because they are "culpable" in ways that liberal jurisprudence does not recognize. *That* story—of a few "bad apples" leading the innocent nation astray—will be persuasively attacked by good journalists, historians, and social scientists (like O'Donnell effectively does) as incomplete, as concealing more extensive complicities, to which its judicial narrators become accessories after the fact.[72]

But the alternative narrative is no less problematic. The law cannot

---

69   Interviews with Argentine Presidential Legal Advisors, in Buenos Aires, Argentina (Aug. 1985).

70   Carlos Nino, *Radical Evil on Trial* 80, 125 (1996). Fear of strong reactions from both Japanese and the world at large also led Occupation authorities to prohibit publication (and even possession) of photographs showing the effects of the Hiroshima and Nagasaki weapons. John W. Dower, "The Bombed: Hiroshimas and Nagasakis in Japanese Memory," in *Hiroshima in History and Memory* 116, 129 (Michael J. Hogan, ed., 1996).

71   Brysk, *supra* note 37, at 124-25.

72   O'Donnell, *supra* note 60, at 263-65.

hope to further social solidarity if its story promises a "happy ending"—by punishing all responsible parties, however numerous. This is a promise on which it simply cannot deliver. Judicial decisions about whom to punish cannot provide anything but the most morally compromised narrative. This is because what is most urgently desired by those seeking a complete accounting (such as the Madres), is a thorough condemnation of *all* those sharing significant responsibility for the atrocities—plus a publicly enforced recollection of enduring "debt" to victims and their families thus incurred.

The courts' credibility in telling a national story, one that will powerfully shape collective memory, is thus alternately threatened by the narrowness or breadth of the narrative framing. The broader framing is politically imprudent, to the point of imperiling the new democratic regime, were a court to try telling it. The narrower framing, however, is politically unpersuasive. It must rely upon distinctions in degrees of culpability likely to be logically weak and morally indefensible, or at least widely perceived as such. Between the broader and narrower story lines, there may be no stable middle ground for courts to occupy.

In seeking to influence collective memory of administrative massacre, then, judges and prosecutors need to be able publicly to acknowledge and explain the law's limits and potentialities, even as they go about performing their more fundamental tasks. More readily than the Durkheimian view, the discursive conception of law's service to social solidarity can confront the differing views about the scope of law's legitimate aims in such circumstances. It can also confront the recalcitrant reality of enduring disagreement, in the aftermath of administrative massacre, over how broadly the lessons of the country's recent horrors should be interpreted. The discursive conception, after all, allows for solidarity despite continuing disagreement about such things as whether the precedent established by the recent past and binding upon the present is fairly applicable to any particular question of public policy that may arise in the future.

It bears mention, in conclusion, that uncritical over-reliance on the purported "lessons of history" is a danger against which the most influential versions of liberalism, such as Kant's, have always been well-guarded.[73]   The notion of a hypothetical social contract, for instance, forces one to start afresh, stripped of historical grievances and prejudices, to reason from a moral point of view, without appeal to prior status as (victimizing) power or (powerless) victim. If anything, liberal theory generally undervalues what can be learned from historical experience and its study, such as the virtue of seasoned judgment.[74] An salutary exception among contemporary liberals was Judith Shklar, who criticized "the patron saints of liberalism" for resting the defense of liberal institutions on ahistorical claims about human nature, rather than simply on a "strongly developed historical memory" of fear and oppression—which any reading of political history would amply supply.[75]

---

73   Immanuel Kant, *Critique of Pure Reason* 313 (Norman K. Smith trans., 1964) ("Nothing is more reprehensible than to derive the laws prescribing what *ought to be done* from what *is done*, or to impose upon them the limits by which the latter is circumscribed."); see also William A. Galston, *Kant and the Problem of History* 36-37 (1975) (contending that Kant, in contrast to much Greek classical thought, "denies that experience can serve as a guide"); Charles E. Larmore, *Patterns of Moral Complexity* 1-5 (1987) (observing Kant's inconsistent views on the usefulness of examples in moral reasoning).

74   For an unusually explicit attempt to employ historiography to this end, see generally Richard E. Neustadt & Ernest R. May, *Thinking in Time* (1990).

75   Judith Shklar, "The Liberalism of Fear," In *Liberalism and the Moral Life* 21, 26-7 (Nancy Rosenblum ed., 1989). Elsewhere she adds, "It is not remembered that the history and present function of rights is the expression of outrage at cruelty." Shklar, "Injustice, Injury, and Inequality: An Introduction," In *Justice and Equality: Here and Now* 13, 24 (Frank S. Lucash ed., 1986).

Chapter 6.

Breaking with the Past,
Through Guilt and Repentance

There is a fourth source of skepticism about the extent to which criminal prosecution of administrative massacre can contribute to collective memory. Is it possible, whether by legal judgment or other means, to infuse shared recollection of moral failure? Still more difficult, is it possible to employ shared recollection of this sort to reconstruct group identity?

We know that a group can create a myth of refounding, a complete break with the past, that does not entail any recognition of responsibility for its wrongs. Such a myth is not based upon the good reasons a group might have for wishing to break with its past in the first place. The German Democratic Republic provides the clearest case. Communist leaders there consistently affirmed, in thousands of speeches and declarations over forty-five years, that their citizens bore no responsibility for Nazism or the Holocaust. These had resulted from fascism and capitalism, with which the East had decisively broken after the War.[1] Such leaders claimed that the new state, in fact, had been founded by a victorious antifascist and anticapitalist movement, which had cleared the country of the reactionary elements (that is, big business) responsible for past horrors.[2]

Denials of this sort, in all their disingenuousness, have been distressingly common in many societies. The legal act of creating a new sovereign entity, where none had before existed, only contributes to the delusion that the past has no claim upon the present. A superficial legal rupture substitutes for a serious moral reckoning.

We also know that collective memory can be based on catastrophe. The role of the Holocaust in Israeli national identity makes that clear.[3]

---

1 Frank Trommler, "The Creation of History and the Refusal of the Past in the German Democratic Republic," in *Coping with the Past: Germany and Austria After 1945,* at 79, 86-87 (Kathy Harms et al. eds., 1990).

2 Only in its final years did East German leaders begin to acknowledge, in part, the responsibility of their people for past injustices. *Id.* at 79.

3 This is a central theme in both Saul Friedlander, *Memory, History, and the*

In fact, it has been quite common for national groups to foster internal cohesion among members by the authoritative telling of stories—sometimes fanciful, often accurate—about the many injustices done to its ancestors by other nations. The "notion of having been victimized by the Germans," notes one leading Europeanist, "became an absolutely indispensable staple of the collective memories of most postwar European peoples, even those significant in number who have in fact benefited from Germany's power and presence during the Nazi era."[4]   As a result, "victimization by the Germans developed into an essential pillar of the 'foundation myth' in these societies."[5]

Criminal prosecution has not often been used to advance this narrative purpose, to be sure. But this is only because it has usually proven impossible to acquire jurisdiction over (that is, get one's hands on) the alleged culprits. Resentment over the wrongs inflicted on one's nation has often, nonetheless, been a fertile source of collective self-definition, and self-assertion.[6] Shared memory of the humiliation represented by the Versailles Treaty was evoked with notorious success by Hitler himself, to resurrect German identity in the aftermath of the First World War.[7] Again, a legal document became the focal point for a national myth of origin, here one of reconstruction on decidedly illiberal foundations.

We know, moreover, that national identity can be constructed on the basis of stories about the moral failings of a society's founders. This is true even when these founders appear otherwise heroic, even

---

Extermination of the Jews of Europe at 113-14 (1993) and Tom Segev, *The Seventh Million: The Israelis and the Holocaust* 223-26 (1993).

4   Thomas Berger, "The Contemporary Power of Memory: The Dilemmas of German Foreign Policy" 11 (Sept. 3, 1995) (paper presented at the Annual Convention of the American Political Science Association).

5   *Id.* In addition to other more subtle forms of collaboration, several occupied countries in Western Europe provided thousands of volunteers each for Germany's Waffen SS. John Keegan, *The Battle for History: Re-Fighting World War II* 102-118 (1995).

6   On the central role of resentment in nationalist movements, see Liah Greenfeld, *Nationalism* 15-17, 222-28 (1992).

7   Erich Matthias, "The Influence of the Versailles Treaty on the Internal Development of the Weimar Republic," in *German Democracy and the Triumph of Hitler: Essays in Recent German History* 13, 22 (Anthony Nicholls & Erich Matthias eds., 1971). For evidence in the autobiographies of Nazi activists, see generally Peter H. Merkl, *Political Violence Under the Swastika* (1975).

superhuman. After all, in ancient Greece, tragic dramas for theatre were written about real events in the remembered past.

> The tragic dramatists of the Greek city-states were ... concerned with reconstituting the history of their forefathers as tragic myth. Prometheus and Io, and later Oedipus and Antigone, belong to an antiquity which fifth century Greeks could recognize as part of a sacrificial struggle for their own collective identity. They are legendary figures.[8]

The life history of such figures, imprinted in collective memory, can function to forge identity and form character in mere mortals. This is partly because the personal frailties of a given founder—his "tragic flaw," in Aristotle's terms—often entail a one-sided exaggeration of a virtue. His life history thus usefully instructs us, his successors, in the merits of moderation and in the continuous need for critical self-assessment even when—perhaps especially when—acting pursuant to our most deeply held ideals and commitments.

What is much less clear, however, is whether national identity can be constructed on the basis of shared acceptance of responsibility for wrongs one's *own* nation has done to *others*. Is it true, as some lament,[9] that memory of one's own grievances against others appears to be virtually the only kind that can provide the mnemonic basis of collective identity? Surely it can be no accident that such founding myths almost invariably offer highly flattering accounts of the nation's early accomplishments and the virtues displayed by its founders. On most recountings, America's myth of origin does not exactly give pride of place to the genocide of the Native American, except perhaps if rendered as "subduing savages."[10]

We are hardly alone in this type of omission. The writing and telling of most national myths of origin entail acts of compulsory

---

8   John Orr, *Tragic Drama and Modern Society* xiii (2d ed. 1989).

9   Peter Novick, oral remarks accompanying presentation of "Pseudo-Memory and Dubious "Lessons": The Holocaust in American Culture" (Apr. 1995) (paper presented at the Project for Rhetoric of Inquiry Symposium, University of Iowa).   Novick proposes this as only a "plausible generalization." Personal communication.

10   Milner S. Ball, "Constitution, Court, Indian Tribes," 1987 *Am. B. Found. Res. J.* 1,8.

"forgetfulness," notes Derrida.[11] This is because the creation of most nation-states has entailed acts of violent dispossession. What must be forgotten in this process is not only the dispossession itself, but also the notions of right, often embodied in customary law, on which prior claims of possession and entitlement were based.

A nation's myths of its origins establish a "cult of continuity," one historian observes: "The greater the origins, the more they magnified our greatness. Through the past we are venerating above all ourselves."[12] Providing such stories with a legal imprimatur, as by official holidays for their commemoration, grants them special authority and solidarity-enhancing impact. One may try to employ such an occasion, like the Bicentennial of the U.S. Constitution, for serious self-criticism of a society's foundational legal commitments.

But such an attempt is likely to be regarded as ill-considered and inappropriate during a festive occasion, even by those otherwise sympathetic to the substance of the criticism, as Justice Marshall learned.[13] What has been here described as historical "balance," a nuanced judgment of our collective strengths and weaknesses in relation to others, is precisely what is *least* welcome at such moments.[14]

---

11 Jacques Derrida, 'Force of Law: The "Mystical Foundation of Authority"' (Mary Quaintance trans.), in *Deconstruction and the Possibility of Justice* 3, 47 (Drucilla Cornell et al. eds., 1992); see also Ernest Renan, "What Is a Nation?," in *Nation and Narration* 8, 11 (Homi K. Bhabha ed., 1990) (contending that to create and unite a nation, such as France, requires inducing its members to "forget" the savage conflicts, as between Protestants and Catholics in the 16th century, that have long divided them). On the exclusionary aspects of leading legal cases establishing American national identity, see Priscilla Wald, *Constituting Americans: Cultural Anxiety and Narrative Form* 22-37 (1995).

12 Pierre Nora, "Between Memory and History: *Les Lieux de Mémoire*," 26 *Representations* 7, 16 (1989).

13 Many editorialists criticized Marshall for his choice of timing, while sharing much of his substantive view. William B. Reynolds, "For the Record," *Wash. Post,* June 11, 1987, at A22; Jack Valenti, "Despite Slavery, a Constitution That Built a Nation," *N.Y. Times,* June 6, 1987, at A27; Edwin M. Yoder Jr., "That 'Defective' Constitution: The Alternative Was a Lot Worse," *Wash. Post,* May 14, 1987, at A25.

14 More precisely, the sort of balance that is sought is aimed exclusively at mitigating one's own wrongs, rather than a disinterested and impartial assessment. Hence, the statement of Masao Horie, head of the Japanese Veterans Association, in response to demands for a parliamentary apology for the country's war crimes: "'At the 50th anniversary of the Dresden firebombing, in which many people died, I didn't hear the Allies apologizing.' And the U.S. dropped atomic bombs on Hiroshima and Nagasaki and killed huge numbers of innocent Japanese people, and never apologized for this.'"

Balance requires a critical disposition that sits uneasily with the attitude of reverence demanded at these moments.

Professional historiography, to be sure, now explicitly distinguishes itself from popular memory on the basis of its more self-critical capacities. In fact, it often prides itself on its willingness to turn a skeptical gaze upon the self-congratulatory memory of the society that sponsors it and upon the more celebratory accounts of earlier historians.[15] Even so, history books for school children have almost everywhere been notoriously silent about the less glorious acts of the famous dead.[16] This is largely because such books are self-consciously aimed at constructing collective memory. A recent study of how Western and Eastern Europeans remember the Holocaust, in textbooks and other media, thus concludes: "In every country, every culture..., irrespective of national character or political ideology ...

Nicholas D. Kristof, "Why Japan Hasn't Said That Word," *N.Y. Times,* May 7, 1995, at E3.

On August 14, 1995, for the first time since the end of the war, the Japanese Prime Minister, "expressed 'heartfelt apology,'" admitting that "Japan had 'through its colonial rule and invasion, caused tremendous damage and suffering to the people of many countries, particularly to those of Asian nations.'" Sheryl WuDunn, "Japanese Apology for War Is Welcomed and Criticized," *N.Y. Times,* Aug. 16, 1995, at A3 (quoting Prime Minister Tomiichi Murayama). The Prime Minister rejected the possibility of compensating Japan's victims, however, stating that such questions had been resolved by treaty with Asian neighbors long ago. *Id.*

15   Nora, *supra* note 12, at 9 ("At the heart of history is a critical discourse that is antithetical to spontaneous memory. History is perpetually suspicious of memory."); see also Yosef H. Yerushalmi, *Zakhor: Jewish History and Jewish Memory* 14-15 (1982) ("Even in the Bible ... historiography is but one expression of the awareness that history is meaningful and of the need to remember, and neither meaning nor memory ultimately depends upon it.").

16   Until recently German textbooks in public schools exhibited "scant interest in the broader circles of complicity involved in murdering millions of men, women, and children." Walter F. Renn, "Federal Republic of Germany: Germans, Jews, and Genocide," in *The Treatment of the Holocaust in Textbooks* 128, 128 (Randolph L. Braham ed., 1987).

Recent U.S. efforts to implement uniform "History Standards," with their modest efforts to qualify an otherwise celebratory account of American history with reminders of slavery and Indian genocide, have been widely rejected. John Fonte, "Flawed History Standards Must Go," *N.Y. Times,* Feb. 19, 1995, at D12. The detention of Japanese-Americans during the Second World War did not appear in high school history textbooks until the 1980s. Rubie S. Watson, "Making Secret Histories: Memory and Mourning in Post-Mao China," in *Memory, History, and Opposition Under State Socialism* 65, 67 (Rubie S. Watson ed., 1994).

self-deception has usually triumphed over self-revelation."[17]

One may thus reasonably "wonder whether a national identity can be built on guilt and repentance, bereft of the ordinary pride of other nations."[18] Opinion surveys suggest that many Germans and Americans are "sick and tired of having to remember"[19] Nazi crimes against the Jews. This prompts one author to observe:

> Most human minds grow weary of negatives. They can absorb only so much repetition of truths that are unwelcome from the beginning. And this psychological reaction suggests that the victims of any vast suffering *should worry over the tactics* as well as the morality of their public protests against forgetfulness.[20]

Whether criminal prosecution is an effective tactic toward this end thus becomes an inescapable question. As Sheldon Wolin observes, "a society which insisted upon periodically reviewing great historical wrongs it had committed would probably invite all the familiar metaphors about 'obsessively picking at its own scabs.'"[21] Perhaps a national culture can "keep its shape," Mary Douglas writes, only by inducing members "to forget experiences incompatible with its righteous image, and ... bring to their minds events which sustain the

---

17   Judith Miller, *One, By One, By One: Facing the Holocaust* 279 (1990); see also Herbert Hirsch, *Genocide and the Politics of Memory* 28 (1995) ("Most nations attempt to avoid honest self-recognition, especially when their past behavior may be viewed as less than morally justifiable.").

18   Francis Fukuyama, "The War of All Against All," *N.Y. Times,* Apr. 10, 1994, §7 (Book Reviews), at 7 (reviewing Michael Ignatieff, *Blood and Belonging,* 1989). German historian Hans-Peter Schwarz proposes a corollary: "'When national consciousness is replaced by consciousness of guilt, patriotism is programmed to degenerate into defeatist pacifism.'" Jürgen Habermas, "Closing Remarks," in *The New Conservatism: Cultural Criticism and the Historians' Debate* 241, 247 (Shierry W. Nicholsen ed., trans., 1989).

19   Donald W. Shriver, Jr., *An Ethic for Enemies: Forgiveness in Politics* 103 (1995).

20   *Id.* (emphasis added).

21   Sheldon S. Wolin, "Injustice and Collective Memory," in *The Presence of the Past* 32, 34 (1989). Wolin is describing and criticizing the views of the French nationalist Ernest Renan for arguing that "a society can ill afford to reexamine collectively a special class of political events [here, Catholic persecution of the Huguenots] in which the members of society feel tainted by a kind of corporate complicity in an act of injustice done in their name." *Id.*

view ... that is complimentary to itself."[22]

To be sure, this view may unduly hypostatize a nation's culture, endowing it with a powerful instinct of self-preservation that protects its "essence" from criticism and reform by its very carriers. Even so, individuals suppress painful experiences from conscious memory through what Freud called "screen memory."[23] There may be an analogue in the process by which historical events enter into (or are filtered from) the memory of an entire society and the national identity of its members.[24] This similarity gives rise, at any rate, to what might be called a psychoanalytical argument for criminal prosecution of administrative massacre. Habermas states it well:

> The dominance of the past, which returns like a nightmare to hang over the unredeemed present, can only be smashed by the analytic power of a form of remembering that looks calmly at what happened without seeing it in morally neutral terms.[25]

This form of remembering and moral analysis is preeminently the task of criminal prosecutors and courts—not scientific scholarship, responded conservative German historians. Their motives are suspect, but their argument is compelling: We should not expect academic historiography to undertake a task alien to and often at odds with its other purposes. If Habermas's concerns with societal self-reckoning are legitimate, they may be misdirected, as a demand upon historical scholarship.

---

22 Mary Douglas, *How Institutions Think* 112 (1986).

23 Sigmund Freud, "Screen Memories," in 3 *The Standard Edition of the Complete Psychological Works of Sigmund Freud* 303 (James Strachey et al. eds., 1962). Elsewhere, Freud quotes Nietzsche approvingly on the mental process involved here: "'I have done that,' says my Memory. 'I could not have done that,' says my Pride, and remains inexorable.   Finally, my memory yields."   Sigmund Freud, *The Psychopathology of Everyday Life* 153 (1914).

24 For a representative statement of this view, see, for example, Carol Gluck, "The Past in the Present," in *Postwar Japan As History* 64, 76 (Andrew Gordon ed., 1993) (noting that often today "students of memory describe how individuals construct and reconstruct their memories in much the same way as nations do their histories, creating what Borges called a 'fictitious past'").

25 Jürgen Habermas, *Frankfurter Allgemeine Zeitung,* Nov. 22, 1985, quoted in Helga Geyer-Ryan & Helmut Lethen, "The Rhetoric of Forgetting," in *Convention and Innovation in Literature* 305, 305 (Theo D'haen et. al., eds., 1989).

More persuasively, Habermas also sees a role for courts. In the aftermath of state-sponsored mass brutality, he implies, courts may do for society at large what psychoanalysis does for individuals. They must unearth repressed memory of historic trauma, forcing the "patient" to work through its enduring ramifications, so that he can confront the present on its own terms, not by acting out of unresolved issues.

Putting even a few prominent individuals on trial can help induce members of a much larger public to confront complicities of their own. This is because the trial—particularly the arguments of the defense, if allowed to open the narrative frame—is sure to put such larger complicities in issue. The resulting self-assessment and self-recognition by ordinary citizens will, in turn, break the neurotic compulsion to repeat the past blindly and uncritically. This, at any rate, is what Habermas implies.

Perhaps. But we should be reluctant to accept any such easy isomorphism, such direct parallelism between the workings of individual memory (over personal trauma) and collective memory (of national trauma). As James Young wisely warns:

> If memory of an event is repressed by an individual who lacks the context—either emotional or epistemological—to assimilate it, that is one thing. But to suggest that a society "represses" memory because it is not in its interest to remember, or because it is ashamed of its memory, is to lose sight of the many other social and political forces underpinning national memory.[26]

---

26 James E. Young, *The Texture of Memory* xi (1993) (focusing on the architecture, artistry, and official rituals of Holocaust commemoration). Psychoanalytic concepts, like "aftereffect" or "return of the repressed," may have some limited heuristic value here, if the metaphorical nature of their usage is acknowledged. Alas, this generally is not the case. The psychoanalytic concepts are simply transposed from the individual to the society with minimal attention to this radical shift in the level of analysis. See, e.g., Eric L. Santner, *Stranded Objects: Mourning, Memory, and Film in Postwar Germany* 4 (1990) (discussing the inability of Germans to remember the past and blaming "the remarkably efficient deployment of a set of defense mechanisms"); Steven Ungar, "Vichy As a Paradigm of Contested Memory," in *Scandal and Aftereffect* 1, 2 (1995) (suggesting that France's postwar "obsession" with the Vichy period is a Freudian "aftereffect," or *nachträglichkeit*, of its failure to "work through" the moral issues raised by extensive French collaboration in Nazi rule and Jewish deportation). Their periodic denigration of the "economic miracle" (and, by implication, the capitalism that produced it) as diversions from the more sober business of societal self-scrutiny in the wake of administrative massacre, is purely rhetorical. Santner, *Id.* at 4; Ungar, *Id.* at 2.

Limits of the Memory Metaphor

Individual memory works in ways different from collective memory. For instance, reliance on written and computer records makes it easier for individuals to forget things, in the knowledge that they can always "look it up." But such records enormously expand the capacity of a national society for preserving memory of its past. Embarrassing documents have a way of turning up at the most 'inopportune' times, in response to the most adamant public denials of what they proceed irrefutably to establish. This is exemplified by the recently uncovered

---

Neither of these authors identifies any analytical or causal connection between market institutions, on one hand, and societal "repression" of unpleasant historical memories, on the other.

The much greater force with which memories of genocide have been officially repressed in Communist societies further belies any such inherent connection between capitalism and memory repression. For a contrast between Communist Party efforts in East Germany to suppress memory of the Holocaust and West German efforts to foster memory of that experience, see Jeffrey Herf, *Divided Memory: The Nazi Past in the Two Germanies* (forthcoming 1997).

Social psychology suggests, moreover, that a measure of economic security, afforded by a society's prosperity, may be necessary before most people will be inclined to examine complex normative issues of personal responsibility, such as those raised in episodes of administrative massacre. See generally Abraham H. Maslow, *Motivation and Personality* (1970) (positing a hierarchy of human needs, beginning with food and shelter, ending in "self-actualization").

Other historians of equally leftist tilt frequently assert that national decline and economic *stagnation*, such as that of postwar Britain, discourage a serious and critical engagement of collective memory with past injustices. For a survey of such views among British socialist historians, see Keith Thomas, "Retrochic," *London Rev. Books,* Apr. 20, 1995, at 7, 7-8, reviewing Raphael Samuel, *Theatres of Memory Vol. I* (1995).

Still others of similar political orientation defend a position very much at odds with the first view above; they contend that Germany's seemingly sincere remorse about its war guilt is a capitalist ploy, calculated to smooth the way for current international commerce, to ensure the success of German exports. For this view, see Jonathan Boyarin, "Space, Time, and the Politics of Memory," in *Remapping Memory* 1, 12-13 (Jonathan Boyarin, ed., 1994); Lothar Baier, *Les bénéfices de la mauvaise conscience,* 68 Le Genre Humain 211 (1988).

But if guilt and repentance were compelled by the "needs" of German capitalism, it is surely puzzling that Japanese political leaders and institutions have proven so reluctant for so long to accept any such responsibility, despite persistent demands for it by trading partners throughout Asia (who are clearly reluctant to become heavily dependent on a neighbor who shares so little of their collective conscience). Takashi Inoguchi, *Japan's International Relations* 109-11, 133-36, 142-47 (1991).

In any event, those who do not share the antipathy of these several authors for market society will be tempted to ask: Which is it? Does capitalism encourage or discourage acceptance of responsibility for war guilt?

documents demonstrating the Japanese government's wartime decision to enslave Asian women as prostitutes for its soldiers.[27]

On account of such differences, the capacity of a society to induce criticism of its culture and institutions may well be greater in many ways than the individual capacity for fundamental self-criticism and identity revision. A particular prosecution for administrative massacre might fail to induce much moral self-scrutiny among its perpetrators and their sympathizers. Yet it might nevertheless inducing considerable scrutiny—among young people and an emergent political leadership —regarding the institutional sources of collective responsibility for that horrendous event.

Conversely, when a society prudently decides not to pursue all those complicit in a large-scale administrative massacre, this decision should not be diagnosed as merely a case of Alzheimer's disease writ large. "Amnesty is lawful amnesia," writes the distinguished literary scholar Geoffrey Hartman.[28] This is the belletristic sensibililty at its most confused, however. The two words do have a common etymology; but etymology is not destiny.

Individual memory can be effectively worked upon without an immediate issuance into concomitant institutional change. Argentina may not have redesigned its political institutions in light of the "lessons" offered by its courts when convicting military officers. But the country currently has the highest per capita concentration of psychiatrists of any society. This suggests that something very widespread is being "worked through," albeit not in public.

When a criminal trial for administrative massacre becomes a massive public spectacle, it can serve as one powerful means to this end. It does so by stimulating debate about the morality of the defendants' conduct and the nature of the institutions they controlled. That has sometimes been precisely the result of prosecutions for

---

27　The documents were discovered in the library of Japan's Self-Defense Agency by historian Yoshiaki Yoshimia, who was prompted (by watching a government spokesman's denials on television) to remember having seen such documents years before. Yoshiaki thereby produced the documentary "smoking gun," requiring Japan's Prime Minister to apologize for the "error." Margaret Scott, "Making the Rising Sun Blush," *Far E. Econ. Rev.*, Mar. 30, 1995, at 50 (reviewing George Hicks, *The Comfort Women: Sex Slaves of the Japanese Imperial Forces* (1994).

28　Geoffrey Hartman, *The Longest Shadow: In the Aftermath of the Holocaust* 46 (1996).

administrative massacre, perhaps its most salubrious result—albeit one uncognizable in doctrinal terms.

The central question thus becomes: How can the criminal law be most effectively deployed, through the dramaturgical choices of prosecutors and judges, to foster national soul-searching of this sort—to stimulate the deliberative criticism of a society's political culture and institutions by its members? In this regard, a major obstacle to this national self-examination is not only the complex psychology of repression and "denial," but simply the number of culpable individuals who remain alive—and fearful of the law's response.

Still, psychoanalytic studies of postwar Germans contend that societal self-analysis, however difficult to induce, is essential to restoring a nation's mental health and solidarity in the aftermath of administrative massacre. "A very considerable expenditure of psychic energy is needed to maintain the separation of acceptable and unacceptable memories," the Mitscherlichs argued.[29] Writing in the early 1970s, they contended:

> What censorship has excluded from German consciousness for nearly
> three decades as a memory too painful to bear may at any time return
> unbidden from the past; it has not been "mastered"; it does not belong to
> a past that has been grappled with and understood. The work of
> mourning can be accomplished only when one knows what one has to
> sever oneself from.... And, without [a meaningful relation to the past],
> the old ideals, which in National Socialism led to the fatal turn taken by
> German history, will continue to operate within the unconscious.[30]

This problem—the "unmastered past"—is faced not only by those who led the nation into disaster, but by those who followed them as well.

---

29 Alexander Mitscherlich & Margarete Mitscherlich, *The Inability to Mourn* 16 (Beverley R. Placzek trans., 1975). One should acknowledge, moreover, that not only perpetrators and bystanders, but even the surviving victims of state-sponsored brutality often wish to forget their most horrific experiences. This suggests that the mechanisms inducing such "forgetting" may operate independently of any "bad faith" on the individual's part. Aharon Appelfeld, *Beyond Despair* 50-54, 72-74 (1995) (describing the author's efforts to hold off traumatic wartime memory by immersing himself in frenetic activity for several years upon leaving Europe).

30 Mitscherlich & Mitscherlich, *supra* note 29, at 66.

If Germans had to live with the unvarnished memory of their Nazi past—even if their personal share in that past was merely in being obedient, fatalistic, or enthusiastically passive—their ego could not easily integrate it with their present way of life. Insistence upon historical accuracy in tackling that area of Germany's past would very quickly reveal that the murder of millions of helpless people depended on innumerable guilty decisions and actions on the part of individuals, and that the blame can by no means be shifted onto superiors ... with such self-evident ease as we Germans at present assume.[31]

Even the *children* of such obedient servants often suffer from their parents' repression of memory, on some accounts.[32] If there is any truth to such analysis, it would follow that thorough self-scrutiny would be especially desirable, for both the individuals involved and for society at large, in the aftermath of administrative massacre. If criminal prosecutions could be tailored to foster that end, so much the better. They would do so by forcing unpleasant subjects onto the agenda of discussion and offering compelling narrative accounts of shared experience.[33]

Theorists of widely variant persuasions distinguish Western modernity from other cultures precisely on the basis of our willingness continuously to attack and revise our intellectual foundations, to question even those commitments seemingly "constitutive" of our collective identities.[34] The capacity for critical self-scrutiny of the most

---

31   *Id.* at 20-21.

32   Jillian Becker, *Hitler's Children* 15 (1989); Anton Kaes, *From Hitler to Heimat* 24 (1989). Kocka offers a more cautious statement of possible relationships: "Without understanding these deficits [that is, parental repression and avoidance of their collaboration] we cannot understand the acuteness of the protest movements of the late 1960s and early 1970s." Jürgen Kocka, "Hitler Should Not Be Repressed By Stalin and Pol Pot: On the Attempts of German Historians to Relativize the Enormity of the Nazi Crimes," in *Forever in the Shadow of Hitler?* 85, 86 (James Knowlton & Truett Cates trans., 1993).

33   Those who commented on the Nuremberg trial at the time sometimes acknowledged this possibility. Robert L. Birmingham, "Note, The War Crimes Trial: A Second Look," 24 *U. Pitt. L. Rev.* 132, 137 (1962) (noting that "psychologically healthy expression of grief and anger may be obtained through a judicial proceeding such as the Nuremberg trials").

34   The view that certain attachments, as to one's ethnoreligious group, are constitutive of the self, and hence ineliminable for purposes of moral reflection, is a central tenet of all nontrivial versions of communitarianism. For opposing views of the self and cultural

thorough sort, to admit that "we were wrong," then, is not altogether foreign to us. In fact, it is clearly a source of pride and self-confidence in those invoking this cultural capacity to distinguish the West from the rest. To tell a *liberal* story about the history of a society that has inflicted large-scale administrative massacre is necessarily to tell a story of rupture and remaking, a story about its efforts to break with what is most reprehensible in its past.

To break with the past—assuming responsibility for its wrongs and a duty to remember them—requires a choice, an exercise of moral autonomy. For communitarians of both left and right, however, such choice is impossible or undesirable. We are necessarily "thrown into" a social world that provides us with constitutive and irrevocable identities, in ways to which the liberal ideal of autonomy is simply deaf. This, if you will, is the alternative hypothesis, against which the comparative history of legal efforts at collective reconstitution must be assessed.

Useful Myths, Discomforting Truths

Those seeking to construct a liberal mythology for their society necessarily labor under a special burden: *their* myth must be truthful, not merely pleasant. There is disagreement over whether, to be truthful, such a story must "correspond" to known facts of political history, or merely "cohere" with other authoritative narratives.[35] In either event, however, truthful stories about the origins of most nation-states cannot be entirely flattering, and so are unlikely to be solidarity-enhancing. It

---

identity in Western society (as infinitely revisable), see, for example, Allan Bloom, *The Closing of the American Mind* 36-39 (1987) (observing that the first thing one learns about non-Western cultures, upon any serious study of them, is their virtually uniform hostility to civilizations other than their own, that is, their ethnocentrism, and their view of their culture's foundational premises as sacred and immune from serious criticism). According to Derrida, postmodernism reflects the West's abandonment of its self-understanding as occupying the center of the world, a self-understanding common among other civilizations. Jacques Derrida, *Margins of Philosophy* 209-19 (Alan Bass trans., 1982); Robert Young, *White Mythologies: Writing History and the West* 19-20 (1990) (parsing Derrida on this point).

35 On the difference between correspondence and coherence in theories of truth, see Alan R. White, *Truth* 102- 21 (1970).

is tempting to say, as leading postmodernists do, that we should therefore "forget" the past, recreate ourselves *ab initio*, periodically refound the republic from scratch.

But simply ignoring discomforting truths about our past will not be useful to liberalism, even if usefulness is to be our guiding star. A national story that left out key facts concerning the enormous harm that the nation had done to others would not encourage the kind of moral self-scrutiny (in light of liberal principles of respect for persons) that is most needed, especially in the aftermath of administrative massacre. Hence we liberals cannot disregard historical injustices our ancestors have perpetrated when using the law to construct mythic narratives encouraging people to take responsibility for their acts. We would betray our principles in the very process of seeking to establish them.

For communitarians, by contrast, things are much easier. The societal value of stories does not turn on their truth; what matters is the significance that such stories have for their tellers and listeners, the meanings derived from these stories for collective identity and direction. In a certain sense, such stories *are* true: they are true as part of the self-definition of the community.[36]

A liberal will thus be troubled by the following story in a way that a communitarian will not. France's state television refused for a decade to show Marcel Ophüls' *The Sorrow and the Pity*, documenting extensive French collaboration in Jewish deportation.[37] When it was finally shown, it was denounced by a prominent senator, himself an ex-member of the Resistance, as "'destroying myths of which the French still have need.'"[38] A philosopher adds, "'what you must understand is that our myths were positive. They enabled France to recoup and rebuild.'"[39]

Such statements—judging myths by their political usefulness, regardless of their truth—necessarily give pause to good liberals. They

---

36 Allan Megill, "Memory, Identity, and Questions of Evidence" 11 (June 23, 1995) (paper presented at the Project on Rhetoric of Inquiry Symposium, University of Iowa). See also Steven Knapp, "Collective Memory and the Actual Past," *Representations* no. 26, 123 (Spring 1989).

37 Marcel Ophüls, *The Sorrow and the Pity* (Mireille Johnston trans., 1972).

38 R.J.B. Bosworth, *Explaining Auschwitz and Hiroshima: History Writing and the Second World War, 1945-1990* 111 (1993).

39 Miller, *supra* note 17, at 141 (quoting Alain Finkielkraut).

reawaken our doubts about the very idea of national mythmaking in a liberal society. They suggest that to be effective for social solidarity, a national myth must necessarily exclude the story of wrongs the nation has done to others. They suggest that a solidarity-enhancing story cannot be about how the nation has acknowledged these wrongs, redressed them, and kept memory of both the wrongs and their redress firmly in its collective consciousness.

If this kind of collective memory is impossible to achieve, practically speaking, then liberalism had best return to its initial Cartesian, hard-core Enlightenment position: that there is no place for national mythology in a truly liberal society, that the notion of liberal memory is an oxymoron. What should hold us together is simply economic interdependence and shared commitment to abstract principles of liberal morality, however imperfectly these have been embodied in our history.

Hence our characteristic ambivalence, our "underlying uneasiness," as Kammen puts it:

> On one hand there is the proof-seeking and critical view of myth as inaccurate or even distorted history. On the other there is an approving notion of socially cohesive legends or stories rich in symbolic meaning, comprised of incidents and characters who are larger than life, regardless of whether they are heroes or villains.[40]

To help effect a needed break with the past, the law can be employed in very different ways. At times, a constitutional convention is an especially fitting device toward this end. At other times, nothing so radical is required. It is simply necessary to take seriously the "law on the books"—particularly the criminal code—as never before: holding former chiefs of state to long-valid legal rules that they flouted indiscriminately, with confidence of impunity.

In asking whether law can help to place guilt and repentance at the center of collective memory, postwar Germany and Japan provide the major tests. Each offers conclusions somewhat at odds with the other. This difference could be summarized by saying that, although the territory of both nations was occupied by the victors, the national mind

---

40   Michael Kammen, *Mystic Chords of Memory* 481 (1991).

was successfully 'occupied' much more in the Federal Republic than in Japan.[41]

In Japan, the U.S. bombing of Hiroshima is commemorated, by several much-visited shrines, as a war crime of unprecedented proportions.   It has had an enormous impact on Japanese self-understanding, by all accounts.   Because of the centrality of Hiroshima to Japanese memory of the period, it has become "virtually impossible," notes one Asia scholar, "to recall that Japan had been waging a war of aggression prior to Hiroshima and Nagasaki."[42]   In contrast, the impact on national memory of the Yamashita and Tokyo War Crimes Trials—widely broadcast to the population—has been virtually nil,[43] until very recently.   Leading Liberal Democratic politicians still continue publicly to deny Japanese culpability for the "Rape of Nanjing" and for Japan's many other atrocities against prisoners of war and noncombatants throughout Asia.[44] The remains of

---

41   This slightly oversimplifies the matter, since serious reassessment by Germans of their nation's wartime misconduct began only some 17 years after the War, that is, with the trials of the Auschwitz guards. Still, it is fair to say, with one recent historian, that "the paradigm shift ... occurring in all the other combatant societies, has never happened in Japan." Bosworth, *supra* note 38, at 186.

42   Norma Field, *In the Realm of a Dying Emperor* 45 (1991).

43   See, e.g., Ian Buruma, *The Wages of Guilt: Memories of War in Germany and Japan* 60-66, 161-66 (1994) (noting the frequent derisory references by contemporary Japanese to "the Tokyo Trial View of History," and that "the trial left them with an attitude of cynicism and resentment"); *The Tokyo War Crimes Trial: An International Symposium* 1948 (C. Hosoya et al. eds., 1986) 194 (noting that "the legal consciousness of the Tokyo trial has not taken root among the Japanese people"); see also Onuma Yasuaki, "Beyond Victors' Justice," 11 *Japan Echo* 63, 71 (1984) (observing that the majority of the Japanese people regarded the Tokyo trial "as an event completely divorced from their own lives"). On the ignorance still prevalent among Japanese youth concerning the country's war crimes, see Gluck, *supra* note 24, at 90 (noting that since young people had received "such minimal instruction in the subject ... they could not be accused of forgetting what they had never been adequately taught"); A. Minhee Lee, "War and Memory," *N.Y. Times*, Mar. 2, 1995, at A22 (observing that "young Japanese ... have little or no idea of the aggression and cruelty that was manifested in the generations before them").

44   On the systematic nature of battlefield atrocities by Japanese troops, see Meirion Harries & Susie Harries, *Soldiers of the Sun* 475-84 (1991). On recent denials of such events by political leaders, see Buruma, *supra* note 43, at 122; James Sterngold, "At Tokyo Shrine to War Dead, a Ritual Persists Despite All," *N.Y. Times*, Aug. 16, 1994, at A8; James Sterngold, "Japan Official Forced to Quit over Remark," *N.Y. Times*, Aug. 15, 1994, at A5. On continuing denials by Japanese law professors, see the remarks of Takigawa Seijiro, one of the defense counsel at the Tokyo trial, in Hosoya, *supra* note

defendants convicted of (and executed for) war crimes at the Токуо trial are housed in official shrines.[45]

Why did the numerous postwar trials of Japan's military leaders for war crimes[46] have so little effect on collective memory of the war and atrocities these leaders authorized? There are several possibilities. First, it might be said that the Japanese, however extensive their war crimes, had not perpetrated anything like the Holocaust, that is, had not sought or accomplished the extermination of an entire ethnoreligious group of their own citizens. On this view, they simply had much less to repent or remember.

Perhaps, but there was still plenty to atone for, had the full record been placed before the Tokyo court. It was not. Much of the most egregious Japanese misconduct, such as biological warfare,[47] vivisection of POWs,[48] and the sexual enslavement of the comfort women,[49] was deliberately excluded from the story the prosecution was allowed to tell.[50] Had the legal narrative encompassed this much wider range of war crimes, and been staged to maximize sympathy for its victims (such as the comfort women, whose marital prospects after the War became

---

43, at 58.

45   Gavan Daws, *Prisoners of the Japanese: POWs of World War II in the Pacific* 375 (1994).

46   The most comprehensive description of these proceedings is offered by Philip R. Piccigallo, *The Japanese on Trial: Allied War Crimes Operations in the East, 1945-1951,* at 39 (1979).

47   Yuki Tanaka, *Hidden Horrors: Japanese War Crimes in World War II* 135-66 (1996); Sheldon H. Harris, *Factories of Death: Japanese Biological Warfare 1932-45 and the American Cover-Up* (1994); Peter Williams & David Wallace, *Unit 731: Japan's Secret Biological Warfare in World War II* (1989).

48   Daws, *supra* note 45, at 360 (concluding that by war's end more than one-quarter of the original 140,000 white Allied prisoners in Japanese custody were dead); Nicholas D. Kristof, "Japan Confronting Gruesome War Atrocity," *N.Y. Times,* Mar. 17, 1995, at A1 (describing medical experimentation by Japanese army physicians on prisoners, involving deliberate exposure to plague, anthrax, and vivisection).

49   Between 100,000 and 200,000 women were involved. Hicks, *supra* note 27, at 19. On their recent damage claims, still pending, against the Japanese state, see Yvonne P. Hsu, '"Comfort Women" from Korea: Japan's World War II Sex Slaves and the Legitimacy of Their Claims for Reparations,' 2 *Pac. Rim L. & Pol'y J.* 97 (1993); Karen Parker & Jennifer F. Chew, "Compensation for Japan's World War II War-Rape Victims," 17 *Hastings Int'l & Comp. L. Rev.* 497 (1994); Janet L. Tongsuthi, '"Comfort Women" of World War II,' 4 *UCLA Women's L.J.* 413 (1994).

50   B.V.A. Röling, *The Tokyo Trial and Beyond* 48 (Antonio Cassese ed., 1993).

nil), the impact on Japanese opinion might have been greater. It might even have resembled that of the Auschwitz trials.

We should not be too quick to attribute Japan's failings, for this reason among others, to any cultural predisposition toward "shame" over "guilt," as some have done.[51] A more thoughtful orchestration of the Tokyo trial could well have elicited a more sympathetic response. To be sure, the Japanese public remains largely unpersuaded by the conviction of its leaders for "waging aggressive war" against the Western Allies.

But the public has grown highly sympathetic to the plight suffered by the fellow Asians whom their leaders colonized, brutalized, impressed (into involuntary military service), and enslaved.[52] Had the Tokyo trial focused not on Japanese wrongs inflicted on those who dropped atom bombs on Hiroshima and Nagasaki, but rather on the industrial rape of the Asian comfort women, or on the human vivisection of Filipino POWs, the trial's impact on Japanese memory would likely have been quite different.

The Allied decision to exclude Emperor Hirohito from prosecution was a particularly significant dramaturgical decision in this regard. This significance has become apparent only following his recent death. Indeed, the decision unwittingly impeded the sort of searching self-examination of national morality and identity that war crimes trials successfully induced in West Germany. The "Tokyo Trial View of History," as progressive Japanese intellectuals derisively label it, became widely accepted by the Japanese populace. This is because the historical narrative promoted by the trial pinned the blame for the country's misconduct exclusively on the recklessness of its military leaders—not on the people themselves or the Emperor they revered.[53]

---

51   Buruma invokes this familiar distinction in connection with Japan after the war. Buruma, *supra* note 43, at 116.

52   An opinion survey in 1994 suggested, for instance, that nearly three quarters of the Japanese population felt that their government had not adequately compensated the Asian peoples subjugated by Japan's prewar and wartime empire. Nicholas D. Kristof, "Many in Japan Oppose Apology to Asians for War," *N.Y. Times,* Mar. 6, 1995, at A9.

53   This view was immediately embraced by postwar textbooks in Japanese public schools. Carol Gluck, "The Idea of Shōwa," in *Shōwa: The Japan of Hirohito* 1, 13 (Carol Gluck & Stephen R. Graubard eds., 1992); see also Saburō Ienaga, *Japan's Last War: World War II and the Japanese, 1931-1945,* at 250 (1979) (noting that books published soon after the war are "full of pacifist sentiment and disdain for militarism").

An historian observes:

> If the villains were clear, so were the victims: not the victims of
> Japanese aggression but the Japanese people themselves, who, it was
> said, "were embroiled" in the war by their leaders ....
>   Th[is] stance was confirmed by both the popular past, in which the
> people appeared as helpless before the state, and by personal memory,
> which viscerally recalled helplessness and suffering. Thus, the stark
> narrative of culpability produced by the "War Crimes Trial view of
> history" in the immediate aftermath of war survived the nearly
> half-century since.[54]

She adds, "had things truly been that simple, and inevitable, the
burdens of Shōwa history would be light indeed."[55] The trial's favored
narrative "had disadvantages since it froze the condemnation of the war
into orthodoxy at a stage when the division of villains and victims
seemed starkly clear."[56] In consequence, "the Japanese remember the
war, not the system that engendered it,"[57] nor their participation in that
system. At the epicenter of that system was the Emperor.

Because the Emperor was worshipped as divine, to hold him
responsible for war crimes would have been to allow mere
humans—foreigners at that—to treat him as if he were a politician like
any other. This would have been to deny his divinity and the
infallibility that it entailed.[58] When the person is not fully distinguished

---

54 Gluck, *supra* note 24, at 83; see also Buruma, *supra* note 43, at 31 (arguing that
MacArthur's decision not to prosecute Hirohito "had serious consequences, for so long
as the Emperor, in whose name the war had been waged, could not be held accountable,
the question of war guilt would remain fuzzy in Japan, and a source of friction between
Japan and its former enemies").

55 Gluck, *supra* note 53, at 12. "Shōwa" refers to the period of Hirohito's rule. Gluck
notes that recent Japanese historiography suggests that:
> The responsibility for war lies far more broadly in society than was earlier
> believed, or hoped .... Vast numbers of ordinary people were entwined in the
> complex mesh of war .... Even those who did not actively march or collaborate
> are now judged as participants. It takes both states and societies—which is to say
> the individuals who comprise them—to make a total war. *Id.* at 13.

56 *Id.* at 12-13 (noting that this narrative "contributed to the emphasis on what the
Japanese people suffered at the hands of the villains in the docket").

57 *Id.* at 13.

58 Kyoko Inoue, *MacArthur's Japanese Constitution: A Linguistic and Cultural
Study of Its Making* 220 (1991); Kosuke Koyama, "Forgiveness and Politics: Japanese

from his "office,"[59] to judge the conduct of the present occupant is necessarily to judge the institution itself. It would also have been to hold responsible the people who worshipped him for failing to question his political judgment when it proved profoundly misguided.[60]

To criticize him was thus to criticize them, that is, their "constitutive," foundational beliefs, and to require profound self-criticism at the level of national identity. That was unlikely to succeed, according to Occupation authorities, particularly MacArthur.[61] In fact, it was likely to provoke mass resistance to the Occupation and its other, less controversial policies.[62]

In any event, the Book of Military Rules informed Japanese soldiers that "'the command you receive from your superior officer is the command you receive from the emperor himself.'"[63] Hence, if it was wrong for soldiers to obey their orders, then it was wrong for the Emperor—by way of his servants—to have issued them. But that conclusion was literally inconceivable, since there was, in principle, no independent standard from which to evaluate the defensibility of the Emperor's conduct.[64] The people supported the "Emperor system," and

---

Experience," in *Bread and Breath* 139, 145-46 (T.K. John ed., 1991).

59 Max Weber, *The Theory of Social and Economic Organization* 330 (A.M. Henderson & Talcott Parsons trans., 1947) (discussing the centrality of this distinction to modern, legal-rational authority).

60 This was what General Douglas MacArthur had in mind when, in contemplating alternative postwar fates for Hirohito, he declared that, "the problem basically is theological." Koyama, *supra* note 58, at 143.

61 On the internal policy debates in this regard, see Robert E. Ward, "Presurrender Planning: Treatment of the Emperor and Constitutional Changes," in *Democratizing Japan: The Allied Occupation* 1, 3-18 (Robert E. Ward & Sakamoto Yoshikazu eds., 1987).

62 *Id.* at 15.

63 Koyama, *supra* note 58, at 158. The insistence on blind, unqualified obedience to superior orders was in fact a recent corruption of the traditional military ethic of Bushido. See Tanaka, *Hidden Horrors, supra* note 47, at 206-11.

64 The most influential study of imperial ideology observes that:
[The Emperor] ... is the centre of all authority and the fountainhead of all virtue, occupying the apical position in a hierarchy... In such a scheme, where everything is based on the idea of an absolute central entity, there is no room for a concept like international law, which is equally binding on all nations.
Masao Maruyama, *Thought and Behavior in Modern Japanese Politics* 19, 20-21 (Ivan Morris ed., 1963). Maruyama also notes that "what determined the everyday morality of Japan's rulers was neither an abstract consciousness of legality nor an internal sense

the Emperor supported (what international law would later categorize as) a war of aggression, involving many war crimes by imperial servants.

"Because Japanese war criminals, whether major or minor, admitted no higher moral authority than the emperor, they seldom if ever expressed guilt in what they had done," writes an historian of postwar Japan. "And certainly in the eyes of Japanese domestic law, no stigma ever attached to their being convicted,"[65] for several Class A convicts promptly reassumed high public office. Japan's famous "system of irresponsibility," reaching downward from the Emperor into every layer of the political system and society at large, remained very much alive throughout the postwar period, on this view.

In sum, to exclude the Emperor from criminal liability was also implicitly to exclude the Japanese people at large from moral responsibility. The precise connection was by no means clear in the minds of Occupation decision-makers or prosecutors, to be sure.[66] Shriver states it succinctly: "A political culture that has long been accustomed to accord unimpeachable and exclusive authority to an Emperor will not generate among citizens much conversation over questions like: 'Is it right or wrong? Who is responsible? What shall we do to change the course of the nation?'"[67]

---

of right and wrong, nor again any concept of serving the public; it was a feeling of being close to the concrete entity known as the Emperor." *Id.* at 13.

65 Herbert P. Bix, 'The Shōwa Emperor's "Monologue" and the Problem of War Responsibility," 18 *Journal of Japanese Studies* 295, 361 (1992).

66 Inoue, *supra* note 58, at 160-220 (discussing how American lawyers and constitutional reformers misunderstood the Emperor's role within the Japanese political system and his centrality to its legitimacy among the public).

67 Shriver, *supra* note 19, at 135-36. Shriver is well aware that any such summary statement inevitably oversimplifies a complex range of differences between cultures. Therefore, he quickly adds, "these questions are rare enough in the conversational culture of the West, and they can virtually disappear in wartime. But they do have roots in Western angles of vision." *Id.* at 136; see also Buruma, *supra* note 43, at 116-17, 294-97 (favoring a religious and cultural explanation of prevailing Japanese attitudes). On the far-reaching ramifications of differences between Japanese and American conceptions of moral responsibility, see generally V. Lee Hamilton & Joseph Sanders, *Everyday Justice: Responsibility and the Individual in Japan and the United States* (1992).

Such culturalist accounts, however, cannot explain the unresponsiveness of Japanese courts to meritorious legal arguments, that is, to the valid legal claims of plaintiffs who have overcome whatever cultural burdens they labored under before

But there is no need to appeal here to the abstraction of political culture.   More concretely, the Allied decision to protect Hirohito "impeded the awakening of the Japanese people's own historical consciousness," as one historian recently noted.   "Many would find it difficult to believe that they had been accomplices in aggression and murder on a near-genocidal scale when the emperor whom they had served so loyally never had to bear any responsibility for his own speech and actions."[68]

Legal stratagems were deployed, quite self-consciously, with a view to teaching the lesson that most Japanese "need not concern themselves with the recent past."[69]   Hence conservatives in the Diet enacted legislation declaring that "War responsibility should not extend to ordinary people who, after the declaration of war, dedicated themselves to duty in a lawful manner in order to conduct the war, obediently following the orders of the state."[70]

The responsibility of the Japanese people could not be seriously examined until it was possible candidly to examine that of their Emperor.   That was judged politically imprudent in the extreme.   His symbolic centrality to the political system was longstanding and continuing.   Examination of Hirohito's wartime role thus did not become possible until his death.

Proustian Justice: The Trial As Aide-Mémoire

Beginning at the Emperor's death, however, a veritable floodgate of personal memory and public discussion has opened in ways that few

---

recognizing and asserting their rights. J. Mark Ramseyer & Frances M. Rosenbluth, *Japan's Political Marketplace* 2-3, 161-66 (1993) (arguing that it is not national culture, but executive and legislative control over the judiciary, which explains the latter's unresponsiveness to legal claims by unpopular minorities).

68   Bix, *supra* note 65, at 330.

69   *Id.*

70   *Id.,* at 330, quoting from *Kanpo gogai*, Dec. 2, 1945, p. 435. Bix concludes, 'Having adopted a "memory strategy" for explaining the past which put all the blame on a few, the governing elites would be conscious of the war responsibility hereafter mainly as a problem to be evaded rather than seriously grappled with.' *Id.* at 312.

had anticipated.[71] A robust discussion of the country's war guilt has now definitely begun, and the courts quickly became a favored forum toward that end. Civil courts, not the criminal law, have provided the primary vehicle to date. They have succeeded, at least, in stimulating precisely the kind of discursive deliberation and civil disagreement here proposed as the necessary foundation of liberal memory and solidarity.

Japanese historians have repeatedly sued their government, for instance, to compel more forthright treatment of the country's war crimes in its school textbooks. Even when their efforts have failed to gain judicial endorsement,[72] they have succeeded in eliciting media coverage, and in putting this uncomfortable issue at least peripherally on the public agenda.[73] The damage claims recently brought by comfort

---

71   Carol Gluck, "Foreword" to Daikichi Irokawa, *The Age of Hirohito* vii, vii (Mikiso Hane & John K. Urda trans., 1995) (noting of the robust public debate following the Emperor's death that "it was as if a dam had broken on thoughts long held but seldom spoken"); see also Kristof, *supra* note 48, at A1, A12 (noting that "half a century after the end of the war, a rush of books, documentaries and exhibitions are unlocking the past and helping arouse interest in Japan in the atrocities committed by some of Japan's most distinguished doctors" including those who became president of the Japanese Medical Association, head of the Japan Olympic Committee, and the Governor of Tokyo).

On recent revelations and public responses, see Shriver, *supra* note 19, at 136-39 (noting the prominent role of the Socialist Party, including its first Prime Minister, and Christian leaders in raising the possibility of an official apology and putting this question on the parliamentary agenda); Gluck, *supra* note 24, at 90 ("The issue of Hirohito's war responsibility occasioned open debate, and polls and letters made it clear that significant numbers of Japanese agreed that the emperor bore some responsibility for the war, although they had seldom before said so in public."); *id.* at 77 ("The standard of acceptable public utterance of personal memories altered, as it seemed to become possible to say things aloud that one had privately felt for years.").

Recent Japanese scholarship supports the conclusion that Hirohito's role in war-related decisions was considerable. Irokawa, *supra* note 71, at xv (concluding that "the emperor [was] the person most responsible for the war") and generally Bix, *supra* note 65.

72   On the mixed results of this litigation, see Lawrence W. Beer, *Freedom of Expression in Japan* 264-70 (1984). In the last two years, in response to complaints by Japan's Asian neighbors, several new textbooks have nonetheless been introduced offering more accurate accounts of Japan's war crimes and the litigation by victims to which such conduct has recently given rise. "Japanese Textbooks Carry War Damage Compensation Issues," *Japan Econ. Newswire,* May 13, 1994, available in LEXIS, News Library, JEN File (quoting one author as saying that he was surprised the Education Ministry did not ask him to cut or rewrite several sections dealing with compensation demands from war victims).

73   Beer, *supra* note 72, at 273 (observing "the increasingly uninhibited media presentation of opposite viewpoints in films and TV programs" resulting from the

women, forced to serve as prostitutes for Japanese soldiers at the front, enjoy enormous public support within Japan.[74] In June 1995, the lower house of Parliament finally approved a resolution of "remorse" for Japanese conduct in World War II.[75]

In other litigation reaching the Japanese Supreme Court, the widow of a postwar military officer sought to prevent the inclusion of her husband's name on a Shinto shrine honoring the country's war dead.[76] The plaintiff, Mrs. Nakaya Yasuko, belongs to a Christian denomination whose leadership had recently acknowledged the church's responsibilities for supporting the War.[77] This public acknowledgment prompted Mrs. Nakaya to object to the "deification" of her husband in a shrine praising the conduct of Japan's wartime soldiers.[78] The trial and first appellate courts accepted her contention that the shrine, construction of which was publicly funded, violated the establishment clause of Japan's Constitution, which mandates the separation of church and state.[79]

In public discussions, Mrs. Nakaya explained that she did not wish to see future mothers and wives deceived by the state into supporting participation by their loved ones in aggressive wars and war crimes.[80]

---

textbook controversies); Saburō Ienaga, "The Glorification of War in Japanese Education," 18 *Int'l Security* 113, 115 (1994) (noting that this litigation "has served as a focal point for a continuing debate over Japan's role in the war ... and the willingness of its government and its people to examine that role and that conduct").

74   A 1994 opinion survey found that by a 4 to 1 margin Japanese voters believe that their government "has not adequately compensated the people of countries Japan invaded or colonized." Kristof, *supra* note 52, at A9. However, some 5 million signatures were gathered for a petition opposing a parliamentary resolution of apology. *Id.*

75   The resolution's language was highly qualified, however, and cannot be considered a genuine "apology" in the Western sense, according to language specialists. Nicholas D. Kristof, "Why a Nation of Apologizers Makes One Large Exception," *N.Y. Times*, June 12, 1995, at A1, A4. Moreover, only 230 members in the 511-member chamber voted for the resolution; the rest boycotted or voted against. *Id.* at A1.

76   Judgment of June 1, 1988, Saikosai [Supreme Court], 42 Minshu 277 (Japan).

77   Field, *supra* note 42, at 121-22.

78   *Id.* at 121-24.

79   Japan's Supreme Court ultimately rejected this view on the grounds that the Veterans' Associations, not the state itself, had established the shrine, and that Mrs. Nakaya suffered no "coercion" as a result of inclusion of her husband's name. *Id.* at 141.

80   *Id.* at 124.

With considerable media attention trained upon them, the courts became the forum in which a struggle was waged for control of memory, that is, over the use of Mr. Nakaya's memory in service of conflicting accounts of the country's conduct during the Pacific war.

In a second trial, also widely publicized, an Okinawan businessman was prosecuted for desecrating the Japanese flag.[81] He was protesting the government's recent insistence that the flag be raised at every public occasion.[82] Okinawans had refrained from so doing for many years following the war, not wishing to identify with a state whose army had been responsible (in the battle of Okinawa) for the murder of hundreds of civilian noncombatants.[83] The state's prosecution of Chibana Shōichi, particularly Shōichi's eloquent defense of his views and act, elicited an unprecedented public debate in Okinawa, where the atrocities during that final retreat (before advancing American troops) had remained unacknowledged.[84] Collective memory of these events has, in consequence of this legal proceeding, been significantly revised.

The Mayor of Nagasaki, Motoshima Hitoshi, finally broke the taboo on public discussion of the Emperor's responsibilities for the War.[85] In response, he was attacked and nearly killed by far-right gangs.[86] But his pronouncement also elicited enormous public sympathy, expressed in many letters endorsing his remarks and praising his courage.[87] A group of citizens formed an organization to support him. They declared:

---

81 *Id.* at 44-45.

82 *Id.* at 52-53.

83 *Id.* at 53-56. Gluck notes:
    Public memory in postwar Okinawa was vigorous and vivid, and the tales it told ... constructed a history with a different political meaning [than on the main Islands]. Subjugated by the Satsuma domain during Tokugawa, Okinawa's ... people were ... made victims twice over, once of the Japanese imperial army, who massacred the allegedly inferior Okinawans as spies, and once of the fighting in one of the bloodiest battles of the Pacific War.
    Gluck, *supra* note 24, at 88. This battle occurred after the inevitability of defeat had become apparent, and some Okinawan civilians wished to surrender. Field, *supra* note 42, at 56-58.

84 Field, *supra* note 42, at 53-66.

85 *Id.* at 178-79.

86 *Id.* at 179-93.

87 *Id.* at 200-20.

As citizens of a nation that imposed immeasurable terror and misery upon the people of Asia in the last war, we believe, in order to gain the trust of the people of the world in international society, that we must reflect with humility on our history of aggression and promote free and wide-ranging debate on the emperor system and the emperor's responsibility for the war. This is because a democratic society must not tolerate taboos of any kind.[88]

In addition to accepting national responsibility for wartime misconduct, this formulation squarely casts the issue in terms of the centrality of open discussion of controversial views (that is, civil dissensus) within a liberal democratic society. Here, the Mayor's supporters invoked the law—constitutional freedom of expression—not to impose their own favored account of collective memory (nor to oppose that of others), but to open up a public sphere for less constrained debate about what such memory should involve. The declaration also accepts the need for placing a recognition of wartime guilt and repentance at the center of collective memory, if not quite at the center of national identity.

Even more than these recent Japanese developments, the postwar German experience belies the pessimism voiced by so many theorists, quoted above, about the capacity to make repentance from a society's historical wrongs the basis of its shared memory.[89] On the fortieth anniversary of World War II's termination, for instance, Federal President Richard von Weizsäcker explicitly affirmed, in a well-received speech, "the Germans' need to continue the discussion of individual moral guilt and to accept history as the basis of national identity and lasting German responsibility."[90]

Opinion surveys suggest that initial German response to the trials

---

88   *Id.* at 233-34 (citation omitted).

89   See *supra* notes 20-22.

90   Lutz R. Reuter, "Political and Moral Culture in West Germany," in *Coping with the Past: Germany and Austria After 1945,* at 155, 179 (Kathy Harms et al. eds., 1990) (citing Federal President Richard von Weizsäcker, Speech Given on the 40th Anniversary of WWII and the Nazi Tyranny (Bonn, May 8, 1985)).

of major war criminals was quite positive[91] and that interest was high,[92] although both declined over time.[93] The surveys also suggest that only from the Nuremberg trial did a substantial majority of Germans learn about the existence of death camps.[94] Nearly a quarter of Germans became aware of the extermination of the Jews in this way.[95] Yet only when the first postwar generation reached adulthood in the mid-1960s was the Holocaust reexamined and discussed in great depth.

Law's Role in "Mastering the Past"

The law played a significant role in the process of "mastering the past." The 1964 prosecution of the Auschwitz guards, and of similar Majdanek officials between 1975 and 1981 for crimes against humanity, captured the imagination of millions of young Germans as virtually nothing about the country's past had done before.[96] "The effect upon the public consciousness was devastating," writes Gordon Craig, "and has not diminished."[97] The Auschwitz prosecution, concurs Ian

91   *Public Opinion in Semisovereign Germany: The HICOG Surveys, 1949-1955*, at 10 (Anna J. Merritt & Richard L. Merritt eds., 1980).

92   *Public Opinion in Occupied Germany: The OMGUS Surveys, 1945-1949*, at 35 (Anna J. Merritt & Richard L. Merritt eds., 1970) (reporting that nearly 80% of German respondents in the American zone indicated that they had read newspaper articles about the trial).

93   Thomas A. Schwartz, *America's Germany: John J. McCloy and the Federal Republic of Germany* 159 (1991); Claudia Koonz, "Between Memory and Oblivion: Concentration Camps in German Memory," in *Commemorations* 258, 262 (John R. Gillis ed., 1994).

94   Koonz, *supra* note 93, at 262.

95   *Id.*

96   Hannah Arendt, "Introduction" to Bernd Naumann, *Auschwitz: A Report on the Proceedings Against Robert Ludwig Mulka and Others Before the Court at Frankfurt* xi, xi (1966); Aleksander Lasik, "Postwar Prosecution of the Auschwitz SS," in *Anatomy of the Auschwitz Death Camp* 588 (Yisrael Gutman & Michael Berenbaum eds., 1994).

97   Gordon Craig, "An Inability to Mourn," *N.Y. Rev. Books*, July 14, 1994, at 43, 44 (reviewing Buruma, *supra* note 43). On the considerable attention given by the German mass media to the 50th anniversary of the Allied liberation of Auschwitz, see Stephen Kinzer, "Confronting the Past, Germans Now Don't Flinch," *N.Y. Times*, May 1, 1995, at A1, A10; Stephen Kinzer, "Germans Reflect on Meaning of Auschwitz," *N.Y. Times*, Jan. 28, 1995, at L5.

Buruma, "was the one history lesson ... that stuck."[98] The foreign attention focused on these trials was no less consequential, for they prompted the 1964 French enactment removing the statute of limitations for crimes against humanity. That change that would permit the prosecution of Barbie and Touvier over two decades later.[99]

In German public awareness, these trials effected a symbolic severing of ties to the past.[100] They evoked and articulated pervasive sentiments of indignation and reprobation, in a way that criminal prosecutions can do with particular efficacy. Through this experience, writes one historian, "Germans constructed a new identity based on a fresh start [and] a clean break with the past.... They forged a new ... identity based on a rejection of Nazism."[101] The memory of judgment by the international community continues to weigh heavily upon the making of German foreign policy in particular, according to specialists in that field.[102]

---

98   Buruma, *supra* note 43, at 149. Traveling in mid-1991, Buruma observed, "[t]he German war was not only remembered on television, on the radio, in community halls, schools, and museums; it was actively worked on, labored, rehearsed. One sometimes got the impression ... that German memory was like a massive tongue seeking out, over and over, a sore tooth." *Id.* at 8.

One should also note the striking contrast between the German Bishops' recent and incredibly blunt recognition of Catholic responsibility for the Holocaust and the refusal of the Polish Bishops to sign the declaration. On the deficiencies of Polish memory in this regard, see Iwona Irwin-Zarecka, *Frames of Remembrance: The Dynamics of Collective Memory* 18, 37-38, 48, 77-78, 92-93, 120, 142-43 (1994).

99   Tony Judt, "The Past Is Another Country: Myth and Memory in Postwar Europe," *Daedalus,* 83, 97 (Fall 1992).

100   These trials became a means by which Germany's "present is to be separated from what preceded it by an act of unequivocal demarcation." Paul Connerton, *How Societies Remember* 7 (1989).

101   Koonz, *supra* note 93, at 262. Even those who think adoption of this new German identity has been a mistake widely concede that it has, in fact, become pervasively established. See, e.g., Christian Meier, "Condemning and Comprehending," in *Forever in the Shadow of Hitler?*, *supra* note 32, at 24, 24 (observing "an identity that has entered our self-comprehension and our imagination and that expresses itself in grief and shame").

102   Thomas Banchoff, "The Past in the Present: Historical Memory and German National Security Policy" (Sept. 2, 1995); Thomas Berger, "The Contemporary Power of Memory: The Dilemmas for German Foreign Policy" (Sept. 2, 1995); Andrei Markovitz and Simon Reich, "Historical Memory and the Sources of German Power" (Sept. 2, 1995) (papers presented at the American Political Science Association Conference).

The lesson would seem to be, *pace* Mary Douglas,[103] that a nation *can* be united and guided not only in the collective memory of its triumphs, but also in shared expiation for its wrongs, in the common commitment neither to forget nor repeat the injustices its predecessors have inflicted on their neighbors. Habermas offers a ringing defense of this conclusion, while alluding to legal concepts of continuity and judgment:

> Can one become the legal successor to the German Reich and continue the traditions of German culture without taking on historical liability for the form of life in which Auschwitz was possible? Is there any way to bear the liability for the context in which such crimes originated ... other than through remembrance, practiced in solidarity, of what cannot be made good, other than through a reflexive, scrutinizing attitude toward one's own identity-forming traditions?[104]

Such invocation of legal language as relevant to historical assessment drew particularly acerbic reproach from Habermas's opponents, who accused him, for instance, of "making himself solicitor general of the kingdom of morality in the province of history," and assigning historiographical matters to a "special court, to which the accused must be extradited."[105]

What Habermas describes as "a reflexive, scrutinizing attitude toward one's own identity-forming traditions" was embraced by President Alfonsín as a central objective of the junta trial and, in fact, of his administration. Attending the trial, Owen Fiss would thus herald it as "an exercise in self-examination," revealing "the nobility of a great nation, prepared to judge itself."[106] In Argentina public discourse often harkens back to grander days of national prosperity. Alfonsín chose instead to distance himself altogether from the country's past. He

---

103   Douglas, *supra* note 22.

104   Jürgen Habermas, "On the Public Use of History," in *The New Conservatism, supra* note 18, at 229, 236 (Shierry W. Nicholsen ed., trans., 1989).

105   Helmut Fleischer, "The Morality of History: On the Dispute About the Past That Will Not Pass," in *Forever in the Shadow of Hitler?*, *supra* note 32, at 80, 83.

106   Remarks of Owen Fiss. Tape of Human Rights and Deliberative Democracy: A Conference in Honor of Carlos Santiago Nino, Presented at Yale Law School (Sept. 23-24, 1994) (also describing the trial as "a people inquiring into what they had done to each other").

portrayed its earlier history not as a golden age and guidepost from which recent leaders had strayed. He depicted it rather as a tale of chronic failure, a story of continuing recrudescence of illiberal vices, displayed not only by elites but by significant segments of society at large: "intolerance of dissent," "inability to compromise," "violence as the preferred response to adversaries," "a conception of social order as requiring the suppression of all conflict," and "authoritarianism as the natural mode of interaction between leaders and led."[107]

This was a crucial component of the story that Alfonsín wanted the courts to tell. It was clearly reflected in the judgment against the juntas.[108]   In his most important public address, the President announced:

> In December 1983 we initiate for the first time an effort at democratization based on the recognition that the key to the past authoritarian regimes lay less in their intrinsic power, than in the possibilities they had of establishing themselves in a political culture generally inclined to accept such authoritarian regimes.
>
> For us, to defend and consolidate democracy means to fight not only against the objective anti-democratic forces, but also against the widespread subjective receptivity of many to such forces, a disposition that has provided the basis of their objective power ....A new stage in our history has begun.[109]

This address was rightly seen at the time as representing a sea change in the country's presidential discourse.[110] Its novelty consisted in its insistence that the source of Argentina's problems lay in its "political culture," as the President put it, rather than in the intervention of foreign states, the constraints of the international capitalist system, or the conspiracies of a corrupt national oligarchy.

Only a few would be prosecuted criminally, but virtually all should

---

107 *Alfonsín: Discursos Sobre el Discurso* 20-22 (Luis Aznar et al. eds., 1986) (translation by author).

108 "Argentina: National Appeals Court (Criminal Division) Judgment on Human Rights Violations By Former Military Leaders (Excerpts)," 26 *Int'l Legal Materials* 317, 327-28 (1987).

109 Alfonsín, *supra* note 107, at 22, 39 (translation by author).

110 See the several responses, later published as a book, along with the speech itself, in *Alfonsín: Discursos, supra* note 107.

accept moral responsibility for having permitted, and often encouraged, the defendants' seizures of power. It was no coincidence that the speech was drafted by Nino, the liberal legal theorist who had traveled widely and shared none of the prevailing nationalist enthusiasms of Argentina's intellectuals.[111]

The Evanescence of Guilty Memory

For several years, at least, it seemed that criminal prosecution in Argentina—its ethical evocations in the public mind—would play a major role in revising national identity on the basis of a complete break with the past, through a reconstitution of the country's political culture on liberal terms, much as occurred in West Germany.

But Argentines ultimately proved reluctant to travel very far down this road. Public support for punishment of even the most unrepentant torturers soon waned, as more pressing problems arose.[112] Only a few years thereafter, state-sponsored torture and murder—now by police, of common criminals—was applauded by many Argentines, including those in prominent public office.[113]

Perhaps least persuasive to conservatives was the President's insistence on the need for a redefinition of national identity, a concept long central to Argentine rightists. Nino himself would later describe

---

111   A related matter must be broached with some delicacy. It is pertinent in this regard that both Nino and Malamud-Goti were Jewish. Argentine nationalism—both its Peronist and Integralist varieties—has always been, and largely remains, deeply hostile toward Judaism and the Jews. See generally Robert Weisbrot, *The Jews of Argentina* (1979) (documenting the history of the Jews in Argentina from the time of the Spanish Inquisition to the rise of Perón). On the myriad forms of nationalist thought among Argentine intellectuals, see Enrique Zuleta Álvarez, *El Nacionalismo Argentino* (1975).

112   Rosendo Fraga, *La Cuestión Militar: 1987-1989*, at 137 (1990) (summarizing opinion survey data reflecting the Argentine public's lack of strong interest in human rights issues during the late 1980s). Two former military officers, notorious for their prominent role in the dirty war and later uprisings, even ran for public office, receiving many votes. One was elected governor of a major province. "Bussi Vuelve a Gobernar la Provincia de Tucumán," *Clarín* (Buenos Aires), Int'l Ed., June 27-July 3, 1995, at 1, 3.

113   Jaime Malamud-Goti, *Game Without End: Terror, Justice and the Democratic Transition in Argentina* 197-206 (forthcoming 1996).

their worldview as positing a

> National Being [that] *does not evolve* with the history of the country; its
> structure is not dependent on the Constitucion, which is seen as a mere
> instrument; nor is its will expressed through the democratic process....
> The military defended the sacrifice of innocent individuals ... as a
> necessary means for *preserving* this National Being.[114]

In short, they defined national identity in a way that made the very idea
of breaking completely with the past to be anathema.

Even one of the principal architects of the trials would ultimately
conclude that the prosecutions of military officers had not stimulated
serious moral deliberation or self-scrutiny.   Rather, the trials had
fostered public embrace of a simplistic division between the guilty and
the innocent, he concluded.[115]

West Germans, too, proved to have second thoughts about their
willingness to base national identity on a complete repudiation of their
country's past.   In the 1980s the country witnessed, in the so-called
"historians' debate," a wrenching reassessment of whether the
Holocaust ought properly to remain at the center of the nation's self-
understanding, even its understanding of German society during the
Third Reich.[116]   The considerable public appeal of the new

---

114   Carlos S. Nino, "The Duty to Punish Past Abuses of Human Rights Put into
Context: The Case of Argentina," 100 *Yale L.J.* 2619, 2633 (1991) (emphasis added).

115   Malamud-Goti, *supra* note 113, at 256-64. It is wrong to suggest, as do some
poststructuralists, that the category structure of law necessarily reflects (and requires)
a binary opposition regarding guilt. Diane Rubenstein, *What's Left?: The Ecole
Normale Supérieure and the Right* 158 (1990) (suggesting that, in French postwar trials
of collaborationists "the use of the binary opposition is to contain guilt to at least one
easily delineated segment of the population that can be purged symbolically"). Perelli
similarly concludes that the junta trial "failed socially and culturally, as it did not enable
people to work out their own experiences of paralyzing terror, repressed guilt, and
projection." Carina Perelli, "Settling Accounts with Blood Memory: The Case of
Argentina," 59 *Soc. Res.* 415, 418 (1992).

116   See generally Richard Evans, *In Hitler's Shadow* (1989) (discussing the West
German historians' debate over how the Holocaust should be remembered). My account
of the debate aims only to show its relevance to the social theoretical concerns of the
present essay. Those concerns, distinct from those of both sides to the dispute, do not
warrant or require endorsement of either. My sympathies are with Habermas and his
defenders. But the social theoretical questions examined here require acknowledging
the difficulties that have been encountered by efforts to use criminal law for constructing
national identity (in Argentina, Japan, and Germany) on the basis of collective guilt. In

interpretations, to judge from responses in the elite press, lay in its assertions of continuity over time and space, its rejection of any need for a total break from the past.

First, German atrocities had not been unique or uniquely horrible. They may have been inspired by early Soviet "experiments" with the Gulag, it was argued, a system that ultimately caused suffering on a greater scale.[117] Subsequent genocides throughout Africa and Asia similarly called into question the long-standing view that the Germans had committed a crime incommensurable with any other, one for which they needed forever to atone, even as other nations mimicked German wrongs without apology. The German experience of administrative massacre, in other words, was not entirely discontinuous with that of other societies, before or since.

Second, until the War began to take its toll, Germans were relatively content with their government. Their economy grew rapidly under Hitler, significantly improving their standard of living. Hence the unofficial memory of these years, quietly preserved by those who lived through them, was considerably more favorable than, and tacitly at odds with, the memory of Nazi rule officially cultivated during the Occupation and thereafter.[118] In fact, German society between the wars displayed trends and trajectories, on all major economic and social indicators, quite similar to those of other West European societies.

In other words, there was considerable socioeconomic continuity both between the Nazi and post-Nazi years within Germany, as well as between German and other Western societies of the interwar period. Insofar as impressive development under Nazi rule had partly contributed to the later postwar economic miracle,[119] there was no need

---

so doing, I concede the significance and inescapability of the neorevisionists' concerns, if not their conclusions.

117 Ernst Nolte, "Between Historical Legend and Revisionism? The Third Reich in the Perspective of 1980," in *Forever in the Shadow of Hitler?*, *supra* note 32, at 12-14 (suggesting that the Holocaust "was the fear-borne reaction to the acts of annihilation that took place during the Russian Revolution"); Ernst Nolte, "The Past That Will Not Pass: A Speech That Could Be Written but Not Delivered," in *supra* note 32, at 22 (suggesting that the Holocaust was inspired by the Gulag).

118 Saul Friedlander, *Memory, History, and the Extermination of the Jews of Europe* 88-92 (1993).

119 Assertions such as this one were particularly offensive to many since they seemed to deny, as Habermas puts it, the "complex connections between the criminality and the

for any *complete* break with the past as the basis of national identity, or national pride.[120]

As in Argentina, the dispute evolved from one between advocates of memory and those of oblivion into a dispute between competing versions of collective memory, conflicting narratives of the nation's past. What is significant for present purposes is not the new scholarly "discoveries" as such, but the apparent receptivity to them, and hence their likely impact on memory.[121] This was a later generation of Germans, both the historians and their public audience, people with no personal complicity. Hence it is impossible to attribute their attitudinal shift purely to self-exculpatory apologetics.

We are thus forced to consider the possibility, as Edmund Burke long ago argued (and as communitarians like C. Taylor and A. MacIntyre seek to remind us), that many people are emotionally constituted in ways that require a sense of connectedness to their country's more distant past, a feeling of continuity with forebears—however puzzling and perverse many of us liberal theorists

---

dubious normality of everyday life under Nazism, between destruction and vital productivity, between a devastating systematic perspective and an intimate, local perspective." Jürgen Habermas, "A Kind of Settlement of Damages: The Apologetic Tendencies in German History Writing," in *Forever in the Shadow of Hitler?, supra* note 32, at 34, 41. On how "Japan's fifteen-year mobilization for war [similarly] created positive technological, technocratic, and institutional legacies for the postwar state," see John W. Dower, "The Useful War," in Dower, *Japan in War and Peace* 9, 32 (1993).

120   Several participants in the historians' debate have observed an alleged trend toward restoring some measure of national "pride" among Germans, a pride incompatible with the "Nuremberg Trial view of history." See, e.g., Hanno Helbling, "A Searching Image of the Past: What Is Expected from German History Books," in *Forever in the Shadow of Hitler?, supra* note 32, at 98, 99 (noting the desire by some for instruction in "a German history that does not have to be read as a prehistory of National Socialism"); Meier, *supra* note 101, at 26 (noting that in 1983 the parliamentary leader of the Christian Democratic Union had suggested "that the Germans should finally 'step out of Hitler's shadow'").

In July 1985, Japan's Prime Minister similarly contended that the "'nation must move from shame to glory'" in order to establish a national identity. Koyama, *supra* note 58, at 160. He blamed its failure in this regard on "'a view of history influenced by the results of the Far Eastern War Criminal Tribunal.'" *Id.*

121   Alan Cowell, "Teaching Nazi Past to German Youth," *N.Y. Times,* June 9, 1995, at A12 (quoting several high school youths, expressing such complaints as, "you can't say: 'I'm proud to be a German.' Beethoven was a German, too, but everything now is seen through the Second World War").

may find this.[122] Shklar thus puts the point more skeptically: "Man, like a vegetable, it seems, requires a root—though why, no one really knows."[123]

On this account, great events in legal history can be, and often are, woven into the larger story. But this must be done seamlessly (in the common law fashion), without ripping apart the rest of the social fabric. Debates about the past then become connected to hopes for the future. This connection "is often deeply felt, but difficult to express in the language of interests and rights," concedes one liberal political theorist.[124]

It follows that trials for administrative massacre, however spectacular their public staging, cannot easily transform collective memory. This is because such trials involve both a radical break with well-settled interpretations of the nation's past—hard enough for many well-meaning citizens—and acceptance of some responsibility by many who have themselves suffered genuine deprivation as a result of the country's recent calamities. To expect this is to expect a great deal.

The new doubts about any need for a complete break with the past, for a national identity founded at "zero hour" upon only the Nuremberg principles and "constitutional patriotism," take the form of an explicitly communitarian theory of collective memory, in the arguments of revisionist historians. Habermas aptly summarizes their claim:

> Without the memory of this national history [preceding 1933] ..., a positive self-image cannot be created. Without a collective identity, the forces of social integration decline. The lamented "loss of history" is even said to contribute to the weakness of the political system's legitimation .... This is used to justify the compensatory "creation of meaning" through which historiography is to provide for those uprooted by the process of modernization.[125]

---

122 Halbwachs viewed collective memory in just such Burkean terms: "The collective memory is a record of resemblances and, naturally, is convinced that the group remains the same ... , whereas what has changed are the group's relations or contacts with other groups ...." Maurice Halbwachs, *The Collective Memory* 86 (Francis J. Ditter, Jr. & Vida Y. Ditter trans., 1992).

123 Judith Shklar, *After Utopia* 107 (1957).

124 Joshua Foa Dienstag, "'The Pozsgay Affair:' Historical Memory and Political Legitimacy," 8 *History and Memory* 51, 59 (1996).

125 Habermas, *supra* note 104, at 235. For an American version of the view that

The argument is that a stable identity—personal and national—rests on an awareness of continuity with a beloved past, whose noteworthy achievements are preserved in collective memory. This view is entirely consistent with Halbwachs's original theory of collective memory and with the Durkheimian conception of mechanical solidarity that it presupposed. Halbwachs claimed that collective memory necessarily "immobilizes time."[126] Hence his very limited and conservative view of commemoration as "reviving the deep traditions of a community that might otherwise be modified over time, as impressions of the past grow vague .... By enhancing the structure of mnemonic imagery, commemoration lends clarity and stability to collective memory."[127] If this were generally true, such memory could never extend to a collective agreement to break decisively with the society's past, unless perhaps this meant returning to some long-lost golden age.

But Halbwachs's claim is not an iron law, and the Israeli experience offers a telling exception. After 1948, national identity initially developed not through memory of victimization by others, but through rejection of features within Judaism and Jewish secular culture

---

Habermas refutes, see Robert Bellah et al., *Habits of the Heart* 152-53 (1985). Habermas's most recent discussion of constitutional patriotism appears in *Between Facts and Norms: Contributions to a Discourse Theory of Law and Democracy* 500 (1996).

126 "Every group ... immobilizes time in its own way and imposes on its members the illusion that, in a given duration of a constantly changing world, certain zones have acquired a relative stability and balance in which nothing essential is altered." Halbwachs, *supra* note 122, at 126. An ethnography of French peasants similarly highlights the fundamental conservatism of collective memory in traditional societies:

The collective memory ... constantly tends to seek permanence, to re-create what is indestructible and so ensure its own survival. It is as if the community needed to lean on its own unchanged past, where the ups and downs of History and the vagaries of modern life disappear .... The present ... is reconstituted by reference to the past—a stable, lasting and well-ordered period, a time outside the reach of Time.

Françoise Zonabend, *The Enduring Memory: Time and History in a French Village* 138-39 (Anthony Forster trans., 1984).

127 Patrick H. Hutton, "Collective Memory and Collective Mentalities: The Halbwachs-Ariès Connection," 15 *Hist. Reflections* 311, 315 (1988) (parsing Halbwachs, *supra* note 122). This view of official commemoration is firmly rejected by contemporary creators and scholars of contemporary public monuments. Young, *supra* note 26, at 14-17 (praising an approach to public monuments that "may save our *icons* of remembrance from hardening into idols of remembrance").

itself. These features were thought to have made European Jews especially vulnerable to such victimization. Few if any efforts at the construction of national identity have been so self-critical, before or since.[128] If there were to be a radical break with the past, it was to entail a break with what being Jewish had meant to the Jews. Specifically, it was to mean a repudiation of millennia of ingratiation of hostile majorities at whose sufferance they existed. It was therefore to mean a sovereign state. The reconstitution of national identity was also to mean an unapologetic attitude toward the exercise of military power in self-defense and a corresponding reassessment of the relative importance of mental and manual labor.[129] "After the Holocaust," write two Israeli philosophers, "history is viewed as radically discontinuous. Memory has the distinct and new role of preserving the sense of this discontinuity."[130]

But this attempted redefinition of Jewish identity on the basis of historical rupture—induced by law, in significant part—made it very difficult for the new Israeli-born generation to sympathize with its predecessor, that is, with the many thousands of Holocaust survivors still among them. The Eichmann trial was intentionally designed to restore a sense of continuity with the past, to extend collective memory in this regard.[131] It would do so by deliberately emphasizing how little the victims could do and how they had resisted nonetheless.[132]

The trial's dramatic focus, in other words, derived from a

---

128 There was ample precedent for this, however, in the Old Testament's appeal to remember the past, given that "many ... biblical narratives seem almost calculated to deflate the national pride" and are by no means "actuated by the normal ... desire to preserve heroic national deeds from oblivion." Yerushalmi, *supra* note 15, at 11.

129 On the repercussions of this transformation for the identity of many American Jews, see generally Paul Breines, *Tough Jews: Political Fantasies and the Moral Dilemma of American Jewry* (1990). See also Barry Schwartz et al., "The Recovery of Masada: A Study in Collective Memory," 27 *Soc. Q.* 147, 151 (1986) (observing that Jewish interest in the Masada story arose only with the rise of Zionism in this century, as it came to symbolize military valor, national resolution, and heroism against high odds).

130 Avishai Margalit and Gabriel Motzkin, "The Uniqueness of the Holocaust," 25 *Philosophy and Public Affairs* 65, 83 (1996).

131 Segev, *supra* note 3, at 348.

132 Segev, *supra* note 3, at 348. The opinion of the district court mentions this resistance several times in the first paragraph alone. *Attorney-Gen. of Israel v. Eichmann*, 36 I.L.R. 5, 18-19 (Isr. Dist. Ct. 1961).

conscious executive decision to rebuild historical links that, although initially repudiated, were now recognized as crucial to solidarity between generations.[133] At the same time, the trial was designed to suggest a new relationship between the Jews and their persecutors: its pedagogic value for Ben-Gurion lay, one scholar suggests, in its capacity to provide "a people that had not experienced sovereignty and was as yet unused to it, the feeling of power and independence that the judicial process imparted."[134]

Liberal Memory As "Constitutional Patriotism"

Perhaps it is only liberal philosophers and liberal social theorists, like Emile Durkheim, Carlos Nino, and the later Habermas, who find it easy to imagine basing their nation's identity entirely on universal values, shared by many others, rather than on memorable experiences uniquely "ours."[135]   But this is an oversimplification of what they actually sought, which was something less abstract: to condemn the past by legal judgment, to be sure, but also to etch into collective consciousness the memory of that very act of condemnation—including the spectacular courtroom events, at Nuremberg and Buenos Aires, by which it was achieved.

Still, it may be, as communitarian theorists imply, that only those already too thoroughly deracinated, feeling little solidarity with fellow nationals, can find firm identity and direction in "critical morality," in the abstract principles for which liberal theorists consider themselves

---

133 The Eichmann trial also convinced American and European Jews that the Holocaust—until then a matter central to Jewish memory, "but not paraded before a general public"—might realistically be made central to international memory. The trial, combined with victory in the Six-Day War shortly thereafter, "created a new openness and pride among Jews about their Jewishness." Michael Schudson, "Dynamics of Distortion in Collective Memory," in *Memory Distortion: How Minds, Brains, and Societies Reconstruct the Past* 350 (Daniel L. Schacter ed., 1995).

134 Michael Keren, "Ben-Gurion's Theory of Sovereignty: The Trial of Adolf Eichmann," in *David Ben-Gurion:* 38, 49 (Ronald W. Zweig ed., 1991).

135 Habermas developed his views on this subject in the context of the so-called "Historians' Debate."   Jürgen Habermas, "Historical Consciousness and Post-Traditional Identity: The Federal Republic's Orientation to the West," in *The New Conservatism, supra* note 18, at 249, 249-67; Habermas, *supra* note 106, at 229-40.

the preeminent spokesmen.[136]   Constitutional patriotism holds that "states should be composed of equal citizens whose ties to one another are purely 'civic' in the sense that each acknowledges the authority of a common set of laws and political institutions." This conception of civic membership would, in effect, "bracket off questions about shared history and common culture and...claim that the basis on which citizens associate is purely political."[137]

This conception is sometimes formulated in explicit opposition to one based in memory: "Memory has been dethroned," writes Todorov, "not to the advantage of forgetfulness but to the advantage of a few general principles and the 'general will.' The same could be said of...law as a whole."[138]   Yet this anti-mnemonic view of "what we share" apparently strikes many as cold and hard-hearted, even after all the horrors that have ensued from repeated efforts to impose a more encompassing, encumbering sense of communal membership.

It is noteworthy in this connection that the speeches drafted by Nino for Alfonsín virtually never invoked the names of Argentina's national heroes, as presidential discourse—in Argentina, as elsewhere—customarily does. The evidence presented here suggests that an effort—by criminal trials, in conjunction with other means—to rewrite a society's myth of origin, in a manner condemning much of its historic past from the standpoint of universal principles shared by other societies, is indeed difficult, but not impossible. Admittedly, it is partly a matter of enjoying favorable conditions. But it is also a matter of making the most of whatever conditions one faces. That is where shrewd dramaturgy has a legitimate role to play.

If the reconstruction of collective memory sought by Nino (for Argentina) and Habermas (for Germany) is possible, surely it cannot be

---

136   An example of such an approach is Habermas's notion of "constitutional patriotism," according to which social solidarity and national identity are to derive directly from the citizen's articulate commitment to moral principles embodied in a liberal constitution, such as that of contemporary Germany. Habermas, *supra* note 135, at 262-66. The approach adopted in the present study views social solidarity arising more circuitously, from the "civilizing process" of disagreement (over such things as the meaning and application of criminal law), channeled by procedural restraints.

137   David Miller, *On Nationality* 189 (1995). On the compatibility of such a form of national identity with continuing forms of ethnic consciousness, see *Id.* at 138 (discussing the views of Michael Walzer and Jonathan Sacks).

138   Tzvetan Todorov, "The Abuses of Memory," 1 *Common Knowledge* 6, 10 (1996).

accomplished through the "quick fix" of criminal trials, however riveting their gruesome details, however profound their momentary impact on opinion surveys. In their most optimistic moments, Alfonsín and his advisor-philosophers hoped that the epiphanic impact of the trial, with its revelations of rampant official lawlessness and the scale of the resulting suffering, would instill a deep and abiding recognition that official respect for individual moral rights was an imperative that could "never again" be compromised.[139] In this, they expected too much. Even the most compelling story, dramatizing the redemption of the disappeared and the resurrection of liberal morality, could not in itself achieve that objective, surely not if predicated on such a thoroughgoing self-criticism.

Peronist opponents sought to portray Alfonsín and his legal advisors as political naifs. But executive leaders were always prudent enough to set certain limits on their Kantian universalism and on their hopes of instilling it in their countrymen. They refrained, for instance, from indicting the juntas under international law for "crimes against humanity." All doctrinal requirements for such an indictment would have been met. But the President and his legal advisers rightly feared that any such reliance on international law would only further stir the passions of Argentine nationalism.[140] For this substantial segment of public opinion, the Nuremberg precedent represented not the triumph of international human rights, but merely the revenge of the Jews. Again, legal strategy was consciously tailored to make the government's favored story more compelling to skeptical publics, to influence collective memory in more persuasive and perduring ways.

Let us now briefly compare the cases. They differ from and resemble one another in several ways. Did criminal prosecution work to unite citizens in community by evoking shared sentiments of indignation? Or did it only further divide society into mutually suspicious subgroups, each adopting the moral universe and favored narrative of prosecution or defense?

In Argentina, the effect was ultimately quite divisive, with family and friends often bitterly at odds over whether "forgetting" was

---

139   Interviews with Argentine Presidential Advisors, in Buenos Aires, Argentina (Aug. 1985).

140   Interview with Jacobo Timerman, in Buenos Aires, Argentina (Aug. 1987).

necessary for (or incompatible with) the restoration of democracy and solidarity.[141] The narrative fostered by Alfonsín's courts failed to win anything close to universal public endorsement for very long, being rejected by both right and left. In this respect, the social impact of criminal prosecution resembled the divisiveness occasioned by the Dreyfus trial.

By contrast, the West German and Japanese experiences display the potentially unifying effect of criminal prosecution on collective memory and social solidarity, but in very different ways. Neither experience, moreover, is entirely consistent with Durkheim's argument. In the Federal Republic since the mid-1960s, criminal trials powerfully united young Germans in repudiation of the complicity of their parents' generation, a complicity represented by the "ordinary men" (camp guards and mid-level officials) finally in the dock.

In Japan, by contrast, the Tokyo and other war crimes trials were widely rejected for their lack of moral "balance," their refusal to frame the story of Japanese "aggression" in the wider context of superpower rivalry in the Pacific (a context permitting Japanese behavior to be characterized as partially defensive). The trial's impact on memory also suffered from its failure to weigh the defendants' authorization of war crimes (against POWs and noncombatants) in relation to analogous Allied crimes (bombing of Japan's civilian population centers).

These trials, in short, united the Japanese populace in substantial rejection of the story they sought to tell,[142] much as the Nuremberg proceedings failed to influence German adults in the same years. The unity achieved among Germans by prosecutions (in the 1960s and 1970s) differed from that achieved among the Japanese not only over whether such trials were defensible. Another difference was equally crucial: the story around which Germans reached consensus was factually accurate, whereas that adopted by the Japanese—frozen in the

---

141 Stories were common, for instance, of courting couples quarreling upon the discovery that one's views on a question were not shared by the other. For a public incident of such discord, see Calvin Sims, "National Nightmare Returns to Argentine Consciousness," *N.Y. Times,* Apr. 5, 1995, at A1.

142 It is nonetheless true, as already noted, that certain aspects of the courts' historical narrative ultimately became all too persuasive to many Japanese, insofar as it exempted them (and the Emperor they worshipped) from any trace of culpability. See *supra* text accompanying notes 52-58.

1940s, unraveling only at Hirohito's death—was not.

The Argentine and Japanese experiences resemble each other in one disquieting way. In both societies, criminal trials exercised considerable appeal for many citizens for the "wrong" reasons. Many Argentines favored prosecution of the juntas not because they had murdered thousands of citizens in the dirty war, but only because they had lost the recent Malvinas/Falklands war.[143]   Similarly, many Japanese were all too happy to see their country's military leadership punished, on account of imprudently involving the country in a costly war it could not win. Far less persuasive to Japanese citizens, however, were the legal arguments for prosecutions of aggressive war-making and the war crimes perpetrated in their name during that conflict.

In both Japan and Argentina, prosecutors were well-aware that the public's antipathy toward the defendants, however superficially consistent with their own, arose from very different concerns—even as prosecutors sought to utilize such public sentiment in support of the law's purposes. This strategy involved a risky gamble, as Argentine prosecutors learned to their painful chagrin. It was unlikely to work for very long in a society deeply divided and politically unstable.[144]

The Argentine trials resembled the post-Nuremberg German ones in an important way that distinguishes them both from the Japanese experience. The Tokyo and Nuremberg trials (as well as other Allied-sponsored war crimes trials throughout Asia and Europe) involved foreigners prosecuting nationals for violations of international law. This approach proved largely unsuccessful in evoking the moral sentiments of nationals in support of the proceedings. By contrast, the prosecutions of Argentina's military rulers, like those of the Auschwitz guards and Majdanek officials, involved nationals prosecuting other nationals for violations of domestic law. This approach proved considerably more effective in generating moral consensus (and mechanical solidarity), especially in the Federal Republic, but also among the substantial majority of Argentines (over ninety percent) who

---

143   Fiascos in strategic and logistical planning caused the collapse of the military regime. This permitted the restoration of civilian rulers (who initiated the criminal proceedings). Andrés Fontana, *Fuerzas Armadas, Partidos Políticos y Transición a la Democracia en la Argentina* (1984).

144   On the depth of social and political conflicts plaguing Argentina since the 1930s, see generally Carlos H. Waisman, *Reversal of Development in Argentina* (1991).

strongly endorsed the junta trial.[145]

In cases involving large-scale administrative massacre, the Durkheimian account of criminal law's contribution to social solidarity has much greater difficulty than the discursive in handling the muddiness of the moral and legal line between accusers and accused. This is because Durkheim saw solidarity arising out of the shared indignation of the innocent many toward the guilty few. But where many thousands bear some culpability for the harm at issue, this premise is invalid. "Coming to terms" with administrative massacre requires some means by which society at large can collectively acknowledge its guilt, collectively repenting its wrongs.

Only when the law is conceived as a forum for public dialogue can it accommodate the possibility (and societal need) for periodic reversal of roles between accuser and accused, for the accusatory finger to be pointed in both directions. This is particularly apt in situations, such as the Nuremberg and Tokyo trials, where accuser and accused, in an escalating cycle of criminality, have become, to some extent, "mutually implicated in each other's ... vices."[146] The objective, as in much modernist theatre, is a "fractured reciprocity whereby beholder and beheld reverse positions in a way that renders a steady position of spectatorship impossible."[147] Only the discursive conception of law's function will allow us to apprehend and appreciate the kind of solidarity that can emerge through such exchanges.

---

145   The greater efficacy of national versus international law in this context confirms Walzer's view that "internal" criticism, based on a society's own moral norms, is almost always more persuasive to citizens than "external" criticism based on universal moral standards, discovered by "prophets" and delivered "from the mountaintop." Michael Walzer, *Interpretation and Social Criticism* 36-66 (1987).

146   Shriver, *supra* note 19, at 74.

147   Barbara Freedman, *Staging the Gaze: Postmodernism, Psychoanalysis, and Shakespearean Comedy* 1 (1991).

Chapter 7.

Constructing Memory with Legal Blueprints?

Political leaders and legal elites often try to use the law to influence social norms, such as those concerning racial tolerance. This is not done entirely in a vacuum. "Successful law and policy try to take advantage of learning about norms and norm change," as Sunstein notes.[1] But little has really been learned about how norms change, except that law's efforts to that end have often failed.[2]

Even when these efforts work, we don't know much about why, i.e., about what distinguishes these situations from others where comparable efforts fell far short. It is tempting to say that law's impact on social norms is real, but gradual, even glacial, hence almost imperceptible. Taking the longer view is also a convenient way for lawyers like myself to dodge the abundant results of social science, showing law's relative impotence here.[3]

Recourse to "the long run" is also misplaced because we know that there are "norm cascades," involving rapid shifts in norms, and "norm bandwagons," where initial change among small groups triggers much larger shifts.[4] Both phenomena appear most conspicuously during rapid transitions in political regimes, as in the former East Bloc and South Africa.[5] Criminal trials for administrative massacre—Nuremberg, Tokyo, and Buenos Aires, for instance—have also frequently occurred in these same, transitional conditions, permitting prosecutors to take advantage of the contemporaneous susceptibility to norm change within society.

One way the law might influence social norms is by shaping how certain events in a society's history—its most normatively-charged

---

1 Cass Sunstein, "Social Norms and Social Roles," 96 *Columbia Law Review* 903, 909 (1996).

2 See, e.g., Gerald N. Rosenberg, *The Hollow Hope: Can Courts Bring About Social Change?* (1991).

3 For a summary of empirical research reaching this conclusion, to varying degrees, see Roger Cotterrell, *The Sociology of Law* 50-64 (2n ed., 1992).

4 Timur Kuran, *Private Truths, Public Lies* 71-73 (1995).

5 *Id.*

events—are remembered. This recalls Durkheim's argument about how prosecution fosters solidarity, by reinvigorating the norms we share, reminding us of their enduring claims. But trials can strengthen social norms about right and wrong only under "normal conditions," Durkheim stressed, those in which commitment to such norms is almost universally shared, awaiting only a symbolically suitable occasion for reasserting itself.

This is precisely what has often been lacking in the immediate aftermath of large-scale state brutality. If criminal law can strengthen a society's normative commitments at such times, the process must be less direct. The law's proper role will be to stimulate a candid discussion of just what these shared norms are, or should be. Solidarity emerges both insofar as agreement is reached in this regard, and also—insofar as it is not—through the very process of discursive engagement over the question. A memorable courtroom telling of the tale of recent horrors can be an effective means to both these ends.

To begin our assessment of this hypothesis, consider the following, from Michel Foucault:

> Memory is ... a very important factor in struggle .... If one controls people's memory, one controls their dynamism.... It's vital to have possession of this memory, to control it, administer it, tell it what it must contain.[6]

Foucault is surely engaged here in willful hyperbole. But it is true that myths of origin (and the collective memory they establish) do not bring themselves into being. "States of origin are conceived as extraordinary only when someone is motivated to point them out and define them as such," writes a sociologist.[7] "The sanctification of social beginnings must be induced and sustained ...."[8] To this end, official "truth commissions," established in the aftermath of administrative massacre, sometimes specifically recommend measures "'to preserve the memory of the victims [so as to] promote a culture of mutual respect and

---

6   Michel Foucault, "Film and Popular Memory: An Interview with Michel Foucault," 11 *Radical Phil.* 24, 25 (1975).

7   Barry Schwartz, "The Social Context of Commemoration: A Study in Collective Memory," 61 *Soc. Forces* 374, 376 (1982) (parsing a statement by Halbwachs).

8   *Id.*

observance of human rights.'"[9]

This is a tall order. Foucault's aphorism, for instance, is surely offered less as a sociological proposition than as a political provocation, less in exhortation than incantation. That no one could mistakenly take his aphorism literally is itself significant and worthy of some reflection.

The political repercussions of the Dreyfus trial dominated French politics for over half a century.[10] Since then, at least, it has been clear that criminal prosecutions can contribute significantly to collective memory of major events in a nation's history and that collective memory of such proceedings can thereby influence national identity.

Much less clear, however, is whether any of these effects may be achieved *deliberately*. This is a fifth reason to doubt whether societies can intentionally employ the law to influence collective memory of administrative massacre.   It may be that collective memory is essentially a by-product—and so too the social solidarity it promotes.

There are certain mental and social states, as Elster observes, that "can only come about as the by-product of actions undertaken for other ends.   They can never, that is, be brought about intelligently or intentionally, because the very attempt to do so precludes the state one is trying to bring about."[11] This is not to deny "the widespread tendency to erect into goals for political action effects that can only be by-products."[12] It is only to say that such efforts are doomed to fail.

---

9   Naomi Roht-Arriaza, "Overview" to *Impunity and Human Rights in International Law and Practice* 147, 158 (Naomi Roht-Arriaza, ed., 1995) (quoting Commission for the Historical Clarification of the Human Rights Violations and Violent Acts That Have Caused Suffering to the Guatemalan People); see also Julie Taylor, "Body Memories: Aide-Memoires and Collective Amnesia in the Wake of the Argentine Terror," in *Body Politics: Disease, Desire, and the Family* 192, 196 (Michael Ryan & Avery Gordon eds., 1994) (observing that the Argentine military "trials were a public and explicit strategy to conclude one historical period and begin another with a decision concerning how to remember").

10   H.R. Kedward, *The Dreyfus Affair: Catalyst for Tensions in French Society* 111-12(1965); Benjamin Martin, "Political Justice in France: The Dreyfus Affair and After" (Sept. 2, 1994) (paper presented at the American Political Science Association Conference).

11   Jon Elster, *Sour Grapes* 43 (1983). There is a fallacy, Elster notes, in "searching for the things that recede before the hand that reaches out for them." *Id.* at 107. Within the class of "states that are essentially by-products," reside phenomena so diverse as sleep, class-consciousness, benevolence, magnificence, the contribution of jury participation to civic education, and self-respect. *Id.* at 43-45, 71-77, 96, 100.

12   *Id.* at 44.

We do not normally legislate what the members of a society ought to remember, after all, although the memory of administrative massacre is a notable exception.[13]

Memory seems to have a mind of its own, as suggested by its frequent verbal invocation as an independent actor or agent. One reads, for instance, that "memory selects from the flux of images of the past those that best fit *its* present needs."[14] Even if memory need not "immobilize time," as Halbwachs thought, perhaps its very dynamism and flux work in slippery ways that elude self-conscious control, including control by liberal elites nominally in charge of an illiberal society, as in Argentina. Hence, Schudson is right to insist on "the incompleteness of this hegemonic process and the social mechanisms that *keep* it incomplete" in liberal societies.[15]

The very act of ordering someone to forget an experience, for instance, necessarily reminds him of the very experience that he must forget—or more precisely, remember to forget. This paradox is inherent in any "official campaign of coercive forgetting,"[16] such as

---

13   Fifteen U.S. states, including California, New York, Illinois, Pennsylvania, and Florida, have legislation mandating or strongly recommending instruction concerning the Holocaust in their public schools. "U.S. Holocaust Memorial Museum, State Requirements and Holocaust Studies" (July 7, 1995). Significantly, though, the Illinois mandate became the focus of "aggressive parental opposition, charging that a small minority was attempting to "'manipulate our children for their political and national purposes.'" Deborah E. Lipstadt, *Denying the Holocaust: The Growing Assault on Truth and Memory* 15 (1993) (quoting a letter from Safet M. Sarich to Winnetka educators (May 1991)).

14   Patrick H. Hutton, "Collective Memory and Collective Mentalities: The Halbwachs-Ariès Connection," 15 *Hist. Reflections* 311, 314 (1988) (emphasis added). Hutton further contends that "memory colonizes the past by obliging it to conform to present conceptions. It is a process not of retrieval but of reconfiguration." *Id.*

15   Michael Schudson, *Watergate in American Memory* 209 (1992) (emphasis added). He elsewhere notes: "In liberal societies and in a porous international system where it is difficult or impossible to curtain one population from the next, instrumentalization [of collective memory] is more often attempted than achieved." Michael Schudson, "Dynamics of Distortion in Collective Memory," in *Memory Distortion: How Minds, Brains, and Societies Reconstruct the Past* 355 (Daniel L. Schacter ed., 1995).

16   On such practices in the former Soviet Union, see Rubie S. Watson, "Memory, History, and Opposition Under State Socialism: An Introduction," in *Memory, History, and Opposition Under State Socialism* 17-19 (Rubie S. Watson ed., 1994). On similar practices in China, see Vera Schwarcz, "Strangers No More: Personal Memory in the Interstices of Public Commemoration," in *Memory, History, and Opposition, id.* at 45, 55. On Czechoslovakia, see Milan Kundera, *The Book of Laughter and Forgetting* 158-59 (Michael Heim trans., 1980).

those regularly employed by "state socialist" regimes. Hence, the law may compel teachers not to offer instruction on certain events. But it can do so only by periodically reminding large numbers of them (in terms calculated to ensure their enduring recollection) of what it is, exactly, that is *so important* for them not to share with their charges.

The "official rewriting of history" in which such regimes engage highlights, unwittingly, the rulers' self-perception that their legitimacy hangs precariously on public acceptance of a particular historical interpretation. This interpretation is often conspicuously inconsistent with others recently foisted upon the public with equal vehemence.[17] (Unfortunately, a pleasing paradox cannot be allowed the last word here: there are vast expanses of the globe where authoritarian states have been all too successful for long periods in inducing collective forgetting of the administrative massacres they have inflicted.)[18]

A converse problem with official orchestration of memory arises in modern liberal societies for the opposite reason: because historical understanding plays *so little* a role in the claims of their rulers to legitimate authority. Official efforts at memory construction by modern liberal societies have hence struck several observers as hopelessly artificial, incongruously sentimental, even absurd. As a French historian laments, in modern Western society:

> *lieux de mémoire* are fundamentally remains, the ultimate embodiments of a memorial consciousness that has barely survived in a historical age that calls out for memory because it has abandoned it. They make their appearance by virtue of the deritualization of our world ... maintaining by artifice and by will a society deeply absorbed in its own transformation, ... one that inherently values ... the future over the past. Museums, archives, cemeteries, festivals, anniversaries, treaties, depositions, monuments, sanctuaries, fraternal orders—these are the

---

17 See, e.g., Steven Ungar, *Scandal and Aftereffect* 18 (1995) (observing of leadership succession in Czechoslovakia that "no longer even a matter of choosing between rival accounts, it was as if each regime irrupted with its own past fully formed. Of course, this invented past was neither natural nor neutral, but rather revised by each regime according to the ambitions on which it grounded its claim to legitimacy").

18 See, e.g., Hedrick Smith, *The Russians* 247-48 (1976) (reporting conversations at an elite Soviet high school with students who, when asked how many people had died in Stalin's gulag, consistently gave estimates in the low hundreds, rather than in the millions).

boundary stones of another age, illusions of eternity. It is the nostalgic dimension of these devotional institutions that makes them seem beleaguered and cold—they mark the rituals of a society without ritual; ... signs of distinction and of group membership in a society that ... tends to recognize individuals only as identical and equal.[19]

In short, market society and its rulers see little need or possibility

---

19 Pierre Nora, "Between Memory and History: *Les Lieux de Mémoire*," 26 *Representations* 7, 12 (1989). Nora's conclusion here embraces the so-called theory of "mass society." *Id.* at 7-9. Rejecting that theory, as I do, entails very different conclusions concerning the possibility of meaningful collective memory within a modern liberal society.

Many now reject the very idea of collective memory, not because shared memory has been shown to be nonexistent or impossible, but simply because they regard it as undesirable under any reasonably foreseeable conditions. In a society divided along socioeconomic or ethnic lines, they imply, the memory of large-scale events—particularly revolutions and general strikes, of course, but major "national" events more generally—must necessarily vary for members of different socioeconomic groups, since such events inevitably impose very different burdens upon each. Any emphasis on what is shared among members of a nation-state necessarily serves to distract attention from these more fundamental socioeconomic divisions among its members, on this view. A weaker version of this view insists that ideas of collective memory and shared national identity have "characteristically been employed to obfuscate and coopt." Peter Novick, personal communication. This version at least admits the possibility of a genuinely shared memory of a common past, one which did not serve conservative political purposes.

Halbwach's idea of "collective memory" is currently all the rage in the human sciences. But its history traces directly to Durkheim, and particularly to Durkheim's preoccupation with social solidarity through moral consensus. This preoccupation is not shared by contemporary theorists, who focus instead on the centrality of conflict, domination, and resistance in modern societies. Randall Collins, "The Durkheimian Tradition in Conflict Sociology," in *Durkheimian Sociology* 107, 107 (Jeffrey C. Alexander ed., 1988) (observing that Durkheim's view of social solidarity has never been as unpopular among sociologists in the seventy years since his death).

Such theorists view the notion of collective memory as possible only at the level of societal subgroups and desirable only as a political weapon against the dominant majority. Deeply influenced by multiculturalism, the study of historical memory in the U.S. is almost entirely hostile to the very idea of a shared national memory among all Americans. This prevalent approach denies the intelligibility of any coherent national narrative in a society riven by divisions of race, ethnicity, and gender.

The present study, by contrast, takes the possibility of a national narrative in such circumstances as an open question, empirical in nature and largely unaddressed (particularly by those who don't much like the idea in the first place). I therefore retain Durkheim's belief in the possibility of a link between collective memory and social solidarity on a national scale. But this approach requires decoupling the concept of solidarity from Durkheim's conception of it. I have sought to do so in examining the discursive engagements fostered by criminal trials for administrative massacre.

for much in the way of collective memory. Combining this point with the preceding, we might be led to conclude that memory construction in modern societies is doomed to failure because historical awareness plays either too insignificant a role in political legitimacy and social solidarity (in liberal democracies), on one hand, or too important a role in that regard (in totalitarian regimes), on the other.

It would follow that collective memory of administrative massacre—in either the West or the East—may be necessarily an unintended consequence, that is, a consequence of something other than the law's efforts to create it. If so, it would be self-defeating for prosecutors and judges, through choice among alternative narrative devices, to aspire to influence such memory directly. In other words, one might ask, with Eduardo Rabossi, Alfonsín's Undersecretary of Human Rights, "is it possible to determine collective remembering or forgetting *by official decree?*"[20] This question seems immediately to invite a negative answer. But that is only because its formulation is too stark and simplified. In fact, there is much that the law can do to influence collective memory (and hence to reconstruct some solidarity after administrative massacre) in powerful ways, I shall suggest.

The Legal Malleability of Collective Memory

One source of skepticism about the law's potential here is the fact that courts, acting in the immediate aftermath of the events they judge, lack historical hindsight. Only such hindsight permits an interpreter to situate events, particularly ones so traumatic and disorienting to contemporaries, within an enduring frame of intelligible context, persuasive to future generations.

To be sure, no historical judgment—even one offered centuries after the events—is immune from periodic revision. But hindsight confers, at least, a much wider perspective than contemporaries enjoy. This advantage facilitates, in turn, formation of "settled judgments" that persist for long periods and that often filter, through the press and mass

---

20   Eduardo Rabossi, *"Algunas Reflexiónes, a Modo de Prólogo,"* in *Usos del Olvido: Comunicaciones al Coloquio de Royaumont* 7, 7 (Yosef H. Yerushalmi et al. eds., 1989) (emphasis added) (translation by author).

media, into popular understanding. This is the most to which historians now aspire.

Lacking such a retrospective vantage point, prosecutors and judges who strive self-consciously for intergenerational didactics are likely to make embarrassing mistakes, as ensuing examples suggest.[21] Only when the defendant is apprehended many years after his offense, as with Eichmann or Touvier, is some such hindsight possible. But even when this passage of time has not compromised the defendant's due process right to a speedy trial, it will often have deprived prosecutors—through statutes of limitations—of the indictments that would let them tell the most accurate and compelling tale, as occurred in the Barbie trial.

In addition, leaders of new democratic regimes generally believe that they must act very quickly against the perpetrators, while the latter's powers are at low ebb, having been just recently removed from office, sometimes in ephemeral disgrace.[22] This need to act quickly—before adversaries can regroup and profit from waning public memory and more recent dissatisfactions with current rulers—is at odds with the need for hindsight. It is thus an obstacle in the prosecutorial search for a narrative that will be persuasive in the long run.

This problem is compounded by the fact that legal judgments necessarily aspire to a degree of finality that historians' interpretations do not. A host of legal doctrines are designed to prevent courts from reevaluating, again and again, particular facts and the issues they raise. These include res judicata, collateral estoppel, stare decisis, double jeopardy, mandatory joinder, statutes of limitations, and restrictive standards of appellate review. For most legal disputes, society's

---

21 Surely the most controversial recent "revision" of judicial historiography proposed by professional historians, although not examined here, is that of Ernst Nolte, Andreas Hillgruber, and other German conservatives. These scholars contend that German military resolve against the Red Army on the Eastern Front, although condemned at Nuremberg as part of the Reich's "waging of aggressive war," must now be seen in retrospect as a crucial first step in the West's defense against what would prove to be a Soviet invasion of Central Europe. That invasion, the German scholars add, would almost certainly have occurred much sooner, and hence have gone much further territorially, but for the persistent valor of German soldiers in combat. For a discussion of this issue, see Omer Bartov, *Hitler's Army: Soldiers, Nazis, and War in the Third Reich* 8-9 (1991); Charles S. Maier, *The Unmasterable Past: History, Holocaust, and German National Identity* 19-23 (1988).

22 Samuel P. Huntington, *The Third Wave: Democratization in the Late Twentieth Century* 231 (1991).

interests in finality are weighty. It is true, of course, that legal disputes continue over the scope and contemporary relevance of a particular precedent, for instance. The opinion's meaning thus often comes to be revised by later litigation. But stare decisis (the duty to follow precedent), as actually employed, tends to provide about as much stability as anyone would want or expect in a modern industrial democracy.

There is no such expectation of relative fixity in the realm of historical understanding, or of the collective memory to which such understanding contributes. Whereas legal judgment is final, collective memory can be fickle.[23] One might say, more sympathetically, that collective memory is necessarily fluid. "The historian no longer poses as a scientist domesticating the past so much as a single participant in a conversation across time."[24] Prevailing understandings of a given event will inevitably change as the interpreters' standpoints move ever further into the hermeneutic horizon.[25] Subsequent events require periodic revision of how earlier ones are remembered.[26] Still later developments alter the concerns that future generations will bring to bear in reexamining the event in question.[27] This process reproduces at

---

23   This is demonstrated, for instance, in the waxing and waning of the reputations of prominent political and intellectual figures over time. Gladys E. Lang & Kurt Lang, *Etched in Memory* 317 (1990); Barry Schwartz, "The Reconstruction of Abraham Lincoln,' in *Collective Remembering* 81 (David Middleton & Derek Edwards eds., 1990).

24   Kenneth Cmiel, "After Objectivity: What Comes Next in History?" 2 *American Literary History* 170, 172 (1990).

25   This terminology is that of Hans-Georg Gadamer. Hans-Georg Gadamer, *Truth and Method* 217, 269, 356 (Garrett Barden & John Cumming eds., Sheed & Ward Ltd. trans., 2d ed. 1986). This observation does not imply that those who did not live through an event are necessarily less likely to understand it. In contemporary France, for instance, surveys suggest that young people have a more accurate understanding of the extent of French collaboration with the Nazi occupation than do their elders. SOFRES Survey, *Libération,* Jan. 9-12, 1986.

26   See, e.g., Henry Rousso, *The Vichy Syndrome: History and Memory in France Since 1944* 10-11 (Arthur Goldhammer trans., 1991) (noting how historical memory of the Vichy period in France continued to change depending on what was at stake at a particular moment).

27   Postmodernists have no special claim of priority to this insight. Gadamer, *supra* note 25; Lucy M. Salmon, *Why Is History Rewritten?* 99-100 (1929); Carl N. Degler, "Why Historians Change Their Minds," 45 *Pac. Hist. Rev.* 167, 174 (1976). Once condemned as a vice, the "intrusion" of the historian's own concerns is now more often seen not merely as inevitable, but even as potentially a virtue. Hence Nora contends,

the societal level what takes place within the lifetime of individual persons. Leading psychologists conclude, on the basis of considerable experimental evidence, that "the way you remember an event depends on your purposes and goals at the time that you attempt to recall it."[28]

If historical writing does not aspire to finality, then, this is not because it lacks the law's authoritative imprimatur. It simply faces powerful obstacles, ones that the law confronts as well. It would thus be wrong to hope for very much from the law's efforts to stamp a particular reading of the recent past into collective memory, in ways likely to long endure. This is especially true when courts seek to base the authority of their historical judgments on the expert testimony of professional historians.

The response of defense counsel to this move is both predictable and devastating. In cross-examining Robert Paxton in the Touvier trial, for instance, defense counsel Trémolet de Villers, says to the witness, "In your book on Vichy France, they say your version of this period is 'revolutionary,' and before you, other historians have had different ideas. Others who come after you will certainly have different ones still. Let us say that you have been one moment in the history of Vichy." Turning then to the jury, he continues, "You are going to judge a *man*. If you make a wrong decision, this is not the same as with Mr. Paxton. Someone else will write another book to say he was wrong, but you will commit a legal error," one that no later legal fact-finder can correct. He concludes: by contrast to the gravity and fixity of legal judgment, "History is only an opinion."

Still, it may not be entirely quixotic to hope that legal judgment might impart some of its presumptive finality to the more ephemeral flux of public memory. In the decade before his death Richard Nixon successfully reestablished himself in the public eye as a respected elder statesman. Could this so easily have happened had Nixon been formally tried and convicted by the Senate, with all the ritual degradation that process would have involved?

---

for instance, that today "a new type of historian emerges who, unlike his precursors, is ready to confess the intimate relation he maintains to his subject. Better still, he is ready to proclaim it, deepen it, make of it not the obstacle but the means of his understanding." Nora, *supra* note 19, at 18.

28   Daniel Schacter, *Searching for Memory* 22 (1996).

The judgments of courts (when tackling conventional legal questions) acquire greater fixity than those of historians. For this reason, it is that much more embarrassing for judges—and threatening to the law's legitimacy—when judicial decisions embodying historical interpretations fail to stand "the test of time." Because our expectations of closure are greater, we are more disappointed by their frustration. Newly discovered information, increased geopolitical constraints, shifting moral sensibilities among the public: any or all of these may require "revision" of the court's allocation of responsibilities, in the form of executive grants of pardons or clemency to those convicted.

Many pardons were granted in Argentina, as well as in Japan, France, and Germany, only a few years after the convictions themselves, in most cases.[29] The courts have seemed, in convicting such defendants, to blame them for their country's recent calamities. Hence a pardon will inevitably be interpreted (as it was in these three societies) not so much as a professional reconsideration of the legal merits of the case, but rather as a political repudiation of a judicial foray into historiography and national narrative. Yet what had made a criminal proceeding so appealing in the first place as "a genre of public discourse," as a forum for memory-practice, was "the key element of symbolic closure provided by the trial's verdict."[30] However desirable they may ultimately be, pardons and amnesties necessarily reopen

---

29 Gavan Daws, *Prisoners of the Japanese: POWs of World War II in the Pacific* 373 (1994) (noting that, due to commutations and clemency, the longest sentence actually served by any Japanese war criminal was less than 13 years and that by the end of 1958 all war criminals were free). The emergence of the Cold War was the decisive consideration in West Germany and Japan. Frank M. Buscher, *The U.S. War Crimes Trial Program in Germany, 1946-1955* 118-19, 143, 150 (1989); Saburō Ienaga, *Japan's Last War: World War II and the Japanese, 1931-1945* 255 (1979); Sakamoto Yoshikazu, "The International Context of the Occupation of Japan," in *Democratizing Japan: The Allied Occupation* 42, 61 (Robert E. Ward & Sakamoto Yoshikazu eds., 1987). In Argentina, the electoral losses of Alfonsín's Radical Party largely accounted for his successor's pardons of the military juntas and other convicted officers. "Argentina: Presidential Pardons," in 3 *Transitional Justice: How Emerging Democracies Reckon with Former Regimes* 528, 528-32 (Neil J. Kritz ed., 1995) (reprinting Argentine Presidential Decrees 1002/89 and 2741/90); on the extensive French pardons and amnesties in 1946 and 1947, which left only the most serious offenders in prison, see B. Gordon, "Afterward," in *Memory, The Holocaust, and French Justice* 193 (Richard Golsan ed., 1996).

30 Robert Hariman, "Introduction" to *Popular Trials: Rhetoric, Mass Media, and the Law* 1-2 (Robert Hariman ed., 1990).

questions (and reverse conclusions) that the law had considered closed.

In its ephemeral flux, collective memory more closely resembles historiography than legal judgment. Neither memory nor history has any strong interest in finality. Neither possesses any institutional mechanisms for attaching itself, over long periods, to any stable resting point. Recent generations of historians, including legal historians, do not presume to provide "the judgment of history." They uniformly disavow such aspirations as hubristic. To claim that one has written "the definitive account" of a period or personage would today be to invite not merely immediate revision, but outright ridicule. Like historical writing, collective memory does not preserve any single, dispositive account of what happened, still less of its meaning. What is remembered evolves with the changing interests and ideals of whoever is doing the remembering, as scholars in several fields have shown.[31]

In interpreting episodes of administrative massacre, judges are more like journalists in this regard than like historians. Journalists must content themselves with uncovering the basic facts and offering them a quick gloss. Historians seek, by contrast, to fit such facts into a larger interpretive framework, encompassing preceding and subsequent events. Later events inevitably alter the meaning of prior ones, disclosing certain features of the historical landscape as far more significant than they appeared to participants at the time, others far less. Judges, like journalists, would have to be outstandingly prescient—in ways their jobs do not conventionally require—if their interpretations are to have an enduring effect on collective memory, in the face of the future's inevitable revision and reassessment. It would be wrong to expect courts, in the immediate aftermath of national trauma, to achieve in this regard what neither the most thoughtful journalism nor the best historical scholarship can expect to accomplish.

But where historians fear to tread, political leaders often enter—and blunder about—quite intrepidly, sometimes employing the law and courts to their ends. After all, political leaders often seek to create, as a prominent French historian notes, "nonevents that are immediately charged with heavy symbolic meaning and that, at the

---

31   Carl L. Becker, *Everyman His Own Historian* 242 (1935); Moses Finley, *The Use and Abuse of History* 31-33 (1975).

moment of their occurrence, seem like anticipated commemorations of themselves; contemporary history, by means of the media, has seen a proliferation of stillborn attempts to create such events."[32]

Vernacular Memory vs. the "Official Story"

Consider several examples of such failed attempts to "lawyer" history (or, more generously, at historiographic lawyering), while the ashes of administrative massacre were still warm. Allied prosecutors at the Tokyo War Crimes trials, for instance, deliberately refrained from indicting Emperor Hirohito—who retained enormous prestige and public approval—in order to make the prosecution of lesser officials more legitimate in the eyes of the Japanese public.[33] Despite this concession to public opinion, the tactic failed, as the trials won little popular support. MacArthur was content, however, to purchase grudging acquiescence, since he feared the alternative to be mass resistance.

Elsewhere, the "vernacular memory" of major events has often proven quite different from, and largely resistant to direct influence by, the public commemorations of events orchestrated by state elites.[34] An ethnography of one blue-collar neighborhood in Buenos Aires, for example, finds that vernacular memory of the dirty war differs from

---

32 Nora, *supra* note 19, at 13; see also Daniel Dayan & Elihu Katz, *Media Events: The Live Broadcasting of History* 68-73 (1992).

33 Ian Buruma, *The Wages of Guilt: Memories of War in Germany and Japan* 176 (1994). Witnesses were even instructed to "'include the fact that Hirohito was only a benign presence when military actions or programs were discussed at meetings that, by protocol, he had to attend.'" *Id.* at 175 (quoting Aristides George Lazarus, defense counsel of one of the generals on trial).

34 Vernacular memory is oral, while legal judgments and elite historiography are written. The dynamics of written and oral communication are so different that this alone may explain much of the distortion when a story is translated from the first medium into the second. Walter J. Ong, *Orality and Literacy:* 69, 74, 105 (1982); see also Mona Ozouf, *Festivals in the French Revolution* 102-05 (1988) (observing how officially staged festivals in France commemorating revolutionary events often escaped police control, becoming violent or carnivalesque); David Cressy, "National Memory in Early Modern England," in *Commemorations* 61, 71 (John R. Gillis ed., 1994) (explaining how by the end of the 17th century, popular memory in England differed substantially from the national commemorations created by the political elite).

"the official story," promulgated by Alfonsín's courts, in several ways: "Most remember orderliness and lack of crime as positive characteristics of the military period, often at the same time as they disapprove of the human rights violations ...."[35] Alfonsín's chief legal advisor ultimately reached an even more pessimistic conclusion: that the courts' judgments proved

> irrelevant to the citizenry's view of its recent political history. This verdict shows that despite the theoretical claim that a judicial determination will establish an authoritative truth, in Argentina judicial decisions lack authoritativeness both in establishing the facts brought to trial and in evaluating these facts. Thus, controversies about what should have been done about past human rights violations continue unabated, with no hope that any arbiter will bring them to an end.[36]

Malamud-Goti's suggestion here that the courts' judgments on the dirty war had no effect on collective memory, however, proved unduly pessimistic.   Even the military leadership would ultimately acknowledge the judicial narrative as authoritative. In April 1995, the head of each of the Argentine armed services finally admitted the responsibility of his respective branch for gross illegality in the dirty war. In his public statement to that effect, Admiral Enrique Molina Pico (Navy Chief of Staff) commented:

> Human justice is imperfect, because it is based on incomplete truth. Nevertheless, the firm and clear judgment of the Supreme Court has established the legal truth by which we abide. That judgment clarifies and makes an accounting of the methods employed—methods denied at the time and until the present—methods that today, in another step toward reconciliation, we admit ....[37]

---

35 Lindsay DuBois, "Popular Memory in Practice and Theory: Reflections on a History Workshop in Argentina" 2 (Mar. 1994) (paper presented at the Latin American Studies Association Conference); see also Elizabeth Jelin, "The Politics of Memory: The Human Rights Movement and the Construction of Democracy in Argentina," 21 *Latin Am. Persp.* 38, 39-46 (1994) (emphasizing the role of memory of political movement militants in curbing contemporary and future human rights violations).

36 Jaime Malamud-Goti, "Punishing Human Rights Abuses in Fledgling Democracies: The Case of Argentina," in *Impunity and Human Rights, supra* note 9, at 160, 164.

37 Enrique Molina Pico, *Clarín* (Buenos Aires), Int'l Ed., May 2-8, 1995, at 7, 7 (translation by author). Molina acknowledged, moreover, that social reconciliation

The Court's judgment, in short, had finally been accepted—at least for its statement of facts, as a point of departure for further discussion between soldiers and civilians over the meaning and memory of these events.[38] The distinguished Argentine journalist Horacio Verbitsky immediately perceived the deliberative potential of Balza's apology:

> From now on, fewer obstacles will block the necessary debate on how this could have happened in Argentina. This debate should be public, involving many voices. And it should eschew both the kind of demonization that casts all the blame upon a few people and the kind of retreat from responsibility in which charges of unequal seriousness are treated as equal.[39]

Efforts to induce collective forgetting may fail in the same ways as efforts to induce collective remembering. In pardoning convicted officers and later praising their "war against subversion,"[40] for example, Alfonsín's successor, President Carlos Saúl Menem, sought self-consciously to diminish memory of the state's criminality during the 1970s. Yet, as Halperin reminds:

> Today when General Videla takes a stroll in the evening, his neighbors cross the street to avoid sharing the sidewalk with him, and this is less a political statement than a reflection of the horror he inspires. It is true that this is small consolation for his victims, and that many of his neighbors' horror is strictly retrospective ....
>
> ... Even so, this kind of reaction has no equivalent in Argentine history since the fall of Rosas [an early dictator] and has important political consequences, first among them, the incredible loss of political clout of the army, that allows [Finance Minister Domingo] Cavallo to be as stingy

---

regarding the dirty war could not be expected shortly, on the simple basis of such confessions by military leadership. *Id.*

38   In fact, it became "hard to find active-duty Argentine officers who identify themselves with the repressive military of the dirty war .... Experts say that civilian control of the military is stronger today than ever in Argentine history." "Argentina's Enlightened Chief of Staff," *N.Y. Times,* Oct. 27, 1995, at A30.

39   Horacio Verbitsky, "Time to Discuss the Dirty War," *Pagina 12,* Buenos Aires, April 30, 1995, translated and reprinted in *World Press Review,* July 1995, at 47, 48.

40   "Menem Expelled from Human Rights Group for Defending State Terrorism," *Latin Am. News Update,* Jan. 1995, at 28, 28.

with officers' salaries as with those of the rest of government, and to privatize or close at will army factories and enterprises, and to abolish the draft without even consulting military opinion (and the military put up with it ....)[41]

These are no small achievements in a society as thoroughly dominated by military power as was Argentina in the preceding half-century. They suggest the continuing impact of the criminal convictions on collective memory. This shared revulsion toward convicted junta members and the attendant ostracism they suffer in their daily life bespeaks a reinvigoration of the social solidarity, founded on liberal morality, that Durkheim longed for, and for which Alfonsín's legal advisors had hoped.

In modern France, persistent efforts by liberal lawyers and officials often failed to influence shared memory of the country's postrevolutionary past. In fact, right-wing nationalism has often expressly sought to distinguish the *pays réel* from the *pays légal*, the "True France" of the people from that officially controlled by republican legal authorities.[42] The virtues of the former have been consistently celebrated by nationalist conservatives precisely for their immunity from the liberalizing influence of the *pays légal*, and the

----

41   Letter from Tulio Halperin Donghi to Author (Feb. 3, 1995). (Halperin is one of Latin America's most distinguished historians.) Alfonsín also reduced the military's budget by over 50% and curtailed staffing considerably at all levels. Andrés Fontana, *"La Política Militar en un Contexto de Transición "* (Mar. 1990) (paper presented at the Schell Center for Human Rights, Yale University). Menem was even able to privatize several public enterprises long controlled by the military, sell off large real estate holdings of the armed forces, and terminate their participation in the Condor II missile development project.

The Madres have continued their weekly marches in the *Plaza de Mayo*, maintaining the issue of the disappeared in the public spotlight. Their "occupation of the main public space of Buenos Aires acquired the force of a ritual of counter-memory." William Rowe & Vivian Schelling, *Memory and Modernity: Popular Culture in Latin America* 228 (1991).

42   This distinction, dating from the Orleanist monarchy, was resurrected in the 1930s by Charles Maurras. Herman Lebovics, *True France: The Wars over Cultural Identity, 1900-1945,* at 136-38 (1992). Ernst Nolte's invocation of the German *pays réel* in the "Historians' Debate" is thus particularly ominous, given the term's prior, consistently anti-Dreyfusard (hence anti-Semitic) usage. Ernst Nolte, "The Past That Will Not Pass: A Speech That Could Be Written but Not Delivered," in *Forever in the Shadow of Hitler?* 19 (James Knowlton & Truett Cates trans., 1993).

secular, cosmopolitan elites who staffed it.[43] But the essential logic of the distinction is politically neutral. In fact, it closely resembles that drawn by "progressive" legal realists in the U.S. between the "law on the books" (bad) and the "law in action" (good).

Social division in modern France was thus rhetorically formulated in terms of a war between those for whom the national identity of France was defined by its law and those for whom it was defined by enduring predispositions and prejudices particularly insusceptible to legal "tampering." Conservative historians were therefore drawn to *early* (that is, prerevolutionary) French law because they viewed it, unlike its degenerate modern variant, as growing naturally and spontaneously from the customs of the French people, reflecting their inalterable essence.[44] These conflicting views of the relation of law to national identity in France took conspicuous expression in its painting, sculpture, and architecture.[45]

The postwar German experience is pertinent as well. Until the late 1940s, American occupation authorities engaged in considerable publicity efforts, including frequent radio broadcasts of the Nuremberg proceedings, to induce the German people to accept responsibility for the wrongs of the Nazi state. That initial effort, admittedly reliant on some rather heavy-handed methods, clearly failed.[46] To establish new

---

43   Lebovics, *supra* note 42, at 137.

44   Keith M. Baker, "Memory and Practice: Politics and the Representation of the Past in Eighteenth-Century France," *Representations*, Summer 1985, at 134, 134. See generally Donald R. Kelley, *Historians and the Law in Postrevolutionary France* (1984) (arguing that French societal struggles over the "proper" way of viewing French history are encapsulated in the disputes over legal philosophy in postrevolutionary France). On similar currents in British legal and political thought, see J.G.A. Pocock, *The Ancient Constitution and the Feudal Law* 275-80 (2d ed. 1987).

45   See generally Jonathan P. Ribner, *Broken Tablets: The Cult of the Law in French Art from David to Delacroix* (1993) (tracing the evolution of legal imagery in French art from the late 18th century to the middle of the 19th century).

46   Koonz provides several examples. Claudia Koonz, "Between Memory and Oblivion: Concentration Camps in German Memory," in *supra* note 34, at 261-62; see also Ron Robin, *The Barbed-Wire College: Reeducating German POWs in the United States During World War II* (1995); James F. Tent, *Mission on the Rhine: Reeducation and Denazification in American-Occupied Germany* 117, 275, 287 (1982). Prosecutors themselves at first devoted little thought to how the first Nuremberg trial might best be designed to educate the German populace. Telford Taylor, *The Anatomy of the Nuremberg Trials: A Personal Memoir* 233-35 (1992). Arendt believed that the German public's "lack of enthusiasm for legal proceedings against Nazi criminals"

models of heroic virtue, many speeches were given commemorating the resistance movement and the personal sacrifices made by its leaders.[47] Yet much German opinion continued to view the wartime resistance negatively, even as treasonous.[48]   The Nuremberg trials greatly influenced *non*-German memory of German crimes, to be sure. This influence was carefully and self-consciously cultivated by the U.S. government, for public and elite opinion regarding the desirability of such trials was at first highly equivocal.   The effort was quite successful.[49]

Even here, however, the ultimate effect on collective memory in the U.S. (and elsewhere) was distinct from that desired. Allied prosecutors, like the Tribunal itself, heavily concentrated on establishing the criminality of German acts involved in "waging aggressive war."   Prosecutors and judges clearly expected that international punishment of such acts to be the central legacy of the trials, and of their professional labors.

Today, after hundreds more aggressive wars, we understand the legacy of Nuremberg quite differently. It is almost universally remembered, both among the literate public and international lawyers, for its contribution to the criminalization of "crimes against humanity."[50]   Hence, even when law succeeds in intentionally

---

during the Adenauer era was at least partly due to the fact that "the West German administration on all levels is shot through with former Nazis." Introduction to Bernd Naumann, *Auschwitz: A Report on the Proceedings Against Robert Ludwig Mulka and Others Before the Court at Frankfurt* xvii (1966).

47   David C. Large, "Uses of the Past: The Anti-Nazi Resistance Legacy in the Federal Republic of Germany," in *Contending with Hitler: Varieties of German Resistance in the Third Reich* 163, 164 (David C. Large ed., 1991). Theodor Adorno described this attitude as "the rancor against re-education." Theodor W. Adorno, "What Does Coming to Terms with the Past Mean?," in *Bitburg in Moral and Political Perspective* 114, 116 (Geoffrey H. Hartman ed., 1986).

48   Large, *supra* note 47, at 166.

49   As Bosch suggests, "the State Department conducted an active program of informing and molding public opinion to favor legal procedures .... The people who were not in favor of or were not interested in the trial method ... changed their positions completely." William J. Bosch, *Judgment on Nuremberg: American Attitudes Toward the Major German War-Crimes Trials* 116 (1970); see also *id.* at 21-39 (illustrating various methods by which this alteration of public opinion was brought about).

50   Two theorists thus recently observe, for instance, that "In 1945 the Holocaust appeared to many people to be a very sad but minor event....only during the [Nuremberg] trial did the enormity of the Holocaust fitfully begin to penetrate the

influencing collective memory of administrative massacre, it often does so in unintended ways.

The Andean highlands offer a second example of the law's unintended effects on the collective memory: here, on the memory of an indigenous people, the Cumbal Indians of Colombia and Ecuador.[51] In conquering the region, Spanish explorers were responsible for many massacres of these Indians. But indigenous memory now focuses instead on Spain's more positive legal legacy: its legislation endowing indigenous communities with rights over designated lands.[52] The Spanish intended this legislation primarily to reduce the territory controlled by Cumbales, that is, to legalize the Spanish conquest and the seizure of native lands.[53] The legislation achieved this imperial objective, of course.

But in the process, it also entitled the Indians to far more territory than subsequent generations of Spanish and *mestizo* inhabitants would wish to acknowledge. This colonial legislation, later adopted as binding by the independent state of Colombia, became the basis for several decades of litigation by Indians against territorial encroachment by more powerful, non-Indian farmers.[54] The tangled history of this litigation has become the centerpiece of native storytelling in the region.[55]

In fact, it has become the focal point of group identity, according to ethnographies of the area.[56] This is because the Cumbales, who no

---

consciousness of those gathered in the courtroom. For most people at the time, the fact that the Germans started this war was their great sin." Avishai Margalit and Gabriel Motzkin, "The Uniqueness of the Holocaust," 25 *Philosophy and Public Affairs* 64, 67 (1996).

51   This analysis is drawn from Joanne Rappaport, *The Politics of Memory: Native Historical Interpretation in the Colombian Andes* (1990) [hereinafter Rappaport, *Politics*] and Joanne Rappaport, *Cumbe Reborn: An Andean Ethnography of History* (1994) [hereinafter Rappaport, *Cumbe*].

52   Rappaport, *Cumbe, supra* note 51, at 5.

53   *Id.* at 2-4.

54   *Id.*; see also Rappaport, *Politics, supra* note 51, at 198-202 (citing pertinent cases).

55   Rappaport, *Cumbe, supra* note 51, at 7 (reporting that "many of the stories I heard ... are couched in the language of jurisprudence or are organized as though they constituted evidence for legal briefs").

56   *Id.* at 26 ("In effect, the European construction of the other, as it is interpreted in law, is basic to an indigenous definition of self.").

longer speak their ancestral Pasto language and who have assimilated other Western ways, must reassert Indian identity—through continuity of lineage with those whose lands were wrongly seized—in order to establish a right to reclaim them.[57] Recounted in ritual gatherings, the legal history of this struggle, by individual family claimants and local Indian leadership, has even become the narrative support for renewed political militancy by the Cumbales against the Colombian state and its majority *mestizo* population.[58] In taking up colonial law to help their people, the Cumbales had first sought only the economic and "material" goal of regaining their lands.

After many decades of such efforts, however, this litigation had significantly strengthened the authority of local governing councils, responsible for allocating regained (and collectively owned) lands. The result was also to strengthen the identification of individual members with the governing institutions of the group, through which such new resources are distributed.[59] Such are the puzzling twists and perplexing turns of the law's impact on collective memory.

Both the Spanish conquistadors and the Nuremberg prosecutors were venturing onto uncharted legal territory. It may be that they were merely shortsighted, that they could in principle have better anticipated the long-term legacy of their efforts. It may not therefore be a *necessary* truth that all such efforts must fail, as Elster's thesis implies.[60] As legal experience (and scholarly reflection upon it) gather over time, it may become possible at some point to say which legal maneuvers work in influencing collective memory and which do not. After all, courts have only recently learned the extent to which *individual* memory can be influenced (and distorted) by therapeutic suggestion,[61] in ways posing enormous problems for legal fact-finding.[62]

---

57 Rappaport, *Politics, supra* note 51, at 185 (noting that "oral tradition is restricted by Indian legislation, which defines the means by which native communities can legitimize their identity"). For a similar story of how long-ignored legal rights, and the lands to which they may offer title, prompted a reconstruction of collective memory and identity among Native Americans in the U.S., see James Clifford, *The Predicament of Culture: Twentieth-Century Ethnography, Literature, and Art* 277 (1988).

58 Rappaport, *Cumbe, supra* note 51, at 7.

59 *Id.* at 10-11.

60 See *supra* note 11.

61 See generally Richard Ofshe & Ethan Watters, *Making Monsters: False Memories,*

Memory, we have learned, can present itself as having been innocently "repressed" from within, when in fact it has been insinuated (sometimes insidiously) from without.

Successful Legal Stagecraft

There is reason to believe that similar fabrication at the *societal* level is equally possible. Here the law is more likely to be the perpetrator of distortion than its victim. Nonetheless, recent studies of collective memory have discovered many instances of successful efforts by officers of the law to influence collective memory in precisely the manner intended.[63]

Within Western Europe, for instance, collective memory of the Holocaust is weakest and least accurate, to judge from opinion surveys and textbook treatments, in precisely those societies that did *not* conduct any (or numerically significant) postwar trials of collaborators, that is, in Austria, Poland, Italy, and the Netherlands.[64]

Psychotherapy, and Sexual Hysteria (1994) (arguing that psychotherapists can unintentionally implant false memories into their patients' minds) and Schacter, *supra* note 28, at 248-279. An influential early study is found in Ernest G. Schachtel, "On Memory and Childhood Amnesia," *Psychiatry*, Feb. 1947, at 1.

62   Cynthia Bowman & Elizabeth Mertz, "A Dangerous Direction: Legal Intervention in Sexual Abuse Survivor Therapy," 109 *Harv. L. Rev.* 549 (1996).

63   On the enduring impact of prosecution upon collective memory in Greece, for instance, see Neil J. Kritz, "The Dilemmas of Transitional Justice," in 1 *Transitional Justice: How Emerging Democracies Reckon with Former Regimes* xix, xxii (Neil J. Kritz ed., 1995) (observing that "nearly twenty years after the conviction of junta leaders who had overseen the torture of hundreds, plans to release them from prison still prompted huge protests").

64   Judith Miller, *One, By One, By One: Facing the Holocaust* 72-73, 111, 153, 210, 285-86 (1990) (suggesting that the trials of quislings elsewhere in Europe, however divisive they may have been, at least clearly revealed, and inscribed in memory, the extent of collaboration to a greater degree than in these four countries). Such legal revelations had considerable influence on the memory of younger generations, especially in West Germany, according to many accounts. See, e.g., Tony Judt, "The Past Is Another Country: Myth and Memory in Postwar Europe," 83, 96 *Daedalus,* (Fall 1992) (observing a relationship between how certain European societies portrayed themselves in the postwar period entirely as victims of German wrongdoing and the fact that their actual "experience with Fascism was left largely unrecorded in public discussion").

On Dutch exaggeration of their wartime resistance to Nazi occupation, see Gerhard

Traditions, we learn, have often been "invented," including legal traditions.[65]   Innovations, in other words, have regularly been presented—surreptitiously but successfully—as a legacy of time immemorial. Common law is especially receptive to this practice; even the most radical innovations, after all, have often been couched as part of a seamless web of evolving doctrine.[66] Legal change can often be

---

Hirschfeld, *Nazi Rule and Dutch Collaboration* (1988); Miller, *supra* note 64, at 111; Peter Hayes, "A Historian Confronts Denial" in *The Netherlands and Nazi Genocide* 521, 522 (G. Jan Colijn & Marcia Littell eds., 1992); Selma Leydesdorff, "A Shattered Silence: The Life Stories of Survivors of the Jewish Proletariat of Amsterdam," in *Memory and Totalitarianism* 145, 161-62 (Luisa Passerini ed., 1992). Austria offers the extreme, limiting case in this regard. Richard Bassett, *Waldheim and Austria* 79-80, 137-38, 158 (1988). Although there were massive purges of public employees and Nazi sympathizers (nearly 500,000 people) in Austria, there were no public proceedings and hence no deliberative airing of issues. Those who were purged were never ostracized. In fact, they were soon pardoned and fully rehabilitated. Frederick C. Engelmann, "How Austria Has Coped with Two Dictatorial Legacies," in *From Dictatorship to Democracy: Coping with the Legacies of Authoritarianism and Totalitarianism* 135, 143-47 (John H. Herz ed., 1982).

On the paucity and political insignificance of postwar trials in Italy, see Roy P. Domenico, *Italian Fascists on Trial, 1943-1948*, at 90-91 (1991); Giuseppe Di Palma, "Italy: Is There a Legacy and Is It Fascist?," in *From Dictatorship to Democracy, Id.* at 107, 116-22.

On the limitations of Polish memory regarding national complicity in the Holocaust, see Iwona Irwin-Zarecka, *Frames of Remembrance: The Dynamics of Collective Memory* 77-78, 92-93 (1994); *Shoah* (Claude Lanzmann, director; Les Films Aleph & Historia Films 1985). On the greater accuracy of school textbooks in countries where trials were held, etching the proceedings into collective memory, see Herbert Hirsch, *Genocide and the Politics of Memory* 28 (1995).

65 Eric Hobsbawm, "Mass-Producing Traditions: Europe, 1870-1914," in *The Invention of Tradition* 263, 263-65 (Eric Hobsbawm & Terence Ranger eds., 1983) (characterizing late-19th-century Europe as a period of particularly fervent efforts to construct national monuments, rituals, and traditions in hopes of overcoming the profound social conflict generated by industrialization).

To be sure, elite efforts to invent traditions and impose them upon populations often fail, and Hobsbawm's influential analysis tells us virtually nothing about when or why such efforts only intermittently succeed.

On such recurrent failures, and the resilience of vernacular memory that they entail, see Raphael Samuel, *Theatres of Memory Vol. I* 17 (1995). Durkheim's preoccupation with solidarity and how it might be reconstructed in modern society was itself an expression of this prevalent concern among 19th-century cultural elites.

66 Reinhard Bendix, *Max Weber* 331 (1960) ("'As a matter of principle it is out of the question to create new laws which deviate from historical norms. However, new rights are created in fact, but only by way of "recognizing" them as having been valid "from time immemorial."'" (quoting Max Weber, *Staatssoziologie* 101 (1956). The legal history of product liability provides a well-known modern illustration of how such unacknowledged, incremental evolution can add up to a veritable revolution.

disguised as continuity, as the preservation or elaboration of practices existing since time immemorial.

In Tudor-Stuart England, collective memory was willfully "shaped by those leaders and preachers who invested particular parts of their history with special meaning," writes an historian of the period.[67] Even in predominantly peasant societies, the historical beliefs of the general public, though not always highly responsive to legal suasion, "are not the pure water of oral tradition, springing unpolluted from the font of popular memory."[68] In fact, they have even been shown to originate in "high" or learned literature. The much-vaunted immunity of popular memory from elite manipulation is largely a populist shibboleth.[69]

Political elites, in particular, often invoke legal history to legitimate their social position and political claims,[70] But elites have not monopolized this practice. In the seventeenth and eighteenth centuries, for instance, British yeomen couched their opposition to private enclosure of common pasture in terms of the eternal birthrights of freeborn Englishmen at common law.[71] Legal doctrines of usufruct

---

MacPherson v. Buick Motor Co., 111 N.E. 1050, 1055 (1916); see also Melvin A. Eisenberg, *The Nature of the Common Law* 58-61, 132-33 (1988) (explaining how Cardozo, in *MacPherson*, changed product liability law by altering the substance but not the form of existing law). On the place of surreptitious invention within legal tradition, see M.T. Clanchy, "Remembering the Past and the Good Old Law," 55 *History* 165, 172 (1970) (observing how French, German, and British legal historians have "all emphasized the flexibility and relative newness of customary law," particularly its ability to conceal innovation).

67   Cressy, *supra* note 34, at 71.

68   Keith Thomas, *The Perception of the Past in Early Modern England* 7 (1983); see also James Fentress & Chris Wickham, *Social Memory* 103-07 (1992) (tracing local Brazilian folklore to European epics); Patrick J. Geary, *Phantoms of Remembrance: Memory and Oblivion at the End of the First Millennium* 12 (1994) 12.

69   The most persuasive evidence of resourceful resistance to official efforts at memory construction are to be found in totalitarian regimes, where the costs of harboring "counter-memory" are greatest. Geoffrey A. Hosking, "Memory in a Totalitarian Society: The Case of the Soviet Union," in *Memory: History, Culture and the Mind, supra* note 65, at 115, 121-22; on similar failures at memory construction in China, see Watson, *supra* note 16, at 13.

70   On the framers' deliberate effort to encourage public reverence for the U.S. Constitution, see Michael Lienesch, *New Order of the Ages: Time, the Constitution, and the Making of Modern American Political Thought* 164-83 (1988).

71   E.P. Thompson, *Customs in Common* 97-184 (1991); see also William Sewell, *Work and Revolution in France: The Language of Labor from the Old Regime to 1848*, at 38-39, 194-95 (1978) (discussing the popular use of medieval corporate legal idiom

proved potent weapons for the poor, since they grounded claims of enforceable right on longstanding memory of social practice, memory as ancient as the commonalty itself. In legal systems heavily reliant on customary law (generally unwritten), memory of customary practices becomes particularly central to legal argument.[72]

This invocation of collective memory to interpret and defend current claims often leads to considerable historical distortion. As one sympathetic scholar concedes, villagers "collectively created a *remembered village* and a *remembered economy* that serve as an effective ideological backdrop against which to deplore the present.... That they do not dwell upon other, less favorable, features of the old order is hardly surprising, for those features do not contribute to the argument they wish to make today."[73]

If "the people" themselves sometimes drop the ball, sympathetic scholars often seek to pick it up and run with it themselves. Hence some self-declared "radical historians" have come to view their vocation as preserving the memory of labor's struggle to organize and legalize union activity, in hopes that the "lessons of the good fight" will not die with those who fought it.[74] The legal history of American labor is today avowedly written from this perspective.[75] Such historians aspire to revive a collective memory of working class struggle that the working class itself has largely forgotten. Their avowed aim is, in part,

---

for formulating political demands in early modern and 19th-century Europe).

72   Bernard Lewis, *History: Remembered, Recovered, Invented* 66 (1975) (noting that in some preliterate societies mental recollection was vital in determining "immemorial rights and privileges").

73   James C. Scott, *Weapons of the Weak* 178-79 (1985). Scott refers here specifically to the legal claims of Malaysian peasants, but his point is of more general relevance. *Id.* at 180.

74   Alessandro Portelli, *The Death of Luigi Trastulli and Other Stories* 1-27 (1991); Marianne Debouzy, "In Search of Working-Class Memory," in *Between Memory and History* 261, 264-74 (Marie-Noëlle Bourguet et al. eds., 1986); Michael H. Frisch, "Towards a People's History: The Memory of History," *Radical Hist. Rev.,* (Fall 1981), at 9, 10. For criticism, see François Furet, *Interpreting the French Revolution* 4-10 (Elborg Forster trans., 1981) (accusing radical historians of endowing obscure, short-lived sects with excessive historical importance in order to establish links between the French revolution, conceived as a myth of national origin, and the partisan preoccupations of such historians).

75   See, e.g., Karen Orren, *Belated Feudalism: Labor, the Law, and Liberal Development in the United States* (1991); William Forbath, *Law and the Shaping of the American Labor Movement* (1992).

to enable future workers to recognize their "own" past in that of the socioeconomic group or category to which the historian seeks to assign them. The nonnarrative character of such historiography, however, makes it singularly inapt for political mythmaking and collective memory, since the "stories" it tells are generally statistical.

Deliberate efforts to cultivate memory date from the Greeks, who devised the art of "mnemotechnics" for impressing places and images on memory.[76] These techniques, passed on to the Romans and in common use among Roman lawyers,[77] were crucial for cultural transmission before the advent of the printing press and the growth of mass literacy.[78] Conversely, the criminal law of ancient Rome had a punishment, the *damnatio memoriae*, entailing the obliteration of any reference to, or symbolic representation of the offender, even from his gravestone.[79]

Today these methods to ensure remembrance or oblivion strike us as terribly artificial. Buy they were understood as essential in preserving cultural inheritances across generations in preliterate societies.[80] Their widespread use was predicated on the idea that the content of our memories—individual and shared—need not be left to chance, and that a society's survival could be furthered by its official adoption of practices by which members periodically remind one another of its greatest achievements and the moral principles they

---

76   Frances A. Yates, *The Art of Memory* 1-4 (1966). On medieval preservation of these methods, see generally Mary Carruthers, *The Book of Memory: A Study of Memory in Medieval Culture* (1990) (discussing medieval preservation of memory); Geary, *supra* note 68, at 20-21 (describing some tools used in the preservation of medieval memory). On the transmission of these methods to the non-Western world, see Jonathan D. Spence, *The Memory Palace of Matteo Ricci* 4 (1984).

77   Fentress & Wickham, *supra* note 68, at 11; see also 1 *Laws of Early Iceland* 187-88 (Andrew Dennis et al. trans., 1980) (noting how medieval Icelandic lawspeakers were to commit their entire law code to memory).

78   For a fictional examination of mnemotechnic transmission of subversive knowledge—Western literary classics—in a postliterate dystopia, prohibiting their publication, see Ray Bradbury, *Fahrenheit 451* (1953).

79   Helga Geyer-Ryan & Helmut Lethen, "The Rhetoric of Forgetting: Brecht and the Historical Avant-Garde," in *Convention and Innovation in Literature* (Theo D'haen et. al., eds., 305, 305 (1989) (citing a 1936 work by F. Vittinghoff).

80   M.T. Clanchy, *From Memory to Written Record: England 1066-1307* 172-77, 297 (Blackwell Publishers, 2d ed. 1993) (1979) (observing of illuminated manuscripts painted by medieval monks, that "the schoolmen were trained to make physical objects create graphic images in the memory to which they attached their abstract ideas").

embody. In traditional societies, after all, members feel a powerful *moral* duty to remember their shared past. In ancient Greece, memory was literally a god (Mnemosyne), the mother of the Muses, hence the source of imagination.[81]

These facts suggest that to contemplate the "intelligent and intentional" creation of collective memory is not oxymoronic. The memory of sentiment, no less of places and images, can be willfully induced by an *aide-mémoire*, as Proust famously suggested.[82] The law might serve, perhaps through annual commemoration of its conviction of official mass murderers, much like Proust's *petit madeleine*. Experimental psychology now offers considerable scientific support for this possibility. It strongly suggests that "the likelihood of remembering ... hinges on the hint or cue that triggers recall—and how it is related to the ... memory trace that was initially recorded."[83] Commemorations of a criminal conviction can be designed to match the traces in which the trial was initially encoded by its intellectual architects.

Some success stories: Israel's secular, socialist founders, in search of a unifying narrative for the new nation, self-consciously sought to make the ancient Masada defenders (who killed themselves as the Roman army lay siege to the beleaguered city) into central figures of national mythology for the modern state. To attain this pivotal place in collective memory, however, the story had to be recharacterized in terms of political martyrdom, for suicide remains contrary to Jewish law. Religious law carried great weight with the substantial population of Orthodox and ultra-Orthodox Jews, whose numbers in Israel have increased significantly in recent years. Only an authoritative legal judgment on the matter enabled the Masada story to become universally accepted as part of the national narrative, as a story whose meaning

---

81   Robert E. Bell, *Women of Classical Mythology* 310 (1991).

82   See generally Marcel Proust, *Swann's Way* (1928) (describing a method of inducing sentimental memory). For Proust, an initially *in*voluntary memory, followed by intense *voluntary* mental effort, could induce the recollection of the individual's prior emotional experience. For the law, an initially voluntary effort (criminal prosecution, periodically commemorated thereafter) would be necessary to induce, in time, the involuntary and spontaneous recollection by a society's members of their—or their ancestors'—prior emotional experience (of shock at the discovery of administrative massacre and of the indignation first felt, individually and collectively toward responsible parties).

83   Schacter, *supra* note 28, at 58-60.

could be shared.[84]

In the Eichmann trial, Hausner's and Ben-Gurion's dramaturgical decisions were highly effective in enhancing *sabra* sympathy for Holocaust victims, a matter on which prevailing sentiment had hitherto been quite ambivalent.[85] Reshaping the young nation's identity was a conscious goal, and the trial was staged with that goal directly in mind.

Perhaps judges within a new democracy, in Latin America or Eastern Europe, could help enhance respect for the rule of law by means more expeditious than simply conducting themselves judiciously. If so, it was entirely reasonable for Argentine legal officials to infer that, during a transition from authoritarianism to democracy, renewed appreciation of the "rule of law" might be deliberately cultivated among the public. This would not merely be done indirectly, by ensuring that judicial officials soberly displayed its perennial virtues. It would also be done more directly, by dramatically affirming the law's principles through the theatrical spectacle of a trial, shrewdly staged to maximal effect.

The Rise of International Memory

Between the Nuremberg trials and those in Buenos Aires, experience and observations had accumulated concerning the impact of criminal prosecution on collective memory of administrative massacre in various places, from Athens to Jerusalem.[86] A process of political learning had occurred; most efforts at prosecution were now preceded by intensive study of preceding ones. In fact, national memory of prior

---

84   Yael Zerubavel, *Recovered Roots: Collective Memory and the Making of Israeli National Tradition* 203-07 (1995).

85   Tom Segev, *The Seventh Million: The Israelis and the Holocaust* 327-30, 338-39, 342 (1993); Sidra D. Ezrahi, "Revisioning the Past: The Changing Legacy of the Holocaust in Hebrew Literature," *Salmagundi,* Fall 1985-Winter 1986, at 245, 260-61.

86   On the prosecution and conviction of Greek colonels for seizure of power, see generally *Amnesty International, Torture in Greece: The First Torturers' Trial 1975* (1977). On the assimilation of that story into the institutional memory of the human rights community, see Margaret Popkin & Naomi Roht-Arriaza, "Truth As Justice: Investigatory Commissions in Latin America," 20 *Law & Soc. Inquiry,* (Winter 1995), at 79, 79-116 (employing experience gained through other investigations to the truth commissions employed in Chile, Honduras, El Salvador, and Guatemala).

efforts had become international memory, through networks of informal assistance from lawyer-activists, legal scholars, and nongovernmental human rights organizations throughout the world.[87]

Alfonsín's advisors were easily able to consult a considerable literature on the Eichmann trial, for instance, and even borrowed (from one analysis of the Israeli judgment) the legal theory of "indirect authorship" used to convict the juntas.[88] In short, as international experience began to accumulate from prior prosecutions of administrative massacre, it became possible to begin discerning "what had worked" in influencing collective memory, and why.

President Alfonsín and his advisors could thus imagine accomplishing, with the junta prosecution, something akin to what Ben-Gurion had achieved—in impact on national self-understanding—with the conviction of Adolf Eichmann, or that accomplished by Chancellors Adenauer, Brandt, and Schmidt through conviction of the Auschwitz guards and Majdanek officials. In all these cases, government prosecutors—with executive prompting and tutelage—were highly self-aware about crafting the proceedings in a fashion calculated to produce maximum impact on collective memory.

To this end, they accentuated certain facts and issues while deemphasizing others—entirely apart from their strictly jurisprudential significance. The resulting decisions have rightly been described as no less "dramaturgical" than doctrinal.[89] More precisely, legal doctrine established only the broadest boundaries within which prosecutors were relatively free to choose their narrative focus in light of dramaturgical criteria.

Alfonsín and his legal advisors, for instance, privately participated in drafting charges against military officers.[90] They also engaged in *ex*

---

87   On the advent and expansion of these international networks, see Kathryn Sikkink, "The Power of Principled Ideas: Human Rights Policies in the United States and Western Europe" in *Ideas and Foreign Policy: Beliefs, Institutions, and Political Change* 139, 153-54 (Judith Goldstein & Robert O. Keohane eds., 1993).

88   The borrowed analysis was that of German legal theorist Klaus Roxin. Roxin, "Sobre la Autoría y Participación en el Derecho Penal," in *Problemas Actuales de las Ciencias Penales y la Filosofía del Derecho* 55 (1970).

89   Segev, *supra* note 85, at 336.

90   Interviews with Confidential Sources, in Buenos Aires, Argentina (Summers 1985 and 1987).

parte discussions with members of the court engaged in trying the juntas, discussions that included the political implications of alternative doctrinal options.[91]   Ben-Gurion similarly interceded, with equal secretiveness, in the prosecutorial decisions concerning the Eichmann trial.[92]

Witnesses in the Argentine junta trial, moreover, were selected not for their eloquence or the severity of their suffering (as Hausner did in the Eichmann trial),[93] but for their regional and social diversity.[94] The goal was to emphasize the breadth of victim class, the fact that repression extended to all provinces and socioeconomic groups. The intended message in this regard, never publicly articulated, was that the dirty war had not been directed primarily at the upper-middle-class university students who chiefly populated the leftist guerrilla movements and fellow-traveling circles of the period.

Rather, the target had been Argentina itself, in all its breadth and diversity. Irrespective of its accuracy (which I do not wish to question), the latter version undoubtedly made for a more receptive audience, especially in the hinterlands, and hence a more felicitous form of collective memory. In a word, it made a better story. In sum, while the law and its spokesmen cannot simply declare what collective memory of administrative massacre shall be, they can significantly influence such memory in subtle and decisive ways.[95]

The real question at present is not whether collective memory of national history *can* be constructed, but whether it ever *cannot*. Ever since the early 1930s, social psychologists have shown that "remembering appears to be far more decisively an affair of construction rather than one of mere reproduction."[96] We have become

---

91   *Id.*

92   Segev, *supra* note 85, at 336, 338, 346.

93   *Id.* at 339.

94   Interview with Luis Moreno Ocampo, Argentine Assistant Prosecutor, in Buenos Aires, Argentina (Aug. 1987).

95   Michael Kammen reaches a similar conclusion, regarding the Declaration of Independence and the American Revolution. Kammen asserts that the development of "collective memory and myth-making ... is partially inadvertent and partially intentional, societal as well as individual in its application, often implicit rather than explicit in its articulation." Michael Kammen, *A Season of Youth: The American Revolution and the Historical Imagination* 211 (1978).

96   F.C. Bartlett, *Remembering* 205 (1932).

conscious, in short, that someone must choose—omitting, combining, rearranging the details of the past in an active way—the stories by which we develop our collective memory and define our national identity. We suspect that shared stories about "our common past" have been influenced by the self-interest of the tellers. And we have learned, with Hayden White, that:

> the historian arranges ... events in the chronicle into a hierarchy of significance by assigning events different functions as story elements in such a way as to disclose the formal coherence of a whole set of events considered as a comprehensible process .... The very claim to have discerned some kind of formal coherence in the historical record brings with it theories of the nature of the historical world ... which have ideological implications ....[97]

Despite White's insinuations here, this process of ideological construction need not be illegitimate, nor necessarily accomplished by sleight of hand. In aspiring to infuse liberal memory, judges may justifiably construe the record of administrative massacre to tell a compelling story vindicating the preeminent liberal virtue: respect for the moral rights of individuals.

The fact that collective memory can be methodically manufactured stands at odds with the orthodox Durkheimian view of law's service to social solidarity, in a way that is not the case with the discursive account.[98] To be sure, Durkheim saw the primary purpose of sociology itself as self-consciously establishing a sort of civic religion, thereby providing the solidarity once created by shared religious commitments. But he viewed the criminal law as already embodying a common morality that was spontaneously summoned up, willy-nilly and unwittingly, by any effort of prosecutors to enforce it—without a

---

97   Hayden White, *Metahistory: The Historical Imagination in Nineteenth-Century Europe* 7, 21 (1973); see also Louis O. Mink, *Historical Understanding* 22-23 (Brian Fay et al. eds., 1987) (noting that there are infinitely many ordering relations among true statements); Roland Barthes, "The Discourse of History," in 3 *Comparative Criticism* 3, 15-16 (1981).

98   Emile Durkheim, *The Division of Labor in Society* 128, 80 (George Simpson trans., 1964) (contending that "states of [collective] conscience are strong only in so far as they are permanent" and that the collective conscience "does not change with each generation, but, on the contrary, it connects successive generations with one another").

thought to self-conscious theatrical strategy.

In contrast, the discursive view admits the limited scope of any such shared morality and the need for prosecutors to be attentive to these limits when seeking to foster collective memory of such divisive events as administrative massacre. The discursive account, in other words, acknowledges that shared moral sentiments in such circumstances cannot be presumed to arise spontaneously, that they must be consciously cultivated through strategic decisions about how the public spectacle might be most compellingly staged.

Many sociologists (of more scientific disposition than the author) would insist, at this point, on going beyond the anecdotes of success and failure to ask a more systematic question: Under what conditions do deliberate legal efforts at memory cultivation work, and under what conditions do they collapse? In a more lawyerly idiom, one would ask: What distinguishes the Eichmann and Auschwitz trials from the Tokyo trials—either in prosecutorial strategy or in environing circumstances —that explains their highly differential impact on collective memory and national identity in Israel, Germany, and Japan?

In my view, the vicissitudes of memory formation simply have not yet been studied sufficiently in particular cases, or even approached with suitable methods, to permit persuasive generalization here. It is possible, nevertheless, to identify at least one key factor impeding the success of any such effort: the fact that the public spotlight is trained so brightly upon participants in such proceedings makes it very difficult for prosecutors and judges to conceal—and to insulate from incisive criticism by defense counsel—their effort to frame the legal narrative in light of the public's anticipated response to alternative tropes and story lines.

Chapter 8.

Making Public Memory, Publicly

What remains uncertain is whether public memory can be fashioned *publicly*, by criminal trial or other means. Even if memory can (to considerable degree) be willfully created, must the fact of its fabrication be obscured from public view in order for such fashioning to be effective? Must prosecutorial decisions about the dramatic staging of a trial for administrative massacre be kept "backstage," in Goffman's terms,[1] never acknowledged in public, for fear of being charged with partisan "manipulation" or with breaching the judicial ethic of impartiality?

In constructing collective memory, can legal officials *explain* what they are trying to do while *doing* it? In such an enterprise, may they lay their cards on the table, or must they necessarily play the game with mirrors? There is reason to fear that any effort to push "on-stage" certain strategic and dramaturgical decisions by courts or prosecutors would only set in motion a self-defeating process: further decisions would still need to be made—inevitably, backstage—about how to produce those parts of the proceeding now being added to the on-stage production, that is, about how to make them seem as if they were really "behind the scenes." Such a process could lead to an infinite regress, ensuring that the most important decisions about how the tale will be told always remain under firm control and shrouded in secrecy.[2]

After all, no one is ultimately deceived by directorial efforts to create the appearance of total spontaneity and improvisation through such devices as a "play within a play," a "play within a film,"[3] or a

---

1 Erving Goffman, *The Presentation of Self in Everyday Life* 111-15 (1973).

2 For one examination of this general problem, see Dean MacCannell, *The Tourist: A New Theory of the Leisure Class* 91-107 (1976) (observing that as more of native culture is put on display for tourists, the more important to natives become those practices and beliefs to which tourists are denied access). Theorists of *cinéma vérité* similarly observe that the most important truths often recede from cinematic view the closer one seems to come to capturing them.

3 For a recent example, see *Vanya on 42nd Street* (Sony Pictures Classics 1994) (directed by Louis Malle, from a David Mamet play and Anton Chekhov's *Uncle Vanya*).

"film within a film"[4] any more than by a "painting within a painting."[5] Although audiences were first shocked and disarmed by such devices, viewers now quickly recognize them as artifices, as involving only the simulation of spontaneity.[6] In fact, we now know that the successful use of such devices always results from meticulous stagecraft and dramatic calculation. So too, with scripted colloquy, disguised as genuine legislative debate. The same proves true of strategic courtroom displays of "refreshing candor."

The problem can be succinctly stated in syllogistic form:

1. In cases of administrative massacre, with the world's eyes trained upon them, prosecutors and judges are inevitably understood to be engaged in "writing history" and influencing collective memory, whether or not they so intend.

2. Writing history is now understood as necessarily involving a choice between alternative interpretive framings, a fact that endows historiography with a similarity to fiction and mythmaking.

3. Thus courts, when engaged in writing the history of administrative massacre, must be understood as involved in mythmaking and partially fictive storytelling. To this end, their narratives—like those of the best contemporary historians—ought to be self-disruptive, periodically reminding readers that the persuasive coherence they seamlessly present is an illusion, secured only by compliance with disciplinary conventions that must themselves be made transparent and subject to critical scrutiny.[7]

After all, judges are not the *only* people engaged in mythmaking and storytelling about these events, the events they presume authoritatively to judge. We are therefore inexorably led to ask: on

---

4   For a recent illustration, see, for example, *Intervista* (Castle Hill Productions 1987) (directed by Federico Fellini).

5   An example is Diego Velazquez's *Las Meninas*, painted in 1656.

6   Umberto Eco, "Semiotics of Theatrical Performance," *Drama Rev.*, (Mar. 1977), at 110-11.

7   For a particularly extreme example of such self-disruptive strategies of historical representation, see Simon Schama, *Dead Certainties: Unwarranted Speculations* 321-26 (1991). For recent programmatic statement, see Robert F. Berkhofer, Jr., *Beyond the Great Story: History As Text and Discourse* 282-83 (1995) (arguing that "any new historical textualization must show how it goes about achieving its representation at the same time as it represents the past as history ... [and] must include multiple viewpoints in addition to ... the author's ... in genuine dialogue").

what basis might *their* favored narratives legitimately acquire the authoritative status of collective memory, a status to which—in proclaiming a trial's "educational value," for example—they clearly aspire and sometimes successfully enjoy for long periods? To disclose the fictive or mythical element of adjudication in such cases—that is, to disclose them publicly and directly—would risk stripping courts of their traditional and generally accepted claim to be authoritative finders of fact and appliers of society's central norms. The present chapter examines that perilous possibility.

Involving courts in the social construction of collective memory does not threaten judicial legitimacy to the extent that might first appear, given a proper understanding of their traditional task. That task is to reformulate continually the community's historical commitments (as reflected in its past political decisions) in their best light, as they bear on contemporary problems at hand. In short, leading legal theory already acknowledges an element of "construction" ineradicably present in the very nature of legal interpretation within a liberal community.[8] Perhaps it is true, then, that the idea that a shared sense of common history can be periodically and willfully reconstructed is not nearly so subversive of "our way of life" as many would suppose.

At least since O.W. Holmes and the legal realists, moreover, lawyers have understood that the same set of brute facts can readily be described and characterized in competing ways—all of these consistent with accepted professional conventions on legal storytelling. For this reason, law students are regularly taught that the most important part of most legal briefs is often not the legal interpretation, but the "statement of facts." In short, the legal profession has managed, over the last half century, to absorb the central tenets of social constructivism without fear that this unmasks either our claims to know anything real or "the rule of law" itself. The intellectual orientation of our profession is by no means radical, to put it mildly. If we can learn this lesson without losing confidence in our social practice, others can as well.[9]

---

8   Ronald Dworkin, *Law's Empire* 228-37 (1986).

9   It is true, of course, that the narrative skill of lawyers is one of the things that laymen most hate about us: the glib facility with which we can, at the drop of a hat, retell the story of a given dispute—consistently with known facts—in ways that disrupt the listener's initial judgments and intuitions, evoking "sympathy for the devil."

Even more than the preceding sources of skepticism, this one must be approached only by way of informed speculation, that is, through speculation informed by such hints and traces (disclosed by participants in these "historic" trials) about how these proceedings were "emplotted." These revelations invariably disclose a troubling pattern: that the contours of criminal prosecution were consciously but secretly tailored in light of perceived public sensibilities, in ways not at all cognizable within doctrinal or jurisprudential terms.

General MacArthur's disclosure regarding his decision to oppose indictment of Hirohito exemplifies this pattern. Despite considerable pressure from members of Congress and American opinion to indict Hirohito, MacArthur based his decision on his fears that such prosecution would evoke mass unrest and organized Japanese resistance to Allied Occupation. Calculations of an equally prudential sort inspired Alfonsín's legal advisors, prosecutors, and judges in many ways, requiring them to maintain an acute sensitivity to perceived shifts in the military's mood as indictments burgeoned in number and the military trials proceeded.[10]

Had MacArthur or Allied prosecutors in Tokyo honestly explained the reasons for their exclusion of the Emperor they would have made a mockery of the trial, discrediting it altogether. One can imagine the public reaction to a candid statement of American policy such as the following: "'any attempt to persuade the emperor to participate in his own 'debunking' should be made in ... a manner ... unknown to the Japanese people and ... give no suggestion of compulsion.'"[11]

Alfonsín's decision to curtail prosecution of military officers on account of their demonstrated restiveness would similarly have been impossible if its rationale had been publicly acknowledged.[12] The President thus felt compelled, in announcing an amnesty barring further

---

10   Interviews with Confidential Sources, Buenos Aires, Argentina (Summers 1985 and 1987).

11   Robert E. Ward, "Presurrender Planning: Treatment of the Emperor and Constitutional Changes," in *Democratizing Japan: The Allied Occupation* 14 (Robert E. Ward & Sakamoto Yoshikazu eds., 1987) (quoting language from an in-house document codifying United States policy).

12   On the considerable backstage wrangling over this and related decisions, see Carlos Nino, *Radical Evil on Trial* 87, 92, 100 (1996) (acknowledging direct presidential intercession to encourage the court, while drafting its opinion in the junta trial, to set limits on future prosecutions of junior officers not directly involved in atrocities).

indictments, to insist publicly that the decision had been in no way influenced by the several military uprisings that immediately preceded it. Although unconvincing to all informed observers, this proclamation proved to be less embarrassing and delegitimating in effect than the more candid alternative.

The resemblance of law to theater is again inescapable here, but in ways rather less flattering than in preceding sections. An effective dramatic performance traditionally camouflages the fact that it *is* a performance, for otherwise we would never be drawn into the story.[13] The actors implicitly deny that they are actors, that they are playing roles—specifically, that these roles are fictive—in order to be persuasive to us.

Moreover, in a highly publicized trial, even more than in a theatrical production, the audience surely would not be as powerfully moved to endorse the drama's ultimate conclusion—and remember its moral implications—if listeners were continuously reminded, at every turning point in the story, of other equally plausible paths that its characters, authors, and directors chose not to follow.[14] A semiotician thus observes that when "theatrical performances, require appreciation of staging, acting, costumes, or sets, [they] draw the attention from the story space to the stage space, and break the spell of referentiality."[15]

Keeping Legal Stagecraft "Backstage"

In order to grip us and draw us into its world, a legal-historical narrative need not represent itself as predetermined by fate, denying the contingent choices of human agency.[16] But for prosecutors and judges

---

13   John Dryden, "Of Heroic Plays: An Essay,' in 1 *Essays of John Dryden* 148, 154-55 (W.P. Ker ed., 1961); J.L. Styan, "The Mystery of the Play Experience," in *Performing Texts* 9, 13 (Michael Issacharoff & Robin F. Jones eds., 1988).

14   Such reminders, however, are commonplace in 20th-century theater. The classic work in this regard is Luigi Pirandello, *Six Characters in Search of an Author, in* Three Plays 3 (Edward Storer trans., 1934), in which the characters converse with the author, the actors with the audience, and the audience with the author.

15   Jean Alter, *A Sociosemiotic Theory of Theatre* 71 (1990) (emphasis omitted).

16   On the problems with representing collective catastrophes, like the Holocaust, as the only possible outcome of preceding historical events, see Michael A. Bernstein, *Foregone Conclusions: Against Apocalyptic History* 95-119 (1994). (arguing for the

publicly to attempt to influence collective memory is to acknowledge the impact upon such memory of political power, which is not equally shared and often illegitimate in the eyes of some. There is some truth in MacKinnon's insistence that "Dominant narratives are not called stories. They are called reality."[17] Can they remain dominant if they are acknowledged *as* narrative, defended as superior to competitors? One wonders.

Admitting the influence of power and self-interest upon how a story is being told undermines its persuasiveness, its asserted claim to represent impartial truth, its "truth-effect" in postmodern idiom. It was sheer power, after all, that permitted the Allies to narrow the narrative frame of the Tokyo and Nuremberg trials, excluding the substantial record of war crimes by the accusers as legally irrelevant. And it was precisely the recognition of this power, of how it thus shaped the story, that led to the lingering charge that the trials were no more than "victors' justice." As Todorov observes, "to be able to judge someone, it is first necessary to defeat him." But this implies "that the law has merely become the mask donned by force."

Of course, all competent litigators privately acknowledge the inexpungibly rhetorical, even fictive, element in their work: the client's story can be told in many ways (for example, with alternative witnesses, lines of questioning, material evidence, and so forth), and the attorney must evaluate the relative risks of each. Yet, when arguing in court, every competent litigator will also "make every effort to disguise the fact that this story is his creation and to present it, instead, as a simple revelation of the objective truth."[18]

We might entertain the possibility, at least, that modern judges—like modernist novelists, dramatists, and painters—might revise their self-conception to acknowledge the performative aspect of their work within the work itself, without undermining the defensibility of their entire enterprise in the process. The scaffolding might, in other

---

superiority in historical fiction and historiography of "sideshadowing"—identification of unrealized possibilities available to historical actors—over foreshadowing of what actually transpired).

17 Catherine A. MacKinnon, "Law's Stories as Reality and Politics," in *Law's Stories: Narrative and Rhetoric in the Law* 232, 235 (Peter Brooks and Paul Gewirtz eds., 1996).

18 Gerald B. Wetlaufer, "Rhetoric and Its Denial in Legal Discourse," 76 *Va. L. Rev.* 1545, 1559 (1990) (reflecting on 12 years experience as a litigator).

words, be left in place—as in some avant-garde architecture.

After all, whereas war memorials were long secretly designed by elites, today the form that they should take is routinely debated in society at large and in the local communities that often sponsor and house them.[19] In fact, the key question in that debate is now whether museum exhibitions, such at the Smithsonian's concerning the end of World War II, should confine themselves to commemoration of what was unequivocally noble in a people's past, or should also seek to stimulate their critical scrutiny of more questionable conduct. Exhibitions of the first sort strive for mechanical solidarity, while those of the second can seek only the discursive variety.

Inserting the storyteller into the legal story—the prosecutor and judge as self-conscious narrators of liberal memory and democratization—may at first appear an impertinence, of a piece with the "self-referentiality" (often a euphemism for self-absorption) of much modern art. But the practice might better be viewed as an expression of modesty, of a willingness to step down from the pedestal of omniscience.

Yet modernist art, unlike legal professionalism, almost entirely repudiates the aim of telling a coherent tale—one with an intelligible beginning, middle, and end, with clear "moral lessons" for its audience. In fact, for modernist culture such aims represent the height of philistinism.[20] Perhaps the first tenet of literary sophistication, after all, is that there is always more to a good story than its moral; it is precisely this "remainder" of doubt and uncertainty—*after* the lessons are learned—that makes the story linger in the mind, makes it more than an instantiation of some abstract theory we already understand and accept. But notions of enduring doubt and inexpungible uncertainty at the story's end do not sit easily with ideas of narrative coherence, whether in the life of the individual or a community. Still less are such notions

---

19 George L. Mosse, *Fallen Soldiers: Reshaping the Memory of the World Wars* 220-21 (1990) (describing the debate in Britain over whether war memorials should take the "liturgical" form of national shrines, in which only commemoration is encouraged, or rather the "utilitarian" form of parks and gardens, focused as much on pleasure for the living as honoring the dead).

20 When once asked by an interviewer "whether your films have a beginning, a middle, and an end," avant-garde director Jean-Luc Godard responded, "Yes, but not necessarily in that order." Martin Jay, *The Dialectical Imagination* 176 (1973).

readily compatible with the desire to make the story of these events into a new myth of national foundation, a kind of secular theology.

Modernist novelists and painters relish their embrace of an antithetical objective: disrupting the illusory *appearance* of coherence and integrity already at the heart of what they see as the "bourgeois perception" of personality and society.[21] Surely, the legal theory of a liberal society should be reluctant to adopt so self-subverting a stance. As Dworkin notes, even in "hard cases," where any interpretation of the parties' respective rights and duties will be controversial, lawyers argue (and judges defend their conclusions) as if only *one* result were ultimately possible at the end of the day.[22]

To admit the equal availability of alternative answers to crucially important legal questions has been considered, by liberals and "critical" skeptics alike, as inconsistent with "the rule of law." By its nature, the law—or so it has been generally thought—can only tell one true story about who is right in a given dispute, can lend its authority to only one of the competing narratives about what happened and about what, legally speaking, it "meant." For example, the legal narrative favored by the Argentine juntas—that they were employing necessarily unconventional methods in fighting a just war against an unconventional enemy—is squarely incompatible with the story put forth by Alfonsín's prosecutors—that no state of war existed and that the defendants ordered the murder of thousands of innocent people, without justification or excuse.

Moreover, lawyers and legal theorists readily acknowledge that the same set of facts, undisputed by either side, can often be conceptualized for legal purposes in several alternative ways, all of these consistent with existing doctrine.[23] A single, harmful act may implicate both civil and criminal law—state, federal, and international. A major crime may encompass several "lesser included offenses."[24] For instance, the "same

---

21   Gerald Graff, *Literature Against Itself* 63-102 (1979); Donald M. Lowe, *History of Bourgeois Perception* 17-33 (1982); Roberto M. Unger, *Passion* 33-34, 297 (1984).

22   Ronald Dworkin, *Taking Rights Seriously* 82-90 (1977). This proposition has been called "the right answer thesis." Dworkin retreated from it slightly in a later work. Dworkin, *Law's Empire, supra* note 8, at 90-96.

23   Steven J. Burton, *An Introduction to Law and Legal Reasoning* 48-53 (1985).

24   James Vorenberg, "Decent Restraint of Prosecutorial Power," 94 *Harv. L. Rev.* 1521, 1524-32 (1981); see also *United States v. Batchelder,* 442 U.S. 114, 123-25

act" of violence by an Argentine officer against a civilian might be legally cognizable as attempted murder, battery, aggravated assault, deprivation of civil rights, a "crime against humanity," or even genocide, on some accounts.[25] Prosecutors have to choose between such alternative conceptualizations of the wrong, on the basis of considerations not governed by law.

Prosecutors can use the same set of facts to tell very different legal stories—all of them inculpatory, albeit in different ways and to varying degree. Hence arises the need for prosecutorial choice and the possibility that such choice might significantly be influenced by dramaturgical considerations of the sort discussed here.

The central issue—the existence of prosecutorial discretion concerning the charging decision—is by no means unique to administrative massacre and routinely arises in other contexts. In fact, a considerable literature now exists on the question of how prosecutorial discretion, given its inescapability, ought to be exercised responsibly.[26] Contemporary legal thought now fully appreciates that those drafting the provisions of criminal law cannot carve up nature at the joints: particular offenses, each with its required elements, are ultimately no more than verbal constructions capturing only certain aspects of a larger tableau of actions and events momentarily under the law's gaze.[27]

Various offenses simply place different aspects of this background into the foreground. Inevitably, the "same" set of events, particularly those involving the coordinated activities of many people over a long period, can be conceptualized in alternative ways. A given historical

(1979) (finding constitutional a statute permitting prosecutors to elect between two offenses, carrying greatly different sanctions, but prohibiting the same conduct).

25   Each of these offenses requires a different mental state: the same act may be prompted by the intent to destroy an ethnoreligious group, which the immediate victim represents in the perpetrator's mind, or simply the individual victim as such, regardless of her ethnoreligious membership. Available evidence in these cases often permits either or both of these characterizations of the defendants' *mens rea*.

26   See, e.g., Vorenberg, *supra* note 24, at 1560-73 (proposing a principled system of prosecutorial discretion).

27   The theoretical foundation for this conclusion lies in the influential work of Ferdinand de Saussure. F. de Saussure, *Course in General Linguistics* 76 (Charles Bally & Albert Sechehaye eds., Roy Harris trans., 1983) (showing that a verbal "signifier" is necessarily arbitrary since the link between it and the "signified" reality it seeks to represent is purely a matter of convention, as revealed by how each particular language divides in different ways the verbally expressible world).

episode can be recounted through a wide range of literary genres and tropes (from epic tragedy to light ironic farce). So too, the same large-scale wrongdoing is often legally cognizable by several alternative offenses, criminal and civil.

We can only hope that, in the interests of due process (that is, the avoidance of retroactivity), at least *some* of our existing legal concepts prove to have captured the morally pertinent features of historically novel forms of wrongdoing, such as those examined here. But virtually no one seriously thinks that, in recognizing the existence of prosecutorial discretion, the conceptual world of liberal law has collapsed.[28]

The attitudes we display toward an historical event, and hence the stories we tell about it, necessarily vary with context. A story reflecting an attitude of simple reverence may be appropriate at moments when the event is apprehended as the foundation of the national myth of origin. So uncritical an attitude would be inapposite, however, when the same event is examined for scientific purposes, such as those of comparative history, sociology, or law. To suggest that such a separation is possible and desirable is to adopt a liberalism of "separate spheres,"[29] according to which the same good or event might have radically different meaning depending on its location within a given domain of social life. On this view, it might well be entirely legitimate to hold our skepticism in abeyance when we wish to celebrate the positive side of our country's past and to remind ourselves of what its members share.

The first problem here is that the proper boundary between such spheres is frequently unclear and subject to contest.[30] In a free society, critically-minded historians do not confine themselves and their discoveries to the archives. In contemporary America, they are virtually always engaged in attacking our national myths of origin, as they understand them, lambasting these as factually inaccurate and/or

---

28 For analysis of how our law deals with one key example of "the redescription problem," as it is generally called, see Michael S. Moore, "Foreseeing Harm Opaquely," in *Action and Value in Criminal Law* 125 (Stephen Shute et al. eds., 1993).

29 Walzer Michael, "Liberalism and the Art of Separation," 12 *Political Theory* 315 (1984).

30 For several discussions of this problem, see the responses to Walzer in *Pluralism, Justice, and Equality,* (David Miller ed., 1996).

morally debased. Moreover, it may breach the legitimate boundary between the spheres of criminal law and national myth-making or identity-formation to harness the first to the yoke of the second.

Also, even when the boundaries between social spheres is clear—and perhaps especially when this is so—it can be quite disorienting, as a simple matter of lived experience, to reequilibrate one's moral gyroscope while shuttling back and forth between them. One will have to do so, after all, several times a day in any modern, liberal society. Whether a coherent "self" is possible in such circumstances is very much an open question (i.e., on any plausible account of personal integrity).

For instance, can Israelis be realistically expected to view the Holocaust, for purposes of establishing national identity and solidarity, as irreducibly unique, yet view it for other purposes (e.g., legal and historiographical) as simply an extreme case of our entire century's quintessential political horror? From the first of these perspectives, the second may seem not merely mistaken but outrageous and unworthy even of discussion. From the second perspective, the first will seem a quasi-theological mystification. Can the same person really hold both views, albeit in different capacities?

Positivist historians may once have believed that their job was to unearth and articulate the true meaning already immanent within historical events. Such people were therefore embarrassed to discover that they were, in fact, imposing conceptual frames that "endow[] a particular sequence with moral closure."[31] But the inexpungibly moral element in storytelling has never been lost upon criminal lawyers, whether arguing for the prosecution or defense. The question has been, by contrast, what the moral of the story should be and whether the legal concepts available for telling it accurately capture the full range of moral complexities. In particular, is it a story of radical evil—one that

---

31   Louis O. Mink, "Everyman His or Her Own Annalist," in *On Narrative* 233, 238 (W.J.T. Mitchell ed., 1981). The embarrassment also arose from the moral skepticism of many such scholars; their suspicion that conclusions about "what justice demands," for instance, were merely arbitrary expressions of personal preference or political power. On a "realist" or even "constructivist" conception of morality, however, there is nothing embarrassing about our having to judge historical events and their perpetrators by moral (and legal) ideas not "immanent" in the historical process or shared by historical actors themselves, but grounded only on reasoned reflection.   Geoffrey Sayre-McCord, "Preface" to *Essays on Moral Realism* at ix, ix-x (Geoffrey Sayre-McCord ed., 1988).

should elicit from us only sentiments of indignation—or is it a story of tragic choices and inescapable moral dilemmas, a narrative evoking more complex and nonjudgmental sentiments?

The point here is entirely compatible with certain postmodernist concerns: with preserving an awareness that many differing stories—all of them offering at least part of the truth—may be told with the same set of brute facts. Its infuriating excesses notwithstanding, postmodernism has at least made us "more aware that there are alternative ways of truth telling, and that we are therefore responsible for the forms we use to tell our truths."[32] Criminal law will be useful for telling some of these stories, tort law (in private actions against torturers, for instance) for telling others. Nonlegal narratives will be necessary to capture still further aspects of any complex political experience. Liberals part company with leading postmodernists only in insisting that the law's several available stories, those receiving authoritative endorsement, not have wildly different "morals."

Acknowledging Legal Artifice

The "narrative indeterminacy" reflected in the exercise of prosecutorial discretion differs substantially from legal indeterminacy of the conventional sort. The latter arises only after the allegations have been formulated, the authorities examined, the legal questions focused, the strengths and weaknesses of alternative answers assessed. Acknowledging publicly the availability of narrative indeterminacy would not undermine the law's legitimacy in the same way as acknowledging the equal availability of alternative "right answers" to the same legal question.

In choosing among alternative defendants and indictments, prosecutors of administrative massacre faced only the less troublesome of these two types of indeterminacy. To admit the existence of narrative indeterminacy—regarding what the story should be about, how its contours should be framed (and which legal questions will thus be asked)—presents no inherent threat to the court's legitimacy, just as the now-widespread acknowledgment of narrative indeterminacy among

---

32   Richard H. Brown, *Society As Text* 3 (1987).

historians is recognized to present no inherent threat to the legitimacy of their endeavors.

It is entirely possible to imagine prosecutors publicly explaining such choices while making them, at least where they are not restricting the scope of prosecution in capitulation to the raw power of potential defendants. Thus far, however, prosecutors have sought to justify the way they exercised such narrative discretion only many years after the events at issue.[33]   To be sure, all this would make the ultimate persuasiveness of the strictly legal story—conviction of particular parties for particular offenses by means of particular testimony—turn explicitly on the persuasiveness of the larger historical frame that underpins it.

But that is already, inevitably, the case, as the legacy of the trials examined here makes abundantly clear. Argentine conservatives, for instance, would never accept the legitimacy of the junta trial—however scrupulous the courts in applying the Alfonsín government's chosen offenses against its chosen defendants—as long as these prosecutorial decisions derived from a larger narrative that conservatives could never endorse (that is, denial of pervasive subversion and unconventional war). This is why the choice of narrative frame must itself be publicly acknowledged and defended. Otherwise, the real issues will never be joined, and the courtroom adversaries will talk past one another, in a "dialogue" of the deaf.

Ideally, liberal memory could be cultivated in a manner consistent with the Kantian "publicity principle."[34]   That principle holds that officials act wrongfully when they adopt policies that they could not persuasively defend before interested publics. This principle would seem to require that if the performative possibilities of trials for administrative massacre cannot be publicly acknowledged without delegitimating the proceedings, then these possibilities should be eschewed, their potential for deliberate shaping of collective memory

---

33   For one such long-belated disclosure, see generally Telford Taylor, *The Anatomy of the Nuremberg Trials: A Personal Memoir* (1992) (explaining how the indictment-drafting committees at Nuremberg decided which individuals should be named as defendants).

34   Immanuel Kant, "Eternal Peace," in *The Philosophy of Kant* 425, 518-25 (Carl J. Friedrich ed., 1993); see also John Rawls, *A Theory of Justice* 133, 177-82 (1973).

left unrealized.[35]

The problem with this response, however, is that Pandora's box is already open. We know, from the historians and anthropologists examined here, that there have been many successful efforts at constructing collective memory. We also know something about how this has been done, and that the law has often provided a potent set of symbolic tools to that end. As a result, it is now impossible for collective memory to develop altogether naively, spontaneously, unreflectively, without self-consciousness.

One Argentine intellectual writes, "memory results only from an *active reworking* of 'what happened' and 'what is recalled about it.'"[36] What at first seems the purest font of mnemonic authenticity—say, a death camp survivor's personal testimony, of the sort on which war crimes tribunals routinely rely—turns out with disturbing frequency to have been unconsciously influenced, as Primo Levi observed, by "information gained from later readings or the stories of others."[37]

Today a prosecutorial decision *not* to employ the full dramatic potential of a criminal trial (as we have come to recognize that potential), so as to avoid the appearance of manipulation, has necessarily become a partly strategic maneuver, taken in light of perceived preconditions for the legitimacy of the proceedings, particularly in skeptical quarters. A prosecutorial decision to minimize

---

35 For recent skepticism about the publicity principle, see Robert Goodin, *Motivating Political Morality* 124-49 (1992); David Luban, "The Publicity Principle," in *The Theory of Institutional Design* (Robert Goodin & Geoffrey Brennan eds., 1996). The principle is most plausibly interpreted, in any event, as requiring the possibility of public justification regarding theory choice, that is, the general principles on the basis of which more particular policies will be chosen, rather than the details of particular policies themselves. This is Rawls's view. Rawls, *supra* note 34, at 175-82, 454-57; see also Scott Altman, "Beyond Candor," 89 *Mich. L. Rev.* 296, 302-03 (1990).

36 Hugo Vezzetti, *"El Juicio: Un Ritual de la Memoria Colectiva,"* 7 *Punto de Vista* 3, 3 (1985) (translation by author) (emphasis added).

37 Primo Levi, *The Drowned and the Saved* 19 (Raymond Rosenthal trans., 1988). Such unintentional reformulation of memory is sometimes more self-conscious, although still without guile. To refresh their memory of traditional practices in preparation for interviews by anthropologists, Cherokee chiefs have been known to "bone up" through books by earlier anthropologists. David Lowenthal, *The Past Is a Foreign Country* 207 (1985). There is some recent neurological and psychological research on the processes by which recall is often made to fit preconceptions of what ought to have happened. See, e.g., Daniel Schacter, *Searching for Memory* 58-61 (1996).

public scrutiny of a legal proceeding, a decision *not* to make it memorable—perhaps to avoid antagonizing still-powerful military officers—could no longer be taken in innocence of this very implication.

Even if one managed somehow to miss the implication oneself, one's critics would be certain to point it out. This occurred, for instance, when human rights activists in Argentina, and their supporters among legal scholars, publicly identified the innumerable ways in which even Alfonsín's initial plans for military prosecutions (that is, even before organized opposition arose from military ranks) stopped well short of what the law allowed, and may even have required.[38]

In short, the telling of legal stories about administrative massacre necessarily confronts the modern condition. That conditions entails "a state of being in culture while looking at culture, a form of personal and collective self-fashioning."[39] Our sense of reality has been affected by the recognition that this sense is itself partly a construction, one that—history suggests—is periodically demolished and reconstructed. It follows that memory-practice, as it is now sometimes called,[40] has become at once transparent and self-conscious (in both the positive and negative senses of the latter term).

We have become acutely aware, moreover, that the fashioning of national identity through cultivation of collective memory is almost inevitably conflictual. Historians remind us that "whenever memory is

---

38 Particularly incisive in this regard is Marcelo A. Sancinetti, *Derechos Humanos en la Argentina Postdictatorial* (1988). Such scholar-activists stress, for instance, that under Argentine law prosecutors have no discretion to refrain from indicting potential defendants against whom evidence has been gathered that is sufficient to justify such indictment. Alfonsín's chief legal advisor acknowledges this. Jaime Malamud-Goti, "Human Rights Abuses in Fledgling Democracies: The Role of Discretion," in *Transition to Democracy in Latin America: The Role of the Judiciary* 225, 236 (Irwin P. Stotzky ed., 1993) (ascribing this commitment to the "full-blooded retributiv[ism]" of the Argentine legal system). For an accessible summary of the legal approach that was favored by the human rights community, see Emilio Mignone et al., "Dictatorship on Trial: Prosecution of Human Rights Violations in Argentina," 10 *Yale J. Int'l L.* 118 (1984).

39 James Clifford, *The Predicament of Culture* 9 (1988). Law's problem here is not unique to law, of course. Walter T. Anderson, *Reality Isn't What It Used to Be* 4 (1990) ("We do not know how to live in a world of socially constructed realities, yet we find it increasingly difficult to live in anything else.").

40 John Gillis, "Memory and Identity: The History of a Relationship," in *Commemorations* 3, 16 (John R. Gillis ed., 1994).

invoked we should be asking ourselves: by whom ... against what?"[41]

Such questions are inescapable in a society like Argentina, because it has "never agreed on its guiding fictions,"[42] as one historian observes. Argentina has even been called, by V.S. Naipaul, a society "without a history, still only with annals."[43] Such erudite distinctions are not merely the preoccupation of poststructuralist theoreticians.[44] At his trial, defendant Emilio Massera invoked the distinction between discovering and declaring brute facts, on one hand, and integrating them into a persuasive national narrative, on the other. He proclaimed: "My critics may have the chronicle, but history belongs to me, and that is where the final verdict will be decided."[45]

The lack of shared sense of a common past—of collective memory, in sociological shorthand—is what makes possible claims of this sort, and precludes their casual dismissal. A Durkheimian focus on criminal law's capacity to invigorate existing consensus on basic morality reaches its limits in such circumstances. For as Gillis observes, "modern memory was born ... from an intense awareness of the conflicting representations of the past and the effort of each group to make its version the basis of national identity."[46]

---

41 Natalie Z. Davis & Randolph Starn, Introduction to "Memory and Counter-Memory", 26 *Representations* 1, 2 (1989); see also Charles Tilly, "Afterward: Political Memories in Time and Space," in *Remapping Memory* 241, 253 (Jonathan Boyarin, ed., 1994) (noting that today "we see the contestation that surrounds every effort to create, define, or impose a common memory—to form a coherent discourse about the origins of a people, the source of citizens' rights, the lessons of previous challenges").

42 Nicolas Shumway, *The Invention of Argentina* 299 (1991).

43 V.S. Naipaul, *The Return of Eva Perón* 151 (1980).

44 See, e.g., Mink, *supra* note 31, at 233 (distinguishing the annalist from the historian on the basis of the former's lack of "a principle for assigning importance or significance to events ... [and] a notion of a social system for whose survival or change some events had more significance than others").

45 *El Diario del Juicio* (Buenos Aires), Oct. 8, 1985, at 25. For discussion of Massera's remark, see Marguerite Feitlowitz, "Night and Fog in Argentina," *Salmagundi*, Spring-Summer 1992, at 40, 71.

46 Gillis, *supra* note 40, at 8.

Competing Views of Collective Memory: Liberal, Communitarian, and Postmodern

Trials for administrative massacre have become one prominent field on which such interpretive conflict over the constitution of national identity and the meaning of national history takes place. Such conflict, based on rival memories of painful recent events, increasingly means that it is no longer possible to advance a particular interpretation of national identity in blissful unawareness of doing so or in the naive belief that one is merely eliciting shared memory and evoking the collective conscience. Thus, it has now become moot whether it is desirable for officers of the court to engage self-consciously in memory construction. Their own sophistication in such matters, the advance of cultural self-awareness in this regard, has made it impossible for them *not* to do so.

That it has become impossible not to try, however, does not mean that success is easy. In fact, it has become harder. Despite loose talk about "the invention of tradition,"[47] the audience, like the performers, is increasingly aware that collective memory can be socially constructed, with legal blueprint in hand. As the public for such proceedings, we have become suspicious of efforts—by judges, prosecutors, or defense counsel—to shape criminal trials with an eye to collective memory, for we will have learned that any effort to organize memory is also an effort at "organized oblivion."[48] We periodically remind ourselves, in fear of being "taken in" by her artfulness, that the teller's reliance on one trope—say, the nation's rise to greatness —necessarily reflects her tacit rejection of another—suppression of subgroups and neighbors, perhaps, who got in its way.

When trying cases of administrative massacre, judges must act willy-nilly as historians—seeking to tell persuasive stories about large-scale events. They thus necessarily confront the obstacles faced by historians themselves in this enterprise. One such obstacle is that to the extent we first find a story coherent and compelling, we are sure to remind ourselves almost immediately that the coherence lies not "out

---

47 *The Invention of Tradition* (Eric Hobsbawm & Terence Ranger eds., 1983).

48 Claudia Koonz, "Between Memory and Oblivion: Concentration Camps in German Memory," Koonz, in *supra* note 40, at 258.

there" in history itself, but rather in narrative conventions about how history ought properly to be written and, more generally, in our assumptions about how the world ought to be apprehended and rendered intelligible.[49] As the audience becomes armed with this awareness, it turns ever more difficult for historians—and hence for judges-as-historians—to pass off their preferred narrative of a recent national catastrophe as definitive, that is, to impart their professional authority to any particular version of collective memory.

The problem is not simply that different stories betray different ideologies. It is that we have even become suspicious of stories themselves, that is, of their capacity to capture and impart important truths.[50] Perhaps, as Hayden White contends, the "value attached to narrativity in the representation of real events arises out of a desire to have real events display the coherence, integrity, fullness, and closure of an image of life that is and can only be imaginary."[51]

But such strictures against the hunger for narrative wholeness are better directed at communitarians than at liberals. Liberal theorists have *always* been hostile to the notion that public narratives, those endorsed by the state and its courts, should seek to satisfy the private longings of its citizens for meaning and wholeness, for "coherence, integrity, fullness, and closure."[52] Thus, despite the postmodernist cast of White's observations, they are entirely consistent with the longstanding aversion of liberal theory to official endorsement of any full-bodied conception of the good life or of the stories by which such a conception will be imparted and remembered.

Postmodernists like White are thus valuable in disclosing the

---

49   Brian Fay et al., "Introduction" to Louis O. Mink, *Historical Understanding* 22-23 (Brian Fay et al. eds., 1987).

50   This key insight of postmodernism has yet to penetrate the current legal scholarship, professedly inspired by it, that celebrates storytelling (and its presumptive superiority over analytical argument).   Patricia Williams, *The Alchemy of Race and Rights* (1991); Lynne Henderson, "Legality and Empathy," 85 *Mich. L. Rev.* 1574 (1987).

51   Hayden White, *The Content of the Form: Narrative Discourse and Historical Representation* 24 (1987); see also Frank Kermode, *The Sense of an Ending* 64 (1967) ("It is not that we are connoisseurs of chaos, but that we are surrounded by it, and equipped for coexistence with it only by our fictive powers.").

52   On liberalism's rejection of this objective, see, for example, Charles E. Larmore, *Patterns of Moral Complexity* 45-47, 69-76 (1987).

dangers of a communitarian conception of collective memory, like that of Durkheim and the authors of *Habits of the Heart*.[53] Such communitarians insist that, as individuals, we are bereft of direction and meaningful attachment if we cannot situate our personal experience within the larger narrative of a community, one that precedes our birth and will endure beyond our death.[54] If liberal law cannot help to provide the needed link between individual and community (as it cannot, they insist), then so much the worse for the law.

Postmodern theorists of history rightly respond that there are necessarily many stories—consistent with known facts—that can be told about the history of a given community and the relations among its subgroups.[55] To insist that *one* such story be shared by all members as constitutive of their identity would thus be factually mistaken and morally indefensible.

That much is consistent with liberal jurisprudence. Where most postmodernists go astray, however, is in their failure to give serious thought to the question of *which* such stories belong within the law, that is, which ought to receive official imprimatur and which, by contrast, ought to remain private matters about which reasonable people may differ.[56] To acknowledge that there are many accurate stories that can be told about the Argentine dirty war, for instance, is not to say that it would be wise for the law to concern itself with arbitrating between them all. This was the hopeless quagmire into which the Barbie trial,

---

53   Robert Bellah et al., *Habits of the Heart* 52-55 (1983).

54   Alasdair MacIntyre, *After Virtue* 194-203 (1981).

55   See, e.g., Nathan Wachtel, "Remember and Never Forget," in *Between Memory and History* 307-08 (Marie-Noëlle Bourguet et al. eds., 1986) (comparing different methods used by Eastern European Jews to preserve their collective memory through the Holocaust); Hayden White, 'Historical Pluralism," 12 *Critical Inquiry* 480, 488 (1986).

56   The failure arises from the consistent refusal of leading postmodernists to admit the defensibility of any distinction between legitimate and illegitimate power.
> We have two schemes for the analysis of power. The contract-oppression schema, which is the juridical one, and the domination-repression ... schema for which the pertinent opposition is not between legitimate and illegitimate, as in the first schema, but between struggle and submission.... Right should be viewed, I believe, not in terms of a legitimacy to be established, but in terms of the methods of subjugation that it instigates.

Michel Foucault, "The Juridical Apparatus," in *Legitimacy and the State* 201, 207, 211 (William Connolly ed., 1984).

under Vergès's prompting, threatened to descend.[57] There are other, more fitting fora—both public and private—for the expression of opposing views about such a society-wide catastrophe and for the critical questioning of particular accounts of its meaning.

This conclusion, however, is not shared by most leading postmodernists. One distinguished anthropologist (of that persuasion) writes of the official reports and legal judgments against the Argentine military, for instance, that the

> well-intentioned effort to expose the terror... [involved] a mode of liberal collective remembering [that] preserves the state in that it monopolizes the public sphere and limits general access to other kinds of remembering, restricting them to the personal, private anguish of individual memories or deferring their public expression to another ... less troubled, time. In this way, political order is preserved and saved from the implications of its own darkest episodes of excess.[58]

Marcus implies that prosecutors cannot choose certain defendants and indictments, that is, certain narrative framings, in light of their own political objectives, without doing an injustice to the "small narratives" of the victims themselves, without forcing these little stories (only as footnotes, perhaps) into liberalism's grand narrative. There will always be other framings, other stories about the dirty war, that are excluded—marginalized, in current parlance—by an official story of

---

57   See *infra* text accompanying notes 108-112.

58   George E. Marcus, "The Official Story: Response to Julie Taylor," in *Body Politics: Disease, Desire, and the Family* 204, 207-08 (Michael Ryan & Avery Gordon eds., 1994). Marcus's title alludes to the Luis Puenzo film, *The Official Story* (Almi Pictures Inc. 1985), which received the Academy Award for best foreign film in 1985. The film was so titled in satiric commentary on the military's public account of disappearances during its rule, described at the time by skeptical Argentines as "the official story." After the junta trial, Argentine intellectuals on the left (like Marcus here) began to employ the term in a doubly ironic sense, to characterize the decision of the courts and the Alfonsín government to apportion responsibility for the disappearances exclusively to a few top military brass. William Rowe & Vivian Schelling, *Memory and Modernity: Popular Culture in Latin America* 228 (1991); Tulio Halperin Donghi, "El Presente Transforma el Pasado: El Impacto del Reciente Terror en la Imagen de la Historia Argentina," in *Ficción y Política: La Narrativa Argentina Durante el Proceso Militar* 71, 78-79 (René Jara & Hernán Vidal eds., 1987). In Spanish, the word *historia* denotes both "story" and "history," and thus connotes a narrative about both the present and the past.

this sort, he insists. Even a liberal story is "repressive" in this sense, notwithstanding its tolerant veneer.

Marcus is *not* simply asserting, with the legal realists, that any private sphere is likely to be a product of legal rules which are themselves publicly created, and hence susceptible to periodic modification. Rather, he asserts that the public-private distinction is inherently repressive, wherever the line is drawn, in that it necessarily marginalizes whatever is made to fall on the private side of this line.

At times, to be sure, official efforts to provide an authoritative account of recent history, even a partly self-critical account, are indeed intended precisely to suppress the public recounting of individual narratives that would prove still more critical and uncomfortable. This was the case, for instance, with the official acknowledgments of wrongdoing by the chiefs of Argentina's armed services in April 1995. These admissions were prompted by a new willingness of retired officers to reveal and publicly discuss their illegal actions.

It was hoped that such individuals would no longer feel impelled by conscience to come forward with details about *particular* atrocities if the armed services at large were finally to admit that it had ordered this *general type* of activity—and had been wrong in so doing. The individual revelations, increasing in frequency and drawing much media attention, were proving particularly embarrassing to President Menem (on the eve of his reelection effort). After all, it was he who had pardoned the junta members and others convicted of ordering atrocities.

Menem was quite candid about the relation he hoped to establish between official acknowledgment of atrocity—in the aggregate, dispensing with gruesome details—and the containment of more personal (and potentially never-ending) revelations by particular "dirty warriors" turned loose cannons. A few days after the official admissions, Menem observed that if these had not happened, "we would have continued until eternity with two out of every three individuals coming forth to make their own declarations."[59]

---

59 *Clarín* (Buenos Aires), Int'l Ed., Apr. 25-30, 1995, at 7. Menem's calculation here was based on a common pattern in Argentine political history. When military officers criticize one another in public, this usually reflects disagreement between organized factions within the corps (each with substantial supporters). When such an internal dispute goes public, it is because one faction suddenly seeks civilian allies in its intramilitary rivalries.

Marcus's critique, his concern over premature closure of debate, is thus well-directed against such policies of Menem, but not against *Nunca Más* or its official authors.[60] In that regard, in fact, his statement must be entirely unpersuasive to anyone committed to a liberal society. Without argument, he summarily denies any meaningful distinction between the proper concerns of the state and those of civil society, between public and private life. The moral bankruptcy of the liberal state, on this account, is presumably demonstrated by the fact that its courts do not provide a forum for every autobiographical introspection—for every narcissistic meandering.

It may be largely true, as concludes a recent study of collective memory in the former East Germany, that "if the past could be worked through, it would happen in smoky pubs and around kitchen tables."[61] It is also true that as time passes, the kinds of stories publicly told about an administrative massacre do change. They often focus less on explaining and judging the "big picture" and more on sympathetically interpreting the myriad forms of human experience involved—for small subgroups, or simply for particular individuals, however idiosyncratic their experience.

Moreover, the courts cannot become aloof to concerns that are primarily "private." For example, they must remain available for civil suits by private citizens seeking redress for the wrongs done them by the state and its torturers, as has been the case in Argentina.[62] To this

---

60   *Comisión Nacional Sobre la Desaparición de Personas, Nunca Más: The Report of the Argentine National Commission on the Disappeared* (1986).

61   Tina Rosenberg, *The Haunted Land: Facing Europe's Ghosts After Communism* 355, 356-94 (1995). Rosenberg is referring especially to a series of personal encounters between a Stasi informer and the colleagues against whom he informed. She adds, "the state could lend its endorsement to a nationwide examination of conscience, but the desire had to come from individuals, as victims confronted their spies and interrogators in more intimate settings." *Id.* at 355.

62   Surviving victims of the dirty war have recovered damages from the Argentine State in a successful effort to enact compensatory legislation. Alison Brysk, *The Politics of Human Rights in Argentina* 86-87 (1994). A November 1994 civil judgment found the federal government and junta members Emilio Massera and Armando Lambruschini each liable for $1 million to the children of a *desaparecido*. Noga Tarnopolsky, "Murdering Memory in Argentina," *N.Y. Times*, Dec. 12, 1994, at A19; See also Tim Golden, "For First Time, U.S. Court to Weigh Claim of Rights Abuses in Foreign Land," *N.Y. Times* A7 (Sept. 2, 1996) (describing continuing litigation in U.S. courts against the Argentine state for unlawful confiscation of private property during the dirty war).

extent, the law must necessarily place its stamp of approval on the "personal" stories of individual victims, as victims. By implication, it marginalizes and occludes other stories, such as those portraying the "victims" as fallen soldiers in the struggle against capitalist imperialism—that is, the story favored by many in Argentina's human rights organizations.

Criminal law, preoccupied with wrongs to public order at large, captures the public imagination at the outset. As Gewirtz notes, "Of all law's narrative arenas, the criminal prosecution most fully engages the public's narrative desires..."[63] Criminal law begins to assume a less salient role over time, while private law, concerned with compensation, tends to wax more prominent.[64] But these private stories are *consistent with* the larger one told by criminal law—and with the liberal lessons that such law, in furtherance of discursive solidarity, seeks to stamp upon collective memory.

The criminal law must necessarily make one story *authoritative*. But it may also, in so doing, *authorize* and thus encourage the telling of other, more personal stories, both within courts and elsewhere in society.[65] That these other stories must be consistent with the grand narrative of liberal memory, constructed by criminal courts, is another form of "enabling constraint."

By limiting the stories that will receive public authorization, the requirement of consistency enables thousands of victims to tell stories that, without such official encouragement, would never publicly be told. Lyotard may be right that "a culture that gives precedence to the narrative form doubtless has no more of a need for special procedures to authorize its narratives than it has to remember its past."[66] But, such

---

63   Paul Gewirtz, "Narrative and Rhetoric in the Law," in *supra* note 19, at 2-3.

64   *Cf.* Michael Geyer & Miriam Hansen, "German-Jewish Memory and National Consciousness," in *Holocaust Remembrance: The Shapes of Memory* 153, 178 (Geoffrey H. Hartman ed., 1994) (arguing that as survivors of the Nazi years have died off and the state has sought to influence collective memory of the period through official rituals of remembrance, "German memory-work became less and less private and individual"). The authors concede, however, that there has been "a broad and swelling stream of confessional literature," allowing later generations to preserve and profit from the distinctive memories of particular individuals. *Id.* at 184.

65   I am grateful to Virginia Dominquez for suggesting this distinction.

66   Jean-François Lyotard, *The Postmodern Condition: A Report on Knowledge* at 22 (Geoff Bennington & Brian Massumi trans., 1984).

is not the culture we inhabit.

Individuals who seek to inject their personal stories into the public realm—stories at odds with currently prevailing official narratives—are free to invoke the law to that end, that is, in a liberal society. In fact, the criminal law can be surprisingly useful in this regard. In April 1995, for instance, Captain Adolfo Scilingo was able single-handedly to reopen Argentine public debate about the dirty war by going public with his story of obeying orders to throw dozens of victims to their deaths from a navy helicopter.[67] Scilingo then pressed criminal charges against the Navy Chief of Staff, Admiral Enrique Molina Pico, for the offense of "concealing evidence of murder."[68] It was Scilingo's official accusation that forced the Chiefs of Staff to reconsider an issue they thought they had long since put behind them (with the 1990 pardons and earlier amnesty statutes). The filing of this legal denunciation quickly led to the first official military admission of wrongdoing and responsibility by all three armed services.[69]

While communitarians lament "the atomization of a general memory into a private one,"[70] leading postmodernists instead decry the opposite danger. Suspicious of all power, they warn against any desire for an authoritative determination of whose stories are most accurate, most important, most deserving of official recognition and collective approval.

A flexible, sophisticated liberalism can absorb the insights and exhortations of both camps. After all, liberal political theory has always been suspicious of state power, and so shares the prevailing postmodernist distrust of any attempt to employ the law to impose a comprehensive national story, one within which every citizen must find personal meaning and his conception of the good. But liberalism need not entirely dismiss the communitarian concern with social solidarity as if it were merely a conservative ploy for suppressing the discordant

---

67 Calvin Sims, "Argentine Tells of Dumping 'Dirty War' Captives into Sea," *N.Y. TIMES,* Mar. 13, 1995, at A1, A8.

68 *"Ratificó Scilingo Sus Denuncias,"* *Clarín* (Buenos Aires), Int'l Ed., Mar. 7-13, 1995, at 8 (translation by author).

69 *Id.*

70 Pierre Nora, "Between Memory and History: *Les Lieux de Mémoire,"* 26 *Representations* 7, 16 (1989).

voices of the powerless—the prevailing postmodernist view.[71] There is a sort of solidarity, based on and arising from civility in the expression of disagreements, that is wholly consistent with the liberal ideal, I have suggested.

When called upon to write national history, liberal courts should not aspire to the anachronistic ideal of a single national story with a single metaphysical "meaning," within which the lives of all groups and individuals find their proper place. Liberal courts thus need not construe their accounts of collective catastrophe as part of some seamless web of national narrative with which no reasonable person may differ. The frequent postmodernist accusation that they fail in this endeavor is misdirected, since the courts have never aspired to accomplish anything so pretentious.

Criminal law must eventually tell only one version of the story, and that version will become authoritative, but only for the criminal law's limited purposes. The serious question is what those purposes are, or ought to be, in cases of administrative massacre, given the somewhat idiosyncratic nature of their contours. Is the criminal law a good device, for instance, in constructing collective memory at such times, if not necessarily in accomplishing its more traditional objectives?

To be sure, the judicial and prosecutorial authors of the story told by criminal law today will often aspire to the larger ambition of influencing collective memory as well. But in so doing, they will be compelled to compete with a multitude of storytellers, offering conflicting accounts about the same events. In this regard, Schudson notes what should perhaps be self-evident, but which each generation must apparently learn anew and today requires vigorous rearticulation:

> In liberal societies, multiple versions of the past can safely coexist. An all-powerful monolithic version of the past will not triumph in a pluralistic society where conflicting views have a good chance of emerging, finding an audience, and surviving. This is not to say that dominant views do not exist, simply that—again, in a liberal society—they are never invulnerable.[72]

---

71   Jennifer Lehmann, *Deconstructing Durkheim* (1993).

72   Michael Schudson, *Watergate in American Memory* 208 (1992).

Consistent with this view, it is important that the judiciary of Argentina, for instance, be able to invoke liberal principles in both holding the juntas accountable for their crimes and also in refuting the larger story they told its citizens for many years about the dirty war and its moral defensibility.

As leading postmodernists rightly suggest (for reasons of their own), we are not always sure that we *want* the courts to attempt authoritatively to establish common understanding of a fratricidal history, be it our own or those of other societies. But this is not because courts cannot, in principle, do so in a manner consistent with liberalism. It is only because the commitment to liberal morality is actually so weak in many quarters. To the extent that many societies retain any strong collective conscience at all, it is not a liberal one: it is not based upon mutual respect for the moral autonomy of all persons.

Hence we may rightly doubt whether the ritual powers of courts, in societies like contemporary Argentina (or Eastern Europe) are adequate to the task of evoking liberal values in parties with radically discrepant, and often profoundly illiberal (ethnic, racialist, or theological) conceptions of "the good" and of national identity. Still, large-scale administrative massacre is not the sort of event in regard to which we feel comfortable about letting a hundred interpretive flowers bloom.[73] There is nothing "fascistic," Lyotard and other postmodernists notwithstanding, in *striving* for some measure of consensus here, even if the law is unlikely to attain it on its own.[74]

There is something about large-scale administrative massacre that brings out the residual positivist—sometimes deeply "repressed," as within postmodernist intellectuals[75]—in virtually everyone.[76] Before

---

73 "In the face of these events," Friedlander notes, "we feel the need of some stable narration; a boundless field of possible discourses raises the issue of limits with particular stringency." Saul Friedlander, "Introduction" to *Probing the Limits of Representation: Nazism and the "Final Solution"* 1, 5 (Saul Friedlander ed., 1992).

74 Jean-François Lyotard, *The Differend: Phrases in Dispute* 56-57 (Georges Van Den Abbeele trans., 1988); Lyotard, *supra* note 66, at 18-40. For commentary on Lyotard's characterization in this regard, see Friedlander, *supra* note 73, at 5 ("The striving for totality and consensus is, in Lyotard's view, the very basis of the fascist enterprise.").

75 See, e.g., Allan Megill, "Memory, Identity, and Questions of Evidence" 29 (June 23, 1995) (paper presented at the Project on Rhetoric of Inquiry Symposium, University of Iowa) (defending the "forensic" or legal approach to historiography, as "a scientific

there is any debate about who is morally or legally responsible for what, about which lessons must be learned by whom to prevent the catastrophe's recurrence, people want to know "the facts." The banners they proclaim through the streets might just as well carry the motto of the nineteenth-century German historian, Leopold von Ranke: to discover the past "as it really was"—a view today treated as the object of ridicule by many professional historians.

Vocally and vigorously, however, a newly mobilized citizenry begins to demand the facts as soon as they are permitted to do so, that is, as soon as the regime that perpetrated the massacre cedes power to those allowing more open public discussion of the past. Hence, "the first indispensable reparation demanded by society after fundamental institutions had been restored," reports the Argentine National Commission on the Disappeared, "was to ascertain the truth of what had happened, to 'face up' to the immediate past and let the country judge."[77]

---

project aimed at getting at justified truth concerning the past," as "more honorable, in its austerity" than various alternatives). Megill is the author of several sympathetic works on postmodernism. Allan Megill, *Prophets of Extremity* (1985). Many within the constructivist left turn suddenly positivist, insisting upon collective memory of their own favored facts, whenever national memory seems to drift in a direction they dislike. See, e.g., Meta Mendel-Reyes, *Reclaiming Democracy: The Sixties in Politics and Memory* 97 (1995) (arguing that "Richard Nixon's surprising reemergence as a respected elder statesman in the decade before his death in 1994...indicates a national desire for reconciliation at the price of forgetfulness.")

76 By "positivist" in this context I refer not to legal positivism but to positivistic philosophy of science, specifically to its notion that knowledge derives from empirical evidence and experience rather than exclusively from a priori categories. It holds, in short, that there exist facts independent of the observer who claims to discern them and of the cultural categories through which they are described. An extreme version of this view is captured in the title of a recent Honduran government report, *The Facts Speak for Themselves: Preliminary Report on Disappearances of the National Commissioner for the Protection of Human Rights in Honduras* (1994).

77 *Nunca Más, supra* note 60, at 428. Similar statements frequently appear during most democratic transitions. In Romania, for instance, the president of the Association of Former Political Prisoners, currently an opposition senator, writes: "'The trial of communism ... pursues restoration of the historic truth, the recuperation of the memory of our past, of the sense of social justice' .... 'All we want is the truth.'" Edwin Rekosh, "Romania: A Persistent Culture of Impunity," in *Impunity and Human Rights in International Law and Practice* 129, 139-40, 142 (Naomi Roht-Arriaza ed., 1995) (quoting Constantin Ticu Dumitrescu). The mandate of the Chilean Truth Commission was "to 'contribute to the overall clarification of the truth about the worst violations carried out in recent years.'" Jorge Mera, "Chile: Truth and Justice Under the

Our most sophisticated theorists today, of course, would counsel such benighted people that the facts are ultimately unimportant, because they can always be plausibly interpreted in competing and inarbitrable ways. Such counsel derives in part from the idea that historical "facts" are utterly insignificant until situated within a proper historical *understanding*, that is, within a coherent *theory* of history. For most leading European intellectuals for most of this century, that meant Marxism. Today, it most often means a recycled existentialism:[78] that we are free—all of us, at any time—to choose whatever we wish as the most congenial genre and temporal framing for emplotting our history (and thereby defining who is "us," for that matter).

To say that leading postmodernists regard such choices as inarbitrable is not to say that they are viewed as undiscussable. Discussion of such matters obviously abounds. Nor is it to say that postmodernists believe discussion of this sort can never produce any agreement. Such agreements have often been reached and maintained for lengthy periods, after all. It is to say, instead, that there can be no rational basis for any such agreement, whether or not an actual agreement on the terms of collective memory is reached by a given society at a particular time.

It is true, moreover, that though the *Madres de la Plaza de Mayo* might swear an oath demanding "nothing but the truth," they do not really desire "the whole truth," not within the public arena. Specifically, they do not desire any serious examination of the extent to

---

Democratic Government," in *Id.* at 172 (quoting the official mandate of the Commission on Truth and Reconciliation); see also *Servicio Paz y Justicia, Uruguay Nunca Más: Human Rights Violations, 1972-1985* (Elizabeth Hampsten trans., 1989), *reprinted in* "Nunca Más Report on Human Rights Violations," 2 *Transitional Justice: How Emerging Democracies Reckon with Former Regimes* 420 (Neil J. Kritz ed., 1995) ("The facts do not only speak, they call out in the midst of an intolerable silence, that is being imposed on the immediate past. Silence has become a cornerstone—placed in the past by the dictatorship and in the present by those who believe that it can assure a peaceful future. But the facts, the victims, are there; they speak or call out to us. There is no future in pretending to be deaf to what they are saying.").

78 Kenneth Cmiel, "After Objectivity: What Comes Next in History?" 2 *American Literary History* 170, 175-77 (Spring 1990). Cmiel observes that leading postmodernist critics of historiography assert that the only acceptable grounds for preferring one historical interpretation over another are moral (or aesthetic). Yet these critics "give no guidance on how ethics (or aesthetics) could inform historical debate." *Id.* at 176. Thus they are "moralists without a morality"—a strange duck. *Id.*

which the excesses of the radical left in the late 1960s brought on the military coups of the 1970s. That very question would imply something sacrilegious to those striving to make the martyrdom of their legally innocent children into a new, authoritative national narrative. The very question, after all, would allow public debate to entertain the possibility that the guerrilla left and its many sympathizers in the universities share some measure of responsibility for what military intervention entailed.[79]

In this respect, at least, the postmodernists are right. Anyone who seeks to base her political demands in the present on claims about a simple, unmediated factual truth concerning the past is being either (naively) ingenuous or *dis*ingenuous. No political program can build unshakeable foundations on unqualified empirical claims about historical truth. Particularly striking in this regard is Lyotard's observation that those who deny that the Holocaust occurred cannot be disproven because they shrewdly shift the terms of debate from the empirical level to an epistemological or methodological plane. At this level of analysis, the question becomes the nonfactual one of whether anyone who has not himself been gassed can provide dispositive evidence on what transpired within these rooms.[80]

Such arguments—both by the "revisionists" themselves and by postmodernists deploying these points to their own ends—would surely strike most citizens in societies victimized by administrative massacre as too clever by half, if not simply obscene. Their reaction does not prove Lyotard wrong, however. Theirs is a moral response, and no moral response can meet an epistemological challenge on its own terms.[81] The significance of their response thus lies elsewhere, in what it says about the extent to which we do not experience a "postmodern condition."

---

79 In academic publications, leading Argentine scholars, including those long identified with the left, now routinely concede the left's partial responsibility in this regard. See, e.g., Guillermo O'Donnell, *Bureaucratic Authoritarianism: Argentina, 1966-1973, in Comparative Perspective* 321-23 (1988).

80 Lyotard, *The Differend, supra* note 74, at 27-31. My interpretation of Lyotard in this regard is shared. See, e.g., Stephen Greenblatt, "Towards a Poetics of Culture," in *The New Historicism* (H.A. Veeser ed., 1989); Alex Callinicos, *Theories and Narratives* 67-70 (1995).

81 Even so, the way we choose our epistemological standards—concerning what should count as a warranted assertion of fact—is not any more arbitrary than how we choose our moral ones.

Recovery of Memory As a Social Movement

In Argentina, El Salvador, and the former Soviet Empire, much of the population rises up in support of the view that there is a bedrock of basic facts—about who did what to how many, when, and in what fashion. These must be authoritatively established, to provide the foundation for any legitimate public discussion of these events. It is not enough that the facts be generally known; they must also be publicly acknowledged, in Thomas Nagel's distinction.[82] When crucial facts are concealed, even for many, many years, each new revelation—often the discovery that a high-ranking perpetrator or collaborator remains in a prominent position—prompts yet another public scandal, and a new round of general debate about whether the country has fully confronted its inner demons, mastered its past.

During democratic transitions, people view the facts—in all their unmediated pretheoretical innocence—as the surest antidote to the flatulent rhetoric, glittering slogans, and radiant abstractions of the authoritarian rulers, recently displaced.[83] A salient feature of the reformist program is a demand that is unabashedly positivist: "getting the numbers right." Hence the recent demand by leaders of an Argentine human rights group: "What we want is the military lists, detailing who kidnapped which person, at what date and for what reason, where that person was taken, where he was killed and where he is buried."[84] Appelfeld states the aim in more lofty terms: "to rescue the suffering from huge numbers, from dreadful anonymity, and to restore the person's given name and family name, to give the tortured

---

82 Nagel defines this acknowledgment process as "'what happens and can only happen to knowledge when it becomes officially sanctioned, when it is made part of the public cognitive scene.'" Lawrence Weschler, *A Miracle, a Universe: Settling Accounts with Torturers* 4 (1990).

83 Judith Miller, *One, By One, By One: Facing the Holocaust* 287 (1990) ("Abstraction is memory's most ardent enemy. It kills because it encourages distance, and often indifference. We must remind ourselves that the Holocaust was not six million. It was one, plus one, plus one ...."). Many recent truth commissions thus emphasize their mandate to identify the fate of individual victims. On the Chilean commission's mandate in this regard, see Mera, *supra* note 77, at 172.

84 Calvin Sims, "Argentina to Issue New List of Missing in 'Dirty War'," *N.Y. Times,* Mar. 25, 1995, at A1, A4 (describing litigation resulting in a federal court order requiring the Argentine government to release any records left by the former military regime that would help identify people who were killed or who had disappeared).

person back his human form, which was snatched away from him."[85]

Public acknowledgment of facts concerning rights abuse is also intensely valued at such times in redress for suppression of speech. "For some, ten years or more had gone by in silence and pent-up anger," reports a member of the United Nations Truth Commission for El Salvador, of the testimony heard from citizens there.[86] "Finally, someone listened to them, and there would be a record of what they had endured."[87] Such official records give voice to the silent. That is precisely what the most distinguished theorists of postmodernism *reject* about them. For such records (and the official efforts to produce them) implicitly "privilege" voice over silence; they insist on trying to "represent" the unrepresentable: the silence of the true victims, the murdered dead.[88]

This social movement for factual recovery, which often adopts "correction of collective memory" as an explicit part of its program, has almost invariably appeared, in one form or another, in the aftermath of administrative massacre: in Russia, the former Soviet Bloc societies,

---

85   Aharon Appelfeld, *Beyond Despair* 39(1995). He adds: "Man as a number is one of the horrors of dehumanization," and by using "the language of statistics" we are following "the murderers' own well-proven means." *Id.* at 28.

86   Thomas Buergenthal, "The United Nations Truth Commission for El Salvador," 27 *Vand. J. Transnat'l L.* 497, 539 (1994).

87   *Id.* As Weschler notes, "Retrospectively, the broadcasting of truth...upends the torturer's boastful claim that no one will ever know...It is essential to the structure of torture that it takes place in secret, in the dark, beyond considerations of shame and account..." Public disclosure ensures that "torturers can never again feel so self-assured—nor their victims so utterly forlorn." Lawrence Weschler, *A Miracle, A Universe,* quoted in Adam Hochschild, *The Unquiet Ghost: Russians Remember Stalin* 20-21 (1994).

88   Bill Readings, *Introducing Lyotard: Art and Politics* 60-62 (1991) (discussing Lyotard's and Derrida's views in this regard). There is an uncomfortable affinity here between the postmodernist claim that the living cannot speak adequately for the dead and that of the Holocaust deniers, to the effect that only those who were gassed can speak adequately about Nazi use of the gas chambers. But it must be acknowledged that postmodernists are by no means the only writers on such issues to insist on the impossibility of representation. See, e.g., Elie Wiesel, *Night* (1960). In an important sense, however, many of the dead speak eloquently for themselves, through their surreptitious diaries of resistance and resignation, maintained even in recognition of their imminent fate. Sara Horowitz, "Voices from the Killing Grounds," in *Holocaust Remembrance, supra* note 64, at 42, 42-58 (describing the secret production and preservation of the *Lodz Ghetto Chronicle* and the *Oneg Shabbes* records of the Warsaw ghetto).

El Salvador, Argentina, Chile, Guatemala, and elsewhere.[89] The state's sympathetic response to this popular upsurge of demand for the facts can take many forms, from official "truth commissions," parliamentary inquiries, town meetings, textbook revisions, and criminal trials to sponsored scholarly inquiry into newly opened government archives. Within the human rights community, there is a thoughtful international debate taking place concerning the relative merits and demerits of these various options.[90]

Criminal courts are by no means the worst forum in which to conduct such inquiries. First, they fragment our settled perception of reality into contending stories and counter-stories. Because they resonate so well with our condition of narrative multiplicity, they provide a congenial institutional venue for confronting that condition and reaching a measure of closure, at least in isolated contests.

Second, the more overtly political branches of government often operate under greater constraints than courts, when asked to confront unpleasant realities and unpopular issues. In postwar West Germany, for instance, demanding prosecution of Nazi war criminals did not exactly mark out the road to a successful political career. Those who advocated such a path, like Kurt Schumacher (leader of the Social Democratic Party in the 1950s), frequently lost their electoral contests

---

89   For discussion of such demands in these societies, see Rosenberg, *supra* note 61, on Czechoslovakia, Poland, and Germany; R.J.B. Bosworth, *Explaining Auschwitz and Hiroshima: History Writing and the Second World War, 1945-1990* 159-60 (1993), on the current interest of Russians in scholarship concerning the number of those killed by Stalin; Thomas Butler, "Memory: A Mixed Blessing," to *Memory: History, Culture and the Mind* 25 (Thomas Butler ed., 1989), on memory movements in Poland and Russia, and the importance of secret Soviet Supreme Court archives to their investigations; Priscilla Hayner, "Fifteen Truth Commissions—1974 to 1994: A Comparative Study," 16 *Hum. Rts. Q.* 597, 611-34 (1994), on recent truth commissions in Africa; Margaret Popkin & Naomi Roht-Arriaza, "Truth As Justice: Investigatory Commissions in Latin America," *Law & Soc. Inquiry* (Winter 1995), at 79, on truth commissions in El Salvador, Chile, and Guatemala; Kathleen E. Smith, "Destalinization in the Former Soviet Union," in *Impunity and Human Rights, supra* note 77, at 113, 124-25, on mock trials against the Communist Party held in Russian schools, universities, and other public fora, charging officials with "crimes against humanity."

90   See, e.g., Naomi Roht-Arriaza, "Conclusion: Combating Impunity," in *Impunity and Human Rights, supra* note 77, at 281, 281-92 (preferring trials over truth commissions, because the former permit victims publicly to confront their oppressors); Aryeh Neier, "What Should Be Done About the Guilty?," *N.Y. Rev. Books,* Feb. 1, 1990, at 32, 34 (defending truth commissions over criminal trials).

for national office. This is scarcely surprising: the Allies themselves had, without extraordinary efforts, managed to indict over 80,000 Germans for war crimes. Over two million German citizens remained Nazi party members by mid-1945, moreover. Mass political support for extensive prosecutions was highly unlikely under these conditions.

Their very insulation from democratic pressures allow courts greater latitude at such times. Still, courts have not generally been preferred or privileged fora for conducting the national self-assessment so needed at such times. This is due to many of the problems examined in this and preceding chapters. Moreover, judicial fact-finding often operates by way of evidentiary presumptions (sometimes irrebuttable), legal fictions, and deliberately "tilted" allocations of the evidentiary burden. These devices are ill-suited for putting the interpretive contestants on a "level playing field."[91] The resulting perception—among defendants and their many sympathizers, especially—that "the game is rigged" is unconducive to discursive deliberation, however defensible such doctrinal devices may be for the limited purpose of ascribing criminal liability.

A second feature of popular sentiment and opinion at such times, equally embarrassing to postmodernism, is the widespread insistence that the facts, once established, be officially recognized as such and recounted *by the state*. In short, the state must tell an "official story," encompassing the entire pertinent period, about the extent and allocation of responsibility. To constitute a story, rather than merely a chronicle or annals, the official account must include a complex series of causal assertions about how the conflagration developed. It must embed these within a normative framework governing the inclusion and exclusion of particular facts and the connections between them.[92] As Hayden White puts it, "narrativity is a mode of description which transforms events into historical facts by demonstrating their ability to function as elements of completed stories."[93]

---

91   This is not to suggest that neutrality is possible or even desirable with respect to the substantive moral standards by which the defendants' conduct will be judged, only that procedural and evidentiary rules should not put either party at an advantage in promoting its view of recent history.

92   On how these features distinguish historiography from a mere chronicle or annals, see Morton White, *Foundations of Historical Knowledge* 222-25 (1966).

93   Hayden White, "The Narrativization of Real Events," in *On Narrative, supra* note

To be truly a story, in short, the state's official account must judge and explain. It must have a "moral," even if the moral does not (as it often cannot) extend to a demand for criminal prosecution of all responsible parties. The state must express remorse and repentance for the acts of its agents, done in its name. It must tell a story that delegitimates the prior regime, the claims made by its leaders and by its contemporary apologists on their behalf.

It must affirm as well-warranted the victims' feelings of resentment and indignation, for this affirmation is the only way for society at large to show that it acknowledges and takes seriously their condition *as* victims.[94] "What contributes to reestablishing their self-respect," Nino observed, "is the fact that their suffering is listened to in the trials with respect and sympathy, the true story receives official sanction, the nature of the atrocities are publicly and openly discussed, and their perpetrators' acts are officially condemned."[95] For the victims and their many supporters, notes Charles Maier, "It is crucial in their eyes that the story of good and evil be told correctly."[96]

The very idea of involving the state in imposing such a single, moralistic metanarrative is, of course, deeply offensive to postmodernist sensibilities. These insist that the postmodern condition is defined precisely by the repudiation of all such grand narratives—including that of the liberal Enlightenment, with its story about the triumph of truth and freedom over superstition, ideology, and intolerance.[97] The

---

31, at 249, 251.

94 Remarks of Martín Farrell. Tape of Human Rights and Deliberative Democracy: A Conference in Honor of Carlos Santiago Nino, Presented at Yale Law School (Sept. 23-24, 1994)

95 Nino, *supra* note 12. Nino rightly adds that this justification for punishment is nonretributive, since any suffering inflicted upon the perpetrators is not designed to "neutralize" that experience by the victims, *see id.*, a notion that Nino found unconvincing.

96 Charles Maier, "Doing Justice, Doing History: Political Purges and National Narratives after 1945 and 1989," 9 (paper presented at "In Memory: Revisiting Nazi Atrocities in Post-Cold War Europe. International Conference to Commemorate the Fiftieth Anniversary of the 1944 Massacres around Arezzo").

97 See, e.g., Berkhofer, *supra* note 7, at 220 ("The good postmodernist prefers fragmenting, differentiating, specifying, particularizing, deconstituting practices to deconstruct the spurious unities and reveal the contradictions of social and textual practices."); Lyotard, *supra* note 66, at xxiv, 30, 39, 72-73 (contending that in the West narrative knowledge has served to legitimate new authorities); White, *supra* note 51, at

discourse of moral judgment and legal condemnation, in this view, is merely one of several conceptual grids that can plausibly be laid upon the facts. It offers simply one among several possible "language games" that skilled rhetoricians can play with such facts.[98] When we tire of one, exhausting its creative or merely disruptive potential, we will switch to another.

"With so many competing and conflicting memories and histories," writes one postmodernist, 'is it not better to banish all metanarrative, to let memory bloom in all its manifestations, true, false, or otherwise? Why should memory necessarily be anchored to any "truth," any reality.' Once detached from that concern, then, "memory...becomes available for any desired ad hoc construction of identity; a coherent national narrative is no longer essential, or even desirable."[99] When constructing collective memory, we can then view a nation's history as just another indeterminate text, one that can be read to mean anything we want it to.

Just as political and professional authorities seek to impose their "regime of truth," they also seek to impose a regime of memory, on this view. We need not accept the invitation to accredit their proferred truths—including their truths in memory—as more legitimate than those offered by others. Memory should not be placed in service of *any* regime, for this is how national narrative becomes a means of control, for imposing uniformity where plurality is acceptable, even desirable. Inquiry into the past should thus be destabilizing of all such impositions and uniformities, on this account. Judicial and other official inquiries into the past, as expressions of state power, cannot do this.

Significantly, however, in the aftermath of administrative massacre, the victims and their families (as well as the substantial portion of society sympathetic to them) characteristically want just such

---

14, 20-25 (arguing that narrativizing always aims at moralizing).

98   Jean-François Lyotard & Jean-Loup Thébaud, *Just Gaming* 49-61, 93-105 (Wlad Godzich trans., 1985).

99 , Richard S. Esbenshade, "Remembering to Forget: Memory, History, National Identity in Postwar East-Central Europe," 49 *Representations* 72, 86 (1995). For an even stronger version of this position, see M. Christine Boyer, *The City of Collective Memory* 3 (1994) (arguing, for instance, that "we no longer dare ... to draw even a partial summing up of the historical or social situation to guide our future actions, to judge our collective project, or to prescribe necessary social transformations... Our postmodern conditions [leaves us] adrift in a sea of fragments and open horizons...")

a moral-legal story, stamped with the state's imprimatur—and brook no other. The victims seek, in short, a new myth of national refounding, a grand metanarrative of liberal redemption, recounting an epic of collective destruction and rebirth—by an authoritative affirmation of their indignation and a corresponding effort to ostracize the perpetrators.

As to social theory, I wish to make both a modest and a not-so-modest claim here. First, in the face of this century's abundant horrors, people are not incredulous toward all metanarratives—only toward illiberal ones. That assertion rightly invites the question: on what basis should we privilege the voice of the victims in this regard over others —including postmodernist intellectuals, who apparently feel no such longings?

Hence the second claim. It is often said that large-scale administrative massacre, from Armenia to Rwanda, defines the quintessential political experience of our century. This assertion is ubiquitous—particularly in social and political theory influenced by the French and Germans. In many ways, it is hyperbole. But insofar as many take it as true, the victims of administrative massacre have come to stand for something larger than themselves. Their condition becomes, in an important (if somewhat imprecise) sense, that of the world in our time. In short, the immediate victims of administrative massacre yearn for a liberal metanarrative, and their political experience is a more direct, intense version of our own. We might then fairly expect to discern in their narrative inclinations a partial guide to telling the story of our era. In craving a liberal metanarrative, they make clear that their "condition" is not postmodern. Insofar as we seek to understand our century and its traumas through their experience, our condition is not postmodern either.

Robert Hughes puts the same basic point more polemically: "Did Václav Havel and his fellow playwrights, intellectuals and poets free Czechoslovakia by quoting Derrida or Lyotard on the inscrutability of texts? Assuredly not: they did it by placing their faith in the transforming power of thought."[100]

Telford Taylor ably expressed the public yearning for an authoritative declaration of both facts and their "moral," in his opening

---

100   Robert Hughes, *The Culture of Complaint* 72 (1993).

statement for the Nuremberg prosecution of Nazi physicians. This yearning is especially acute where the normal instruments of criminal sanction appear inadequate, their purposes mocked.

> The mere punishment of the defendants, or even of thousands of others equally guilty, can never redress the terrible injuries which the Nazis visited on these unfortunate peoples. For them it is far more important that these incredible events be established by clear and public proof, so that no one can ever doubt that they were fact and not fable; and that this Court ... as the voice of humanity, stamp these acts, and the ideas which engendered them, as barbarous and criminal.[101]

It is not necessary or sufficient, in other words, that everyone feel emboldened to tell his personal story, to seek private catharsis in unburdening himself of his horror by sharing his memories with whoever will listen. There is also a powerful and pervasive desire at such times, to which new democracies often rightly respond, that such private accounts be woven together into a larger narrative about the period as a whole, and etched into collective memory.

The Argentine Commission on the Disappeared thus incorporates in its final report the tales of dozens of particular victims, by way of lengthy quotations from their personal testimony.[102] This noble effort to do justice both to the private, "subjective" dimension of the victims' suffering, however statistically unrepresentative, and to the larger institutional apparatus of repression responsible for such suffering is perhaps the greatest strength of *Nunca Más*, its textual aid to liberal memory and solidarity.[103]

---

101 1 *Trials of War Criminals Before the Nuernberg Military Tribunals* 27 (1946) (opening statement in *United States v. Brandt*).

102 *Nunca Más, supra* note 60, at 12-75.

103 Marcus's critique of this document, shows no awareness of its considerable attention to the "phenomenological" experience of individual victims, the "local narratives" that postmodernists universally applaud. Marcus, *supra* note 58, at 204-08. In fact, Marcus's critique—offered as a sympathetic response to Taylor's critique—evinces no sign whatsoever of his having read the report itself, which has long been available in English.

Perelli makes an antithetical objection, that "the collective dimension of repression tends to be lost in this bleak recitation of individual pain and despair. There [is] no place in this narrative for the common people," who have not been tortured or detained, but who have been victimized nonetheless by the regime's "culture of fear." Carina

Still, this very effort creates another dramaturgical dilemma: the stories most likely to stay in public memory (and so to be selected by prosecutors and commission members) will be the most extreme. The most extreme stories are necessarily idiosyncratic. Their unrepresentativeness thus evokes criticism—entirely plausible, albeit primarily from the defendants and their sympathizers—that collective memory has been willfully distorted, historically unbalanced by the state's efforts to influence it. But this is just to say that there is a place, in orchestrating the prosecutorial script, for prudent use of understatement, a conventional rhetorical device with which all competent litigators (like other good storytellers) are intimately familiar.

Again, courts of law are not necessarily the best forum for this sort of official narrative, albeit not altogether useless. Korean former comfort women are beginning to learn, for instance, that although the law may accord them rights to monetary compensation, there is no legal right to an official apology—in international law, Japanese law, or anywhere else. There is no legal right, one might say, to authoritative correction of collective memory. Official truth commissions, such as the recent Chilean one, may *choose* to offer a formal apology on the government's behalf for the acts of its agents.[104] But apology is not the remedy that the law—civil or criminal—affords for the wrongs suffered.

The law reviews are already full of creative arguments for overcoming legal obstacles to damage claims by the comfort women.[105] Yet journalists who interview such plaintiffs in depth report that what

---

Perelli, *"Memoria de Sangre*: Fear, Hope, and Disenchantment in Argentina," in Boyarin, *supra* note 41, at 50. Such conflicting indictments and exhortations simply suggest that these authors are criticizing the legal system for failing to solve problems beyond its ken, and that they are thus making unreasonable demands upon it. Liberal theory owes them an account of why these demands are unreasonable, an account consistent with its own defense of a role for liberal courts in constructing collective memory of such events.

104 Mera, *supra* note 77, at 172 (discussing the formal apology issued by Chilean President Aylwn on behalf of the government for acts of its agents).

105 See, e.g., Yvonne P. Hsu, "'Comfort Women' from Korea: Japan's World War II Sex Slaves and the Legitimacy of Their Claims for Reparations,' 2 *Pac. Rim L. & Pol'y J.* 97 (1993); Karen Parker & Jennifer F. Chew, "Compensation for Japan's World War II War-Rape Victims," 17 *Hastings Int'l & Comp. L. Rev.* 497 (1994); Janet L. Tongsuthi, "'Comfort Women' of World War II,' 4 *UCLA Women's L.J.* 413 (1994).

they most passionately desire is simply an official recognition by the Japanese state of the facts concerning what it did to them, and an apology for having done so. "I am not interested in money," one such woman insists, "because no emotion can be bought with money."[106] Some of these women even regard the idea of money as offensive, as do family members of the disappeared in Argentina, on the grounds that it treats the wrong as merely civil, rather than criminal in nature. (Serious crime, after all, has always been thought to offend against public values that make it incommensurable, hence partially uncompensable, in monetary terms.)

These women seek compensation from the Japanese government primarily as a definitive acknowledgment of state responsibility. Hence their continuing opposition to the government's recent compromise: a *private* foundation to help compensate surviving members of this group, involving no official participation beyond encouragement of private donations.[107] What the victims want is an authoritative narrative, an "official story," as the remedy for the wrongs they have endured.[108]

A criminal trial, particularly, is not well-designed for establishing

---

106 Peter McGill, "War Crime Victims Unite to Shame Japan," *Independent* (London), Jan. 28, 1995, at 6 (quoting Mrs. Son Shindo, age 73), available in LEXIS, News Library, Curnws File. The organization of Korean former comfort women, as well as other sympathetic rights organizations, rejected a government proposal for a privately funded trust, since this proposal did not involve any official recognition of responsibility and was thus unresponsive to their "demand that the historical record be set straight." Margaret Scott, "Making the Rising Sun Blush," *Far E. Econ. Rev.*, Mar. 30, 1995, at 50; see also Naomi Roht-Arriaza, "Punishment, Redress, and Pardon: Theoretical and Psychological Approaches," in *Impunity and Human Rights, supra* note 77, at 13, 21 (noting the greater importance of such "symbolic redress" than monetary compensation to many victims of administrative brutality).

107 "South Korean Group Seeks Compensation for Comfort Women," *Asian Pol. News*, Apr. 10, 1995, available in LEXIS, News Library, Curnws File. The private foundation has been titled the "Asia Peace and Friendship Fund for Women," a name that in no way suggests any wrongdoing on the part of the Japanese government. *Id.* In fact, a government spokesman expressly described the fund's purpose, at its creation, as "an expression of sympathy." Many comfort women and their legal advocates understandably felt that such statements, and the policy they sought to justify, merely added further offense to injury. Andrew Pollack, "Japan Pays Some Women From War Brothels, but Many Refuse," *N.Y. Times*, Aug. 15, 1996, at A5.

108 To this end, the litigation, in conjunction with diplomatic pressures, has been useful in eliciting from the Japanese government several tentative steps toward an official apology, including a personal apology from the Prime Minister while visiting South Korea.

society-wide consensus over the interpretation of tremendously controversial events. Klaus Barbie's defense counsel, Jacques Vergès, was surely correct when he observed:

> A trial is an event. It provokes, it creates drama, a spectacle desired by others, and it is up to us to create the image to our own liking. And by creating the image, I mean not manipulation but giving significance to the facts in our possession ....[109]

Such a debate could prove quite salubrious for a society at these times, breaking silence at last on central questions of national morals. The lessons that Vergès sought to teach were certain to be contested: that Barbie's acts paled in comparison to subsequent atrocities of purely French doing, wrongs that warrant a more central place in the country's collective memory.[110]

Shared memory is unlikely to result from treating the defendant as a coequal participant in shaping the terms of debate. But such debate can itself contribute to social solidarity (of the discursive variety) precisely by way of the civil engagements it engenders.

The Barbie trial had been initiated at the strenuous and persistent prompting of Nazi hunters Serge and Beate Klarsfeld, who viewed it chiefly as an opportunity to demonstrate publicly (and sear into France's collective memory) the extent of the nation's voluntary cooperation in the extermination of French Jewry.[111] Yet under the clever promptings of Vergès, the French were ultimately asked to accept responsibility for *all* of their major twentieth-century massacres, as in resisting independence movements in Algeria and other former colonies.

The *special* evil of the Holocaust, and hence the special evil of French collaboration in it, was thus to be effectively neutralized.[112] It

---

109   Jacques Vergès & Étienne Bloch, *La face cachée du procès barbie* 32-33 (1983) (translation by author).

110   On Vergès's legal and political strategy in this regard, see Alain Finkielkraut, *Remembering in Vain: The Klaus Barbie Trial and Crimes Against Humanity* xxix-xxx (Roxanne Lapidus & Sima Godfrey trans., 1992); Erna Paris, *Unhealed Wounds: France and the Klaus Barbie Affair* 146 (1985); Guyora Binder, "Representing Nazism: Advocacy and Identity at the Trial of Klaus Barbie," 98 *Yale L.J.* 1321, 1355-72 (1989).

111   Serge Klarsfeld, *Vichy-Auschwitz* 8 (1983); Paris, *supra* note 110, at 110-29.

112   Finkielkraut, *supra* note 110, at 34-44, 52-53; see also *id.* at 34 (arguing that

had been that evil which, in the view of Klarsfeld and many Jews, justified both the creation of a Jewish state and the moral imperative of strong French support for its survival.[113] By the end of the trial, however, defense counsel had managed to turn the narrative tables to a considerable extent, in the judgment of certain observers,[114] irrespective of the strictly legal result—the defendant's conviction.

A criminal trial—unless it really *is* a Stalinist show trial—differs crucially from a theatrical production in that there is no single stage "director." There is always a serious danger that the courtroom narrative might suddenly take an unexpected direction at the defendant's persuasive urging, a direction unfavorable (even deeply embarrassing) to the prosecution. Such a turn would surely shake the firm Durkheimian foundations of the entire endeavor, by preventing the trial from serving its proper, orderly, preordained, consensus-affirming functions.

But the possibility that the defendant's proffered counternarrative might actually prove at least partly persuasive, at least briefly convincing, is unthreatening to the discursive account of law's service to solidarity.[115] In fact, it is precisely the genuine uncertainty of result that gives a *liberal* show trial both its normative legitimacy and the dramatic intensity so conspicuously absent where conviction on all charges is a foregone conclusion. This feature of legal storytelling is also consistent with the postmodernist point that stories can always turn out differently than they do, that their ending is always uncertain and contestable.

The defendant's efforts to project his own interpretation of disputed events ensure that such proceedings are as likely to stir national controversy as to still it. The interpretation favored by Barbie and Vergès, after all, could appeal to the considerable self-interest of many elder Frenchmen, including President Mitterand himself,[116] in

---

Vergès's narrative framing strove to depict "Hitler's racism as [a] symptom of Western racism and imperialism").

113   For this point and general guidance on postwar French politics, I thank Professors Rosemarie Scullion and Sarah Farmer.

114   Finkielkraut, *supra* note 110, at 44, 66.

115   On discursive solidarity, see Chapter 2, "Solidarity Through Civil Dissensus."

116   Mitterand worked as a civil servant for the Vichy regime for 18 months. Until the early 1980s, he maintained a close friendship with René Bousquet, a former Vichy

suppressing any close examination of their wartime activities. Insofar as Vergès successfully redirected its narrative focus, Barbie's trial was not likely to foster much "mechanical solidarity," the social integration supposedly enhanced by punishment of one whose conduct is universally despised.[117] After these trials, "'our collective memory is a battlefield, a place of combat,'" observes philosopher Bernard-Henri Lévy.[118] But that is not so sorry a fate—and surely an improvement over forty years of coerced silence—provided that the ensuing verbal combat adheres to the discursive equivalent of the *jus in bello*.

Loose talk about the need for national storytelling may tend to conjure up the denizens of some homogeneous enclave—gathered around the tribal fire—responding together on cue, in laughter and tears. In modern societies, telling stories that resonate identically in all quarters is much more problematic. When citizens gather at all to this end, they are likely to disagree about how the story goes. Someone is certain to be accused of having "missed the point." This recalcitrant reality is inevitably reflected as well in *legal* storytelling, the narrative of the courtroom—even when all agree that the tale is a tragedy, that it recounts a national failure of the first order.[119] It is wrong to expect the law to provide the nation with narrative coherence at such times, if "coherence" is understood to entail stilling argument over "the moral" of the story.

Judicial efforts to tell a persuasive national story, one that resonates in the personal experience of all who lived through the period, cannot assume that the audience constitutes a traditional *gemeinschaft*.[120] Even so, judicial efforts at national storytelling are not

---

police official responsible for organizing the Jewish deportation. Bousquet was ultimately charged with crimes against humanity. A recent book establishes the President's close wartime affinities with the far-right. Pierre Péan, *Une Jeunesse Française* 315-22 (1994).

117 Emile Durkheim, *The Division of Labor in Society* 70-71 (George Simpson trans., 1964).

118 Miller, *supra* note 83, at 147.

119 One author observes that this is perhaps the single point of agreement in the national stock-taking following the dirty war: that Argentina is a "has-been" nation and that what requires explanation is why its early democratic and economic promise, prior to 1930, was not later realized. Carina Perelli, "Settling Accounts with Blood Memory: The Case of Argentina," 59 *Soc. Res.* 415, 415 (1992).

120 For communitarian arguments explicitly linking the possibility of meaningful

inevitably condemned to failure, for neither is modern Western society a *gesellschaft*—an agglomeration of lost souls, doomed to find their personal experience of the period utterly unintelligible and incommunicable to their fellows.

The least we might fairly expect from courts, at such trying times, is a stimulus to democratic dialogue between those who wish us to remember very different things. A courtroom may not be the optimal place for such a dialogue to occur, still less to be resolved. But a courtroom is one place where it might fruitfully begin or be carried forward. If its initiation is impeded by the jurisprudence of formalism, then we should doubt the value of this professional orientation at such times.

The real question, then, is whether modern courts can, by widening the acceptable scope of legal discourse, effectively influence collective memory of administrative massacre by telling liberal stories about it. Whether any of the six skepticisms I have identified in this book prove to be insurmountable obstacles to the law's deliberate influence on collective memory thus depends, in part, on how we conceive the law itself and the proper social function of courts.

In the contemporary world, then, collective memory must inevitably be fabricated in the face of public awareness about its constructed character. This fact is far more easily accommodated by the discursive than by the Durkheimian account of law's contribution to social solidarity. The former stresses the inevitability and salubriousness of the collective soul-searching that often follows a society's experience of administrative massacre. It also highlights the

---

collective memory to the survival of premodern social structures, and specifically to Ferdinand Tonnies' social theory, see Richard Terdiman, *Present Past: Modernity and the Memory Crisis* 44 (1993) (noting that "*gemeinschaft* is the paradise of memory"). See also Edward Casey, *Remembering* 7 (1987) (arguing that it "is regrettable that reminiscing as a social practice has faded from style.... In a more leisurely age ... [it] was a frequent feature of family gatherings and other social settings"); Sheldon S. Wolin, "Injustice and Collective Memory," in *The Presence of the Past* 32, 32-33 (1989) (describing modern Western democracies as forming "an anti-mnemonic society" that, unlike "mnemonic societies," displays no deference to custom or tradition). Such communitarian lamentations about the loss of memory through social change resemble those of 12th-century monks, who decried the spread of writing for seeming "to kill living eloquence and trust and substitute for them a mummified semblance [of memory] in the form of a piece of parchment." M.T. Clanchy, *From Memory to Written Record: England 1066-1307* 296-97 (Blackwell Publishers, 2d ed. 1993) (1979).

courtroom's utility as a forum for vigorous debate about the meaning of such events and their implications for the redefinition of national identity.

Public memory can be constructed publicly if the law advances social solidarity by ventilating and addressing disagreement, rather than concealing it—by acknowledging and confronting interpretive controversy, not suppressing it. Durkheim's account, in contrast, inevitably views any profound disagreement about how criminal law ought to be applied in such circumstances as reflecting, and perhaps contributing to, a lack of social solidarity.[121] When the courtroom becomes a forum for expression of deep disagreement about the meaning of the society's fundamental values, the criminal law necessarily fails to provide the solidarity that is its primary social function, on this account.

In sum, today many wish to use prosecutions for administrative massacre to help enhance the solidarity so essential in the aftermath of these events. To that end, trials should be orchestrated in light of more adequate understanding of social solidarity itself, that is, of its proper place within a liberal society. In this respect, contemporary theorists of deliberative democracy offer greater guidance than Durkheim's sociology of law.

Dramatic Genres for Legal Narrative

Certain literary genres prove better than others in choosing particular facts—among all chronicled ones—and arranging them into a national narrative that can effectively foster discursive solidarity and liberal memory. I have suggested in passing that the stories that litigants seek to tell in prosecutions of administrative massacre tend to correspond at least roughly with the genres of the "morality play" and "tragedy." Prosecutors put forth the former; defense counsel, the latter. The courtroom drama hence tends to become, to great extent, a

---

121 W. Paul Vogt, "Durkheim's Sociology of Law: Morality and the Cult of the Individual," in *Emile Durkheim: Sociologist and Moralist* 91 (Stephen P. Turner ed., 1993) (Durkheim "claimed that except in pathological circumstances 'all ordinary consciences' agree on what is right and wrong, on the gravity of particular wrongs, and therefore on what ought to be a crime and what its punishment should be.").

conflict about which such genre best fits and justifies the facts of recent history. Which genre provides the most suitable framework for historical interpretation and public understanding of these horrors? Neither of these genres, however, is particularly congenial for fostering the sort of civil dissensus that enhances social solidarity of the discursive variety.

Both genres, when well-executed, are too successful in achieving resolution and closure before the curtain falls, in tying up loose ends, in leaving no moral "remainder."[122] It is this remainder, however, that provides the impulse for continued discussion and public deliberation after the end of the proceeding. The genre best suited to cultivating discursive solidarity in the aftermath of administrative massacre is therefore the "theater of ideas."[123] The task for the court is to prevent the other genres and their professional advocates, however persuasive in strictly doctrinal terms, from altogether overwhelming the judicial role in shaping liberal memory, a role best served by recourse to this third dramatic form.

Every literary genre has particular conventions for representing the world. "The function of genre conventions," writes Culler, "is essentially to establish a contract between writer and reader so as to make certain relevant expectations operative and thus to permit both compliance with and deviation from accepted modes of intelligibility."[124] Hence, "the use of a given dramatic form is in some sense a proposal to elicit a given kind of response."[125] This response involves a measure of sympathy for certain characters and antipathy toward others—or ambivalence toward them all.

The purpose of genre-choice in the present context is little different from "real" theater. This is because of how social life, particularly in the courtroom, involves no small measure of role-playing and thus is

---

122   I employ here the terminology of Bernard Williams. "Ethical Consistency," in *Problems of the Self* at 177-79 (1973).

123   Although it has many predecessors, this genre largely originates in the dramas of Henrik Ibsen, George Bernard Shaw, and Bertolt Brecht. Its current leading representative is Tony Kushner, who has employed its conventions in virtually all of his plays.

124   Jonathan Culler, *Structuralist Poetics* 147 (1975).

125   Elder Olson, *Tragedy and the Theory of Drama* 168 (Wayne State Univ. Press 1966) (1961).

not entirely discontinuous with theatrical performance.[126]   This connection implies, for instance, that "when we describe real-life events as tragic, we emphasize ... [how] the event in life seems organized in the manner of the tragic form in drama."[127]   In our attempts at understanding the world, "we structure real experiences in the same way that tragedy organizes them in drama."[128]

In the morality plays of the early Elizabethan period, the characters functioned allegorically, representing the various virtues and vices.[129] These dramas were "intended to convey a lesson for the better conduct of life," in the words of one interpreter.[130] They were "to serve a ritual social purpose," notes another, "to demonstrate and therefore to verify Christian doctrine."[131]   The simplifications of character, plot, and worldview that they involved were considered necessary for rendering learned theological themes accessible to a largely illiterate audience.[132]

Morality plays were not mere sermons or theological arguments. They were "concerned more amply with moving the emotions, not merely with impressing on the mind clear and distinct ideas."[133] It was this feature that enabled them "to elicit pleasure and/or to purge passions," to "exert an ideological action on the spectators, reinforcing their common faith."[134]

This reinforcing of common faith provides the link to Durkheim's

---

126   Goffman, *supra* note 1, at xi; Eco, *supra* note 6, at 113.

127   Richard H. Palmer, *Tragedy and Tragic Theory* 9 (1992).

128   *Id.*

129   Robert Potter, *The English Morality Play* 105-55 (1975); James A. Reynolds, *Repentance and Retribution in Early English Drama* at v (1982) (noting that "the major characters, through both speech and action, correspond to specific agents of good and evil in the morality tradition").

130   2 J. Payne Collier, *The History of English Dramatic Poetry to the Time of Shakespeare* 259 (AMS Press 1970) (1831); see also Clifford Davidson, *Visualizing the Moral Life: Medieval Iconography and the Macro Morality Plays* 4-13 (1989).

131   Potter, *supra* note 129, at 16. "In each case we have a ... tangible substantiation of higher principles. In each case the Truth comes true. In each case we have a drama ... with a positive and reinforcing conclusion." *Id.*

132   On the central aim of popularizing Christian moral teachings, see David N. Beauregard, *Virtue's Own Feature: Shakespeare and the Virtue Ethics Tradition* 28-29 (1995); David M. Bevington, *From Mankind to Marlowe: Growth of Structure in the Popular Drama of Tudor England* 48-67 (1962).

133   Beauregard, *supra* note 132, at 29.

134   Alter, *supra* note 15, at 39.

view of criminal prosecution. After all, prosecution was to serve as a public ritual for awakening and consolidating the collective conscience, the content of which increasingly consisted, he believed, of our "common faith" in ideas of respect for individuals and their rights.[135]

Today, however, the weakness of the morality play as a genre for social drama and mnemonic didactics is relatively clear. It lies in the polarity of the conclusion: the unequivocal triumph of the unflinchingly good over the unregenerately evil. One will be tempted to respond, of course, that in cases of large-scale administrative massacre this proves almost entirely accurate as a rough characterization, at least, of the central *personae*—the mass murderers and the murdered—and of their predominant features.

But when complicity in such crimes is widespread throughout a society, because of diffuse support or connivance enjoyed by the immediate perpetrators, the simple bipolarity of the morality play is inadequate. Specifically, its genre conventions offer poor guidance for a society in need of a deeper and more far-reaching process of self-reckoning. That need has surely been present in all of the situations examined here, and is sometimes even widely acknowledged.

Like modern melodrama, the morality play displays a psychological structure that is "monopathic," in the words of one scholar.[136] Since it is based "on the victor-victim polarity, there is no counter-feeling to offset the dominant emotion: the approval of victory easily expands into the delights of self-congratulation."[137] This pattern has been especially conspicuous in the Argentine reaction to the junta prosecution and in Japanese response to the Tokyo Trial, as we have seen. In morality plays, as in the melodramas of mass culture, "victory is not tempered with the rigors of cost accounting, nor defeat with the reckoning of spiritual growth."[138]

In the wake of administrative massacre, the very success of the prosecution in eliciting and purging the punitive passions via the genre conventions of the morality play thus constitutes at once its deepest

---

135   See Chapter 1, "Crime, Consensus, and Solidarity," *supra* text accompanying notes 16-18.

136   Robert B. Heilman, *Tragedy and Melodrama* 87 (1968).

137   *Id.*

138   *Id.*

failure. It fails as a vehicle for generating discursive solidarity between current accusers and former sympathizers of the accused. This failure is especially problematic where the crimes of the accused recently received pervasive sympathy from the accusers themselves or, more precisely, from a substantial segment of the public whom the prosecutorial accusers represent.

Where the prosecution aims to change the audience's beliefs and memories, rather than to confirm existing ones, other genres are more promising as dramatic vehicles for legal narration of recent events. Tragedy immediately recommends itself in this regard. This is not so much because such events are clearly "tragic" in the lay sense of involving terrible suffering and misfortune. Rather, a tragic framing of events suggests itself because of the complexity that this dramatic genre admits in the distribution of wrongdoing and blame.

The story becomes, instead, one about how good and evil people are to be found on both sides of the conflict, and about how good people on each such side were made to suffer by evil people on the other. This story will tend to implicate the accusers (and those for whom they speak), depriving them of "clean hands" and weakening confidence (even self-confidence, at times) in their moral standing to accuse and to judge.

This effect of tragic drama upon its audience has been noted and decried at least since Rousseau. He contended (as a recent commentator observes) that in tragedy

> the passions are made more attractive, while virtue becomes the preserve of special kinds of beings. ... Men are softened ...; they hear vice, adorned with the charms of poetry, defended in the mouths of villains; they become accustomed to thinking of the most terrible crimes and to pity those who commit them ....[139]

This softening effect follows directly from an essential feature of tragedy as a literary genre. A drama scholar thus writes:

> While the stresses of melodrama can unite an audience against a common

---

139   Allan Bloom, "Introduction" to *Jean-Jacques Rousseau, Politics and the Arts: Letter to M. D'Alembert on the Theatre* at xi, xxv (Allan Bloom trans., 1960).

enemy and a common evil, those of tragedy can be more painful because they are difficult or impossible to resolve. You can throw rotten eggs at the villain of melodrama, a gesture impossible in tragedy, whose villain hides inside your own head.[140]

This effect was exactly that sought by Vergès, for instance, in pointing the accusatory finger at France itself, and its postwar foreign policy in particular: to hide inside the head of the national audience, disrupting the tranquility of its desired *dénouement*.[141] In seeking to soften up the judgmental passions of an audience, the idiom of *tu quoque* offers a congenial device. It has hence been prominent in defense narratives —not only at Nuremberg and Tokyo, but also in the more recent trials (Buenos Aires, Paris, and Lyon) examined here.

The question then proves to be whether it is possible to render the historical narrative more complex in this fashion—as the intended basis for collective memory—without thereby also undermining the *legal* result. After all, only the defendants can be convicted and imprisoned, not "society" at large. A tragic framing of their clients' conduct and circumstances appeals to defense counsel precisely because of how it weakens the plausibility and persuasiveness of such a conclusion to the legal story. The moral complexity of the tale is brought to the fore—and deployed to maximal theatrical effect—in hopes of enervating the audience's initial moral passions, which are often (as in the trials of Barbie and the Argentine juntas) intensely punitive.

Classical tragedy displays a second drawback, for present purposes. It ends with the restoration of the cosmic order that has been disrupted by the characters and events.[142] This tranquility serves to "transcend the carnage" with which such plays commonly end. But this purified state of peacefulness, offered only by grace of the gods, has been widely and rightly thought to render such endings unpersuasive to modern audiences—even irrelevant to the modern condition. That condition is said to be "characterized by fragmentation rather than by

---

140   J.L. Styan, *Drama, Stage and Audience* 72 (1975).

141   See *supra* text accompanying notes 108-122.

142   Palmer, *supra* note 127, at 150 (noting that "tragic theorists persistently advance the idea of a cosmic order upset by the character's actions but restored at the play's end").

the ever-uniting synthesis."[143] A dramatic form that "asserts ... the ultimate unity of the moral order"[144] is surely not well-calculated to stimulate continuing discussion at the end of the play or proceeding; it is thus poorly suited to foster discursive solidarity among parties to such a much-needed discussion.

Rendering the national narrative as tragedy thus overcomes the weakness of emplotting it as melodramatic morality play. But it does so only by introducing serious, perhaps insurmountable obstacles to justifying severe punishment for a limited few. A tragic emplotment is likely to fail, in any event, because its genre conventions require a concession of wrongdoing and an expression of remorse by the central character—the defendant. Such concessions have been almost entirely absent in prosecutions of administrative massacre. The exception of Albert Speer, in this respect, only serves to reveal the extreme rarity of such a response.[145] In short, the defendant himself generally proves unwilling to assume the mantle of tragic hero, insofar as this requires disclosing a "tragic flaw."

The closest that most defendants will come to satisfying this genre convention is to allege that their acts were determined by fate, by bad luck—a common theme in classical tragedy.[146] Hence the recurrent claim of Eichmann and even higher-ranking Nazi officials, for instance, that they were mere "cogs" in an organizational machine, one that would have produced identical effects without them. If their absence would have made no difference, then their presence must be viewed as merely a matter of moral luck, they imply.

To foster discursive engagement between the parties (and their

---

143 Murray Krieger, *The Tragic Vision* 6 (1960). An influential argument for this view is espoused in Georg Lukács, "The Sociology of Modern Drama," *Tul. Drama Rev.*, Summer 1965, at 146 (Lee Baxandall trans.).

144 Krieger, *supra* note 143, at 6. "The cathartic principle itself, in maintaining that pity and fear are not merely to be aroused but to be purged, is evidence of the need in tragedy to have dissonance exploded, leaving only the serenity of harmony behind." *Id.* at 3; see also Robert Brustein, *The Theatre of Revolt* 4 (1964) (observing that in the traditional "theatre of communion," including the works of Sophocles and Shakespeare, "traditional myths were enacted before an audience of believers against the background of a shifting but still coherent universe").

145 Gitta Sereny, *Albert Speer: His Battle with Truth* (1995).

146 Dwight Furrow, *Against Theory: Continental and Analytic Challenges in Moral Philosophy* 68 (1995).

respective followers), the court must resist the narrative framings offered by the antagonists, passing judgment only on their legal arguments. Whatever legal conclusion is ultimately reached on the merits, the story enacted within the public drama of the courtroom (and thus infused in collective memory) should be one that serves the needs of what I have called discursive solidarity. To this end, the most suitable dramatic genre is surely the "theater of ideas."[147] Its leading theorists spoke explicitly of the "theater as tribunal."[148] The affinities this suggests make it defensible to consider, the merits of the tribunal as theater.

The drama of ideas involves, writes George Bernard Shaw, "the introduction of the discussion and its development until it so overspreads and interpenetrates the action that it finally assimilates it, making play and discussion practically identical."[149] The effect is that

> the drama arises through a conflict of unsettled ideals rather than through vulgar attachments, rapacities, generosities, resentments, ambitions, misunderstandings, oddities and so forth as to which no moral question is raised. The conflict is not between clear right and wrong: the villain is as conscientious as the hero, if not more so: in fact, the question which makes the play interesting (when it *is* interesting) is which is the villain and which the hero.[150]

In fact, notes a scholar, "the dramatist may feel so ambivalent about both sides ... that he refuses to permit either to score a clear victory."[151] Such principled irresolution should not be confused with mere indecisiveness. Both "high" tragedy and "low" melodrama, whatever their differences, resemble each other in this crucial respect: questions about "which is the victor and which the vanquished ... cannot

---

147 ، For studies on major exemplars of this tradition, see *Ideas in the Drama* (John Gassner ed., 1964).

148 Timothy J. Wiles, *The Theater Event: Modern Theories of Performance* 75 (1980) (quoting Erwin Piscator).

149 George Bernard Shaw, "The Quintessence of Ibsenism," in *Major Critical Essays* 1, 146 (1932).

150 *Id.* at 139.

151 Vivian Mercier, "From Myth to Ideas—and Back, in Ideas in the Drama," *supra* note 147, at 42, 46.

afford to be left in doubt."[152]

Bertolt Brecht's "alienation effect" can contribute to this process of deliberate disruption. This is because such "alienation allows both players and audience to deliberate upon the action with full awareness of how events"—including the events on stage—"are manipulated."[153] Cross-examination by opposing counsel can be viewed as a theatrical device in the public drama for ensuring that the testimony of a given witness, no matter how initially sympathetic, is subjected to such an alienation effect. Brechtian drama, remarks Roland Barthes, is thus "a theatre that invites, requires explanation, but does not give it; it is a theatre that provokes History, but does not reveal it, that poses the acuity of the problem ... but does not solve it."[154]

The drama of ideas does not involve mere intellectual debate between embodied representatives of abstract ideas. Emotions play a key role. These are not the emotions of uncritical sympathy with some characters and unqualified loathing of others (as in the melodrama), but rather "'the sense of justice, the urge to freedom, and righteous anger.'"[155] No identifiable hero ("proletarian" or otherwise) is allowed to monopolize these noble sentiments, moreover. The dramatic result is to achieve a great degree of moral complexity without succumbing to the cosmic resolution and resulting tranquility of classical tragedy.

Surely this is the dramatic form most hospitable to the courtroom, especially when the defendants view their conduct as just and honorable and are prepared to defend it publicly as such. This was particularly true of Argentina's military trials. By enforcing the adversarial structure of the proceeding and the civility-rules governing it, the court can induce the antagonists to engage each other's historiographical interpretations. If dramatic catharsis and social connection are to result,

---

152 *Id.*

153 Frederick Burwick, *Illusion and the Drama* 6 (1991); see also Wiles, *supra* note 148, at 86 (describing "the theatrical reality of Brechtian actors observing and commenting upon the characters they play before a critical audience which judges rather than empathizes").

154 Roland Barthes, "Brecht, Marx, et l'historie," *cahiers de la compagnie Madeleine Renaud/Jean Barrault* 21, 23 (1957); see also Wiles, *supra* note 148, at 75 (noting that Brecht "left his plays unresolved so that his audience would seek to solve problems outside the theater, in the world").

155 Wiles, *supra* note 148, at 76 (quoting Bertolt Brecht).

they must emerge from this very process of civil dissensus, rather than from any hope of its immediate resolution by the court.

To orchestrate the trial in this way does not require that we regard ` the architects of genocide as "men of ideas," although they themselves—from Adolf Hitler to Ramon Camps—have often viewed their lives in just this way. It requires only that we provide them with the occasion to demonstrate the moral bankruptcy of their ideas and acts, when publicly subject to critical scrutiny and examination. To the extent that such defendants altogether fail to persuade anyone of their crack-pot historical theories, prosecution of them will easily evoke the righteous indignation of the collective conscience, much as Durkheim hypothesized. To the extent that the defendants succeed in remaining persuasive to significant numbers of fellow citizens, those citizens will at least be drawn into discursive solidarity, through civilized debate, with others whose views they oppose, debates modeled on those initiated and observed in court.

The dilemma thus becomes: how to *authoritatively resolve* the legal question of the defendants' criminal liability, while expressly holding open larger questions about collective memory that the court now admits as legitimately open to debate within the forum it provides. How can judges, by telling liberal stories in their opinions, effectively influence collective memory of administrative massacre, while nonetheless disavowing any professional monopoly over questions of historical meaning? If courts are to seek to tell the national story, their conviction of the defendants must somehow confirm the liberal narrative without imposing complete closure on it. In the present study, I seek only to bring this tension more clearly to the surface of our discussion and to clarify its terms.

Conclusion

The central purpose of criminal prosecution remains the deterrence of, and retribution for serious wrongdoing. Anyone who proposes adding other functions rightly bears the burden of proving that these additions are consistent with these older and enduring aims. This study contends that there is no reason to assume any such incompatibility. In part, at least, this is an empirical question. As such, it can best be answered by examining the historical record of deliberate efforts to influence collective memory through prosecution of administrative massacre. The present study has approached the question in these terms.

In the trials examined here, efforts to shape the story of administrative massacre take place in several venues, often simultaneously, within the courtroom and in society at large. The dynamics of disagreement can be quite different on each such level. But I have not chosen to dwell on these differences. On the contrary, I have stressed the close relationship between what goes on within the courtroom and beyond it. This is because in such trials both sides are playing a two-level game: legal and political, doctrinal and historiographical. When the game is well-played, each move is calculated with both audiences in mind.[1] Both sides seek to tell a legal story than can be woven into the fabric of collective memory, necessarily rewriting aspects of national history in the process. Each side tells the tale of what happened between the litigants in a manner designed to situate that story within contrasting accounts of how the country was brought to the point where such things could happen.

It remains to be seen whether liberal courts can entirely reconcile the traditional, delimited functions of criminal law with the dramaturgical demands of monumental didactics. But from the prior discussion it should be clear, at least, that criminal courts *have* often shaped collective memory of such national tragedies as administrative massacre. It is equally clear that prosecutors, defense counsel, and executive officials have sought to influence judicial conclusions toward this end, sometimes successfully. Such successes, and the promise they

---

1   I shall reserve for another venue the temptation to develop the game-theoretic implications of this fact.

hold out, ensure that courts will continue to be drawn willy-nilly into the process of memory construction.

These successes also ensure that we, the audience, will nevertheless be increasingly wary of the resulting potential for their political manipulation, injustice to defendants, distortion of the historical record, and fostering dangerous delusions of purity and grandeur. If courts have already been thrown into these bracing waters, the principal task for liberal sociology and jurisprudence is to teach them to swim.

To this end, I have found it necessary to explore what liberalism might learn from selective strands in postmodernism, especially postmodernist theories of narrative and collective memory. To the dismay of many postmodernists themselves, no doubt, I have sought to tame their insights in ways permitting acceptance of these by liberal legal and political theory. Conversely, liberals may doubt whether postmodernism can be so easily de-fanged. Most liberals are—quite understandably, in my view—utterly repelled by postmodernism's more extravagant versions, which are cognitively relativist, morally nihilistic, and politically anarchistic.

In accentuating the negative, in emphasizing the problems inevitably to be confronted, I mean only to emphasize that the courts cannot perform so large a job on their own. In so doing, I wish to suggest how the many nonlawyers engaged in other media of memory-practice might target their own contributions more pointedly toward compensating for the criminal law's particular weaknesses.

In addition, the preceding analysis may help sensitize prosecutors and judges involved in cases of administrative massacre to both the perils and promise that such cases present for cultivating liberal memory and solidarity,[2] to exploit the promise and confront the perils

---

2   See, for example, the pending United Nations proceedings against Bosnian Serbs and Rwandan Hutus, as well as the current trial in Ethiopia against 44 former military leaders. All three trials involve indictments for war crimes and crimes against humanity. S.C. Res. 955, U.N. SCOR, 49th Sess., 3453d mtg., at 2, U.N. Doc. S/Res/955 (1994) (establishing an international tribunal for prosecuting violators of international humanitarian law in Rwanda"); S.C. Res. 827, U.N. SCOR, 47th Sess., 3217th mtg., at 2, U.N. Doc. S/Res/827 (1993) (establishing an international tribunal "for the sole purpose of prosecuting persons responsible for serious violations of international humanitarian law committed in the territory of the former Yugoslavia"); *Office of the Special Prosecutor, Transitional Government of Ethiopia, The Special Prosecution*

more directly than they otherwise would do. I am acutely aware of having raised far more questions than I have answered. My modest hope has been to open up consideration of a question not presently on the agenda of liberal jurisprudence and to recast some existing issues of legal sociology in a new light.

As a tool for the construction of collective memory of administrative massacre, criminal prosecution has both the strengths and weaknesses here identified. It does some things rather well, other things only passably well, and makes an utter hash of still others. Despite frequent, energetic assertions that the problems are "inherent" in the law or liberalism,[3] that case has nowhere been effectively made, or even seriously argued. When we examine the actual cases, those discussed here, the obstacles we encounter are localized, discrete, historically contingent: this statute of limitations, that definition of the elements of an offense, the other jurisdictional quirk.

From all this we should no more conclude that criminal trials are inevitably insignificant as a font of liberal memory than that they are uniquely potent instruments toward that end. Discussion of such trials by both legal scholars and those in the human sciences, I have suggested, has frequently been characterized by overgeneralization: by exaggerated claims for the pedagogical value of these proceedings no less than by hyperbolic dismissals. The present study has sought to show the need for greater subtlety and discrimination in our judgments here.

Process of War Criminals and Human Rights Violators in Ethiopia (1994) (mandating the establishment of an historical record of the abuses of the Mengistu regime and bringing those criminally responsible for human rights violations and/or corruption to justice).

3   See, e.g., Lawrence Douglas, "Film As Witness: Screening 'Nazi Concentration Camps' Before the Nuremberg Tribunal," 105 *Yale L.J.* 449 (1995) (attributing Nuremberg's failure as historiography to the doctrine of precedent); Letter from Professor Herbert A. Strauss to Professor Eric Stein, in "Correspondence on the "Auschwitz Lie"," 87 *Mich. L. Rev.* 1026, 1027 (1989) (pointing out the absurdity of lawyers and judges still applying law handed down from the Nazi period and arguing that this absurdity is "inherent in legal forms of thinking"); Nancy Wood, "Crimes or Misdemeanours? Memory on Trial in Contemporary France," 5 *French Cultural Stud.* 1, 21 (1994) (suggesting, on the basis of the Touvier trial, that "the 'limits of juridical logic' impose necessary restrictions on the historical, educative and commemorative functions of law"); Paul Thibault, "La Culpabilité Française," *Esprit* 24 (Jan. 1991) (arguing that the very nature of legal judgment necessarily oversimplifies issues of historical explanation and moral assessment.)

Perhaps the modesty of my verdict in this regard will, at least, temper the overly ambitious reach of my historical and theoretical purview. But some readers will surely find my qualified endorsement of liberal law's potential too inconclusive, even willfully equivocal. Though a lawyer by training, I confess to being—by intellectual temperament—less of a problem-solver than a problem-finder and a problem-clarifier. This book thus seeks primarily to clarify and define the nature of the issues at stake. I can only hope and encourage others of my profession—more given to moving and shaking the world— to take up the challenge that, rightly understood, these problems continue to present.

To cultivate liberal memory in the aftermath of administrative massacre requires that courts treat easy cases as if they were hard ones. This is because legal concepts and doctrines will often have lost their normal connection to the underlying moral and political issues at stake. This means that judges must allow both prosecutors and defense counsel to paint with a broader brush (as they have demonstrably done, in any event), to widen the spatial and temporal frame of courtroom storytelling in ways that allow litigants to flesh out their competing interpretations of recent history, and to argue these before an attentive public. Only in this way can the debate within the courtroom be made to resonate with the public debate beyond the courthouse walls. Just as hard cases can make bad law, so too easy cases can make for poor drama (i.e., within the genre of the theatre of ideas, as a basis for discursive solidarity).

The result will be to make the prosecution's case, however strong on strictly doctrinal grounds, more vulnerable to refutation by contextualizing historical arguments that courts would normally disregard as legally irrelevant, excluding all evidence proffered in their support. The side whose story has greater "fit" with existing rules would no longer win hands-down on that account, for fit must be weighed against other values, especially those of robust public deliberation and memory-practice.[4]

---

4   My argument here differs from Dworkin's, in which "fit" is devalued against other objectives when legal rules look very bad from a moral point of view. Ronald Dworkin, *Law's Empire,* 256-57 (1986). In my cases, the applicable legal rules themselves (against murder, for instance) are morally unproblematic. They are nonetheless traded off against other important values—to justify punishment more persuasively to more

What will be lost by prosecutors in terms of enhanced vulnerability will be gained, many times over, in the judgment's ultimate persuasiveness as the foundation for collective memory of the disputed events. This will often mean a slower, more circuitous route to judgment, dramaturgically designed as much to raise public understanding about the underlying morality of criminal law as to view these particular defendants in its light.

The response to both the Argentine junta members and the Japanese generals would thus have had to be that: first, even on their utilitarian assumptions about morality, their respective reactions to the leftist guerrilla (mass torture of nonguerrillas and disappearances) and to Western imperialism (Japanese war crimes throughout Asia) were grossly "disproportionate" to the threat in question; and second, the criminal law of a liberal society and international community must, in any event, reject such utilitarian calculations when they conflict with the most fundamental moral rights of persons—to life, liberty, and physical integrity. Therefore, for example, Barbie's murder of seven French Jews, ostensibly in order to save a larger number of gentile Frenchmen, could not be excused as a lesser evil. The French courts rightly responded in this fashion.[5] These judicial responses help to set the terms for the ensuing debate in society at large.

A "slam dunk" conviction, summarily condemning the defendants as "radical evil" incarnate,[6] is certain to shut off the very dialogue that most needs to be initiated among fiercely hostile opposing camps of political partisans, ready to renew their genocidal efforts (or avenge those of their more successful adversaries) at the first opportunity.

The path that I propose could have made military trials not merely more compelling as public spectacle, but more urgently demanded by the Argentine public, permitting them to go forward without the amnesty and pardons. It could also have done more to educate morally the Argentine populace about the issues dodged during the dirty war.

---

people, and thus to shape collective memory. Fit will be compromised most clearly regarding legal rules on admissibility of evidence and the customary scope of fact-finding.

5   Sorj Chalandon, "My Colleague Told Me: You Must Choose Seven Jews," in *Memory, the Holocaust, and French Justice* 137 (Richard J. Golsan ed., 1996).

6   This view of the Argentine junta defendants is reflected, for instance, in the title of Carlos Nino's posthumous book, *Radical Evil on Trial* (1996).

"Pedagogically-motivated taboos"[7] make not only for poor historiography, as German revisionist historians rightly warn. In the longer run even, they even make for poor pedagogy. Opening the law at such times to the full range of moral and historical arguments that we use in real life to govern and judge our actions would have better served the ends of legal didactics, social solidarity, and political reform.

Only in this way, by ensuring that all antagonists feel they have received a fair hearing, can the courts hope to impart a measure of professional authority—however limited—to their judgments, weaving their strictly legal conclusions into a plausible and relatively capacious narrative about the country's recent conflagration. To insist on punctilious judicial adherence to any notion of legal formalism at such times is to guarantee the failure of courts to cultivate liberal memory when this objective is vital to successful democratization.

Because courts do not conventionally have authority to resolve issues of collective memory and national mythology, conventionalist accounts of judging would not authorize judges to address them. This stricture would apply even to passages of an opinion that no reader would take for anything but dicta and to testimony that no observer would mistake as anything but "general background."[8]

Judicial conventions should be revised accordingly. By simply applying "the rules laid down," without extended discussion and defense of the principles on which they rest, formalist approaches to judicial process shut off the very discussion that is most needed, when judging the conduct of those who do not share the law's assumptions.[9] Formalist judging assumes that widespread societal agreement on fundamentals already exists, when agreement at such times is conspicuously absent, and when steps toward its construction—through reasoned debate and persuasion—are so imperative.

---

7 Saul Friedlander, *Memory, History, and the Extermination of the Jews of Europe* 66 (1993) (summarizing arguments of the revisionists).

8 For a discussion of this sort of conventionalism, its close relation to what others call legal positivism, and its limitations as a conception of the judicial role, see Dworkin, *Law's Empire, supra* note 4, at 114-50.

9 Although discursive democratization is ill-served by formalist judging, that approach has paradoxically produced most laudable results (in judicial resistance to wicked law) *during* periods of authoritarian rule. Mark J. Osiel, "Dialogue with Dictators: Judicial Resistance in Argentina and Brazil," 20 *Law & Social Inquiry* 481, 493-95, 522-26, 533-45(1995).

As Sanford Levinson observes, many theories of punishment *"assume* ... the existence of a single community organized around a coherent moral code reflected in its criminal law."[10] Because people thus essentially agree about morality, the courtroom need not become a forum for extended debates about its nature and demands. Correspondingly, judges need not examine its ambiguities when applying the legal rules embodying it to what the law regards as easy cases.

But whether any such shared moral code exists and whether it is accurately reflected in the community's criminal law prove to be highly problematic propositions in the historical circumstances where large-scale administrative massacre occurs. By no means are they to be casually assumed. Even when most people largely agree in their moral judgments, this "conventional morality" may often be uncritical, that is, less rationally defensible than the liberal morality formally embodied in the criminal law applicable to the defendants' conduct.

Such was very much the case in several of the episodes examined here, such as the German and Argentine. Levinson's observation thus suggests a vital link between legal positivism and consensualist sociology: the latter presupposes a societal agreement on basic morality that is thought to be reflected in rules of positive law, rules that should therefore generally be applied in a straightforward, syllogistic fashion—the hallmark of formalist judging.[11]

This link between legal positivism and consensualist sociology suggests common weaknesses in any effort to employ either perspective for guiding and assessing the law's response to administrative massacre. Only nonformalist conceptions of the judicial role, by encouraging litigants to examine the law's underlying moral principles and social

---

10   Sanford Levinson, "Responsibility for Crimes of War," 2 *Phil. & Pub. Aff.* 244, 249 n.10 (1973). Levinson is specifically referring to the view of Henry M. Hart, Jr., in "The Aims of the Criminal Law," 23 *Law & Contemp. Probs.* 401, 413 (1958).

11   The philosophy of legal positivism by no means logically entails the judicial practice of mechanical formalism. H.L.A. Hart, *The Concept of Law* 121-50 (1961). But as a practical matter of judicial self-understanding, the close affinity between legal positivism and formalism is often difficult to disconfirm. See generally Lon L. Fuller, "Positivism and Fidelity to Law—A Reply to Professor Hart," 71 *Harv. L. Rev.* 630 (1958). Fred Schauer, a leading positivist, acknowledges that there is plainly an affinity between legal positivism and rule-based decision-making. Fred Schauer, "Rules and Rule of Law," 14 *Harv. J.L. & Pub. Pol'y* 645, 676 (1991).

low courts some legitimate latitude to stimulate this broader public deliberation, or to initiate it where memory remains At such times, legal analysis can be confined within narrow, formalistic terms only at the cost of sacrificing all public persuasiveness and societal resonance.

In short, as an approach to judging, legal formalism tacitly relies on the conclusions of Durkheimian sociology. To concede the absence of the moral consensus that Durkheim presupposed is to concede the limitations of any judicial philosophy that rests upon his foundations. In the deeply divided societies where administrative massacre occurs, it is too much to hope (in a Durkheimian spirit) that, through criminal law, judges can easily elicit shared sentiments of liberal morality in ways that all will endorse. Durkheim himself believed that only in "normal" societies does criminal prosecution summon up the collective conscience unproblematically.[12] The societies in which large-scale administrative massacre occurs are, virtually by definition, "pathological" ones (in his terminology).

Even so, it is not too much to hope that courts in such societies might make full use of the public spotlight trained upon them at such times to stimulate democratic deliberation about the merits and meaning of liberal principles. In the ensuing debate, with the recent memory of official intolerance and repression firmly in everyone's minds, liberal morality will do very well on its own. That debate can signally contribute to the special sort of solidarity—through civil dissensus—to which a modern pluralistic society may properly aspire.

This conclusion is implicit in the more eloquent statement of Henri Glaeser, the son of one of Touvier's victims, in his remarks to the French jury. "'My father was not judged by anyone. He was arrested, thrown five hours later against a wall, and assassinated.'"[13] The present forum offered a striking contrast, notwithstanding the vigorous controversy within it. "'I am happy to find myself in front of a court

---

12 On Durkheim's quite idiosyncratic understanding of these terms, many-probably most-Western societies displayed profoundly pathological features. I am grateful to Domenick LaCapra for this reminder.

13 Laurent Greilsamer, *"Le procés de Paul Touvier devant la cour d'assises des Yvelines: 'mon père, lui, un ne l'a pas jugé ...',"* Le Monde, Apr. 10, 1994, at 13 (translated in Wexler, *supra* note , at 220).

that is democratic, engaged in an adversarial debate where everyone can speak, anything can be said, even by the accused.'"[14]

---

[14] *Id.* French procedure facilitates such debate by allowing a defendant's surviving victims formally to join the criminal proceeding as parties. Argentina's criminal procedure has long allowed a similar form of "joinder."

Appendix

Collective Memory in the Postwar German Army

Consider, in conclusion, a final example of an effort to use the law, with some success, to influence shared memory and group identity in the face of all six obstacles discussed above. It is useful, in evaluating the preceding argument, to observe the interaction between these obstacles in a single case. It is also fruitful to observe how the argument applies beyond the collective memory of an entire society to that of particular institutions within it.[1]

I hypothesize that any large institution employing law to influence the collective memory of its members will confront the six problems examined above. In most societies, the army is considered an institution with which its members must strongly identify in order to elicit from them the supreme sacrifices sometimes expected in its service. Thus, army leadership virtually everywhere employs periodic rituals, commemorating the country's military successes, to invigorate the collective memory of its soldiers, with a conscious view to inspiring them to comparable future feats.

To elicit courage, combat cohesion, and self-sacrifice from their soldiers, armies need heroes and the memory of their accomplishments. How, then, was the West German armed forces, newly reconstituted after the Second World War, to meet these universally acknowledged requirements? Could a coherent narrative of institutional identity, consistent with liberal principles, be fashioned under such circumstances? The postwar civilian leadership set out to try.[2] The problem, in short, was:

---

1 For a discussion of how formal organizations, certain professions, and particularly the judiciary develop institutional memory in ways partially independent of memory formation in society at large, see Maurice Halbwachs, *The Collective Memory* 160-65 (Francis J. Ditter, Jr. & Vida Y. Ditter trans., 1992).

2 The ensuing discussion draws from Donald Abenheim, *Reforging the Iron Cross: The Search for Tradition in the West German Armed Forces* (1988). For further discussion of the subject, see James Diehl, *The Thanks of the Fatherland: German Veterans After the Second World War* (1993).

The disasters of German history compelled the leaders of the West German armed forces to examine the past, a demand that worked against the formation of a tradition free of problems. Other countries in the twentieth century seemed quite willing to select the best from their pasts and ignore their failures, or to idealize their defeats into victories.... [But] any attempt by the Bundeswehr to interpret its history in perhaps a less harsh light would be interpreted by its critics as an act of restoration.[3]

This problem established the terms of debate. Was there anything worth remembering, besides the mistakes of the past? Could those mistakes themselves become the exclusive basis of the army's institutional identity? At one extreme were the "re-educators," such as Adenauer's Defense Minister Baudissin, who wanted to decree "an official image of history,"[4] establishing a new ideal of the "citizen in uniform" and denying the existence of any distinctively military virtues, exemplified and enshrined in Germany's military past.

This legal decree was to celebrate as heroes the officers in the July 20th plot against Hitler and the earlier Prussian tradition of military reformers, who had sought to preserve some professional independence from political manipulation by civilian leadership.[5] The "traditions decree," as it came to be known, was to refrain from honoring even ordinary soldiers, innocent of atrocities, who obediently and unquestioningly served the Nazi state in its aggressive wars.[6] The decree would prohibit relations (via veterans' associations) between retired Wehrmacht officers and active duty officers in the new Bundeswehr.[7] It would even prohibit the flags, standards, and traditional pageantry employed during (but also long before) the Third Reich.[8]

At the other extreme were the conservatives, who viewed the army's institutional continuity, reinforced by enduring insignia and intergenerational relations between retired and active-duty officers, as

---

3 Abenheim, *supra* note , at 198.

4 *Id.*

5 *Id.* at 200.

6 *Id.* at 211.

7 *Id.* at 213.

8 *Id.* at 211.

necessary for organizational solidarity.[9] They doubted the possibility of "decreeing" collective memory by executive order, given the inevitable autonomy of custom and tradition from legal mandate. They questioned the suitability of the July 20th conspirators as models of military morality, in all but the most exceptional circumstances. They resisted ostracizing either Wehrmacht officers or enlisted personnel who had served honorably at the front, been innocent of atrocities and ignorant of the extensive criminality occurring elsewhere, and so "'took another path of obedience out of honest conviction.'"[10]

From the late 1950s until the mid-1980s, an extensive debate ensued between the advocates of these two views, both within civilian leadership (of the Christian Democratic and Social Democratic Parties) and between these civilians and the officer corps.[11] Several drafts of the traditions decree were widely discussed and two versions ultimately issued, in 1965 and 1982.[12] How were the six problems confronted and addressed?

First, although only the highest ranking Wehrmacht officers were to be prosecuted or purged,[13] the question inevitably arose of whether to stigmatize in other less stringent ways officers, noncommissioned officers, and enlisted personnel who were to remain in service and assume even greater rank under the Federal Republic's newly formed Bundeswehr. Would these soldiers be wronged, in any serious sense, if denied public recognition—in the traditions decree and the ceremonies it would sanction—of their dutiful service and considerable sacrifice for their country? After all, as Abenheim observes: "Despite the political failings and crimes of the military leadership, the soldiers of the Wehrmacht had fought well against terrible odds. They had mastered their operational craft on the battlefield and in the staff room,

---

9   *Id.* at 213.

10   *Id.* at 190 (quoting Major Schütz).

11   *Id.* at 256-82.

12   *Id.* at 282. Until this point, I have largely equated the law's likely response to administrative massacre with criminal prosecution. The legal procedure involved in the German traditions debate, however, involved an executive order, with discussion focusing on what its content should be. The significance of this difference for the law's relative success or failure in influencing collective memory cannot be examined here.

13   *Id.* at 39.

and, until the very end, the Wehrmacht retained its cohesion."[14]

Many leaders thought it unfair to deny the loyal service and sacrifices of these individuals any place in collective memory and associational life of the army. The 1965 decree sought a compromise: to condemn the Wehrmacht, as an institution, and its leadership for the role it played in the Nazi state, in traditional war crimes, and in the "new" international crime of waging aggressive war, but to exonerate and even praise the courage of the less-aware rank and file, including intermediate-level officers.[15]

The 1982 decree abandoned this compromise.[16] Historical research in the preceding years made it impossible to sustain any such distinction between the criminality of the very top leaders and the innocence of middle and lower ranking officers, now discovered to have been deeply involved in the slaughter of the Jews.[17] The eventual retirement in the 1970s of officers who had served in the Wehrmacht and SS facilitated this revision of the decree.[18] Solidarity within the army, and a salubrious relation between it and civilian society, now seemed to permit, if not require, a more unequivocal condemnation of wartime wrongdoing by German soldiers, without fear of unfairness to those whose reputations and family names would thereby be besmirched.

Second, concerns about distorting the historical record continuously infused German debate over the traditions decree. Historians, serving actively as consultants throughout, were charged with finding in German military history "individuals and deeds worthy of emulation" for preservation in the army's collective memory.[19] Some historians balked at this agenda, asserting that "it was against the essence of historical scholarship," which must allow for changing interpretations over time, "to 'decree' an image of history."[20] Certain

---

14   *Id.* at 293.

15   *Id.* at 208-12, 279-81.

16   *Id.* at 271-81.

17   See, e.g., *id.* at 275-76 (discussing the research of Manfred Messerschmidt, Chief Historian of the Military Historical Research Office in Freiburg).

18   *Id.* at 229.

19   *Id.* at 265.

20   *Id.* at 205; see also *id.* at 197 ("'Historical thinking rightly defends itself against falsifying history for a specific political purpose.'" (quoting historian Gerhard Ritter)); *id.* at 195 ("'The person who believes in tradition ... is ... conservative.... [H]e imposes

drafts were similarly condemned as "too long for a decree and too short as a history."[21] In search of military heroes, the 1965 decree turned to early Prussian reformers and the July 20th conspirators.[22]

But later research revealed that the Prussian reformers never accepted the postwar soldierly ideals of "freedom in obedience" and moral autonomy from superior orders. Historians now claimed that "there had never been ... [any] good soldierly traditions of political thought and responsibility in the German armed forces."[23] Moreover, as historians began to uncover the coparticipation of Wehrmacht units with SS killing squads, and as these discoveries began to enter into wider political discussion, the initial decree's distinction between "the guilt of certain individuals and groups and the enduring integrity of the institution appeared ever less credible."[24] Historical learning, first harnessed to provide evidentiary support for the original decree, thus came to undermine its legitimacy and proved to be its ultimate undoing. Rather than authoritatively shaping collective memory, the law had to catch up with it, and historians' impact upon it.

Third, there was the issue of how broadly to read the lessons of the July 20th conspiracy as a precedent to guide future generations of military leaders. These wartime officers, who had plotted Hitler's death, were still seen by many Germans nearly as traitors.[25] But young cohorts in the officer corps, especially after 1968, began to display considerable sympathy for the conspirators and to participate actively in the official ceremonies commemorating their acts.[26] More conservative, elder officers continued to hold that however necessary those acts of rebellion against civilian leadership may have been, the

---

his ideas and those of his time on the past .... [But] [h]istory ... seeks to comprehend problems in their own time, neither as symbols nor as spiritual and moral values. It does not support tradition ...." (quoting historian Meier-Welcker)).

21   *Id.* at 205.

22   *Id.* at 186.

23   *Id.* at 276.

24   *Id.* at 231.

25   *Id.* at 213-16. On the different forms of German resistance during the Third Reich, see *Contending with Hitler: Varieties of German Resistance in the Third Reich* (David C. Large ed., 1991).

26   Abenheim, *supra* note 2, at 192 (observing that the yearly celebration of the *Attentat* proved popular among the younger soldiers).

circumstances that justified them were too unique and unsusceptible of repetition to warrant elevating the conspirators, by legal decree, into the archetype of military morality.[27] Such a move would risk inviting future disobedience by officers to lawful commands from civilian superiors whose ideology officers did not share or whose strategic judgment they did not respect.

These fears were partially confirmed when mutinous French officers invoked the precedent of the July 20th conspirators to justify armed resistance to official French policy favoring Algerian decolonization.[28] The question became whether the military resistance to Hitler, commemoration of which was to be incorporated into the army's institutional memory by decree, provided a faulty analogy to current predicaments in the postwar world.

Then there was the fourth problem of breaking decisively with the past through acknowledgment of guilt and repentance. Those who perceived a strong need for institutional continuity found this break impossible. The 1965 traditions decree sought to pay obeisance to their concerns: "'Tradition is the handing down of the valid heritage of the past. The maintenance of tradition is a part of military education. It opens the way to historical examples, experiences, and symbols; it should enable the soldier better to understand and to fulfill his mission today and tomorrow.'"[29] Academics such as Gerhard Ritter remained dissatisfied with this concession, however, warning that "overemphasis on the negative aspects of history ... posed a threat to the political integration of the [former Nazi] soldier in society."[30] A refusal to honor the past's great achievements would "'destroy contemporary self-confidence,'" they complained.[31]

Yet even the 1965 decree, with all its compromises, stressed that for military memories and traditions properly to endure required their compatibility with universalistic Western principles, embodied in constitutional and international law.[32] One provision thus provided that

---

27   *Id.* at 196.

28   *Id.* at 193.

29   *Id.* at 208 (citation omitted).

30   *Id.* at 197.

31   *Id.* (quoting Professor Gerhard Ritter).

32   *Id.* at 281.

"'the measure for the understanding and maintenance of tradition is the Basic Law [the Constitution] and the tasks and duties which it assigns to the Bundeswehr. The Basic Law is the answer to German history.'"[33] Another provision stipulated that "'the duties of the soldier—loyalty, bravery, obedience, [and] comradeship ... achieve their moral standing in our time by being bound to the Basic Law.'"[34]

Such legal commitments marked a decisive "break with the past"[35] in the self-understanding of the German officer corps, as one historian notes. He concludes, with regard to the army's recognition of its war guilt, that its twenty-five years of internal debate over the traditions decree and its revisions "represented an attempt among professional soldiers to address the past in an intelligent and responsible fashion ... further remarkable because no other major social group in West Germany underwent a similar process of historical self-examination."[36]

Fifth, could German leaders realistically hope to shape the army's collective memory by means of legal decree? Perhaps a high-ranking officer was right to observe, in half-serious self-deprecation, "'one really has to be a German to decree in writing what a tradition must be.'"[37] Many participants in the intragovernmental debate protested that the Defense Ministry ought to allow the Bundeswehr to form its own traditions without interference from above.[38] From this standpoint, collective memory was (what I have called, following Elster) a necessarily unintended consequence.[39]

But the possibilities and limits of shaping institutional memory by decree itself became an explicit subissue in the debate among the politicians, officers, and historians. One side held that "all artificial

---

33   *Id.* (citation omitted).

34   *Id.* (citation omitted). This language reflected the arguments of people like Meier-Welcker, a German historian and participant in the official debate, who contended that "[t]he values of the present must be the sole measure of the spiritual direction of the Bundeswehr; only they could guide the choice of what was worthy of tradition." *Id.* at 196.

35   *Id.* at 281.

36   *Id.* at 295.

37   *Id.* at 185 (quoting General Gerd Schmückle).

38   See, e.g., *id.* at 269 (referring to the 1979 White Paper in which Defense Minister Hans Apel contended, "[t]radition ... cannot be planned. It has to grow").

39   Jon Elster, *Sour Grapes* 43 (1983).

attempts to found tradition would inevitably alienate people; instead, one should allow tradition to grow of its own accord."[40] Others responded that this was a false dichotomy, that "'tradition is neither "grown" in place nor made artificially. Rather it can and should be guided, awakened, and planted through many sensible deliberations.'"[41] Despite the doubts of many, two generations of German political leaders—in part through the "traditions debate" itself—proceeded to try.

Sixth, to a considerable extent, the decision regarding how the law ought to shape collective memory, and hence organizational solidarity, was made *publicly*, with full consideration of the views of the very people whose memories were to be influenced. That there was a robust debate, over many years, among all interested parties is perhaps the most striking feature of how the postwar West German military handled the question of collective memory. This discussion primarily took the form of a flurry of interagency memoranda, white papers, and decision memoranda. But it exhaustively explored the strengths and weaknesses of virtually every conceivable answer to the question, and regularly found a forum in the elite press, if only rarely in the mass media.

Despite the view of some that shared memory and tradition must—almost by definition—be noncontroversial, a vigorous controversy nonetheless developed (involving hundreds of high-ranking officers, party leaders, military lawyers, and historians) concerning what the content of the army's institutional memory ought to be and how its memories ought to be symbolized and commemorated.

This experience suggests, in short, that it is possible to use the law to influence collective memory about administrative massacre in the face of all the obstacles examined in this book.

---

40 Abenheim, *supra* note 2, at 197 (describing the views of Percy E. Schramm).

41 *Id.* (quoting Professor Werner Conze).

Index

About the Author

Mark Osiel is professor of law at the University of Iowa. His articles have appeared in the *Harvard Law Review, Law and Social Inquiry,* and the *University of Pennsylvania Law Review,* among other journals. He is also the author of *Obeying Orders: Military Discipline, Atrocities and the Law of War.*